AUSTRIAN MINISTRY FOR
ECONOMIC AFFAIRS AND LABOUR
ECONOMIC POLICY CENTER

STRUCTURAL REFORMS IN THE CANDIDATE COUNTRIES AND THE EUROPEAN UNION

EDITED BY
HEINZ HANDLER

VIENNA, JULY 2003

IMPRESSUM:

ISBN 3-901676-36-8
Owned and Published by the Austrian Federal Ministry for Economic Affairs and Labour, Economic Policy Section
A-1010 Vienna, Stubenring 1, Tel. ++43-1-71100-0

Layout: Waltraud Schuster-Götz, Sylvia Vana
Cover: Christian Berschlinghofer

Printed by the Austrian Federal Ministry for Economic Affairs and Labour

CONTENTS

Preface 1

Conference Contributions 1

Key Messages on the Lisbon Strategy and the Integration of the Acceding States into the Community's Economic Policy Co-ordination Processes
Heinz Handler and Heinz Scherrer 4

Stuctural Reform Needs in the Candidate Countries
Willem Buiter 14

The CEECs in an Enlarged Europe: Patterns of Structural Change and Catching-up
Michael A. Landesmann 28

1. Introduction 28
2. Macroeconomic catching-up and broad patterns of structural change 31
3. Convergence and divergence in manufacturing structure 38
4. Productivity, wage rates and unit labour costs 48
   4.1. Productivity 54
   4.2. Wage rates 55
   4.3. Unit labour costs 55
5. Trade performance and trade specialization 57
   5.1. Current accounts: structures and developments 57
   5.2. Trade specialization in manufacturing 60
6. The allocation of foreign direct investment across branches 69
7. The role of educational attainment and labour market developments with regard to different skill groups 73

8. Summary 78
9. References 80
10. Appendix 85

Differences and Similarities Between CCs and the EU - a CC Perspective
András Inotai 88

Kick-off Papers 105

The Context for Reform: The Preconditions for Sustainable Growth and the Convergence Challenges
Matthew Salter 106
1. Overview 106
2. General economic context, and the challenge of real convergence 108
3. Structural challenges 114

Real Exchange Rate Developments in the Accession Countries
Peter Part 120
1. Introduction 120
2. Recent real exchange rate developments 121
   2.1. (Real) exchange rate developments and exchange rate regimes 121
   2.2. Inflation developments: the Balassa-Samuelson effect and impacts related to the transition to market economies 126
   2.3. (Unit) labour cost developments and real exchange rate appreciation 129
   2.4. Capital flows and current account sustainability 131
3. Conclusions 132
4. References 133

Assessment of Product Markets in the Candidate Countries
Lars Östling 134
1. Introduction 134
2. General economic background 135
3. Productivity and the structure of the economy 142
4. Economic integration 149
5. Business environment 156
6. Foster a knowledge-based economy 159
7. Reform priorities in the Candidate Countries 162
8. Summary 165
9. References 165

Agriculture in Candidate Countries
Christophe Blanc 168

Financial Sectors in EU Acceding Countries - Stylized Facts and Challenges
Reiner Martin, Giacomo Caviglia and Christian Fehlker 176
1. Introduction 176
2. Key features of AC financial sectors affecting efficiency 180
3. Integration of AC financial sectors 184

Labour Markets, Labour Market Policies and Challenges in the Candidate Countries
Christina Burger 189
1. Introduction 189
1.1. Evolution of labour market challenges in the transition period 189
1.2. EU-requirements concerning the labour market 191
1.3. Where do they stand and where are they going: the Lisbon strategy 193

2. Key issues in employment policy 199
2.1. Tax-benefit-systems 200
2.2. Wage bargaining systems 210
2.3. Labour market regulation 220
2.3.1. Employment protection legislation 220
2.3.2. Working time 225
2.3.3. Self employment 229
2.3.4. Female labour participation and employment rates 230
2.4. Education and skills 231
2.4.1. School education 232
2.4.2. Skills 236
2.4.3. Active labour market policy 237
3. Conclusions and Summary 240
4. References 240
5. Annex: Determination of wages 245

The Quality of Public Finances in the Acceding Countries
Kari Varis and Lauri Taro 250
1. Introduction 250
2. The structure of public finances 252
3. Macro-economic stability of public finance 257
4. Preliminary findings 259
5. References 261

Demographic Outlook and Pension Reform Challenges in the Accession Countries
Micheline Lambrecht, Felix Lowinski, Dominique Simonis, Patrick van Brusselen 262
1. Aim 262
2. The demographic outlook 263
3. Macroeconomic context 266
3.1. Growth performance 266

3.2. Breakdown of growth into its various components 272
3.3. Recent growth performance 276
3.4. Labour markets: participation and employment rates 278
3.5. Economic dependency ratios 281
4. Main characteristics of pension systems 284
5. Medium to long-term growth prospects and implications with respect to the sustainability of public pension schemes 289
6. Conclusions 291
7. Annex 295

Education and Training in Acceding Countries

Ana Martinez and Esther Gordo 309
1. Challenges for Education and Training Systems in the EU: The Lisbon Targets 309
2. The Economics of Education 310
2.1. Policy implications 311
3. Education in Candidate Countries 313
3.1. Overview 313
3.2. Resources allocated to education: Public expenditure on education 315
3.3. Structural issues 318
3.4. Output and Quality of Educational systems 319
3.4.1. Educational attainment 319
3.4.2. Participation at Education 327
4. Conclusions 337
5. References 338

R&D and Innovation

Helge Sigurd Naess-Schmidt 341
1. Well educated work force 343
2. Entrepreneurship 346
3. Fierce competition 347
4. Financial sector conditions 347

5. Macro stability 348
6. Infrastructure of research networks and co-operation between private and public sector 349
7. Broad brush indicators of innovation 350

EPC-Report 355

Key Structural Challenges in the Acceding Countries: The Integration of the Acceding Countries into the Community's Economic Policy Co-ordination Processes
Economic Policy Committee 356
Preface 356
Key Messages 358
1. The context for meeting the strategic Lisbon goal 366
2. Labour market reforms 375
3. Product markets 380
4. Financial market reforms 386
5. Improving the quality and sustainability of public finance 390
6. Fostering the knowledge-based economy 402
7. Environmental and social sustainability 411
8. Implications for the Lisbon strategy and integration of the acceding countries into EU structural reform processes 413
9. Annex 421
10. References 426
11. Members of the EPC Working Group on Enlargement 429

Appendix 431

Authors 432

List of Abbreviations 434

Index 437

Publications by the Economic Policy Center 445

PREFACE

In November 2002, the Economic Policy Committee (EPC) of the EU established a (temporary) Working Group on Enlargement, which I had the honour to chair. The mandate of the group was to discuss and evaluate, in the light of the Lisbon agenda, the consequences of enlargement on structural economic policies in East and West, and in particular on the Community's economic policy co-ordination processes. As envisaged, the group reported back to the parent EPC at the end of April 2003. The report is intended to guide ECOFIN Ministers in their discussions on the structural policy issues resulting from accession.

To back up the report, the members of the Working Group prepared "kick-off papers" on several topics covered by the final report. As much effort has been put into these papers, they are made available in this volume to a broader public readership.

Moreover, the Austrian Ministry for Economic Affairs and Labour, in co-operation with the EPC Secretariat organised a round-table discussion in Vienna on "Structural Reforms in the CCs and the EU". One of the aims was to present the preliminary findings of the Working Group and to receive opinions from the Candidate Countries (CCs). The meeting was designed to have an active participation of some 50 experts and officials from East and West and no passive audience. Introductory speeches were given by renowned professors with affiliations to policy-related institutions. Their papers are also included in this volume.

Finally, the EPC report on "Key structural challenges in the acceding countries: the integration of the acceding countries into the community's economic policy co-ordination processes" is reprinted in the current publication.

The Candidate Countries (CCs), inspired by the Copenhagen economic criteria and the Lisbon goals, have already achieved solid progress in structural and institutional reforms. However, progress has not been consistently strong across all countries and areas. Given the aspirations of the Lisbon agenda, most countries in either region face adjustment needs in the labour market and unresolved problems in terms of the sustainability of public finances, in particular the pension and health-care systems. In most countries, there is scope to further improve the functioning of product markets and to accelerate the transition to the knowledge-based economy. The range of problems is enormous and the spectrum of instruments is broad - but this is true for both, the CCs and the current EU Member States. The continuation and acceleration of the structural reform process - interacting with growth and stability-oriented macroeconomic policies and exchange rate strategies - is essential for the successful integration of all CCs into the EU economy. The benefits of economic integration into the enlarged EU market can be fully delivered only if in the acceding countries implementation of consistent and comprehensive policies of structural reform continue in a broad range of policy areas. It is crucial to maintain the current reform momentum, also in case of temporary lower growth performance, to avoid any risk of jeopardizing the overall target of structural reform.

This publication would not have been possible without input by the members of the Working Group on Enlargement and the background work by Heinz Scherrer from the EPC Secretariat and Christina Burger from the Ministry. I cordially thank all persons involved for their contributions.

Heinz Handler

CONFERENCE CONTRIBUTIONS

Key Messages on the Lisbon Strategy and the Integration of the Acceding States into the Community's Economic Policy Co-ordination Processes

Heinz Handler and Heinz Scherrer

The Ecofin ministers in November 2002 underlined their commitment towards continuing, with the support of the EPC and the Commission, the surveillance of progress with economic and structural policies in the acceding countries. The aim of the work of the EPC's Working Group on Enlargement is to support the efforts of the acceding states to devise structural reform agendas to achieve rapid real convergence, in the light of the Lisbon goal for the EU *"to become the most competitive and dynamic knowledge-based economy in the world, capable of sustainable economic growth with more and better jobs and greater social cohesion"*. It should be a first step towards integrating the acceding states, after enlargement, into the multilateral surveillance by the Council under the Treaty, in line with the mandate from the Ecofin ministers of 5 November 2002. By providing advice and oversight for the Council it should help in concentrating the EU's monitoring on priority areas where reform challenges are most evident.

Joining the EU is but one step on the way to full economic integration into the EU. Most acceding countries in their Pre-Accession Economic Programmes (PEPs) have outlined structural reform strategies conducive to their future integration into the Union's economic policy co-ordination processes and notably the Lisbon strategy. Embracing the policies needed to achieve the Lisbon objectives will enhance the catching-up process and help draw the full economic benefits from an enlarged EU. Lisbon means: raising employment rates, increasing productivity and growth to enhance international competitiveness. The continuation and acceleration of the structural reform process - interacting with growth- and stability-oriented macroeconomic and exchange rate strategies as well as sound public finances - is essential for the successful integration of the acceding states into the EU economy and raising their economy's potential growth rate.

Measured by per capita income in purchasing power standards, in most acceding countries catching-up over the past five years has been limited. Catching-up to income levels achieved in the EU will be a long-term process, but the challenge is to make the process irreversible through sustainable policies in the medium to long-term narrowing the productivity gap and the gap in employment rates vis-à-vis the EU Member States. Also the development of unit labour costs in some countries has been rather dynamic. As a matter of emphasis, for the acceding states to promote sustainable real convergence and to support the EU-25 in achieving the Lisbon goals the following issues are of particular importance in the current juncture:

- **Raise employment and increase incentives to work**. Even greater efforts than in the EU-15 will be needed in the EU-25 in order to achieve the Lisbon employment goals. Whilst for the EU, the average employment rate has been rising, this is not the case for many acceding countries. In most acceding countries, unemployment has remained unacceptably high. A key challenge for the acceding states is therefore to reduce the high unemployment rate, especially long-term unemployment, for certain groups especially the youth and the low skilled, and regional disparities, and increase employment rates for older workers. Measures key to "more and better jobs" include:
  - increasing the incentive effects of tax and benefit systems, in particular for low wage earners,
  - removing unemployment traps ("increase incentives to work"),
  - strengthening wage developments, maintaining the link between productivity growth and wages,
  - improving employment flexibility through a thorough review of employment protection legislation,

  - focusing on precisely targeted, effective and efficient active labour market policies.

  Such reforms will determine how fast the acceding countries converge towards the EU's Lisbon employment targets.

- **Strengthen competition and efficiency in goods and services markets**. There are still several sectors in goods and services markets where competition in the acceding countries needs to be strengthened. Productivity growth in the acceding countries can be increased by a further shift in the sectoral composition of the economy to sectors with a higher value added Open markets and greater competition are a catalyst for innovation and help businesses grow. Across all sectors, for enterprise and entrepreneurship to thrive, measures to improve the business environment are key. The following should be priorities for further action:
  - In some countries, more progress is needed to strengthen competition rules and establish independent competition authorities.
  - Despite good progress, significant deficiencies need to be addressed in most countries in regard of the regulatory burden on business, the effective implementation and in some countries the design of judicial reforms, and the quality and administrative capacity of the central and local authorities.
  - In a number of countries, incomplete market exit provisions should be addressed, in particular through the improvement of bankruptcy legislation and procedures.
  - After accession, particular attention will have to be devoted to comply to internal market obligations, notably with respect to quickly achieving the EU Directive transposition rate targets.
  - State aid should be overhauled and re-directed towards horizontal measures.

The implementation of competition policies should be a core subject of monitoring. Restructuring of the **agricultural sector** remains an urgent priority. In many acceding countries subsistence farming, where income does not derive from the sale of agricultural products, but from welfare payments which provide no incentives for change, might slow down the modernisation process.

- **Continue financial market reforms.** Bank restructuring and privatisation have added to financial sector stability in the Candidate Countries. The following further reforms have been identified as being important for further action:
  - Continued reforms to deepen and widen the financial sector are required so as to avoid credit constraints and foster faster real convergence.
  - The rapid implementation of EU financial services regulation is crucial.
  - The availability of low cost loan and early stage risk capital financing for SMEs should be a central priority.
  - Good progress has been made in putting into place adequate regulatory and supervisory capacities, but certain persisting weaknesses have to be addressed.

- **Improve the quality of public finance.** The Ecofin ministers in their meeting with their counterparts from the Candidate Countries on 5 November 2003 noted that reaching sound fiscal positions for some of the acceding countries will clearly require efforts over and above those described in the PEPs. In addition, the acceding countries should enhance the efficiency of public spending and revenues by institutional and structural reforms. In order to foster a growth-enhancing environment providing sufficient space and incentives for private sector development, there remains the need to re-assess the structure of budget revenue and expenditure.

Specifically:

- On the revenue side, challenges should be addressed, such as the narrow tax base that characterises several acceding countries, and weaknesses in tax collection and administration.
- On the expenditure side, specific attention should be devoted to investment in key areas (such as R&D, and human capital) to underpin future competitiveness and growth, as well as addressing the need for norms for expenditure control at subnational level of government.
- It is essential that the use of EU structural funds will be focused on those types of investments most conducive to long-term productivity gains, particularly human and knowledge capital, as well as on basic infrastructure.

- **Continue pension and health care reforms.** Ageing populations could induce dramatic changes in potential growth rates. In the light of the Lisbon agenda:
  - As a response to the expected increase in old-age dependency rates, policies to increase the workforce, notably amongst women and older workers, are key.
  - In line with the three-pronged strategy developed by the Ecofin Council to prepare for the budgetary effects of ageing (i.e. debt reduction, raising employment rates, and reform of pension systems), in view of the current parameters of their pension systems (for example pension expenditure as a share of GDP), many acceding countries will have to implement comprehensive reform strategies. Those will have to include initiatives aimed at offsetting the effects of ageing via productivity improvements, and reforms of the basic parameters of public pension systems (e.g. the retirement age, the replacement age, or the contribution rate), with a view to improving incentives to work and to strengthening the actuarial link between contributions and benefits.
  - Due to growing GDP as well as technical progress and product innovation, health-care expenditures are expected to grow fast.

Containing such expenditures, while providing effective coverage, will imply steps to raise the efficiency of the health-care systems.

- **Accelerate the transition to the knowledge-based economy.** In light of the Lisbon strategy, some important challenges remain for the educational systems of many acceding countries. Low levels of investment in R&D and IT may hamper the catching-up of the acceding countries with the EU mainstream and their increase in productivity levels.
  - The acceding countries should continue educational reforms, and improve their education and training systems in terms of educational attainment, skilled human resources as well as R&D and innovation performance.
  - More focus should be devoted to technology transfer and gradual product and process improvement.

It is crucial for the acceding countries to maintain the current reform momentum, even in the event of lower growth performance. There should be a determined attempt in the acceding countries to mobilise public opinion to build or maintain political reform constituencies amongst the various stakeholders backing the drive to catch up.

Economic policy co-ordination processes

Within the EU, a number of economic policy co-ordination processes have been developed to foster economic reform and provide for appropriate peer pressure:

- The **Broad Economic Policy Guidelines**, which are at the centre of economic policy co-ordination and which reflect and guide all other co-ordination activities at EU level. They are specific about misalignments, structural imbalances and issues of competitiveness. The Council in December 2002 decided that in future the BEPGs should focus on the medium-term economic policy strategy, and should only be reviewed every three years (set-up of the improved economic policy co-ordination cycle see Annex 2). In the intermediate years, the focus should be on implementation;

- Other policy co-ordination processes which deal with specific economic policy areas, such as employment (**the Luxembourg process**), structural reforms and competitiveness (**the Cardiff process**), the macro-economic dialogue with the social partners (**the Cologne process**) and pension reforms (**the open method of co-ordination on pensions**);
- The **Lisbon strategy** with the Commission's annual synthesis report leading to the Spring European Council on economic reform.

The existing policy co-ordination processes, notably the Cardiff process, the Luxembourg process, the Lisbon process and the BEPGs cover all economic aspects which are relevant for the present and future Member States. The acceding countries will have to be integrated into all the existing processes in the course of 2004/2005 as appropriate.

Several working groups of the EPC will have to extend their work to cover the acceding countries (for example the EPC's Ageing Working Group to include those countries into their next round of common projections for public spending on pensions, health and long-term care for the elderly in 2004/5, and the EPC's Working Group on Output Gaps).

Annex 1: Key Lisbon targets and objectives

The Lisbon strategy entails a variety of targets and objectives, agreed not only at the Lisbon Council itself (March 2000), but also at Stockholm (March 2001), Göteborg (June 2001) and Barcelona (March 2002). Not all are quantified or time-specific, but those which are include:

Employment:

- an overall employment rate of 67 per cent in 2005 (Stockholm) and 70 per cent in 2010 (Lisbon);
- a female employment rate of 57 per cent in 2005 (Stockholm) and 60 per cent in 2010 (Lisbon);
- an employment rate for workers aged 55-64 of 50 per cent in 2010 (Stockholm);
- an increase of 5 years by 2010 in the average effective retirement age (Barcelona); and
- available childcare by 2010 for 90 per cent of pre-school children over three, and 33 per cent of children under three (Barcelona).

Research and innovation:

- R&D spending of 3 per cent of GDP by 2010, with two thirds of the total coming from business (Barcelona); and
- 100 per cent of schools to be connected to the Internet by 2002.

Economic reform:

- full implementation of the Risk Capital Action Plan by 2003, and of the Financial Services Action Plan by 2005 (Lisbon);
- a transposition rate into national law for Internal Market directives of 98.5 per cent (Stockholm);
- no Internal Market directives to be more than two years overdue in their transposition (Barcelona);

- open energy markets for business customers in 2004, and subsequently for domestic users (Barcelona);
- cross-border energy transmission capacity equal to at least 10 per cent of installed production capacity by 2005 (Barcelona); and
- a single European sky by 2004 (Barcelona).

Social cohesion:

- halve by 2010 the number of early school-leavers not continuing with further education (Lisbon); and
- reduce by 2010 the numbers living at risk of poverty (Barcelona).

Environment/sustainable development:

- visible progress on reducing greenhouse gas emissions by 2005 (Göteborg);
- an indicative target for electricity generated from renewable sources of 22 per cent of gross electricity consumption in 2010 (Göteborg); and
- Combating Climate Change: meet the indicative target of 22% for the contribution of electricity produced from renewable energy sources to gross electricity consumption by 2010 (Göteborg).

Annex 2: Flowchart of the improved economic policy co-ordination cycle

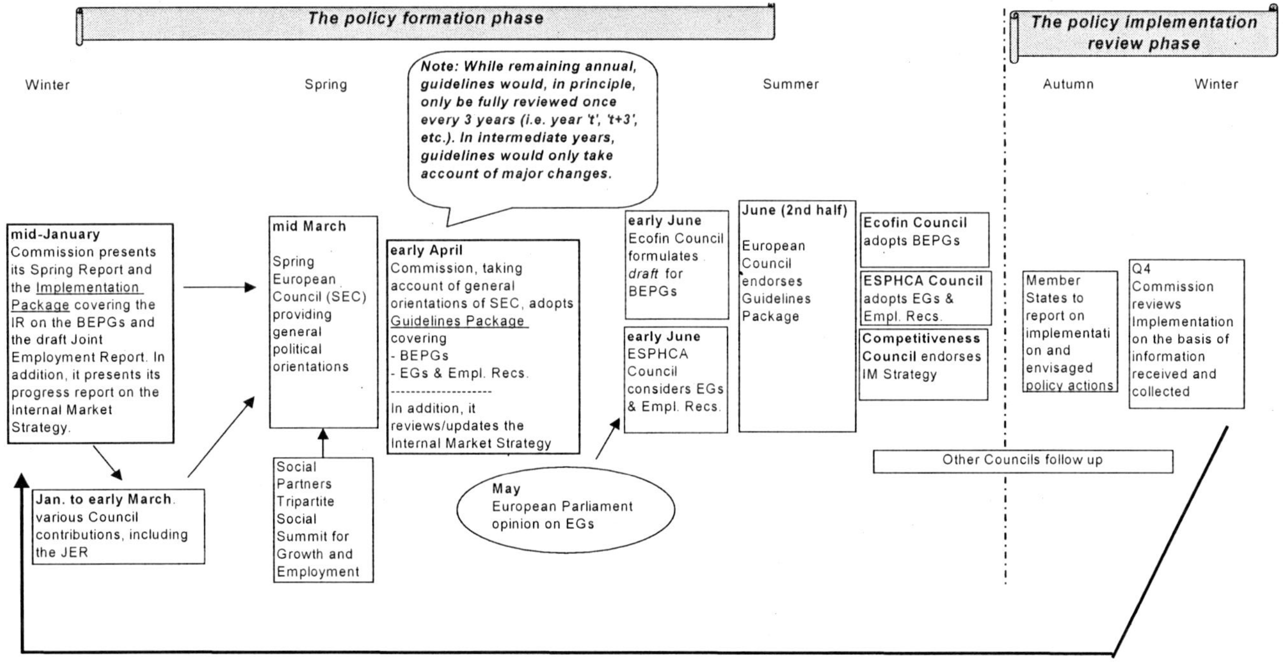

STUCTURAL REFORM NEEDS IN THE CANDIDATE COUNTRIES

WILLEM BUITER

Introduction

The next enlargement of the EU is to include a large number of transition countries (the three Baltic countries, the Czech Republic, the Slovak Republic, Hungary, Poland and Slovenia in May 2004; Bulgaria and Romania hope to join in 2007).

For the objective of catching-up with EU average living standards, these countries will need rapid growth over a sustained period and face two types of challenges:

1. macroeconomic challenge: managing the fiscal - monetary policy mix in light of potential EMU accession
2. microeconomic/structural reform challenge: boosting competitiveness through deeper institutional reforms, in particular in the enterprise, agriculture, infrastructure and banking sectors.

On average, the PPP per capita income in accession countries equals 40 per cent of the EU average, which shows a large potential for catching-up

With enlargement, the population of the EU will increase significantly, its GDP will increase only marginally. Average income in the enlarged EU will therefore arithmetically be significantly lower than in the old EU (this will be the case even if no one in either the old or the enlarged EU is worse off!). This is a long way of saying that the newcomers are much poorer than the existing members.

Graph 1: GDP per capita in PPP terms, population and GDP in EU15 and Candidate Countries

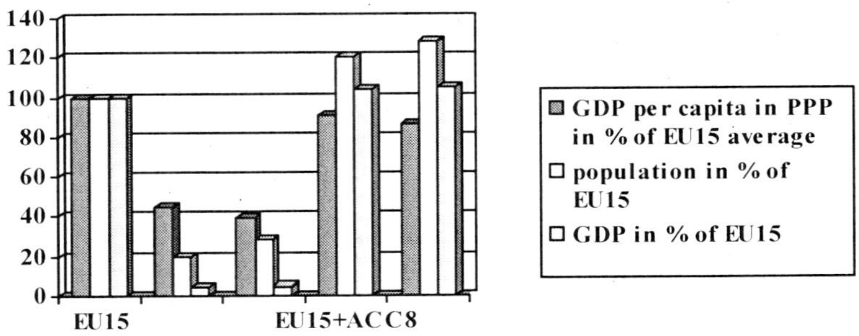

Only three of the transition countries that are to join the EU reach at least 50 per cent of the EU average real per capita income (Czech Republic, Hungary and Slovenia); the Slovak Republic is close at 48 per cent.

Graph 2: Per capita GDP in PPP as % of EU GDP, 2001

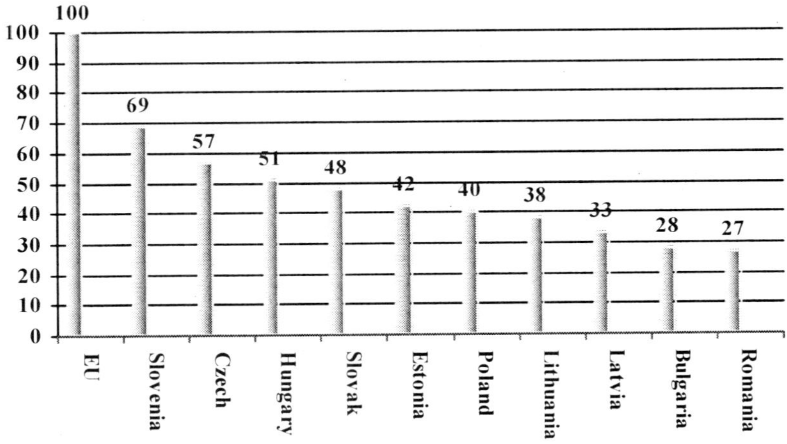

At the time of their accession, the Southern countries (Greece, Portugal, and Spain) were relatively richer with incomes per capita in purchasing power parities between 60 and 70 per cent of the EU average at the time.

Convergence with the EU level of income per capita will require sustained growth rates over a long period of time

It would take on average between one and one and a half generation (25 years) for the Central and Eastern European Countries to fully converge with the average standard of living in the EU, if they were to record a positive annual growth differential of 3 per cent vis-à-vis the existing members.

Table 1: How long will it take for CEEC to converge to EU if growth differential...

	50%	**75%**	**100%**
Czech Rep	na	9	19
Estonia	6	20	30
Hungary	na	13	23
Latvia	14	28	38
Lithuania	10	24	34
Poland	8	22	32
Slovak Rep	2	16	26
Slovenia	na	3	13
Romania	24	37	43
Bulgaria	20	34	41

In order to reduce the duration of the catching-up period for full convergence to twenty years, assuming the average annual GDP growth rate of the EU is 2 per cent, the accession countries would have to record growth rates ranging from 5 to 10 per cent per annum on average!

Table 2: By what rate do CEEC need to grow for convergence to occur in 20/30 years, assuming EU15 grows at 2% pa?

	100% target		**75% target**		**50% target**	
	20	**30**	**20**	**30**	**20**	**30**
Czech Rep	4.9	3.9	3.4	2.9	na	na
Estonia	6.5	5.0	5.0	4.0	2.9	2.6
Hungary	5.5	4.3	3.9	3.3	na	na
Latvia	7.8	5.8	6.2	4.8	4.1	3.4
Lithuania	7.1	5.4	5.6	4.4	3.5	3.0
Poland	6.8	5.2	5.3	4.2	3.2	2.8
Slovak Rep	5.8	4.5	4.3	3.5	2.2	2.1
Slovenia	3.9	3.3	2.4	2.3	na	na
Romania	9.1	6.8	7.7	5.7	5.5	4.3
Bulgaria	9.7	6.4	7.1	5.4	5.0	4.0

The accession countries are facing significant macroeconomic challenges on the road to E(M)U accession; this is even more emphatically the case if they wish to adopt the Euro as soon as possible

Despite a good performance in terms of GDP growth in recent years, which shows their resilience in the face of the slow-down in the EU (the prime destination for their exports), the CEECs record large fiscal and current account deficits and in a couple of cases (including Hungary) also continued high inflation.

Table 3: Macro-data of the CEECs

	Growth	**Average inflation**	**Fiscal balance**	**Current account balance**
Bulgaria	4.5	5.9	-0.8	-4.3
Czech R	2.0	1.8	-7.3	-5.3
Estonia	5.8	3.6	1.2	-12.6
Hungary	3.3	4.8	-9.9	-4.2
Latvia	6.1	1.9	-2.5	-7.8
Lithuania	6.7	0.3	-1.2	-4.8
Poland	1.3	1.7	-5.7	-3.6
Romania	4.9	22.5	-2.7	-3.6
Slovak	4.4	3.3	-5.5	-8.2
Slovenia	2.9	7.5	-2.9	1.8

Monetary policy will be mainly focused on bringing inflation down to sufficiently low levels permit the CEEC countries to meet the inflation requirement for EMU membership.

Graph 3: Bringing down inflation

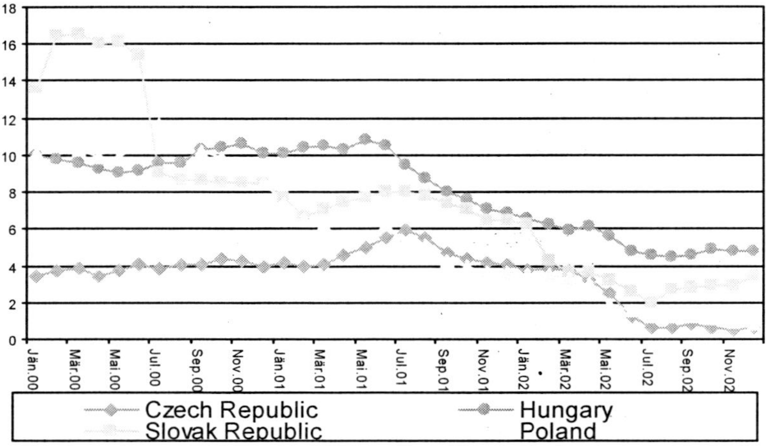

Fiscal tightening will be necessary for CEECs to fulfil the fiscal criterion. This will be all the more difficult because their relatively high structural deficits are partially driven by EU accession-related public investment needs (as well as by excessively large public administrations and high public sector wage pressures).

Table 4: General Government balance in per cent of GDP

	2001	**2002**	**2003**
Czech Republic	-5,1	-7,3	-7,1
Hungary	-4,6	-9,9	-5,7
Poland	-5,4	-5,7	-6,0
Slovakia	-3,9	-5,5	-4,9

Despite the progress achieved in recent years to qualify as functioning market economies, the remaining structural reform challenges that must be met to achieve rapid growth, are significant in many ways.

They concern mainly four areas:

1. in the enterprise sector: completing the restructuring and privatisation process, improving the investment climate, and introducing labour market flexibility
2. in the agricultural sector: developing functioning land markets and pursuing the restructuring of farms and agro-enterprises
3. in the infrastructure sphere: deepen commercialisation, liberalisation, and tariff reform
4. in the banking sector: improving the structure, efficiency and depth of f inancial intermediation

An illustration of this situation is given by the structure of GDP in the ten accession countries compared to that of the EU: the former still have larger agricultural and industrial sectors than the current members of the EU, so that services represent only 60 per cent of total output to be compared to 70 per cent in the EU.

Graph 4: Structure of GDP

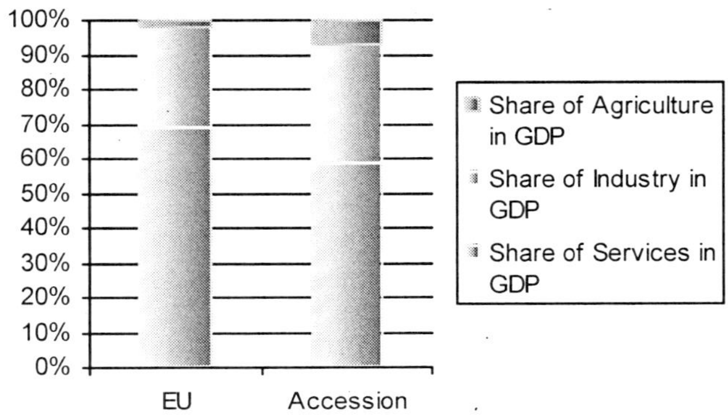

Based on the indicators maintained by the EBRD, the environment of enterprises needs to be further improved in the accession countries in order to promote the potential for growth

In the enterprise sector, the remaining challenges concern large-scale privatisations, enterprise restructuring and corporate governance. As regards corporate governance, the CEEC countries are still relatively far away from the standard of market economies.

Table 5: Enterprise reforms

	Share of GDP produced in the private sector (mid 2001, in %)	Large-scale privati-sation	Small-scale privati-sation	Governance & enterprise re-structuring
Czech R	80	4	4+	3+
Estonia	80	4	4+	3+
Hungary	80	4	4+	3+
Latvia	70	3+	4+	3-
Lithuania	75	4-	4+	3
Poland	75	3+	4+	3+
Slovak. Rep.	80	4	4+	3
Slovenia	65	3	4+	3
Bulgaria	70	4-	4-	2+
Romania	65	3+	4-	2

Note: Figures in the last three columns of Table 5 are to be read according to the classification system for transition indicators, which is a stylised reflection of the judgement of the of the EBRD's Office of the Chief Economist; the scale ranges from 1 - little progress achieved in terms of transition to market economy - to 4+ - standards and performance typical of advanced industrial economies)

As far as the business environment is concerned the main remaining obstacles have to do with almost all the dimensions surveyed in the BEEPS, despite the progress achieved in the recent years: finance, taxes, regulations, judiciary and in some cases corruption.

Graph 5: Business environment

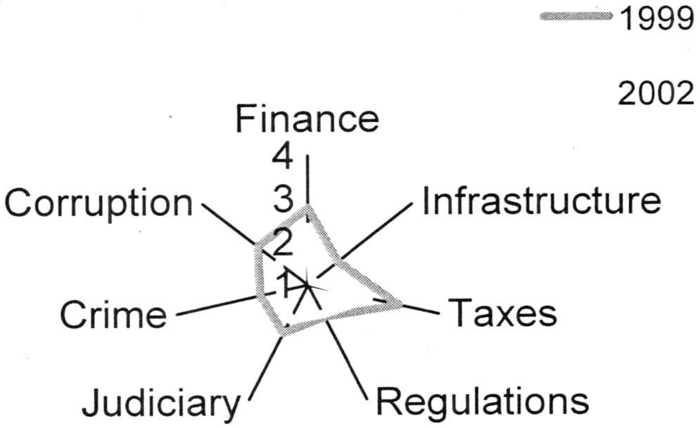

The high level of unemployment across the region points to its partially structural nature and calls for the introduction of more flexibility in the labour market, beyond the requirements of the acquis communautaire.

Table 6: Unemployment remains high across the region

	Unemployment as % of labour force, 2002
Czech Rep.	9,8
Estonia	10,4
Hungary	5,8
Latvia	12,2
Lithuania	16,3
Poland	18,1
Slovak Rep	18,8
Slovenia	6,5
Bulgaria	16,8
Romania	8,1

Efficiency gains can also be expected from pursuing reforms in the agricultural, infrastructure and energy sectors.

While the share of agriculture in GDP and employment remains high compared to the situation in the EU, the reform challenges are significant as far as the following aspects are concerned: establishing clear property rights to land, restructuring semi-subsistence farms, improving market institutions and access to finance.

Table 7: Agricultural reforms

	Share of Agri in GDP	Share of Agri in Emplt	Price & Market	Land Re-form	Agro pro-ces-sing	Rural Finance	Rural Institu-tions
Czech Rep	3.9	5.2	8	9	10	9	9
Estonia	6.3	7.4	9	9	9	9	9
Hungary	4.1	4.8	8	9	10	9	9
Latvia	4.5	13.5	9	9	9	9	9
Lithuania	7.5	19.6	8	9	8	7	8
Poland	3.3	18.8	8	9	9	7	8
Slovak Rep	4.5	6.7	8	8	9	8	7
Slovenia	3.2	9.9	9	9	10	8	8
Bulgaria	14.5	11.3	9	8	8	7	8
Romania	12.6	42.8	7	8	8	6	6
EU-15	2.0	4.3	n/a	n/a	n/a	n/a	n/a

Note: Figures in Table 7 range from 1 to 10; 10 equals the standards of advanced market economies, including competitive markets, large-scale private farm ownership, privatised agro-processing, an efficient financial system, and well-functioning rural institutions

Further progress in terms of commercialisation, liberalisation and tariff reform will be necessary to reform infrastructures, and in particular railways and roads which are lagging behind.

Table 8: Infrastructure reforms

	Telecoms	Power	Railways	Roads
Czech Rep.	4	3	2+	2+
Estonia	4	3	4+	2+
Hungary	4	4	3+	3+
Latvia	3	3	3+	2+
Lithuania	3+	3	2+	2+
Poland	4	3	4	3+
Slovak Rep.	2+	4	2+	2+
Slovenia	3	3	3+	3+
Bulgaria	3	3+	3	2+
Romania	3	3	4	3

Note: Figures in table 8 are to be read according to the classification system for transition indicators, which is a stylised reflection of the judgement of the of the EBRD's Office of the Chief Economist; the scale ranges from 1 (little progress achieved in terms of transition to market economy) to 4+ (standards and performance typical of advanced industrial economies)

Finally there is a substantial potential for improving energy efficiency in accession countries as their energy intensity levels are much higher compared to those observable in western countries (i.e. France, UK and USA).

Graph 6: Energy intensity in accession countries

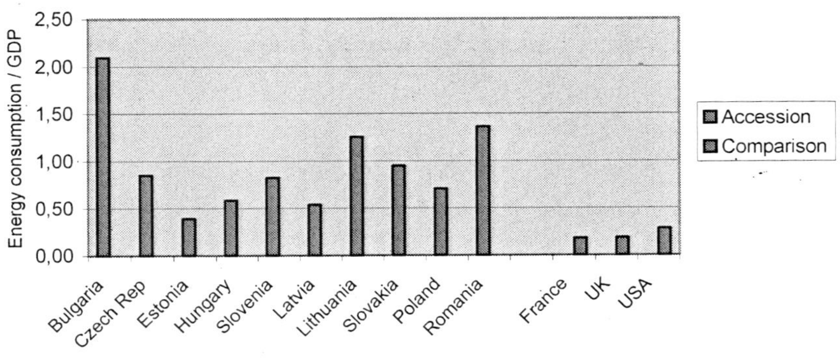

However, reforms in the infrastructure field will put a considerable burden on the public finance of the accession countries as they will have to spend an estimated 2-6 per cent of GDP per annum to meet transport infrastructure and environmental compliance costs; the EU will help meet much, but by no means all of the financial cost. EU aid is often in the form of matching funds.

Table 9: Infrastructure needs and fiscal constraints

	Transport investment needs, € million (% GDP p.a.)	Environment compliance costs, € million (% GDP p.a.)	Capital Expenditure, % 2001 GDP
Czech Rep	10,203 (1.0)	6,600-9,400 (0.7-1.0)	5,6
Estonia	628 (0.7)	4,406 (4.9)	3,5
Hungary	10,166 (1.2)	4,118-10,000(0.5-1.1)	3,6
Latvia	1,990 (1.7)	1,480-2,360 (1.2-1.9)	3,2
Lithuania	2,322 (1.2)	1,600 (0.8)	1,6
Poland	36,423 (1.4)	22,100-42,800 (0.7-1.4)	3,1
Slovak Rep	6,543 (2.0)	4,809 (1.4)	n/a
Slovenia	5,774 (1.9)	2,430 (0.8)	2,8
Bulgaria	5,278 (2.4)	8,610 (3.9)	4,0
Romania	11,211 (1.8)	22,000 (3.4)	n/a

The financial sector also needs to be further reformed in order to develop and be able to fulfil its intermediation function, which is still very weak compared to the EU

The banking sector faces important challenges, as the level of credit as a share of GDP in accession countries was, in the best case, equivalent to half of the level observed in the EU; these challenges include: bank restructuring and privatisation, further consolidation and efficiency improvements, and increasing the menu of financial services

Table 10: Financial sector reforms

	Domestic Credit (% GDP, end yr)	Domestic Credit to Private Sector (% GDP)	Interest rate spread (in %)
Czech Republic	46.5	24.4	4.0
Hungary	52.8	31.5	2.7
Poland	31.2	18.4	8.5
Slovak Republic	58	27.6	5.3
Average accession countries	38.7	23.6	5.8
Euro- Area	136.8	n/a	3.5

Even without any prior as to whether the main channel of intermediation should be the banking sector of capital markets, the development of capital markets is necessary; stock market capitalisation in accession countries represented less than 20 per cent of GDP in 2001, compared to at least 60 per cent in the EU.

Graph 7: Stock market capitalisation, % of GDP in 2001

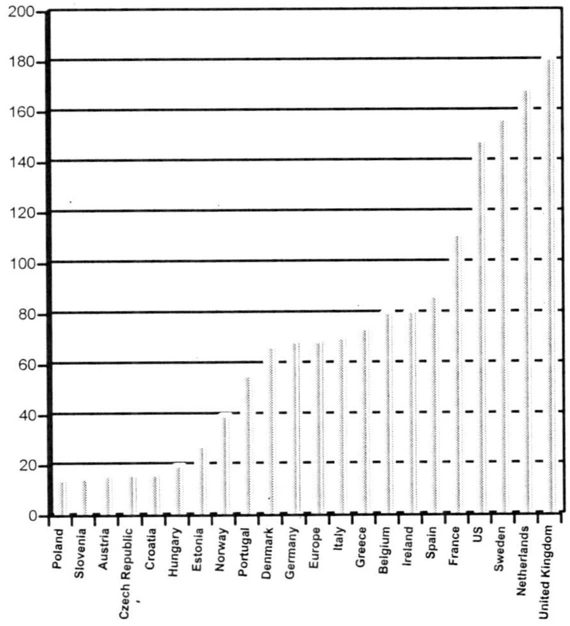

The institutional investor is still weak, even if the situation varies greatly in the EU, and many accession countries need to implement pension reforms and changes to the legislative framework for securities, pension and investment funds, as well as life insurance.

Graph 8: Financial assets of institutional investors, 1999

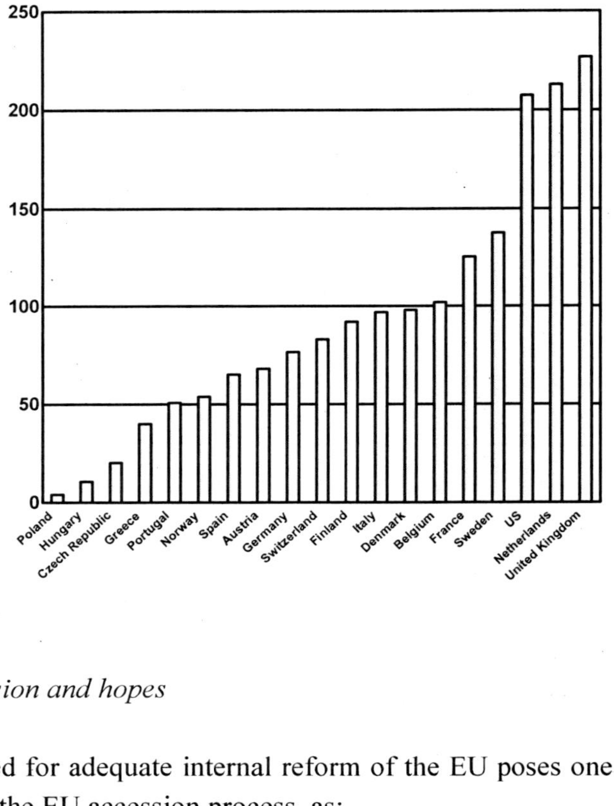

Conclusion and hopes

The need for adequate internal reform of the EU poses one of the main risks to the EU accession process, as:

1. there is a widespread belief that the voting mechanism adopted in Nice is not adequate;
2. the Common Agricultural Policy will have to be reformed when accession countries are granted equal treatment, unless the EU budget is increased;
3. the rules for allocation of structural funds might change as well, so

that poorer existing members can keep more of their current transfers.

Other risks include:
1. weakening political support in the EU 15 and the Candidate Countries;
2. incomplete transition and "reform fatigue" in many Candidate Countries (including governance and public administration);
3. the financing of the EU budget, though not posing a threat to the enlargement process, might become a problem after 2006.

There are some hopes however, so I end with the following rosy scenario:
1. ease into EU by 2004;
2. followed by an easy slide into EMU as soon as possible after EU accession;
3 public finances will become more sustainable thanks to fiscal restraint and EU transfers;
4. steady real convergence will take place (real GDP per capita, economic structures, relative prices).

THE CEECS IN AN ENLARGED EUROPE: PATTERNS OF STRUCTURAL CHANGE AND CATCHING-UP[1]

MICHAEL A. LANDESMANN

1. INTRODUCTION

In this paper I shall present an overview of structural developments which have been taking place in countries of Central and Eastern Europe (CEECs) and discuss some of the qualitative patterns of catching-up which we observe across the region. Since the beginning of the transition in 1989, the CEECs have gone through a dramatic process of systemic change and structural adjustment in which their integration into trade and production links with Western Europe has played a major role. EU enlargement will of course be a major step in this process towards full integration, but the basic outlines of the division of labour which is emerging in this "enlarged Europe" have already become visible prior to that.

Underlying the analysis is a theoretical model (see Landesmann and Stehrer, 2000 and Stehrer, 2001) which attempts to combine a model of catching-up with international trade specialization and thus falls into the category of the dynamic modelling of trade and growth (for other approaches, see Krugman, 1986, Grossman and Helpman, 1991, Taylor, 1993). The basic outlines of the model are simple and have been guided by the "stylized facts" observed in growth patterns of successful and less

---

[1] The paper draws heavily on joint work with my WIIW colleague Robert Stehrer. A previous version of the paper, "Evolving Competitiveness of CEEC's in an Enlarged Europe" (written jointly with Robert Stehrer from the Vienna Institute for International Economic Studies (WIIW)), was published in Rivista di Politica Economica, No. I-II, January-February 2002, pp. 23-87.

successful catching-up economies. Such economies start off with substantial productivity (and product quality) gaps and such gaps are not the same across all industrial branches. Typically, the gaps are greater in the technologically more advanced branches and less in the technologically less demanding ones. This has the following implications: full catching-up has a longer way to go in the technologically more advanced branches and this can be interpreted in two ways. On the one hand, it is "more difficult" to catch up fully in such branches as it requires a much greater effort in learning, skill acquisition and often a big jump in organizational and managerial capacities; on the other hand, it means that the scope for differential productivity growth (and for product quality upgrading) between the "technology leader" and the catching-up economy ("the laggard") is higher where the initial gap is larger.

This is a simple application of the Gerschenkron hypothesis ("advantage of backwardness") which states that the "potential" for growth is highest where the "initial gap" is the highest (Gerschenkron, 1962). This principle has, of course, been widely applied at the aggregate level and is the background for the much tested "convergence" hypothesis in the many recent aggregate growth studies (for a survey of such studies see Temple, 1999). What is special in our model is that we apply this principle at the industrial level with the implication that those industries have the greatest potential for productivity growth and product quality upgrading that start off with the biggest "initial gaps". Of course, as pointed out early on by Abramovitz (1986), actual growth is not necessarily equal to potential growth as countries (and in our case industries) might not be able to exploit this potential. Abramovitz emphasized here the importance of "social capabilities", i.e. a wide range of institutional and behavioural requirements which are necessary such that actual catching-up comes as close as possible to potential catching-up. This analysis opens a wide range of possible catching-up patterns. In the case of our more disaggregated analysis it also means that the **dynamics of comparative advantages** which determines a country's position in the international division of labour can follow quite different patterns for catching-up economies. At a more concise level, the dynamics of specialization advantages and disadvantages is determined by the timing of "switchovers" in the comparative cost structures across industrial branches. Here the dynamics of relative productivity growth rates and of wage rates across industrial branches plays a decisive role. We have examined these patterns of comparative advantages across the historical experiences of a wide range of catching-up economies in a number of analytical and empirical studies (see Landesmann and Stehrer, 2001, and Stehrer and Wörz, 2001) and show that the approach gets also validated in the analysis of patterns of catching-up and trade specialization of CEECs after the transition.

In an extension of this approach, it is possible to show that the allocation of **foreign direct investment (FDI)** across industrial branches is similarly affected by the dynamics of comparative advantages although in this context we also emphasize the role which price-cost margins (Schumpeterian profits) play in determining (particularly foreign) investment activity[2]. FDI flows in turn provide a conduit for a speeding up of technology transfer and hence for a partial endogenisation of productivity catching-up across branches. Just as the model implies that the range of experiences with respect to catching-up patterns and hence of the positions that economies occupy in the international division of labour can be quite wide, this is borne out by the diversity of experiences we observe in Central and Eastern Europe.

[2] Foreign direct investment - through technology transfers - in turn affects the dynamics of catching-up and hence the dynamics of trade specialization. See Landesmann and Stehrer, 2003, for an attempt to extend our theoretical model by endogenizing foreign direct investment flows and its impact.

We shall now give an overview of the structure of the paper: Section 2 discusses shortly catching-up processes at the macro-level and summarizes the broad patterns of structural shifts (across the primary, secondary and tertiary sectors) which we observed since the beginning of the transition. Section 3 takes a closer look at structural change within the manufacturing sector and reveals at this level some of the interesting emerging patterns of industrial specialization of CEECs. Section 4 reports on the main determinants of industrial cost competitiveness, i.e. productivity, wage rates and labour unit costs and shows in which industry groupings (lower-tech, resource-based, higher-tech) the strongest inroads were made in relative productivity and unit cost developments. Section 5 discusses trade performance und uses various classifications guided by industrial organization and skill content criteria to show the qualitative pattern of trade specialization emerging in CEECs in relation to the European Union (EU). Section 6 gives some evidence on FDI allocation across industrial branches and section 7 looks at the educational attainment in the CEECs and at labour market developments in CEECs in particular in relation to the positions of different skill groups. The argument here is that the positions of skill groups reflect the patterns of catching-up and industrial specialization discussed in the previous sections of the paper. The concluding section provides an outlook on the impact which EU enlargement will have on the further integration processes between Central and Eastern and Western Europe.

2. *MACROECONOMIC CATCHING-UP AND BROAD PATTERNS OF STRUCTURAL CHANGE*

In this section we shortly discuss the main features of macroeconomic growth of the CEECs relative to the EU-15 and review the patterns of structural change which took place in the CEECs at the broad sectoral level. As is well known, all transition economies experienced dramatic dramatic declines in GDP and employment in the early phases of transition (Janos Kornai coined these the "transformational recessions") and most of the economies also experienced further - at times sharp - interruptions in their growth processes due to delayed corporate restructuring and banking crises (often called "secondary transformational recessions") and/or macroeconomic imbalances, most often caused by unsustainable current account deficits. However, taking the group of the 8 accession countries[3] together we can see in Graph 1 that the countries have moved towards what appears to be - on average - a rather steady growth path since about 1994. The average hides of course volatility at the individual country level which have already been mentioned and this picture also persists over the most recent period (see Graph 2). However, the combined long-term trend in GDP is, furthermore, significantly above that of the EU-15 (the growth differential over the period 1994-2002 amounts to 1.3% per annum for GDP growth and 2.6% per annum for GDP/employment which we shall refer to as macro-productivity). The greater growth differential in productivity than in output in the accession countries compared to the EU-15, is due to the worse employment performance of the accession countries over the period. The pattern is even more marked if we just look at manufacturing (right-hand side of Graph 1): there the differential in output growth between the group of accession countries and the EU-15 over the period 1994-2002 amounts to 4.6% per annum and for productivity (output/employment) to 7.0%. Thus, we can say that, if we look at the group of accession countries as a whole, they have embarked from about the mid-1990s onwards upon a catching-up process with the current member countries of the European Union.

[3] Czech Republic, Hungary, Poland, Slovakia, Slovenia and the Baltic states.

Graph 1: Growth of GDP, manufacturing production, employment and productivity in the ACs and the EU

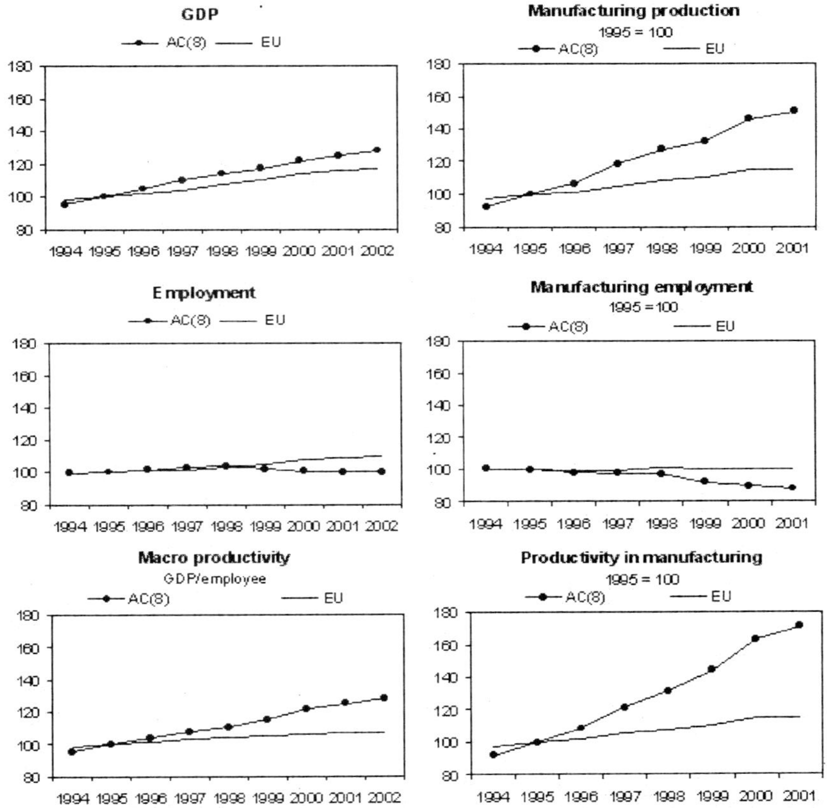

Source: wiiw database incorporating national statistics, Wifo and wiiw calculations using AMECO.

Furthermore, and we now move to the main topic of this section, strong shifts took place at the broad sectoral level which can be interpreted as structural convergence with more advanced Western economies. These broad shifts can be summarized under the headings "deindustrialization" and "tertiarization". It is well known that the Communist economies emphasized industry at the cost of services and, furthermore, service activities were often supplied within big industrial combines, which meant that these service activities were classified under industry. With the transition a strong move towards the expansion of the service sector took place and a scaling-down of the industrial sector. With respect to agriculture a somewhat more complex picture emerged which will be discussed below.

Graph 2 and Graph 3 demonstrate the evolution over the period 1989 to 2000 of the shares of the three classic sectors (agriculture, industry, services) in value added and employment respectively. Graph 4 allows a comparison of the sectoral employment structures after a decade of adjustment between the CEECs and two groups of EU countries, the "EU-North" (composed of Belgium, France, Germany, UK) and the "EU-South" (composed of Greece, Portugal, Spain). We can observe the following tendencies:

De- and re-agrarization

In general, there was a tendency in most of the CEECs to reduce the size of the agricultural sector; however, there were exceptions to this: in some economies the share of the labour force in agriculture (and in Romania even the absolute number) has actually increased. This is true for Bulgaria and Romania, while for all the other CEECs there were losses in the shares (and dramatic losses in absolute numbers) of agricultural employment.

Graph 2: Comparison of CEECs' value added structures in 1989, 1993 and 2000

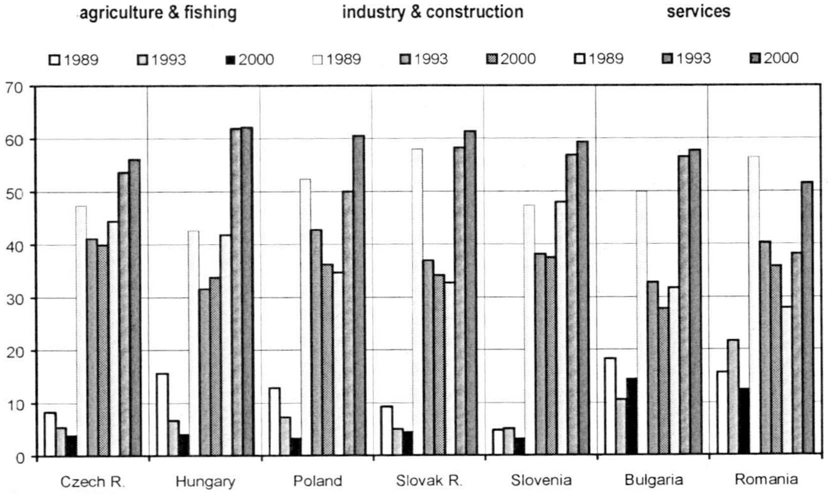

Source: WIIW

Graph 3: Comparison of CEECs' employment structures in 1989, 1993 and 2000 (based on registration data)

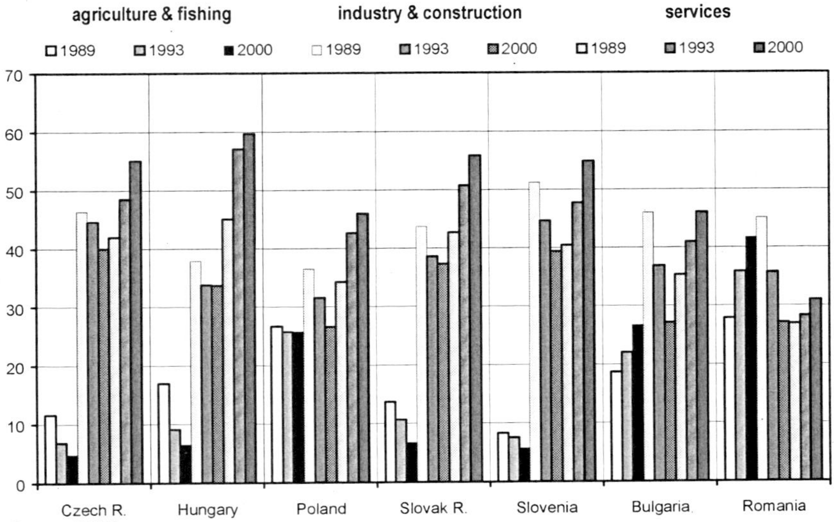

Source: WIIW

Graph 4: CEECs' employment structures compared with EU-North and EU-South, 2000 based on LFS

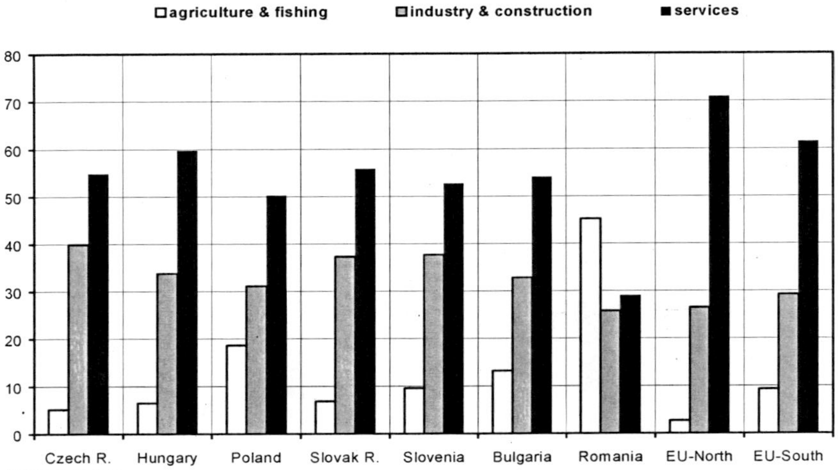

Source: WIIW

Interestingly, the economies with the larger agricultural sectors (Poland, Bulgaria, Romania) had smaller percentage declines (or even increases) in the employment shares of this sector compared to the countries which started off with a smaller agricultural sector (Czech and Slovak Republics, Hungary, Slovenia). Hence, regarding the "primary sector", the transition brought about processes both of "deagrarization" as well as - in some countries - of "reagrarization". The second type of pattern should be considered a transitory phenomenon, resulting from the severe employment crisis in the industrial sector (especially in countries such as Bulgaria and Romania) and - so far - the limited absorption capacity in the services sector (for more details on this, see Vidovic, 2002). There are also interesting discrepancies in the movements of value added shares and employment shares in agriculture: In value added, the shares of the agricultural sectors are declining in the most recent period also in those economies in which there were previously signs of "reagrarization" (Bulgaria and Romania); this trend supports the view that the phenomenon reflects mostly the dramatic overall jobs crisis in these countries.

Deindustrialization

Broadly, one can also speak of a general process of "deindustrialization" with falling absolute employment levels in the industrial sectors (comprising manufacturing, mining, water and electricity supply, construction). In share terms, however, there are some interesting exceptions to the general decline of employment in the industrial sector. In Hungary the employment shares of the industrial sector have recovered after the initial drop at the beginning of the transition and value added shares have risen again in Hungary and the Czech Republic and stabilized in Slovenia. In relation to both the EU-North and the EU-South, some of the CEECs maintain, also at the end of the first decade of transition, a high share of industry in both value added and employment (for employment shares compared to EU-North and EU-South see Graph 4). There are again differences in value added and employment shares: the Czech Republic and Slovenia, followed by the Slovak Republic and Hungary, are the countries with the highest employment shares in industry, while the Czech Republic, Slovenia and Romania, followed by Poland, are the countries with the highest shares in value added. These differences reflect, of course, differences in relative sectoral productivity levels, e.g. the extremely low productivity level in Romanian agriculture would push up industry's share in value added in spite of its own low level of productivity. The levelling-off of relative employment losses in manufacturing in some of the CEECs (such as Hungary and Poland) and persistence of manufacturing's relatively high value added shares could be an indication of the attractiveness of some of the CEECs as locations for some of Europe's manufacturing industries within the context of an overall European division of labour.

Tertiarization

As regards the "tertiary sector", there are clear signs of a catching-up process of the CEECs in the relative size of this sector (although, just as in the West, the changes are partially due to statistical reclassifications and sourcing out of service activities previously undertaken within the other sectors). Again, the relative increase of the importance of the services sector in the CEECs over the last decade has not necessarily been in line with the size of the initial gap (relative to the Western European employment structure). Thus, countries such as Hungary, Slovenia, Slovakia and the Czech Republic experienced very substantial increases in the shares of the services sector, while countries such as Romania and Poland where the initial shares of the services sector in overall employment were relatively low, experienced rather modest share increases. In absolute terms, the employment gains in the services sector were, however, far from sufficient to compensate for the employment losses in the other two sectors.

3. Convergence and Divergence in Manufacturing Structure

Let us now look more closely at the ongoing structural change within the manufacturing sector in the CEECs. We use data from The Vienna Institute for International Economic Studies (WIIW) industrial database, which reports several variables at the NACE rev. 1, 2 digit level (DA-DN) for seven Central and Eastern European Countries. In this paper, we restrict the analysis to the period 1993-2000, i.e. after the transformational crises. The data, which are mostly collected from national sources, are likely at times to be inconsistent over the years (e.g. as data sources changed or for methodological reasons, such as coverage of the small enterprise sector). To overcome these problems we tested the series for significant changes in the growth rates to check when a structural break was indicated by using dummies in the estimates on growth rates. If this procedure indicated a significant break the data series was adjusted accordingly.

Let us first get an overview of growth processes in aggregate manufacturing over the period 1993-2000, i.e. after the immediate impact of the "transformational recession". Graph 5 shows the trend (per annum) growth rates of output, employment and labour productivity. We can see that trend employment growth over this period in manufacturing was negative in all of the transition countries. It ranged from -8.1 and -7.1% in Bulgaria and Romania to -1.4% in Poland. Output growth was even more diverse, with negative growth over that period in Bulgaria and Romania and a wide spectrum of growth rates amongst the "more advanced" of the Candidate Countries. The relatively high growth rates in manufacturing output in Hungary (11.9) and Poland (9.4) are particularly striking with rather modest trend growth in the other three economies. (Labour) productivity growth results directly from the difference in output and employment growth and shows again a quite wide range of diversity, with Hungary and Poland again the forerunners driven by high output growth, followed by a range of economies with per annum average growth rates in labour productivity of 5-7%. It is clear from these figures that the relationship between output and employment growth is quite differentiated across the transition countries and, most likely (as would be seen if the time series were analysed more closely) unstable across time, reflecting major periods of restructuring and other periods when labour hoarding takes place in the wake of output declines.

Graph 5: Growth rates of employment, output, and productivity (1993-2000)

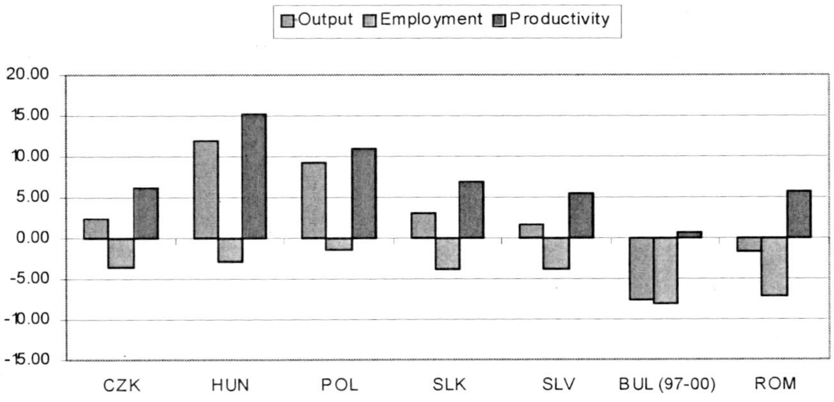

We now move on to present a qualitative picture of the ongoing structural changes within manufacturing. For this purpose we do not report developments in all the 14 industries contained in the database but aggregated the industries into three broader categories (note that these do not cover all manufacturing industries).

- **low-tech, labour-intensive industries:** food products, beverages and tobacco (DA), textiles and textile products (DB), and leather and leather products (DC)
- **resource-intensive industries:** wood and wood products (DD), coke, refined petroleum products and nuclear fuel (DF), chemicals, chemical products and man-made fibres (DG), and other non-metallic mineral products (DI)
- **medium- to high-tech industries:** machinery and equipment (DK), electrical and optical equipment (DL), and transport equipment (DM)

Table 1 reports data on employment and output shares (both at prices 1996 and at current prices) and the wage structure for the seven Central and Eastern European Countries and Austria as the benchmark.[4] Further Table 2 shows deviations of the variables from Austria in percentage points.

One can see that all countries started in 1993 with high shares in low-tech industries relative to Austria. In employment Hungary and Poland with more than about 20 and 16 percentage points above Austrian shares were the countries with the highest shares in low-tech industries. The lowest deviation from Austria can be observed for the Czech Republic. This corresponds to the data on output shares (either at current or constant 1996 prices). With regard to employment shares in medium-/high-tech industries only the Czech Republic and Slovakia showed initially higher employment shares than Austria, reflecting a strong position of

---

[4] An average of EU economies would have been preferable for this comparison, but Austria was singled out as a benchmark country for reasons of data availability.

the engineering sector in these two economies. In terms of output shares, the medium-/high-tech sectors had in all countries lower output shares than the benchmark Austria (although for some countries these deviations were quite small). In the resource-intensive sectors the shares relative to Austria are smallest on average both in terms of employment and output shares.[5]

More interesting than these starting values are, however, the trends over time. Employment shares in low-tech sectors have been declining slightly in the Czech Republic, Hungary, Poland, Slovakia and Slovenia but have increased dramatically in Bulgaria (from about 30% to about 43%) and in Romania. On the other hand one can see slight increases of employment shares in the medium-/high-tech sectors in the Czech Republic and very large increases in Hungary (from 23% to 32%). Relative to Austria all countries except the Czech Republic and Hungary now show lower employment shares in medium /high-tech sectors than in 1993. For the resource-intensive sectors there are no clear trends across countries and changes are small.

These trends in employment shares can either result from changes in output or changes in (labour) productivity (ignoring possible interactions between these two variables). Compared to Austria the output shares of low-tech industries at constant 1996 prices have fallen dramatically in the Czech Republic, Hungary, Poland and Slovakia and remained almost stable for Slovenia. On the other hand the shares of these industries compared to Austria have risen in Bulgaria and Romania from nine to about 16%.[6] This shows a clear pattern of specialization amongst the CEECs. Regarding the medium-/high-tech sectors one can see the opposite tendencies for output measured at constant prices. Hungary increased its share dramatically from about 17% to more than 55%,

[5] One reason for this pattern is the relatively large share of resource-intensive industries in Austria.

[6] It is, however, interesting to see that the output shares of the low-tech industries at current prices have fallen in all countries (most strongly again in Hungary and the Czech Republic), the difference to the constant price output shares being driven by changes in relative prices.

the Czech Republic from 25% to 36%, and Slovakia from 18% to about 33%. In the other countries output shares of high-tech industries also increased, but at lower rates and remained more or less stable in Bulgaria. The rising share of high-tech output in Romania is due to the decreasing share of resource-intensive industries (especially chemicals and chemical products (DG)). Output shares of high-tech industries at current prices were rising in all countries except for Bulgaria and Romania. Again a clear and diverse pattern of industrial specialization gets revealed.

Table 1: Changes in the structure of manufacturing - 1993 and 2000

	Employment shares			Output (at prices 1996)			Output structure (at current prices)		Wage structure	
	1993	2000	Employment growth (p.a.)	1993	2000	Output growth (p.a)	1993	2000	1993	2000
Austria[1)]										
Low-tech	19.64	18.21	-2.39	20.51	17.08	2.36	21.59	16.91	84.57	79.35
Resource-intensive	17.00	16.17	-1.79	23.66	20.72	3.00	23.30	21.74	103.01	104.86
Medium-high-tech	29.22	30.66	-0.17	27.08	34.05	9.23	26.74	33.08	108.48	112.32
Czech Republic[2)]										
Low-tech	24.65	22.69	-4.80	27.07	19.94	-0.81	28.31	22.39	88.54	83.20
Resource-intensive	14.22	17.16	-1.72	20.60	18.00	1.97	18.59	18.60	105.63	113.70
Medium-high-tech	31.53	33.05	-3.28	25.60	36.35	7.76	26.37	30.16	99.46	106.84
Hungary										
Low-tech	39.20	36.95	-3.91	34.73	16.64	1.83	34.66	19.17	85.44	77.15
Resource-intensive	16.55	15.27	-4.11	27.58	11.28	-0.73	25.95	17.18	124.54	133.67
Medium-high-tech	22.67	32.01	1.32	16.70	56.80	24.40	18.61	46.76	101.93	111.51
Poland[2)]										
Low-tech	35.56	33.08	-2.59	34.86	27.49	5.61	35.91	30.53	88.55	81.92
Resource-intensive	15.63	16.82	-0.54	21.76	19.56	7.31	22.80	20.07	106.47	110.55
Medium-high-tech	26.22	22.70	-3.51	19.22	24.40	12.10	18.64	23.09	105.16	113.94

Table 1 (continued)

Slovakia										
Low-tech	27.52	26.85	-0.03	26.38	17.83	-0.78	25.22	18.52	85.59	85.60
Resource-intensive	17.08	16.18	-1.27	24.27	20.87	2.94	25.26	19.61	111.33	103.71
Medium-high-tech	31.70	28.62	-1.68	18.10	32.90	9.99	18.46	27.29	95.74	105.39
Slovenia[2)]										
Low-tech	29.21	26.08	-3.83	27.10	23.67	0.11	26.78	23.65	95.44	86.41
Resource-intensive	14.29	15.40	-0.89	18.90	19.63	1.76	20.09	18.35	110.85	113.48
Medium-high-tech	26.84	25.88	-2.69	25.29	29.61	4.30	25.51	28.94	97.20	101.06
Bulgaria										
Low-tech	29.22	43.28	-3.73	29.82	31.37	-4.15	32.67	29.60	97.38	81.21
Resource-intensive	13.46	14.22	-8.61	25.58	31.72	-2.26	25.25	36.66	128.30	135.91
Medium-high-tech	29.21	22.31	-13.33	14.59	13.58	-6.82	17.82	12.39	105.94	102.52
Romania										
Low-tech	32.05	37.90	-4.80	29.54	33.71	0.09	33.77	29.95	86.96	76.62
Resource-intensive	15.60	15.49	-7.54	28.76	23.11	-5.06	24.49	26.72	110.97	114.15
Medium-high-tech	28.92	24.66	-9.63	14.42	18.77	1.65	19.79	14.75	103.96	127.10

Notes: 1) 1999 instead of 2000 for output at prices 1996 and current output. - 2) 1999 instead of 2000 for current output

Table 2: The structure of manufacturing and growth in relation to Austria (difference in percentage shares and growth rates) - 1993 and 2000

	Employment shares			Output (at prices 1996)			Output structure (at current prices)		Wage structure	
	1993	2000	Employment growth (p.a.)	1993	2000	Output growth (p.a)	1993	2000	1993	2000
Czech Republic[2)]										
Low-tech	5.01	4.48	-2.42	6.56	2.86	-3.17	6.72	5.48	3.97	3.86
Resource-intensive	-2.78	0.99	0.07	-3.06	-2.72	-1.04	-4.71	-3.13	2.62	8.83
Medium-high-tech	2.31	2.39	-3.12	-1.47	2.30	-1.47	-0.37	-2.92	-9.03	-5.48
Hungary										
Low-tech	19.56	18.74	-1.52	14.22	-0.43	-0.53	13.07	2.26	0.87	-2.19
Resource-intensive	-0.46	-0.90	-2.32	3.93	-9.44	-3.73	2.65	-4.56	21.53	28.81
Medium-high-tech	-6.54	1.35	1.49	-10.38	22.75	15.17	-8.13	13.68	-6.55	-0.81
Poland[2)]										
Low-tech	15.92	14.87	-0.21	14.35	10.41	3.25	14.32	13.62	3.98	2.57
Resource-intensive	-1.37	0.65	1.25	-1.89	-1.16	4.30	-0.50	-1.66	3.46	5.68
Medium-high-tech	-3.00	-7.96	-3.34	-7.86	-9.65	2.87	-8.10	-9.99	-3.33	1.62

Table 2 (continued)

Slovakia										
Low-tech	7.87	8.63	2.35	5.87	0.75	-3.14	3.63	1.61	1.02	6.25
Resource-intensive	0.08	0.01	0.53	0.62	0.15	-0.06	1.96	-2.13	8.32	-1.15
Medium-high-tech	2.48	-2.04	-1.52	-8.98	-1.16	0.76	-8.28	-5.79	-12.74	-6.93
Slovenia[2)]										
Low-tech	9.57	7.86	-1.45	6.58	6.59	-2.25	5.19	6.75	10.86	7.06
Resource-intensive	-2.71	-0.77	0.90	-4.76	-1.09	-1.25	-3.21	-3.38	7.84	8.62
Medium-high-tech	-2.38	-4.78	-2.52	-1.78	-4.45	-4.93	-1.23	-4.14	-11.29	-11.26
Bulgaria										
Low-tech	9.58	25.07	-1.34	9.31	14.29	-6.52	11.08	12.70	12.81	1.86
Resource-intensive	-3.54	-1.95	-6.82	1.92	11.00	-5.26	1.95	14.92	25.29	31.05
Medium-high-tech	-0.01	-8.36	-13.16	-12.49	-20.47	-16.05	-8.92	-20.69	-2.54	-9.80
Romania										
Low-tech	12.40	19.69	-2.41	9.03	16.64	-2.27	12.18	13.04	2.39	-2.73
Resource-intensive	-1.40	-0.68	-5.75	5.10	2.39	-8.06	1.19	4.98	7.96	9.29
Medium-high-tech	-0.30	-6.00	-9.46	-12.65	-15.28	-7.58	-6.96	-18.33	-4.53	14.78

Notes: 1) 1999 instead of 2000 for output at prices 1996 and current output. - 2) 1999 instead of 2000 for current output

With respect to the wage structure one would expect that on average wage rates are relatively higher in the higher-tech sectors (e.g. by the assumption that the skill intensity is higher for these sectors or the higher productivity of these sectors). However, the general picture in 1993 was that average wages have been highest in all countries in the resource-intensive sectors and lowest in the low-tech sectors. Comparing this with the year 2000 we can indeed see a catching-up of relative wage rates in the medium-/high-tech branches and a falling-behind in the low-tech branches. The question for comparative costs is whether such changes proceed above or below relative productivity level adjustments which will be explored in the next section of the paper. One can also find a trend towards a convergence of wage structures (e.g. compared to the Austrian as a representative of a Western European wage structure) although this process seems to be slow.

Note that the analysis of output and employment patterns already points towards our initial (Gerschenkron) hypothesis that specialization patterns of catching-up economies may get directed towards the medium-/higher-tech branches (as was the case especially in Hungary) where initially the gap might have been the largest. This requires the fastest catching-up in areas in which the initial gaps are the highest and this in turn depends on the existence (or mobilization) and utilization of "capabilities" (to use Abramovitz' terms) to facilitate such differential catching-up. This was apparently not the case in Bulgaria and Romania and the experience in this respect was also quite differentiated amongst the other (more advanced) Candidate Countries. We now turn to the productivity and cost side of production in order to look at the development of productivity gaps and the evolution of comparative cost structures more directly. After that we study the emerging patterns of trade specialization.

4. *PRODUCTIVITY, WAGE RATES AND UNIT LABOUR COSTS*

Not only productivity matters for competitiveness but also wage rates play their role in shaping relative cost structures and hence the competitive position of different industries from the cost side. In Table 3 we have summarized the data again for the three types of industries (low-tech, resource-intensive, and medium-/high-tech).

Using the same database as before, we focus now on productivity, wage rates and unit labour costs. For productivity levels, we use employment and data on output which are first expressed in national currency units (NCU) at prices 1996. For comparative analysis these can be converted either by using nominal exchange rates (EXR) or PPP rates (PPP) for the year 1996.[1] Output for industry i in country c in year t is denoted as $PR_{i,t}^{c}$. Data on wages and salaries $W_{i,t}^{c}$ are first obtained in NCU at nominal values. These data are converted into a common currency (euro) using either current EXR or current PPP.[2] Data on employees $E_{i,t}^{c}$ refer to average employment levels over the years.

---

[1] For this analysis we are constrained to using PPP rates for GDP as a whole. For selective countries we have been able to obtain industry-level unit value ratios to adjust for industry level differences in price levels, but this database is not large enough to allow the more extensive comparative analysis presented here.

[2] One might ask why one should look at wage rates also in PPP terms as one is interested in comparative actual wage costs. The reason could be that one might want to conjecture what wage costs would be when price levels between the CEECs and the EU have converged. One could see such a comparison as an exercise multinationals might be interested in if they want to judge relative wage cost differentials also for the longer run when the severe undervaluation of the CEECs' national currencies would get eroded. In this case, workers would still ask at least for the same real wage rate as they now obtain, an estimate for which would be the wage rate at PPP rates.

Labour productivity $LPR_{i,t}^{c}$ is calculated as $LPR_{i,t}^{c} = \frac{PR_{i,t}^{c}}{E_{i,t}^{c}}$.
Further, unit labour costs are defined as

$$ULC_{i,t}^{c} = \frac{LPR_{i,t}^{c}}{W_{i,t}^{c} / E_{i,t}^{c}}$$

In Tables 3 wage rates, productivity levels and unit labour costs are compared to Austria (= 100). The variables for Austria have been calculated analogously. Table 3 presents the data using the nominal exchange rates (EXR) conversion and in Table 4 the gaps are derived from PPP comparisons (both wage rates and productivity levels). The difference between the two tables thus reflects the development of the ratio between the exchange rate and the PPP rate. In the following, we shall discuss first the three variables expressed at exchange rates.

Table 3: Nominal productivity and wage at EXR and unit labour costs - 1993 and 2000

		Wage			**Nominal productivity**			**Unit labour costs**[1)]		
		1993	**Growth rate**	**2000**	**1993**	**Growth rate**	**2000**	**1993**	**Growth rate**	**2000**
Czech Republic	Manufacturing total	7.79	8.80	14.42	13.93	0.04	13.97	18.76	8.76	34.65
	Low tech	8.50	8.77	15.93	16.44	-0.74	16.63	18.47	9.52	33.76
	Resource intensive	6.97	8.95	13.34	15.72	-4.81	13.88	20.47	13.76	66.95
	Medium-high tech	7.36	9.63	14.25	11.47	2.52	13.46	21.66	7.11	35.48
Hungary	Manufacturing total	11.22	0.69	11.77	18.22	7.79	31.45	22.82	-7.51	13.49
	Low tech	12.02	0.87	12.70	17.28	3.04	21.10	27.92	-2.58	23.65
	Resource intensive	11.52	0.94	12.52	16.79	-2.41	14.29	39.73	2.95	40.41
	Medium-high tech	10.73	1.53	11.87	13.91	13.52	49.93	28.72	-12.39	9.23
Poland	Manufacturing total	7.94	9.60	15.54	15.58	2.98	19.19	20.10	6.62	31.96
	Low tech	8.43	9.56	16.64	15.89	3.16	19.89	22.43	6.40	33.56
	Resource intensive	7.86	9.47	15.44	14.40	1.48	16.69	23.96	7.99	39.53
	Medium-high tech	7.88	10.28	16.35	11.54	6.32	17.87	28.33	3.96	36.19
Slovak Republic	Manufacturing total	6.71	6.71	10.74	15.42	-2.74	12.72	13.51	9.46	26.18
	Low tech	7.13	8.38	13.12	17.78	-5.37	12.56	14.53	13.75	34.60
	Resource intensive	6.16	6.14	9.38	12.27	0.49	12.10	17.57	5.65	26.75
	Medium-high tech	5.98	7.97	11.41	9.17	2.92	22.63	20.55	5.05	24.37
Slovenia	Manufacturing total	21.65	4.98	30.67	27.60	-3.15	22.15	43.87	8.12	77.46
	Low tech	27.51	4.04	37.22	34.58	-1.91	30.89	52.18	5.95	71.76
	Resource intensive	23.86	4.51	34.70	33.90	-5.55	29.43	41.70	10.06	77.00
	Medium-high tech	19.63	5.39	28.49	28.02	-0.21	27.57	41.55	5.60	69.04

Table 3 (continued)

Bulgaria	Manufacturing total	4.24	0.86	4.51	6.72	-3.31	5.33	13.49	4.18	18.07
	Low tech	5.57	-0.78	5.20	7.61	-3.13	6.15	16.30	2.35	19.91
	Resource intensive	5.05	-0.65	4.70	7.45	-2.47	5.30	19.22	1.82	19.36
	Medium-high tech	4.31	0.07	4.19	3.49	-1.12	3.36	26.51	1.19	27.05
Romania	Manufacturing total	2.93	2.98	3.61	5.34	-2.03	4.63	10.08	5.01	14.31
	Low tech	3.27	1.63	3.67	7.05	1.03	7.90	11.13	0.60	11.38
	Resource intensive	2.77	3.80	3.55	6.10	-3.54	4.37	9.92	7.34	15.83
	Medium-high tech	2.88	5.46	4.24	2.61	2.37	3.11	20.68	3.09	25.23

[1)] Defined as wage at EXR/Productivity in PPP 1996

Table 4: Productivity, wage and unit labour cost gaps at PPP - 1993 and 2000

		Wage			Productivity			Unit labour costs[1)]		
		1993	**Growth rate**	**2000**	**1993**	**Growth rate**	**2000**	**1993**	**Growth rate**	**2000**
		(AUT=100)								
Czech Republic	Manufacturing total	28.91	3.62	37.26	41.51	0.04	41.62	47.59	4.49	65.16
	Low tech	31.58	3.59	41.16	48.96	-0.74	49.55	47.18	5.80	65.52
	Resource intensive	25.89	3.77	34.46	46.82	-4.81	41.35	54.62	7.91	135.73
	Medium-high tech	27.32	4.45	36.81	34.18	2.52	40.11	54.94	3.75	71.73
Hungary	Manufacturing total	28.28	0.59	29.47	49.16	7.79	84.84	61.52	-9.29	32.11
	Low tech	30.29	0.77	31.79	46.61	3.04	56.91	77.35	-7.21	50.04
	Resource intensive	29.05	0.85	31.33	45.28	-2.41	38.55	101.45	-3.34	71.86
	Medium-high tech	27.05	1.43	29.72	37.52	13.52	134.69	72.10	-13.34	22.62
Poland	Manufacturing total	22.61	5.40	33.00	39.48	2.98	48.63	51.12	3.76	66.52
	Low tech	24.01	5.36	35.34	40.27	3.16	50.39	56.98	2.92	68.02
	Resource intensive	22.41	5.27	32.79	36.48	1.48	42.30	55.17	5.47	79.70
	Medium-high tech	22.44	6.08	34.72	29.24	6.32	45.29	76.72	0.30	74.89
Slovak Republic	Manufacturing total	24.22	3.59	31.14	49.70	-2.74	41.02	50.23	3.33	63.41
	Low tech	25.72	5.26	38.04	57.31	-5.37	40.49	56.77	5.74	80.61
	Resource intensive	22.22	3.01	27.20	39.57	0.49	38.99	58.58	4.29	79.69
	Medium-high tech	21.59	4.84	33.07	29.56	2.92	72.95	77.68	-1.13	58.35
Slovenia	Manufacturing total	43.39	2.51	51.74	49.35	-3.15	39.60	86.60	2.28	101.61
	Low tech	55.13	1.57	62.79	61.83	-1.91	55.22	105.14	1.19	107.08
	Resource intensive	47.81	2.05	58.53	60.61	-5.55	52.62	77.83	6.41	110.56
	Medium-high tech	39.34	2.93	48.06	50.10	-0.21	49.29	83.22	-1.95	81.52

Table 4 (continued)

Bulgaria	Manufacturing total	7.19	-6.90	4.44	31.45	-3.31	24.94	79.32	-5.24	54.96
	Low tech	9.45	-8.54	5.12	35.63	-3.13	28.80	90.06	-5.56	66.33
	Resource intensive	8.56	-8.40	4.63	34.88	-2.47	24.80	100.58	-5.98	64.10
	Medium-high tech	7.30	-7.69	4.13	16.34	-1.12	15.75	135.35	-5.38	87.53
Romania	Manufacturing total	15.67	-2.91	12.79	29.04	-2.03	25.20	51.51	1.09	55.60
	Low tech	17.50	-4.26	13.02	38.37	1.03	43.01	49.34	0.35	48.14
	Resource intensive	14.82	-2.09	12.57	33.17	-3.54	23.80	56.65	1.79	66.37
	Medium-high tech	15.44	-0.43	15.05	14.19	2.37	16.93	99.40	4.05	123.16

1) Defined as wage at PPP/Productivity at PPP

4.1. PRODUCTIVITY

Expressed in nominal exchange rates all countries showed a large gap in 1993. The best performing country was Slovenia, reaching a productivity level of about 27% (relative to Austria). Bulgaria and Romania only reached a productivity level of about 5% to 6% of the Austrian level.

There are however differences when looking at industry groups. In all countries the gaps to Austria were the largest in the medium-/high-tech industries and smallest in the low-tech industries, the measured difference in the productivity gaps between these two sets of industries was generally between 5 and 10 percentage points.

Over time rapid changes in these patterns occurred. All countries experienced positive productivity growth from 1993 to 2000 (see Graph 5 earlier in the paper). But not all countries succeeded in closing the gap relative to the benchmark Austria. In aggregate manufacturing only the Czech Republic, Hungary, and Poland had higher productivity growth than Austria. All other countries had lower productivity growth and thus the gap widened.

But here again there are marked differences across types of industries. Hungary closed the gap in the high-tech industries with a (per annum) rate of closure of the gap of 15% and reached a level of about 50% that of Austria. Similarly, Poland closed the gap most rapidly in the high-tech sector with a rate of 6% and the Slovak Republic of 2%. Slovenia and Bulgaria were falling back relative to Austria in all three sectors, but the gap widened more (at a higher rate) in the low-tech and resource-intensive industries than in the medium-/high-tech industries. Finally, also Romania succeeded in closing the gap in the low- and the medium-/high-tech industries but started from an extremely low level.

Thus information on productivity catching-up seems to confirm in most instances the Gerschenkron hypothesis at the industrial level, i.e. that faster rates of catching-up can be achieved in industries in which the initial gaps were higher.

4.2. Wage rates

With respect to wage rates one can observe the following pattern. First, the gaps in wage rates are much more even across sectors than was the case with productivity. The gaps in wage rates (at current nominal exchange rates) extended from Slovenia with a level of about 20% the Austrian wage rate level in 1993 to Romania with only 3%. Second, and this is a very important point for the comparative cost dynamic, the growth (or closure) rates for wage rates were much more similar across sectors than was the case for the (differential) productivity growth rates.

4.3. Unit labour costs

The relative movements of wage rates and productivity determine the evolution of unit labour costs which is, of course, an important measure of the general (cost) competitiveness of countries but more importantly, for our purposes, of the relative competitiveness of different industries.

Looking at the dynamics, we can see that in aggregate manufacturing the wage versus productivity growth was such that over the period 1993-1999 unit labour costs were rising (relative to Austria) in the Czech Republic, Poland, Slovak Republic, and Slovenia. They were falling quite strongly in Hungary and Bulgaria, but for quite different reasons as a comparison of productivity and wage rate movements at both current and PPP exchange rates shows. In Hungary this was due to a very strong performance in relative productivity growth and very moderate relative wage growth (at current exchange rates), while in Bulgaria there was actually a fall in the productivity position (relative to Austria) but combined with a much sharper fall in relative wage levels (again measured at the current exchange rate and this was due to a sharp devaluation of the Bulgarian currency).

Differences in the dynamics across industry groupings are remarkable especially for those sectors in which countries experienced large productivity growth rates (as wage growth is rather similar across sectors). Especially Hungary reduced relative unit labour costs in the medium-/high-tech sectors from 66% (the Austrian level) in 1993 to about 22% in 1999.

The important point which emerges from cross-industry comparisons is that for some countries the productivity catching-up (closure of the gap) is rather rapid in the medium-/high-tech industries in which the initial gaps were the highest. We reiterate the important point that this pattern very much confirms the "Gerschenkron hypothesis" as applied to the industry level (and as stated in the introduction of the paper). For other countries no such differential productivity catch-up can be observed; in the language of Abramovitz, such countries either did not have the "capabilities" or did not mobilize these to make use of the high learning (and technology transfer) potential in those industries in which the initial technological gaps were the highest. On the other hand, we observe that the pattern of wage catching-up (or wage growth) is much more even - than productivity growth - across sectors, and hence comparative cost structures move in favour of those sectors which experience faster productivity catching-up; in Hungary and to a lesser degree also in a number of other CEECs these are the medium- to high-tech sectors. This is exactly the pattern which was also found in research on the dynamics of comparative costs across a much wider range of catching-up economies (see Landesmann and Stehrer, 2001). Let us now move on to examine whether these underlying patterns of comparative cost dynamics get also revealed in the evolving trade structures of CEE economies.

5. *Trade Performance and Trade Specialization*

In this section we start with an overview of broad sectoral patterns of trade performance and then move towards a more detailed qualitative examination of trade specialization. As will be seen below, the analysis of evolving patterns of trade specialization will turn out to be consistent with the previous observations regarding the dynamics of differentiated productivity catching-up (across countries and industries) and the implications drawn from this regarding comparative cost dynamics. To complete the analysis of trade performance, we shall show that indicators of product quality up-grading (measured by the closure of export price gaps) also support the picture drawn here regarding the evolution of comparative advantage dynamics across the different CEE economies.

5.1. Current Accounts: Structures and Developments

We shortly review the broad outlines of the current accounts in the CEECs. Table 5 shows the four broad components of the current accounts (all expressed in per cent of GDP) over the period 1989-2001. We can see that all countries (with the exception of Slovenia) experienced at times dramatic - and unsustainable - deficits in the current accounts. In general, the CEECs are performing better in the trade accounts on services than on goods. However, at closer examination (see Römisch, 2001 and Graph 6), it emerges that this good performance in services trade is predominantly due to the **travel account**, i.e. tourism income, which is a very strong net contributor to the current accounts in countries such as the Czech Republic, Slovenia, and - potentially - Bulgaria. Also the **transport services** sector contributes positively in many CEECs to the current account due particularly to the wage cost advantages in road haulage. In **other services,** in which financial, insurance and all types of **business services** (accountancy, marketing, consultancy, etc.) are the main components, the CEECs are predominantly net importers. In previous studies, it has been shown that in the business services area, advanced economies retain a strong comparative advantage vis-à-vis catching-up economies after they have lost comparative advantages even in relatively advanced areas of manufacturing (such as in electronics). We thus expect the net import position in the business services area to persist between the CEECs and the advanced countries of Western Europe in the longer run. To some extent high deficit positions in these areas (especially in financial services) get reduced in those countries which were most successful in attracting foreign firms to set up local subsidiaries.

The income accounts also show mostly a negative balance (again with the exception of Slovenia) which is mostly due to high interest payments on debt as well as - in countries which managed to attract a lot of FDI such as Hungary - the repatriation of profits. In most countries there is a positive balance on transfers.

Table 5: Current account in per cent of GDP

		1989	1990	1991	1992	1993	1994	1995	1996	1997	1998	1999	2000	2001
Czech Republic	Current account balance	1.56	-0.97	4.47	-1.02	1.30	-1.91	-2.63	-7.14	-6.73	-2.20	-2.66	-5.28	-4.65
	Balance on Goods	1.30	-0.72	1.33	-6.38	-1.50	-3.36	-7.07	-9.89	-9.24	-4.57	-3.46	-6.09	-5.43
	Balance on Services	0.63	0.44	3.15	4.98	2.89	1.19	3.54	3.33	3.33	3.37	2.18	2.75	2.69
	Balance on Incomes	-0.31	-0.60	-0.17	0.02	-0.34	-0.05	-0.20	-1.25	-1.49	-1.91	-2.45	-2.67	-2.73
	Balance on Transfers	-0.07	-0.08	0.17	0.35	0.25	0.31	1.10	0.67	0.67	0.91	1.07	0.72	0.82
Hungary	Current account balance	-4.93	0.38	0.80	0.87	-8.96	-9.42	-5.55	-3.71	-2.15	-4.89	-4.33	-2.85	-2.13
	Balance on Goods	1.84	1.05	0.57	-0.13	-8.42	-8.76	-5.47	-5.85	-4.29	-5.00	-4.53	-3.77	-3.89
	Balance on Services	-2.45	1.51	1.83	1.76	0.56	0.63	3.54	5.32	4.95	3.78	2.89	3.80	4.16
	Balance on Incomes	-4.75	-4.30	-4.14	-3.36	-3.09	-3.48	-4.13	-3.22	-3.11	-3.98	-3.40	-3.38	-2.87
	Balance on Transfers	0.43	2.11	2.55	2.60	1.99	2.19	0.51	0.04	0.30	0.31	0.70	0.49	0.47
Poland	Current account balance	-1.73	1.21	-3.40	-1.80	-3.34	0.73	4.18	-0.95	-2.99	-4.32	-7.45	-6.31	-4.07
	Balance on Goods	0.29	3.75	0.36	0.55	-2.89	-0.97	-1.50	-5.69	-7.86	-8.66	-9.27	-8.36	-6.62
	Balance on Services	-0.28	-0.25	0.37	0.41	0.44	0.06	0.11	-0.15	0.21	-0.31	-1.05	-1.07	-0.55
			-5.64	-3.72	-4.74	-3.95	-3.06	-0.48	-0.25	-0.32	-0.36	-0.51	-0.48	-0.51
	Balance on Transfers	9.32	3.36	0.93	0.82	0.56	0.68	0.43	0.70	0.80	1.23	1.04	1.07	1.13
Slovakia	Current account balance					-4.44	5.00	2.67	-9.56	-8.56	-9.01	-4.86	-3.62	-8.58
	Balance on Goods					-7.77	0.39	-1.19	-11.18	-9.76	-10.70	-5.41	-4.66	-10.43
	Balance on Services					2.82	4.95	3.45	0.85	0.95	0.73	1.08	2.23	2.34
	Balance on Incomes					-0.32	-0.79	-0.07	-0.22	-0.58	-0.72	-1.49	-1.80	-1.53
	Balance on Transfers / Balance on Incomes	-3.77				0.83	0.46	0.48	0.99	0.83	1.67	0.97	0.60	1.04
Slovenia	Current account balance	8.99	2.98	1.02	7.40	1.51	3.98	-0.53	0.17	0.06	-0.75	-3.90	-3.37	-0.36
	Balance on Goods	1.59	-3.50	-2.07	6.32	-1.22	-2.34	-5.08	-4.37	-4.26	-4.03	-6.20	-6.28	-3.31
	Balance on Services	7.61	6.56	3.81	1.44	2.96	4.47	3.08	3.36	3.46	2.51	1.81	2.41	2.66
	Balance on Incomes	-0.82	-0.68	-0.84	-0.73	-0.41	1.18	0.96	0.70	0.22	0.14	-0.12	-0.14	-0.40
	Balance on Transfers	0.61	0.61	0.12	0.37	0.18	0.67	0.51	0.48	0.65	0.62	0.61	0.64	0.68
Romania	Current account balance	5.34	-8.73	-3.51	-7.99	-4.45	-1.42	-5.00	-7.28	-6.06	-7.10	-4.13	-3.69	-5.91
	Balance on Goods	4.77	-8.96	-3.83	-7.25	-4.28	-1.37	-4.45	-6.99	-5.61	-6.28	-3.53	-4.56	7.48
	Balance on Services	0.52	-0.46	-0.48	-0.86	-0.44	-0.57	-0.92	-1.09	-1.17	-1.56	-1.20	-0.69	-0.55
	Balance on Incomes	0.04	0.42	0.05	-0.44	-0.55	-0.43	-0.68	-0.87	-0.91	-1.06	-1.15	-0.77	-0.84
	Balance on Transfers		0.28	0.76	0.57	0.81	0.94	1.04	1.68	1.64	1.80	1.76	2.33	2.96
Bulgaria	Current account balance	-2.78	-1.99	-0.95	-4.19	-10.15	-0.33	-1.51	1.63	10.06	-0.48	-5.03	-5.57	-6.11
	Balance on Goods	-2.56	-1.31	-0.39	-2.47	-8.19	-0.17	0.28	1.22	3.09	-2.99	-8.35	-9.33	-11.56
	Balance on Services	0.82	0.32	-1.06	-1.11	-0.53	0.11	0.50	3.33	8.13	2.93	2.43	4.01	4.02
	Balance on Incomes	-1.18	-1.19	-0.35	-1.11	-1.78	-1.99	-3.30	-3.96	-3.43	-2.23	-1.43	-2.55	-2.24
	Balance on Transfers	0.13	0.19	0.85	0.50	0.34	1.72	1.01	1.04	2.28	1.81	2.32	2.30	3.68

Source: WIIW Database; own calculations.

Graph 6: Net balances of CEECs in components of services trade, 1993-2001

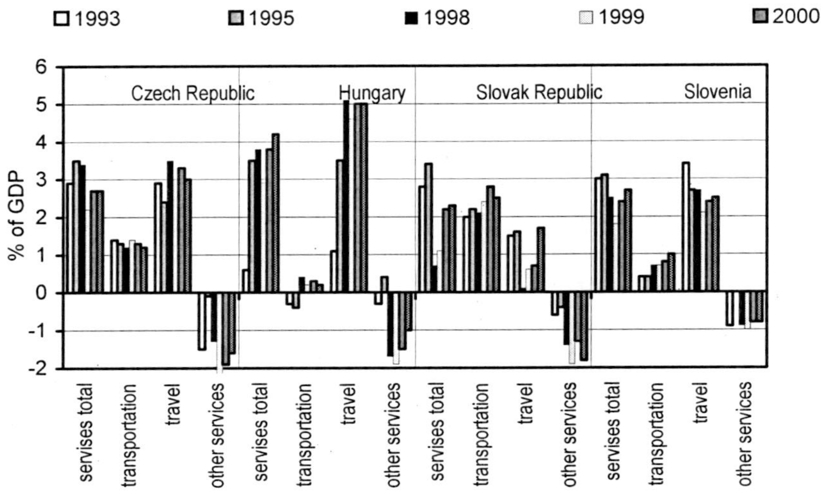

Source: WIIW.

Although a differentiated analysis of the non-manufacturing parts of the current accounts across the CEECs would be very interesting in itself we shall now - for reasons of space - move towards a mote detailed examination of trade specialization within manufacturing.

5.2. TRADE SPECIALIZATION IN MANUFACTURING

In order to analyse structures and tendencies of trade specialization of CEECs within manufacturing we use the COMEXT database which collects all trade with the EU countries as reporting countries. The database includes data at a very detailed (8-digit) level. The very detailed level will be used in section 5.3 when examining relative export prices as indicators for relative product quality. In this section we shall examine trade structures at the level of industry groupings which themselves are constructed as aggregates of industries defined at the 3-digit NACE level. The industry groupings used are the same ones which were defined for the series of European Competitiveness Reports (see European

Commission, 1999 and 2000) and the WIIW Competitiveness study (WIIW, 2001).

Earlier studies (see e.g. Landesmann, 2000) have shown that the Central and East European countries' trading structure with the EU-12 started in 1989 with a profile typical of less developed economies: the representation of exports of the labour-intensive industrial branches was above-average (in relation to EU imports as a whole), in the capital-, R&D- and skill-intensive branches below-average (particularly in the latter two), while the representation of exports of energy-intensive branches was above-average - which reflected the heritage of cheap energy supplies within the CMEA. Over time, important changes took place in the CEECs' export structure to the EU and in the revealed comparative advantage indicators (RCAs) in the different categories of industries. The most remarkable change took place in Hungary: from sizeable deficits in its export structure in the areas of capital-, R&D- and skill-intensive industries, these deficits either eroded completely or turned into surpluses. This pattern was followed in a much less spectacular manner by the Czech Republic and Poland, where deficits in the representation of skill-, R&D- and capital-intensive branches were also reduced. For these economies and also for the Slovak Republic the relatively strong presence of energy-intensive branches declined substantially, while this was not the case with Romanian and Bulgarian exports to the EU (particularly in the latter case, dependence upon energy-intensive exports to the EU increased markedly until 1998). Also the picture with respect to labour-intensive industries was remarkably different in the cases of Romania and Bulgaria, on the one hand, and the CEEC-5 on the other: in the first two, labour-intensive branches became the predominant segment of their exports to the EU, while the dependence upon labour-intensive branches got somewhat reduced in the other countries.

Discontinuity in statistics does not allow us to present a full analysis of patterns of trade specialization going back to 1989 and we focus instead on the period 1995 to 2000 (from 1995 onwards 15 EU reporting countries are represented in the COMEXT database and consistent CN-NACE classification converters can be used). As mentioned above, we shall employ for this analysis a qualitative grouping of industries (derived from an aggregation of 3-digit NACE industries) which was being used in the EU Competitiveness Reports and has hence the advantage of immediate comparability with the analysis conducted there for the EU member countries. Two "taxonomies" are applied: one based on the use of cluster-analytic techniques where industries are clustered (and industry groupings identified) by the use of a number of industrial organization and input use criteria (**taxonomy 1**). This led to the distinction of five industry groupings: mainstream, labour-intensive, capital-intensive, marketing-driven and technology-driven. In the other taxonomy (**taxonomy 2**) industries are grouped by skill intensity (low-skill, medium-skill/blue-collar, medium-skill/white-collar, high-skill). The correspondence between NACE 3-digit industries and the two taxonomies can be seen in Appendix Table 9 and more detail on the underlying methodology can be obtained from Peneder (2001).

In Table 6 we have calculated (in Table 6 a) for taxonomy 1 and in Table 6 b) for taxonomy 2) the percentage points by which certain industry groupings are more or less represented in the export structures of the CEECs compared to the export structure of the EU Northern countries (all EU countries except for Spain, Portugal and Greece). The figures for the EU Southern cohesion countries have been similarly calculated as differences in the percentage representation of their exports to the EU in the different industry groupings relative to that of the EU-North. Finally for the EU Northern countries the actual percentage representation of the industry groupings in their total (intra-EU) exports are presented. In Graph 7, we have picked out the shares in countries' exports to the EU of those industry groupings where the qualitatively most striking differences can be observed: the labour-intensive and technology-driven groupings of taxonomy 1 and the low-skill and the high-skill groupings of taxonomy 2.

We can see the following:

- In general there is still a relatively stronger representation of the labour-intensive branches in the CEECs export structures to the EU (compared to the EU Northern countries' export structures). For Poland, Bulgaria, Romania and the Baltic states this dependence is very strong - in fact much stronger than for the EU-South, and for Bulgaria, Romania, Latvia and Lithuania this dependence has, furthermore, sharply increased over the period 1995 to 2000. For the other countries, this "over representation" of labour-intensive branches - relatively to the advanced EU member countries - has declined, for some quite sharply. For Hungary a (branch) specialization in this direction no longer exists.
- With respect to technology-intensive branches, which accounted for about 33% of EU Northern EU exports, the CEECs started off in 1995 (earlier figures would indicate that this was even more the case before that) with sizable "deficits" in these areas. Over the period 1995 to 2000 these deficits have declined substantially in Hungary, the Czech and Slovak Republics, Estonia (in fact, in Hungary and Estonia they have turned into surpluses), and in Poland more mildly. In Bulgaria, Romania, Latvia and Lithuania these deficits have remained at very high levels and in most cases have further increased.
- The picture is similar if we look at the two extreme categories of **taxonomy 2**, i.e. the relative representation of low-skill- and high-skill-intensive industries respectively in the countries' export structures to the EU. Again we can see that the CEECs all started off with an over-representation of the low-skill-intensive branches in their exports to the EU (just as the Southern EU countries did). This over-representation fell quite dramatically in the case of a number of CEECs (the Czech and Slovak Republics, Hungary, Poland, Slovenia and Estonia), but again remains at a very high level in Bulgaria, Romania and Lithuania.
- In the high-skill industries, deficits remain in all CEECs (as they do in the Southern EU countries) but the picture shows again quite a bit of differentiation across the CEECs, so that the percentage differ-

ences (to EU-North) are below 10% in the case of the Czech and Slovak Republics, Hungary and Slovenia.

Thus the picture which emerges is of strong differentiation across the CEECs by a number of indicators of revealed comparative advantage (see also the WIIW Competitiveness Report, WIIW, 2001, for further indicators and analysis) in their structures and, furthermore, tendencies of trade specialization. While some of the CEECs have reduced dramatically (or even lost completely) their inter-industry specialization towards labour-intensive, low skill branches and made some inroads into technology-driven and skill-intensive branches, others show clearly that their specialization structures got "locked in" (at least so far) in the labour-intensive, low-skill sectors. We take this as support of our basic hypothesis that catching-up patterns can give rise to "comparative advantage switchovers" if countries can utilize the high potential for productivity growth (and, as we shall see below, of product quality upgrading) in industries in which the initial technological (and product quality) gaps are rather high. Alternatively, countries which cannot utilize this potential remain locked in a specialization pattern which remains the typical one between (technologically) advanced and less advanced economies.

Table 6: Export structure of CEECs compared to EU-North and EU-South

a) Export shares (taxonomy I - factor intensities) - differences to EU-North

	Czech Republic		Hungary		Poland		Slovak Republic		Slovenia		Bulgaria		Romania	
	1995	**2000**	**1995**	**2000**	**1995**	**2000**	**1995**	**2000**	**1995**	**2000**	**1995**	**2000**	**1995**	**2000**
1 mainstream	7.65	8.95	-0.83	-3.42	-4.37	-0.56	-1.34	2.02	6.96	7.84	-10.32	-8.95	-7.28	-5.13
2 labour-intensive	14.37	8.13	11.11	2.07	25.88	19.44	13.59	8.90	16.64	12.58	10.46	21.50	32.33	35.84
3 capital intensive	0.36	-4.10	-3.09	-10.15	1.70	-3.35	13.79	1.96	-5.52	-3.09	25.41	16.53	3.68	-7.99
4 marketing-driven	-6.22	-4.47	-1.07	-4.85	-5.44	-2.73	-7.80	-4.94	-7.99	-5.01	-0.58	-0.03	-2.59	3.08
5 technology driven	-16.16	-8.51	-6.12	16.35	-17.77	-12.80	-18.24	-7.95	-10.10	-12.32	-24.97	-29.05	-26.14	-25.79

	Estonia		Latvia		Lithuania		EU-South		EU-North (Shares)	
	1995	**2000**	**1995**	**2000**	**1995**	**2000**	**1995**	**2000**	**1995**	**2000**
1 mainstream	-10.66	-12.24	-14.21	-15.27	-14.88	-12.46	-6.60	-7.37	21.67	20.82
2 labour-intensive	27.39	18.06	20.75	46.93	22.49	34.18	12.37	1.84	11.39	11.60
3 capital intensive	8.01	-5.51	31.36	7.99	22.38	9.33	-3.23	2.56	23.81	23.37
4 marketing-driven	-8.00	-6.33	-10.90	-8.12	-6.26	-3.63	4.56	7.00	15.53	11.62
5 technology driven	-16.73	6.01	-27.00	-31.53	-23.74	-27.42	-7.11	-4.02	27.60	32.59

b) Export shares (taxonomy II - skill intensities) - differences to EU-North

	Czech Republic		**Hungary**		**Poland**		**Slovak Republic**		**Slovenia**		**Bulgaria**		**Romania**	
	1995	**2000**	**1995**	**2000**	**1995**	**2000**	**1995**	**2000**	**1995**	**2000**	**1995**	**2000**	**1995**	**2000**
1 low skill	6.54	-3.32	9.41	-7.79	17.08	4.77	12.68	1.42	3.94	-0.08	38.28	45.81	38.06	36.64
2 medium skill/ blue collar	7.33	16.52	3.92	9.36	11.27	20.15	5.80	13.82	12.85	16.61	-13.42	-14.23	-3.90	-5.40
3 medium skill/ white collar	-7.11	-8.09	-2.34	0.92	-14.05	-11.91	-5.43	-7.53	-6.39	-7.20	-11.90	-20.14	-19.28	-17.64
4 high skill	-6.77	-5.11	-10.99	-2.49	-14.30	-13.01	-13.05	-7.71	-10.40	-9.34	-12.96	-11.44	-14.87	-13.60
	Estonia		**Latvia**		**Lithuania**				**EU-South**		**EU-North (Shares)**			
	1995	**2000**	**1995**	**2000**	**1995**	**2000**			**1995**	**2000**	**1995**	**2000**		
1 low skill	13.29	4.01	3.68	2.10	19.75	22.05			23.36	14.88	29.41	26.97		
2 medium skill/ blue collar	2.76	7.95	3.08	24.77	-5.28	-1.34			1.67	-2.75	19.59	20.56		
3 medium skill/ white collar	-7.50	3.26	11.25	-9:75	4.07	-3.56			-11.49	-7.28	32.00	33.62		
4 high skill	-8.55	-15.21	-18.00	-17.12	-18.53	-17.15			-13.54	-4.85	19.00	18.86		

Note: Differences of export shares between CEECs and EU-South to EU-North; export shares for EU-North.
Source: Comext data base and own calculations

Graph 7: Shares of different industry groupings in exports to EU

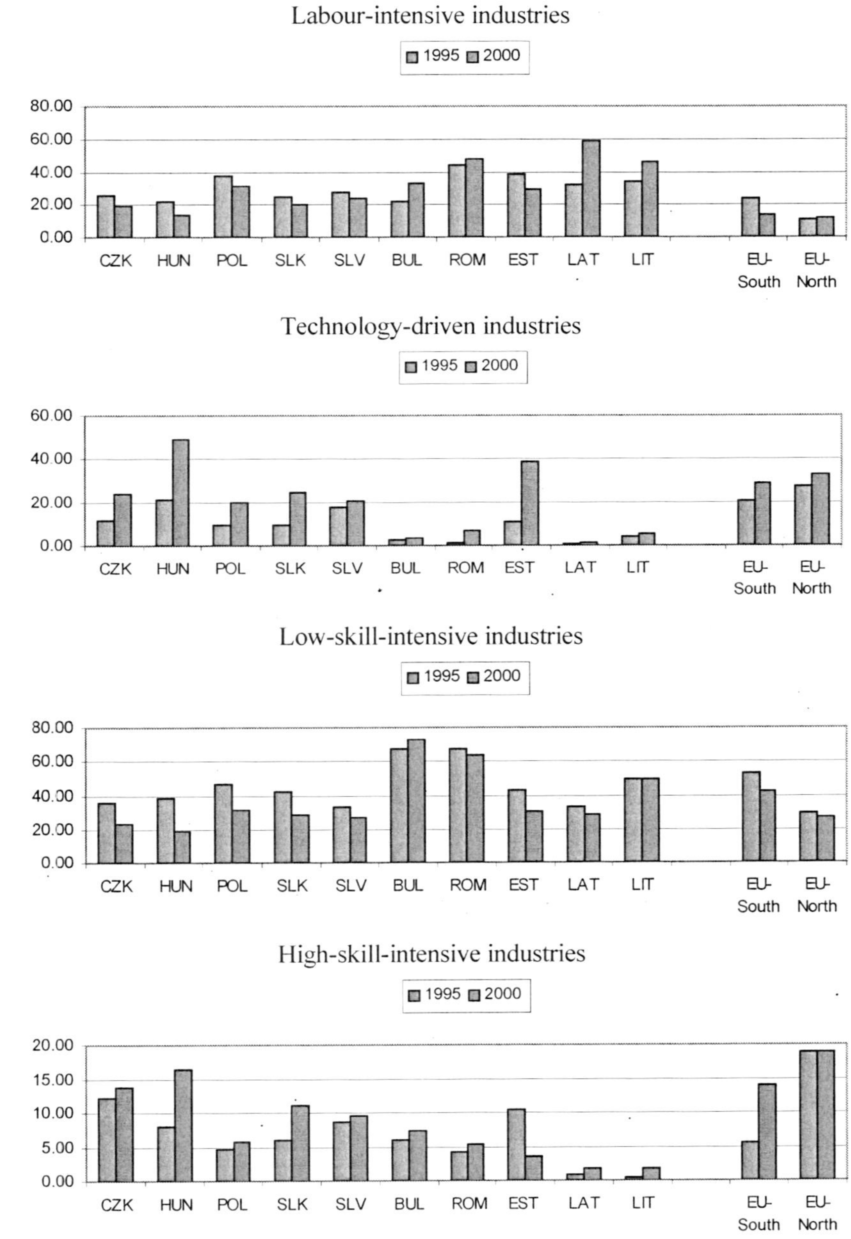

Source: Comext database; own calculations

However, we have still to be cautious at this stage: What we have analysed in this section was a distinct pattern of **inter-industry specialization** which emerges in trade between the CEECs and the EU. However, the analysis of inter-industry specialization is only one aspect of trade specialization; the other would be **intra-industry specialization**, i.e. the specialization on particular production stages or on product quality segments within an industry. For reasons of space, we are not going to present the results from detailed analysis of patterns of "vertical product specialisation" which we have undertaken, i.e. the specialization on particular production stages or on product quality segments within an industry. For this we refer the reader to the results reported in Landesmann and Stehrer (2002). The results support the Gerschenkron hypothesis with respect to strong upward movements in the vertical (i.e. product quality) structure of intra-industry trade, particular in those industries where the initial "product quality gaps" were large, in the case of the advanced CEE economies.

In this context, let us also point out that there is well-established strong evidence (see Landesmann, 2000 and WIIW, 2001) for **growing intra-industry trade** between the more advanced CEECs and the EU. This is in line with the "new" trade theory which suggests that trade among industrialized countries is motivated by product differentiation and economies of scale. Measured by Grubel-Lloyd indices, intra-industry trade has been most pronounced in EU trade of the Czech Republic, Slovenia and Hungary whereas it has been lowest in Latvia, Lithuania and Romania. Compared with the early period of transition (and even more so with the pre-transition period), intra-industry trade between the more advanced CEECs (the Czech and Slovak Republics, Hungary and Poland) and the EU has increased further whereas it has more or less stagnated in Bulgaria and Romania. Judging also by the high shares in exports and imports, intra-industry trade (including outward processing trade) has been of particular importance in textiles as well as in electrical, optical and transport equipment. Again, the evidence on the levels and rates of change of intra-industry trade points towards a strong differentiation amongst the CEECs.

6. *THE ALLOCATION OF FOREIGN DIRECT INVESTMENT ACROSS BRANCHES*

We finally look at two important factors which are generally regarded as important in determining the course of catching-up and the pattern of specialization of the Central and Eastern European countries. We refer here, firstly, to the role of foreign direct investments (FDI) as important carriers of technological and managerial know-how transfer and, secondly (in section 7), to the role of human capital whose existence is seen as crucial in facilitating the adoption of new technologies and as influencing a country's pattern of trade and industrial specialization.

There is broad agreement in the literature that FDI plays an important role in restructuring and in improving competitiveness (see the general evidence world-wide e.g. in UNCTAD, 2001, Barrel and Holland, 2000, and for the CEECs, see e.g. Hunya, 2000). Table 7 reports data on FDI stocks in 2000 for seven Central and Eastern European countries. These data were collected from national sources and/or foreign investment agencies. As there are methodological problems in comparing the data across countries (especially for Hungary and Poland) we shall only discuss the structure of FDI within the countries.

Manufacturing industry has been an important target of FDI in most Candidate Countries attracting nearly half of the inward FDI stock as of end-2000 (exceptions are the Baltic states and no data are presented for Bulgaria and Romania in Table 7). The sectoral distribution of FDI is highly uneven, reflecting the varying attractiveness of individual branches for foreign investors as well as differences in the privatisation policies pursued by the individual Candidate Countries (see Hunya, 2000). Generally FDI inflows have been high in both the domestically oriented food, beverages and tobacco industry (DA) especially in the Czech Republic, Hungary, Poland, Slovakia, Latvia and Lithuania, in some natural resource-based industries such as non-metallic mineral products (DI), as well as in export-oriented branches such as electrical, optical (DL) and transport equipment (DM) industries.

Table 7: Foreign direct investment (FDI) stock in manufacturing industry, 2000 (USD million)

NACE	Activities	Czech Republic[1)]	Hungary	Poland	Slovak Republic	Slovenia	Estonia	Latvia	Lithuania
DA	Food products; beverages and tobacco	1125.6	918.4	4961.9	229.0	38.5	128.2	100.2	269.3
DB	Textiles and textile products	203.6	142.6	254.4	20.6	12.7	78.6	32.5	108.6
DC	Leather and leather products	4.1	22.8	17.2	15.3	12.4	.	1.8	0.3
DD	Wood and wood products	89.7	40.4	240	17.1	5.6	93.6[3)]	57.9	33.0
DE	Pulp, paper & paper products, publishing & printing	587.7	159.4	1470.3	105.9	191.6	.	17.9	25.2
DF	Coke, refined petroleum products & nuclear fuel	210.9	515.9[2)]	.	151.6	.	6.0	0.0	42.8
DG	Chemicals, chemical products and man-made fibres	398.0		1285.1	117.1	173.2	49.6	38.1	.
DH	Rubber and plastic products	104.2	176.7	591.4	21.3	141.4	6.3	10.5	26.7
DI	Other non-metallic mineral products	1467.8	233.6	2785.7	97.9	73.3	.	23.7	37.6
DJ	Basic metals and fabricated metal products	624.2	194.6	403.4	819.2	88.5	22.3	25.7	11.6
DK	Machinery and equipment n.e.c.	218.7	199.1	317.1	80.4	144.7	18.5	21.5	7.4
DL	Electrical and optical equipment	662.2	680.6	1575.1	80.0	122.4	16.6	5.9	53.0
DM	Transport equipment	989.5	366.0	5167.7	122.3	133.9	39.1	1.3	48.1
DN	Manufacturing n.e.c.	100.5	38.3	393.5	7.8	4.5	.	8.1	7.9
D	Manufacturing	6786.7	3688.4	19462.8	1885.4	1142.7	567.7	345.0	671.5
	FDI total	17552.1	10104.0	45772.0	3692.2	2808.5	2645.4	2081.3	2334.3

Notes: 1) 1999. - 2) Includes DF+DG. - 3) Includes DD+DE.

Remarks: Czech Republic: equity capital, reinvested earnings, loans. Hungary: nominal capital based on corporation-tax declarations.
Poland: equity capital, reinvested earnings gross; projects over USD 1 million capital based on PAIZ data. Slovak Republic: equity capital, reinvested earnings - in the corporate sector. Slovenia: equity capital, reinvested earnings, loans. Estonia: equity capital, reinvested earnings, loans. Latvia: equity capital, reinvested earnings, loans. Lithuania: equity capital, reinvested earnings, loans. Croatia: equity capital.

Source: National banks, Statistical Offices and Foreign Investment Agencies.

Using again our previous classification into low-tech, medium-/high-tech, and resource-intensive industries and looking at the shares of sales from FIEs (enterprises with some degree of foreign ownership; for details on this database see Hunya, 2002) in total industry sales, we can see that in all four countries depicted in Graph 8 the FIEs account for a higher share of sales in the medium-/high-tech than in the low-tech or the resource-intensive branches. This is quite consistent with the picture of structural change and trade specialization depicted for the more advanced of the CEECs in the previous sections of this paper.

Graph 8: The share of FIEs in different industry groupings (1999 in %)

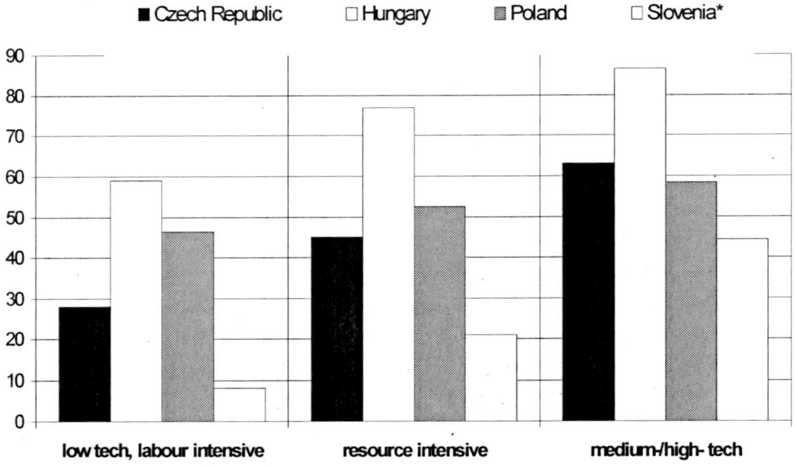

* Slovenia without tobacco.

Overall, there are two points we want to make with regard to FDI:

- The presence of FDI across CEECs remains very uneven and hence the role it can perform in facilitating the up-grading of the CEECs' industrial structures will actually be performed to different degrees. This is compatible with a picture of differentiated catching-up patterns across the CEECs as pointed out in the previous sections of the report.

- The distribution of FDI across branches (although this point needs further elaboration which will not be undertaken in this paper) indicates that FDI is attracted also to branches which can be classified as medium-/high-tech and thus plays a role in the productivity and quality up grading process in these branches (for further evidence on the impact of foreign ownership involvement in further productivity improvements and export performance in CEECs, see Hunya, 2002).

7. *THE ROLE OF EDUCATIONAL ATTAINMENT AND LABOUR MARKET DEVELOPMENTS WITH REGARD TO DIFFERENT SKILL GROUPS*

It is well known that the large cumulative employment drops in the CEE region since 1989 has been reflected in falling labour force participation rates in all CEECs. A comparison between the transition countries covered here and the EU-15 shows that, despite these considerable falls, participation rates are still higher than the EU average (68%) in the Czech Republic, Slovakia and Romania, similar to the EU-15 level in Poland, and lower than in the EU in Hungary and Bulgaria. Employment rates (total number of employed relative to the population aged 15-64) also show a wide range, from close to 70% in Romania and the Czech Republic (in 1998) to 54% in Hungary. A comparison of employment rates in CEECs and the EU in 1998 shows that the average CEE-7 rate stood at 62.7%, slightly higher than the EU average of 61%. Furthermore, the gender gap in employment rates remained smaller in the CEECs compared to most countries in the EU. Unemployment rates amounted to between 9% and 19% in the CEECs by the year 1999 which reflects the development of the labour force (particularly the participation rate) on the one hand and that of employment levels on the other. Unemployment rates across the region have reached a range not dissimilar to the EU in the early 1990s.

The labour market structure of the accession countries with respect to skill levels and educational attainment must be seen against the background of these changes in participation rates. A first glance at comparable data across CEECs and a comparison with EU Northern and EU Southern economies reveals high shares of upper secondary education (see Table 8).

The data presented in Table 8 were collected from national labour force surveys and compared to data for European countries reported in European Commission (2001). Although there are methodological difficulties these data provide a rough overview of the structure of educational attainment.

Table 8 shows that most countries have a share of lower upper secondary educational levels in the working-age population of about 30% (lowest in the Czech Republic with 24%) which is at more or less the same level as for the EU Northern countries. Higher shares are only reported for Bulgaria and Romania with more than 40%. This can be compared to the EU Southern countries which show a share of almost 60%. With respect to the other aggregates the Central and Eastern European countries have on average higher shares of upper secondary and much lower shares in tertiary education than the EU Northern and even slightly lower shares in tertiary education than the EU Southern countries.

Table 8: Educational shares

		Czech Rep.	Hungary	Poland	Slovenia	Slovak Rep.	Estonia	Latria	Lithuania	Bulgaria	Romania	EU-South	EU-North
Population													
Age group 15-64 by education													
< upper secondary	%	23.8	38.5	33.1	33.9	28.8	26.2	30.6	31.3	43.9	43.2	58.0	28.6
upper secondary	%	67.0	50.3	58.3	53.9	63.5	51.3	55.3	36.8	42.7	49.9	29.2	49.5
Tertiary	%	9.1	11.2	8.6	12.1	7.6	22.5	14.1	31.9	13.4	6.9	12.8	21.9
Labour force													
Age group 15+ by education													
< upper secondary	%	10.4	18.4	15.8	20.7	9.4	12.4	13.8	12.4	22.9	35.7	54.9	23.5
upper secondary	%	77.8	65.4	71.9	62.8	80.0	58.5	66.7	44.9	56.8	55.9	28.3	51.6
Tertiary	%	11.8	16.2	12.3	16.5	10.6	29.1	19.4	42.6	20.3	8.4	16.8	24.9
Employment													
Age group 15+ by education													
< upper secondary	%	8.8	17.4	14.8	19.9	6.9	10.7	12.7	11.4	19.2	36.8	54.7	22.3
upper secondary	%	78.7	65.5	71.3	62.8	80.7	57.4	66.3	42.6	57.7	54.4	28.2	51.8
Tertiary	%	12.6	17.1	13.9	17.3	12.4	31.8	21.0	45.9	23.1	8.7	17.1	25.9
Unemployment													
Age group 15+ by education													
< upper secondary	%	26.7	32.4	20.8	31.9	19.8	23.9	20.8	18.0	39.0	20.0	56.1	38.0
upper secondary	%	69.2	64.1	75.0	62.9	77.2	65.1	69.5	57.4	53.0	75.6	29.5	48.7
Tertiary	%	4.1	3.5	4.2	5.3	2.9	11.0	9.8	24.6	7.9	4.4	14.4	13.3

Source: Employment and labour market in Central European countries, European Commission, 2001 and own calculations.

However, the shares of different educational groupings in the labour force and in employment can differ from those in (working-age) population as participation rates differ across countries and educational levels. Whereas the relative shares between population, labour force and employment across the different educational groups corresponds roughly for the EU Southern and EU Northern countries, there are bigger differences in relation to the Central and Eastern European countries. The share of lower upper secondary educational levels in the labour force and in employment is in most cases much below the share in total population which reveals a very low participation rate. Correspondingly the relative shares of people with upper secondary education and tertiary education in the labour force and in employment are relatively higher.

The skill structure of unemployment similarly reflects this picture and also differs from the EU Northern and EU Southern countries. People with upper secondary educational levels amount to about 60% to 70% of unemployed compared to 30% in EU-South and 50% in EU-North. On the other hand the share of people with lower upper secondary level is lower (the reason might be the lower participation rate) whereas the share for people with tertiary education is much lower. Unemployment rates are particularly low amongst the persons with tertiary education, even in comparison with the EU Southern and EU Northern countries. This points towards a structural problem, i.e. the lack of highly-skilled workers/employees. However, these data mask further severe deficiencies with respect to particular occupations. E.g. the EBRD (2000) reports a lack of skills especially in managerial and other high-skilled employment which corresponds to the relatively low shares in tertiary education.

Graph 9 shows the evolution of employment levels by skill groupings (ISCED classification) for three of the CEE Candidate Countries. The compilation of this dataset from national labour force surveys (LFS) was laborious and the data series have different starting points as the compilation of LFS data started at different dates in the different economies. The uniform picture which emerges is that there were strong

The uniform picture which emerges is that there were strong negative employment developments in the lowest skill categories while there were positive labour market pressures for the higher skill groupings (mostly those with tertiary education, in some countries those with upper secondary educational levels).

Although the above definitely requires much more detailed analysis, the evidence obtained with regard to strong labour demand pressures for the highly skilled in the transition countries is consistent with the picture of a catching-up process with qualitative up-grading which has been developed in the earlier sections of this paper.

Graph 9:

Czech Republic: Changes of employment in skill categories

(Index: 1993 = 100)

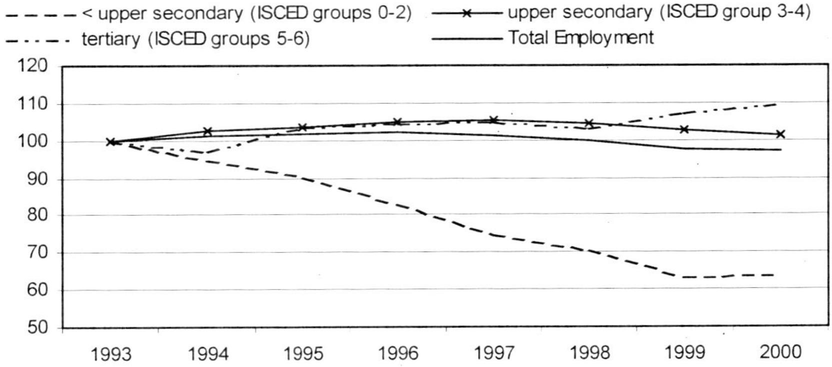

Hungary: Changes of employment in skill categories
(Index: 1992 = 100)

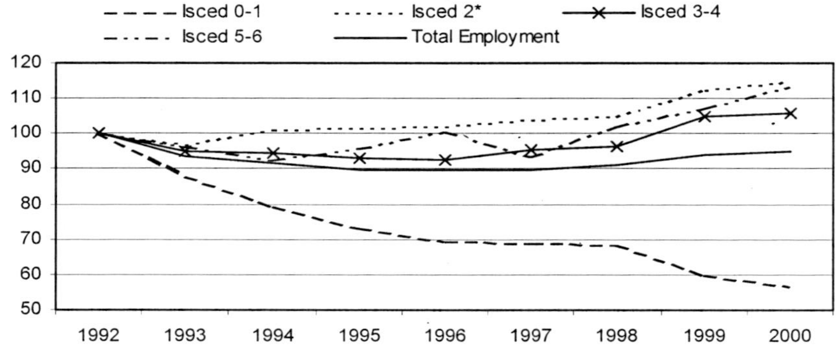

Poland: Changes of employment in skill categories
(Index: 1993 = 100)

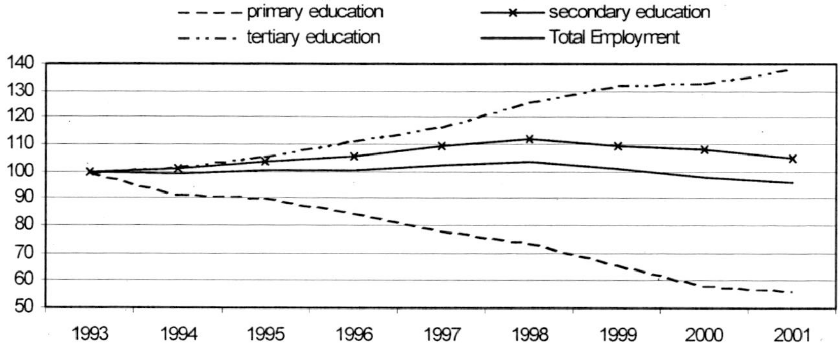

8. *Summary*

This paper has attempted to analyse the evolving patterns of industrial specialization in Central and Eastern Europe. We have shown that a differentiated picture emerges, with some countries catching up relatively fast in technologically more sophisticated branches and also improving their positions in intra-branch product quality. This picture is compatible with an analytical approach in which the potential exists to turn comparative advantages in favour of those areas in which initially bigger gaps (in productivity and product quality) exist. This is an application of the Gerschenkron hypothesis ("advantage of backwardness") at the industrial level. However, the existence of such a potential does not automatically imply its utilization (a point which Abramovitz emphasized). The approach makes room for a wide diversity of qualitative catching-up patterns and evolving positions of catching-up economies in the international division of labour. This is what we observe with respect to the countries in Central and Eastern Europe where one set of countries got (so far) "locked in" in a rather traditional pattern of trade and industrial specialization (in low-skill, labour-intensive branches), while other CEECs (to varying degrees) show a much more dynamic pattern of integration into the European division of labour.

We have substantiated this picture of diversity by analysing first the broad patterns of structural change in Central and Eastern Europe (section 2) and then the changes in employment and production structures within manufacturing (section 3). We then moved towards examining the evidence for a dynamically evolving structure of comparative advantage with a detailed assessment of differential patterns of productivity and unit (labour) cost growth across branches (section 4) as well as with an analysis of the evolving structure of trade specialization (section 5). Finally, we sketched the roles of foreign direct investment (section 6) and of the existence and utilization of educational attainment (section 7) as important factors in determining the positions of individual countries (the analysis could similarly be extended to regions) in the evolving division of labour in the European economy as a whole. We could show that the picture concerning labour demand for different skill groups supports our analysis with respect to the up grading of industrial structures in the more advanced of the CEE Candidate Countries.

As regards EU enlargement, our analysis shows clearly that different CEECs are in different positions with regard to their achieved levels of catching-up, and this refers not only to overall levels but - probably more importantly - to the qualitative nature of their structural transformations and their positions in cross-European trade structures. We expect such differentiation to have a bearing on how they will cope with the additional adjustments required by the accession process itself and on what footing they will be able to participate in the integrated structures of the enlarged European economy. This, of course, also has implications for the instruments which will be required to deal with the problems of cohesion which will get further accentuated not only as a result of the accession process itself but as a result of the existence of a set of other economies which are highly integrated with the EU but will not join in the first round.

Differentiation across regions shows a similar picture of differentiation across countries (see Fazekas, 2002). Again, some regions are catching up in terms of industrial up grading, they are very successful in attracting FDI which accounts for a large share of overall exports, while other regions remain "locked in" in low-skill areas of production, with low shares of well-educated personnel and little evidence for up grading. Regional differentiation constitutes thus a great challenge for cohesion policies in the Candidate Countries.

9. *REFERENCES*

Aiginger, K. (1997), "The use of unit values to discriminate between price and quality competition", Cambridge Journal of Economics, vol. 21, pp. 571-592.

Abramovitz, M (1986), "Catching-up, forging ahead and falling behind", Journal of Economic History, vol. 46, pp. 385-406.

Aturupane, C., Djankov, S., Hoekman, B. (1999), "Horizontal and vertical intra-industry trade between Eastern Europe and the European Union", Weltwirtschaftliches Archiv, vol. 135, pp. 62-81.

Baldone, S., Sdogati, F., Tajoli, L. (2001), "Patterns and Determinants of International Fragmentation of Production: Evidence from Outward Processing Trade between the EU and Central Eastern European Countries", Weltwirtschaftliches Archiv, vol. 137(1), pp. 80-

104.

Barrel, R., Holland, D. (2000), "Foreign direct investment and enterprise restructuring in Central Europe", Economics of Transition, vol. 8(2), pp. 477-504.

Burgstaller, J., Landesmann, M. (1999), "Trade Performance of East European Producers on EU Markets: an Assessment of Product Quality", The Vienna Institute for International Economic Studies (WIIW), WIIW Research Reports, no. 255, Vienna.

European Commission (1998), "The Competitiveness of European Industry. 1999 Report", Working document of the services of the European Commission, Luxembourg.

European Commission (1999), "European Competitiveness Report 1999", EC. (See http://europa.eu.int/comm/enterprise/enterprise_policy/competitiveness/index.htm)

European Commission (2000), "European Competitiveness Report 2000", EC. (See http://europa.eu.int/comm/enterprise/enterprise_policy/competitiveness/index.htm)

European Commission (2001), "Employment in Europe 2001. Recent Trends and Prospects", European Commission, DG Employment and Social Affairs.

EBRD (2000), "Transition Report 2000. Employment, Skills, and Transition", London.

Fazekas, K. (2002), "Regional labour markets in Hungary and EU accession", paper presented at the Workshop on "Economic Integration and Regional Development - EU Experience and Expected Effects in Eastern Europe" at The Vienna Institute for International Economic Studies (WIIW), 6/7 June 2002, Vienna.

Fontangné, L., Freudenberg, M. (1997), "Intra-Industry trade: methodological issues reconsidered", Document de Travail, 97-01, CEPII, Paris.

Gerschenkron, A. (1962), "Economic Backwardness in Historical Perspective", Harvard University Press, Cambridge Mass.

Greenaway, D., Hine, R., Milner, C. (1994), "Country-specific factors and the pattern of horizontal and vertical intra-industry trade in the UK", Weltwirtschaftliches Archiv, vol. 130, pp. 77-100.

Grossman, G.M., Helpman, E. (1991), "Innovation and Growth in the Global Economy", MIT Press, Cambridge.

Havlik, P., Landesmann, M., Stehrer, R. (2001), "Competitiveness of CEE Industries: Evidence from Foreign Trade Specialisation and Quality Indicators", The Vienna Institute for International Economic Studies, WIIW Research Reports, no. 278, Vienna.

Havlik, P. et al. (2001), "Transition Countries in 2001: Robust Domestic Demand, Concerns About External Fragility Reappear", The Vienna Institute for International Economic Studies, WIIW Research Reports, no. 277, Vienna.

Hunya, G. (2000), "Foreign direct investment in CEEC manufacturing", in: Landesmann, M. (ed.), "WIIW Structural Report. Structural Developments in Central and Eastern Europe", The Vienna Institute for International Economic Studies (WIIW), Vienna, chapter 5.

Hunya, G. (2000), "Integration Through Foreign Direct Investment. Making Central European Countries and Industries Competitive", Edward Elgar, Cheltenham, UK.

Hunya, G. (2002), "Recent Impacts of Foreign Direct Investment on Growth and Restructuring in Central European Transition Countries", The Vienna Institute for International Economic Studies (WIIW), WIIW Research Reports, no. 284, Vienna.

Jansen, M., Landesmann, M. (1999), "European competitiveness: quality rather than price", in: Fagerberg, J. et al. (eds.), "The Economic Challenge for Europe: Adapting to Innovation-based Growth", Edward Elgar, Cheltenham, UK.

Krugman, P. (1986), "A technology gap model of international trade", in: Jungenfeldt, K., Hague, D. (eds.), "Structural Adjustment in Advanced Economies", Macmillan, New York.

Landesmann, M. (2000), "Structural change in the transition economies, 1989-1999", in: Economic Survey of Europe, United Nations Economic Commission for Europe, no. 2000 (2/3), pp. 95-123.

Landesmann, M., Stehrer, R. (1999), "Convergence Patterns at the Industrial Level: the Dynamics of Comparative Advantage", The Vienna Institute for International Economic Studies (WIIW), WIIW Working Papers, no. 11.

Landesmann, M., Stehrer, R. (2000), "Industrial specialisation, catching-up and labour market dynamics", Metroeconomica, vol. 51(1), pp. 67-101.

Landesmann, M., Stehrer, R. (2001), "Convergence patterns and switchovers in comparative advantage", Structural Change and Economic Dynamics, vol. 12, pp. 399-423.

Landesmann, M., Stehrer, R. (2002), "The CEECs in the Enlarged Europe: convergence patterns, specialisation and labour market implications", Research Report 286, The Vienna Institute for International Economic Studies, July.

Landesmann, M., Stehrer, R. (2003), "A (nearly) comprehensive model of the dynamics of international economic integration", WIIW Working Paper, forthcoming.

Landesmann, M., Stehrer R., Burgstaller, J. (2000), "Catching-up at the industrial level - Prospects for the CEEC's", in: "Structural Developments in Central and Eastern Europe", WIW Structural Report, The Vienna Institute for International Economic Studies, printed in Bratislava.

Peneder, M. (2001), "Entrepreneurial Competition and Industrial Location", Edward Elgar, Cheltenham, UK.

Römisch, R. (2001), "Trade in Services in the Central and East European Countries", The Vienna Institute for International Economic Studies (WIIW), WIIW Research Reports, no. 274.

Stehrer, R. (2002), "Dynamics of Trade Integration and Technological Convergence", Economic Systems Research, 14(3), 219-244.

Stehrer, R., Wörz, J. (2001), "Technological Convergence and Trade Patterns", The Vienna Institute for International Economic Studies (WIIW), WIIW Working Papers, no. 19.

Taylor, M.S. (1993), "Quality Ladders and Ricardian Trade", Journal of International Economics, vol. 34(3-4), pp. 225-243.

Temple, J. (1999), "The New Growth Evidence", Journal of Economic Literature, vol. XXXVII, pp. 112-156.

UNCTAD (2001), "World Investment Report", United Nations, Geneva.

Vidovic, H. (2002), "The Services Sectors in Central and Eastern Europe", The Vienna Institute for International Economic Studies (WIIW), commissioned study.

WIIW (2001), "Competitiveness of Industry in CEE Candidate Countries", Report to the European Commission, DG Enterprise, Final Report, July 2001; available on the EU DG Enterprise Web Site.

10. Appendix

Table 9

WIFO Taxonomies		*Taxonomy I*	*Taxonomy II*
	NACE rev. 1	**factor inputs**	**labour skills**
Meat products	151	4	1
Fish and fish products	152	4	1
Fruits and vegetables	153	4	1
Vegetable and animal oils and fats	154	4	1
Dairy products; ice cream	155	4	1
Grain mill products and starches	156	4	1
Prepared animal feeds	157	4	1
Other food products	158	4	1
Beverages	159	4	1
Tobacco products	160	4	1
Textile fibres	171	3	1
Textile weaving	172	2	1
Made-up textile articles	174	2	1
Other textiles	175	1	1
Knitted and crocheted fabrics	176	1	1
Knitted and crocheted articles	177	1	1
Leather clothes	181	2	1
Other wearing apparel and accessories	182	2	1
Dressing and dyeing of fur; articles of fur	183	2	1
Tanning and dressing of leather	191	4	1
Luggage, handbags, saddlery and harness	192	4	1
Footwear	193	4	1
Sawmilling, planing and impregnation of wood	201	2	2
Panels and boards of wood	202	2	2
Builders' carpentry and joinery	203	2	2
Wooden containers	204	2	2
Other products of wood; articles of cork, etc.	205	2	2
Pulp, paper and paperboard	211	3	3
Articles of paper and paperboard	212	1	3
Publishing	221	4	3
Printing	222	4	3
Coke oven products	231		
Refined petroleum and nuclear fuel	232	3	3
Nuclear fuel	233		
Basic chemicals	241	3	3

Table 9 (continued)

Pesticides, other agro-chemical products	242	5	3
Paints, coatings, printing ink	243	1	3
Pharmaceuticals	244	5	4
Detergents, cleaning and polishing, perfumes	245	4	3
Other chemical products	246	5	3
Man-made fibres	247	3	3
Rubber products	251	1	1
Plastic products	252	1	1
Glass and glass products	261	1	1
Ceramic goods	262	2	1
Ceramic tiles and flags	263	3	1
Bricks, tiles and construction products	264	2	1
Cement, lime and plaster	265	3	1
Articles of concrete, plaster and cement	266	1	1
Cutting, shaping, finishing of stone	267	2	1
Other non-metallic mineral products	268	1	1
Basic iron and steel, ferro-alloys (ECSC)	271	3	1
Tubes	272	1	1
Other first processing of iron and steel	273	3	1
Basic precious and non-ferrous metals	274	3	1
Structural metal products	281	2	2
Tanks, reservoirs, central heating radiators and boilers	282	4	2
Steam generators	283	2	2
Cutlery, tools and general hardware	286	4	2
Other fabricated metal products	287	1	2
Machinery for production, use of mech. power	291	1	4
Other general purpose machinery	292	1	4
Agricultural and forestry machinery	293	1	4
Machine-tools	294	2	4
Other special purpose machinery	295	1	4
Weapons and ammunition	296	1	4
Domestic appliances n. e. c.	297	1	3
Office machinery and computers	300	5	4
Electric motors, generators and transformers	311	1	3
Electricity distribution and control apparatus	312	5	3
Isolated wire and cable	313	1	3
Accumulators, primary cells and primary batteries	314	1	3
Lighting equipment and electric lamps	315	1	3
Electrical equipment n. e. c.	316	2	3

Table 9 (continued)

Electronic valves and tubes, other electronic comp.	321	5	3
TV, and radio transmitters, apparatus for line telephony	322	5	3
TV, radio and recording apparatus	323	5	3
Medical equipment	331	5	3
Instruments for measuring, checking, testing, navigating	332	5	3
Optical instruments and photographic equipment	334	5	3
Watches and clocks	335	4	3
Motor vehicles	341	5	2
Bodies for motor vehicles, trailers	342	2	2
Parts and accessories for motor vehicles	343	3	2
Ships and boats	351	2	2
Railway locomotives and rolling stock	352	2	2
Aircraft and spacecraft	353	5	4
Motorcycles and bicycles	354	1	2
Other transport equipment n. e. c.	355	1	2
Furniture	361	2	2
Jewellery and related articles	362	2	2
Musical instruments	363	4	2
Sports goods	364	4	2
Games and toys	365	4	2
Miscellaneous manufacturing n. e. c.	366	4	2

	Taxonomy I :	**Taxonomy II :**
Industry clusters:	1. Mainstream	1. Low-skill industries
	2. Labour-intensive industries	2. Medium-skill/blue-collar workers
	3. Capital-intensive industries	3. Medium-skill/white-collar workers
	4. Marketing-driven industries	4. High-skill industries
	5. Technology-driven industries	

Source: M. Peneder (2001), "Entrepreneurial Competition and Industrial Location", Edward Elgar, Cheltenham, UK.

Differences and Similarities Between CCs and the EU - A CC Perspective

András Inotai

First of all I want to thank the organisers and also the Economic Policy Committee for the invitation and for the possibility to share with you some of my experience and personal remarks concerning the economic development, structural changes and problems in the acceding countries and in a wider European Union. I would like to make altogether nine points.

1. The environment of the enlargement in which most of the structural changes are expected to take place in the coming years. The environment of this enlargement differs to a significant extent from the previous enlargements, for many reasons. First of all, it is a "big bang" enlargement. There will be up to ten countries, eight of them from Central and Eastern Europe that will enter. Of course, as in many other cases, it is a fundamentally politically motivated "big bang" enlargement. That is no problem, the European Union is not just an economic actor, but also a political actor. And all the previous enlargements had had political motivations, some to a larger, and some to a smaller extent. But the problem today is the low level of awareness of the economic consequences of the political decision. While during the Mediterranean enlargement, these economic consequences were fully taken into account, in the sense that the European Community was prepared financially and provided large sums in regional and structural aid for the new and less developed countries, this kind of balance is largely missing in the framework of the coming enlargement. This imbalance may create a number of problems both for the acceding countries at least until the end of 2006 and for the present member countries.

Secondly, the enlargement is taking place most probably and unfortunately in a Western Europe which has very low economic growth rates. There are no encouraging signs at the moment that the situation would be dramatically improving in 2004 and 2005.

Third, there is an accumulated reform pressure in some of the EU member countries, particularly in those countries which used to be the engine of the European integration process - mainly Germany but also in some other, mainly large countries.

Also, in addition, the reform needs are not less important on the integration level. A number of EU policies, from institutional reforms to common agricultural policy up to the future of the budget, should be revisited and reconsidered not after 2007, but most probably at the moment of enlargement, and not only because the enlargement takes place.

And finally, of course, Europe is not isolated from world developments and global challenges that certainly make some further and fundamental impacts on the shaping of a new and enlarged European Union.

2. For obvious political reasons, the acceding countries have been put into one basket. However, it would be extremely not only simplified but dangerous to think that these countries are homogeneous. There are quite important differences both on the macroeconomic level, and even more if you look at the microeconomic structures and the institutional level. Let me just mention the latest figures published by Deutsche Bank Research a couple of days ago. National growth rates for 2002 and 2003 are between 1.3 percent for Poland and 6.7 percent for Lithuania. The Consumer Price Index is 1.1 percent for the Czech Republic and over 5 percent in the case of Hungary. The fiscal balance is between almost a balanced situation in Estonia to up to 9 percent of the GDP deficit in the case of Hungary, and this year it will be almost 6 percent in the Czech Republic. Current account balance and unemployment is from 6 percent in Hungary up to almost 20 percent in some other acceding countries. And in addition, most of these figures can change, sometimes very quickly, to the better or to the worse. So the sustainability of this process is also a very important issue.

3. When talking about the accession of the Central and Eastern European Countries to the European Union, I think we miss the real point. The point is not to join. That will happen on 1 May 2004 according to the present situation. What I am much more interested in is not the moment of accession, but the **continuity of the integration process, that is membership**. How will these countries have a sustainable membership in the EU. And not only sustainable but also successful. All the efforts, and all the structural changes should focus on how to achieve these major goals.

4. What are the pillars of sustainable growth? For the time being I think that it's quite clear that in all countries sustainability of growth has to be based on export-orientation and it has to be investment-driven and not consumption-driven. That was the case in most of the countries for a long time. However, most recently there was a deviation, I would say even aberration, from this healthy path of sustainable development in some countries. For various reasons, ranging from facing the consequences of global economic downturn, domestic economic problems of transition to short-term and short-sighted party-politics, private consumption became the basic engine of growth. This growth pattern is already showing a number of negative consequences. It does not mean, of course, that private consumption cannot increase. It has to, and under normal economic conditions, it can also increase. However, it should not outpace the general rate of economic growth. If a country has a 5 percent growth rate, there is relatively large manoeuvering room to increase private consumption by 3 percent, and still investment-driven and export-driven economic growth can easily be sustained.

5. If we talk **about export-oriented and investment-driven sustainable growth**, then we have to look at these two factors in more detail.

Looking at the trade and export development of most of the Candidate Countries, the traditional classical trade theory can be challenged in a number of areas.

First, there is of course a correlation between developments or growth rates on the main export markets of Central and Eastern Europe and the growth rate in Central and Eastern Europe itself. However, one can see that even in 2002 in most CEE countries exports were resistant to the downturn or recessionary trends in Western European markets. While in the EU total imports fell by 3 percent, exports from the Czech Republic, Poland, Hungary and Slovakia increased between 5 and 10 percent to the European Union. Despite the uniquely high level of dependence on Western Europe, these countries could increase their market share and could maintain their dynamic export development. The explanation mainly lies in the rapidly growing competitiveness. It was not the case a decade ago, when a much lower level of "dependence" from Western European import markets was not able to prevent the immediate negative impacts on growth in Central and Eastern Europe in case of declining or sluggish growth in Western Europe.

Also the theory on the so-called training ground has been challenged. The sequencing was not what many experts had been proposing at the beginning of the 1990s. Their advise was to give priority to the CEE market, where the transition economies were expected to be more competitive. And once a higher level of competitiveness will have been reached, to say, in 10 to 15 years, then these countries could be able to enter the Western European market. Just the opposite happened. In this context, Central (and partly Eastern) Europe followed the East-Asian model. All the East-Asian economies first became competitive on the US market, and then, in the second stage, they could prove their competitiveness also on other markets, including the regional ones. To focus more on the regional market is likely to happen in the coming years, once most of these countries will become members of the EU.

The different structural specialisation of the CEE countries must also be mentioned. Some countries are certainly defying the traditional Heckscher-Ohlin model that, being at a lower level of development, they should specialise on labour-intensive or raw-material-intensive products, and that they should import more technology-intensive, skill-intensive goods. This is certainly not the case for Hungary, not the case for the Czech Republic, to a lesser extent for Slovakia. It is, however, very much the case for the Baltics, excluding services, and particularly for Southeastern Europe. Thus, there are very clear structural differences among the individual CEE countries. Based on international classification, almost two-thirds of total Hungarian exports to the EU consist of so-called technology-intensive goods, although we can discuss what is meant by "technology-intensive goods". This share is about 50 percent for the Czech Republic and Slovakia, it is about 40 percent for Slovenia, 35 percent for Poland and less than 10 percent for the Baltics.

The unit price of exports is an additional important indicator of structural differences and different levels of competitiveness. On the German market, which is the most important export market for all of these countries, these differences are more than obvious. Final manufactured goods account for 75 to 90 percent of the total exports of the CEE countries to Germany. In 2001, one ton of Hungarian exports of final manufactured goods to Germany was 2.5 times more "valuable" than one ton of Czech exports and 4 times more "valuable" than one ton of Polish exports. The deeper one is digging into the micro-level, the more differences can be identified. And some of these differences are sustained differences, which need a relatively long time to be changed.

The last point concerning the critical remarks on classic trade theory is the trade balance. If there is free trade between two countries on different levels of development, traditional trade theory says that the more developed country has to have a surplus, provided that the less developed country is not an exporter of raw materials, oil or gold, which is certainly not the case in Central and Eastern Europe. In the trade of some CEE countries with the EU just the opposite can be seen. The Czech Republic, Slovakia and particularly Hungary have a noticeable to remarkable trade surplus with the EU. In turn, they register a substantial trade deficit with some developing countries, as a result of increasing trade among and within large multinational companies. To a large extent, international trade has become a flow of commodities and services between and within companies, and stopped to follow the classic pattern of trade between states. This change has important consequences for the competitiveness, for the competitive location of industries and services, which brings me to another point still on the trade issue, which is the future of trade relations in an enlarged EU.

There is a frequently heard argument that, provided that we already have free trade in industrial goods and also a large part of agricultural trade is liberalised, we cannot count with tremendous trade creation effects after enlargement. I do not fully subscribe to this view. First, there are still some areas of trade in agriculture which are not yet part of the free trade. Second, membership and, more importantly, participation in the internal market, create highly reliable conditions for longer-term business contacts, with obvious positive implications for the development of bilateral trade relations. In addition, there will be a large increase of trade in the service sector, which has been very much neglected also in economic research until now. Also I think that higher growth rates in Central and Eastern Europe and, in the medium term, hopefully larger EU resources which will flow from the structural and cohesion funds towards Central and Eastern Europe will have a trade-creating effect. However, in the short term, the most important trade-creating effect will be generated by the liberalisation of trade among the new member countries. CEFTA is a free trade area on paper only. In fact, there have been a large number of protectionist measures which time by time have been applied in bilateral flow of specific commodities (agriculture, steel, petrochemicals, other semi-manufactured goods, etc.). However, at the very moment of membership trade policy will stop to be made in Warsaw, it will not be made in Prague, and it will not be made in Budapest either. It will be made in Brussels. In consequence, on the first day of membership in the EU, there will be no trade barriers among the new member countries, resulting in rapidly increasing regional trade volumes and, not less importantly, in further structural changes in the still protected industrial sectors and agriculture as well.

6. Concerning **foreign direct investments**, I would like to make two sets of remarks.

First, and particularly in the more developed countries of the region, there is a clear change on the horizon. FDI had practically in the last decade three different patterns. It started in Central Europe by making use of low-skilled labour. Then it went to a second stage which is higher-skilled labour, mainly in the car industry and also in part of the computer industry and electronics. Now it has reached a third level which affects R&D-intensive activities. No question that, for various reasons, the largest profit can be obtained in the latter case.

There is another change, too. Some countries which started with bold and open privatisation have practically come almost to an end of this process. Therefore the question is: how can they get new, fresh investments which they undoubtedly need in order to sustain the rapid modernization and catching-up process. There are two possibilities to maintain the dynamic inflow of FDI. One is greenfield investments, for which the conditions have to be created and to which I will come back to immediately. The second is, what is missing in many statistics, which, however, became a major source of investment: the reinvestment of profits which were made by foreign companies in a given country. The older the co-operation with FDI, the earlier foreign investors came to a given country, the higher is the likelihood that they have already generated profit, and they started to invest (a large) part of the profit into expanding and fostering activities in the host country. According to modest estimates, if a country has a stock of 30 billion dollars of FDI and if FDI is working at an average profitability of just 8 percent, which is most probably an underestimation, then annual profits amount to about 2.4 billion dollars. If 30 or 40 percent of this profit is transferred, repatriated, still at least 1.5 billion dollars remain in the country for reinvestment.

Another question here, of course, is and that is a real challenge, how to upgrade the activities of FDI in a given country. It implies practically three things. It means technological upgrading, how to increase the technology-intensity of FDI. It raises the issue of how to increase the value added FDI is producing in a given country. And, finally, and in the longer term, the most important issue is how to create a production and distribution network between large foreign companies and small- and medium-sized companies as subcontractors. When I talk about small- and medium-sized companies I have in mind both foreign and domestic small- and medium-sized companies. I do not make any distinction between domestic and foreign companies. Where I do make a distinction is whether a given small- or medium-sized company is working in the given accession country or is working still in Western Europe so that most of the inputs that a large company is using is imported. With higher and sustainable level of development, these imported inputs are expected to be gradually relocated to the given host country of the large international company.

The second set of remarks concerns the development of FDI after enlargement. I think it will be very interesting to look at the regional pattern and specialisation of FDI. At the moment we have three different patterns. One is when the same foreign company is working in several of the acceding countries and is doing practically the same job, producing the same things, either for exports or for the domestic market. The second is when a large foreign company has its regional headquarters just in one country and tries to provide or supply the regional market from this centre. And the third and most advanced pattern is when a foreign company is active in several countries, with a clear pattern of specialization based on the competitive advantage of different locations. In this way, it is contributing not only to the establishment of regional production networks but also to higher intraregional trade flows as well. This pattern will certainly experience a dynamic growth in the next period.

However, competition for FDI will remain strong among the CEE countries, just as there is competition for FDI among the present EU member countries as well.

7. Sustaining and strengthening of competitiveness is, in my view, the most important policy objective of the CEE countries in a situation in which they have already entered the second stage of economic transformation, which I would call sustainable growth in a sustainable modernisation process. It is unavoidable that in such a situation some previous conditions which, in an earlier stage, made these countries a favourable location for production and also for some service activities, are changing. Wages are increasing, not only because the countries are at the threshold of membership in the EU, but also for other, partly short-term political and election considerations.

The question is of course to what extent the productivity keeps on growing. If productivity growth is outpacing wage growth, as it was the case in the previous years, there is no problem. Unfortunately, some countries seem to have forgotten about this basic relationship. All Central European countries made a number of mistakes, some made them earlier, some made them later, and unfortunately those who made them later did not learn from the mistakes of those who made them earlier. It started in Poland, was followed by the Czech Republic. And from none of these errors did the Hungarian economic policy learn in the last years. And not because the economists did not make warnings, but because, unfortunately, economic policy became to some extent the prisoner and to some extent the victim of short-sighted party-political factors and populism.

The second issue is appreciation of the currency. It is an absolutely normal development, in all countries which were successful in the catching-up process. High productivity growth generates appreciation while speeding up the catching-up process. However, if there is a sudden appreciation, to say of 8 to 10 percent in a year, the competitive position may be shaken. This is even more the case, if the appreciation is accompanied by wage pressure. And, in addition, all this happens in a world and European economy which is not growing dynamically. In this situation, the achieved and apparently cemented comparative advantages of a country may be easily undermined.

There is one more and basic issue to be shortly addressed. It is the question of widespread and fundamental structural reforms which are required to create the longer-term conditions for sustainable competitiveness. Unfortunately, and similar to most Western European countries, they have not been started in the years in which the growth was high. It is an economic and political commonplace (and common sense) that large-scale economic and structural reforms are easier to be introduced when a country has a sustainable high growth than when the growth rate is declining or when one has to struggle with a number of macroeconomic imbalances.

These reforms become the more relevant the more initial productivity reserves are being eaten up. Beyond the well-known statistical impact, that growth rates decline with higher levels of development, increasing wages and appreciating currencies limit the influence of productivity increases on strengthening competitiveness. Therefore, a solid competitive position needs other factors to be given more attention to. First of all, total production costs have to be restructured by decreasing the job-related expenditures on the one hand, and by cutting taxes, on the other. Unfortunately, the years of high economic growth have not been used to develop the necessary reforms.

Two other deficits I would like to mention which should be the precondition or the framework conditions for sustainable competitiveness. One is investment in physical infrastructure, and the other is investment in human capital. Some of the more developed Candidate Countries already face a shortage of skilled labour. And there is foreign, and increasingly also domestic capital which would like to expand the production, but the main barrier to expanding, and even more, to upgrading production is the lack of skilled labour, and to some extent also the missing infrastructural network.

Let me mention just one example. If you compare a map of Hungary, but you can also do it with some other country, showing the geographic expansion of FDI in the country, and another map which indicates the development of physical infrastructure exemplified by the highway construction, the two maps to a large extent overlap each other. So FDI is geograpahically expanding up to the point to which the physical infrastructure is adequate. Both human capital and physical infrastructure should be high-priority goals of the government economic policies in CEE countries.

What we sometimes, however, forget about: competitiveness, is that it has some non-economic factors as well, which have got enhanced relevance in the last years. I would like to mention just two of them. One is the quality of public administration. You may be extremely productive in your factory. However, if you go out with your products or services to a market and on the way from the factory to the market you face a number of barriers - bureaucratic barriers, administrative barriers and other barriers - then it turns out that although you might be the best, the highest competitive producer in the world, but you will not become competitive once you reach the given market due to the fact that your competitors have been facing less bureacratic hindrances or had been supported by a better (if you want, more competitive) public administration.

The second new element which is a non-economic factor of sustainable competitiveness. It is social cohesion, which is much more than peace in the workplace and lack or low number of strikes. Particularly in small countries, social cohesion has to be considered to be a priority factor of competitiveness.

Here I would like to make a small remark on the catching-up process as measured in GDP per capita terms. I know that there is no better and more comprehensive indicator for the catching-up or the lagging-behind process. However, I think that we should give more attention to two other factors. One is the so-called convergence indicator, which is based on a set of 50 or 60 indicators developed by Deutsche Bank Research. At regular intervals, Deutsche Bank Research prepares and publishes a regional comparison based on convergence indicators. According to this survey, and taking the EU level as 100, the gap between the EU average (let alone between some less developed member countries) and some CEE countries is much less pronounced than indicated by GDP-per capita-based analyses. This indicator is above 70 percent in the case of Slovenia, Hungary and the Czech Republic. It is 65 percent in the case of Poland, about 60 percent in the case of Bulgaria, and between 65 and 70 percent in the case of the Baltic countries.

But what should be even more reliable, and, unfortunately, there has not been made any such comparison until now, although it would be, I would say, imperative looking at this in the Lisbon agenda of the EU, is the assessment of those factors of the catching-up process which tell something about the future. While GDP per capita data reflect the past and the present, new, future-oriented indicators are needed to describe the potential dynamism of growth in the transition countries. In this context, the objectives fixed in the Lisbon agenda may be useful indicators. According to the objectives formulated in this document, Europe should concentrate on R&D, on human resources development, on a higher level of competitiveness, a higher level of employment, etc. If we include into our surveys such factors as the level of general education, human resources endowment, research- and technology-intensity of production, expenditure on research and development, but also some non-economic factors strongly influencing competitiveness, as social cohesion, flexibility of the society, flexibility of the labour market, or flexibility of the administration, then, in fact, we could come to a comparative picture, in which at least some of the acceding countries would be in a better position than some of the present member countries. Such a general assessment would be extremely important and urgent to look at and to (jointly) shape the future of Europe.

8. Evidently, the continuity of the catching-up process is not automatically granted. There are some fears that this process may be broken or interrupted in the next few years. I am convinced that we have to deal with them. Not with all of them because some of the fears, once a country enters the EU, seem to be to a large extent either unjustified, or if they are justified, it is not because of entering the EU, it is because some of the basic reforms have not been made before entry. We have free trade. We have a liberalised commodity market. We have a large liberalised capital market. I do not think there will be tremendous price rises after joining the EU. I do not think there will be a higher level of unemployment either as a direct consequence of membership. If, however, some of the structural problems in some accession countries have not yet been solved, and have been postponed for the first years of membership, higher unemployment may be the result. It would, however, be fundamentally mistaken to blame for such an adverse development the EU. Also I do not share the view or the fear that small- and medium-sized companies will massively go bankrupt. As a general experience, these companies cannot be thrown into the same basket. There are very different kinds of small- and medium-sized companies. Some of them are export-oriented, some are part of the subcontracting network of large multinational companies, some of them are specialised just on the local services. They will not be affected adversely. Some of them may be affected but mainly those which did not develop a competitive performance and did not enter the international market, because they remained in or became captured by the large and over the 1990s rapidly growing domestic market. The most important problem small- and medium-sized companies are already facing, is the increasing need for capital concentration, as a major precondition of sustainable competitiveness. In fact, it is impossible that one million small ventures will remain in the country of ten million inhabitants if you want to sustain economic growth and remain competitive.

Here I would like to make one more remark, and that is about the support of SMEs. Should small- and medium-sized companies be artificially supported? The underlying positive argument is making reference to the success of small- and medium-sized companies in northern Italy, in Austria, in southern Germany, in Bavaria or in Baden-Württemberg, and maybe in some other parts of the world. The situation in Central and Eastern Europe at the beginning of the 21st century is fundamentally different in two aspects, and that is why the old patterns do not seem to work. One is generated by the development history of such companies. At some (remote) time in the past, they started with a one-man firm, then after ten years, if they were successful, a family firm was established, in 20 years it developed into a small-scale firm, in 40 years it may have reached the status of a medium-scale firm. New firms in CEE countries generally do not have 40 years for such a development. Either a firm is successful at the beginning or in a very short time, or it is likely to disappear. The other is linked to national protection. German, Austrian or Italian SMEs, had been developing for a long time in the national economic framework. Markets were strictly national ones or only partially open. In addition, at critical stages of the firms' development process tariffs and non-tariff barriers could be introduced (or maintained) CEE firms do not have this kind of instrument, since they have to work and survive in conditions of free trade - and there is no way back from free trade. As a result, I would not say that government economic policies should not devote attention to the development of small and medium-sized companies, but certainly not with the methods which are not in compliance with the requirements of the 21st century.

Concerning accession to the EU, there are certainly two real fears. One is that, mainly in the first years after accession, regional differences within the individual acceding countries may be increasing. The explanation is quite simple. The adjustment and absorption capacity of the more developed parts of the country is higher. They will most probably be able to attract more of the resources, both domestic and foreign, and use them with higher level of efficiency and within a shorter period. Also, they are likely to be more successful in applying for EU funds. The temporarily growing development gap does not, however, mean that the less developed parts of the given country will not develop as compared with their previous level of development. It is a key task of the government to keep this development process under control, but not by constraining the more efficient regions but to provide support to increase the absorption capacity of the less developed ones and speed up the spillover process from more to less developed areas. Namely, it is obvious that the modernization process must not be undermined by uncontrollable social strains or conflicts. After a short transition period, particularly a small country, cannot manage a largely polarised economy, divided between highly developed and highly underdeveloped regions.

The most real threat, however, is the budgetary crunch in all of the CEE countries. All of them have already a budget deficit in terms of GDP which in most cases is much higher than the one fixed by the Maastricht criteria. After membership, the budget will have a number of additional burdens. Some of them will be burdens which are connected with the preparation of successful membership. There will be some areas where the preparation will not be finished by 1 May 2004, and therefore the financial or budgetary implications will burden the budget also later. Then there will be some anticipated payments which have to be made by the central budget, that is e.g. the direct payments to farmers, which will be paid by Brussels ex post, but you will have to provide this money in 2004 already. In addition, up to 30 per cent of agricultural support may added from the central budget to the farmers. Moreover, there will be also some anticipated payments including co-financing for the structural funds. At the same time, everybody who enters the Union will be committed to observe or to adjust to the Maastricht criteria. In consequence, it is hardly probable that the rapid (and today unforeseen) increase in budgetary income can create the financial capacity needed to cover all the additional costs mentioned. Therefore, some or even a fundamental restructuring of the budget is unavoidable. And just in this point will the governments face the most serious challenge. In which areas should the necessary cuts be made? If, as it used to happen in the past, the "savings" will hit those areas which are considered to be the guarantee of the medium- and long-term competitiveness of these countries, namely human resource development and health, then the CEE countries' future and sustainable growth may be undermined.

9. Both the enlarging EU as well as the current and future member countries are expected to face critical years. Three basic challenges can be shortly mentioned. One is that the enlargement must not undermine the critical minimum level of internal cohesion in the enlarged EU. All present and future member countries take the responsibility for it. Second: there is a heterogeneous group which will join the EU in 2004. Cross-country differences are not limited to structural features or to macroeconomic performance indicators. The basic difference seems to be much more in the adjustment capacity of the individual countries. Some countries will be more successful because they will be able to adjust in a better way; some others may feel really as second-class members, not because they are treated as second-class members but because they feel unable to cope with the new challenges. This may create a very difficult situation concerning the third condition, that the enlargement

enlargement process has to remain open to further members. If the internal cohesion is threatened, and if some countries feel unsuccessful in the enlarged EU, it will be very difficult to create the necessary political will and public support for the continuation of the enlargement process. If, however, the enlargement is not continued, Europe will get a number of additional problems. To avoid them and have the right answers at the right time has to become a common task and responsibility for all of us, governments, policy-makers, societies alike.

Kick-off Papers

THE CONTEXT FOR REFORM: THE PRECONDITIONS FOR SUSTAINABLE GROWTH AND THE CONVERGENCE CHALLENGES

MATTHEW SALTER

1. OVERVIEW

The forthcoming enlargement of the EU will contribute to the urgency of the economic reform programme. As well as generating opportunities, enlargement also poses challenges to established patterns of production, employment, finance, consumption and trade. To meet these challenges and to realise the opportunities of enlargement, ongoing reform is vital. Not only will engagement with the Lisbon reform agenda increase the rate of real convergence and growth in the candidates, but it will also bring benefits to the whole of the EU.

The Copenhagen European Council, held at the end of last year (December 2002), paved the way for 10 new Member States to join the EU on 1 May 2004, increasing the EU market from 370m consumers to 450m. The expansion of the Single European Market provides considerable opportunities for the European economy, associated with the increased supply potential as the Candidate Countries become fully integrated with the EU, and increased demand as their income levels rise towards EU-15 levels. But it also poses challenges in terms of the reorganisation of patterns of production, consumption and trade that will be needed if the full potential of enlargement is to be realised.

To meet these challenges, it is vital that the economies of both the accession countries and the EU-15 have the ability to respond to the increased competitive pressures and changing patterns of comparative advantage. Ongoing economic reforms in both existing EU Member States and accession states are therefore desirable to ease adjustment to new patterns of economic activity.

This can be achieved through engagement with the EU's economic reform agenda, as set out at the Lisbon Council. The Lisbon programme puts the focus of reform on raising productivity and employment by improving the efficiency of labour, product and capital markets. Work on the Lisbon agenda is of course already underway in many Candidate Countries, and follows naturally from the economic reforms they have already undertaken since 1989. The shift from a centralised regulatory approach towards a more flexible but co-operative policy-making will be even more appropriate to the increased diversity of an enlarged EU. The Lisbon methods of benchmarking and peer review will enable the rapid dissemination of best practice across the enlarged European Union, thereby enhancing the dynamism of the enlarged Single Market.

Economic Reform in the accession countries is important for the EU

The economic development of Central and Eastern Europe provides potential for productivity gains and growth among existing EU Member States. The reforms indicated by Lisbon will help the EU Member States in their own right, but also help the EU to better respond to the shifting patterns of trade and production prompted by EU enlargement. Both the EU and the accession countries need to put policies in place that promote flexible and rapid reallocation of resources that will ease the adjustment process. In the EU, labour markets will need to be flexible enough to respond to increases in supply from the candidates and also to respond to the fact that the demand for labour may well decline in some industries, but increase in other industries, perhaps requiring a different skill set. Capital markets will also need to respond to the changed and changing productive potential of a larger Single Market.

It is important however to recognise that areas of comparative advantage will evolve over time. Relative wages in the Candidate Countries will converge towards EU levels as their economies develop, which will shift their advantages away from labour-intensive industries. Economic reform in the EU and candidate states will facilitate adjustment to such changes in comparative advantage, and improve the ability of economies to grow and create employment.

This paper aims to give a general background to the challenges that lie ahead for accession states as they prepare for membership of the European Union, and their integration with EU procedures and processes. The next section of the paper, describes the wide gap in prosperity between the EU-15 and the accession states, and the size of the challenge of real convergence; a process which is likely to last for more than a generation. The subsequent section sets out some of the key structural challenges for the accession states, focussing on the large gap between the EU-15 and accession states in employment structure, overall employment rates, and the gap in productivity and wage costs.

2. *General Economic Context, and the Challenge of Real Convergence*

Current prosperity levels

Although the economies of central Europe have changed significantly over the past decade, the process of convergence with their western neighbours has barely begun. Taking account of differences in purchasing power, GDP per capita in the Candidate Countries in negotiations, is around 45% of the average EU level. Within this figure there are large divergences between the candidates, as the following graph shows.

Graph 1: GDP per capita in PPS, 2001 (EU-15=100)

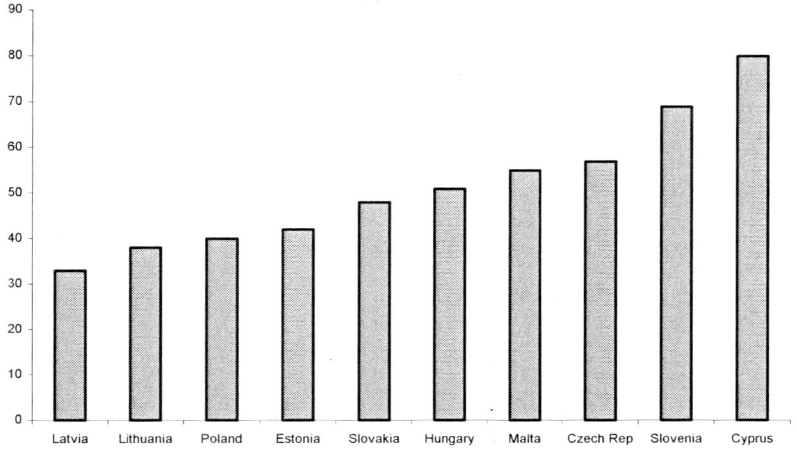

Source: Commission Strategy Paper (2002)

Cyprus and Slovenia are in fact as prosperous as some of the poorer current EU Member States, yet the Baltics and Poland have a GDP per head which is less than 45% of the EU average. It is significant that Poland accounts for around 50% of the population and GDP of the ten leading candidates.

Against this background, it should be noted that this is not the first time that the EU has admitted countries with lower levels of economic development than current Member States. The lessons from previous enlargements which admitted less prosperous members is useful for underlining the challenges ahead, and is a subject covered later on in this section.

Convergence over the last ten years

Most of the candidates generally succeeded in the 1990s in creating a stable macroeconomic environment and in implementing some of the structural reforms required to become market economies. This success has been rewarded with steady economic growth in most of the accession states (see following graph), but it is evident that convergence with

EU income levels has been slow and uneven.

Graph 2: Convergence with the EU-15, GDP per capita (EU-15=100)

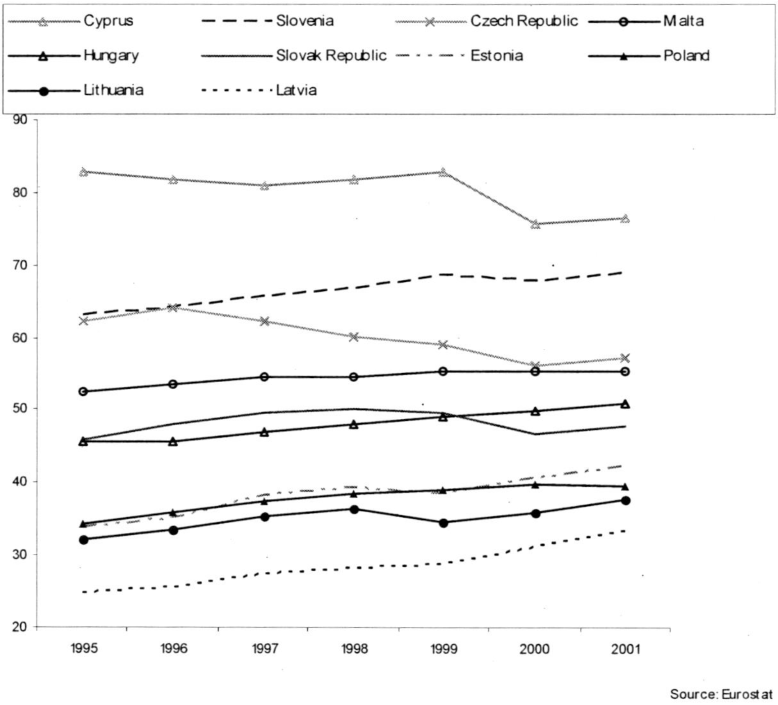

Real convergence in the future

Using a rather stylised set of assumptions[1], it is possible to derive a mechanistic long-term outlook for convergence trends of the accession states towards the EU-15 average. These assumptions can be used to calculate the number of years it will take to reach a certain threshold of the EU-15 income level, such as 75%. The following table shows the effect of using these specific assumptions:

---

[1] Assumption for EU growth (2.6%) based on the forecast for 2004 in the Commission's Autumn 2002 Economic Forecasts. Assumptions for Candidate Country growth based on 2004 forecasts in Commission's Autumn 2002 Forecasts for Candidate Countries. Prices assumed to be constant.

Table 1: Years to reaching 75% of the average of EU-15 in GDP per capita in PPS

Bulgaria	36
Cyprus	1
Czech Republic	24
Estonia	25
Hungary	18
Latvia	26
Lithuania	38
Malta	32
Poland	50
Romania	55
Slovakia	22
Slovenia	7
Turkey	71

For most candidates, convergence to 75% of the EU average is unlikely in the short to medium term. Indeed, convergence is likely to take one or two generations for some of the candidates, and any perceptions of instant prosperity on the point of acceding to the EU are naively misplaced. This is perhaps unsurprising, given the lessons from the process of convergence of past accession states (see following section).

Though very stylistic, these results are similar to the conclusions in the Commission's report (DG Ecfin, November 2001) on *"Real Convergence in the Candidate Countries"*, which stated that *"what is clear from that exercise is that for many countries catching-up even to levels of just 75% of the EU average will probably be a process spanning over more than one generation"*.

But perhaps the most noteworthy point is the sensitivity of the results to the assumptions made. Assumptions regarding the growth rates are crucial for the rate of convergence, and as the following simple example shows, small changes in growth rates can affect the speed of convergence by more than a generation.

Table 2 shows the effect of lowering the growth rate assumptions in the candidates by 0.5%.

Table 2: Years to reaching 75% of the average of EU-15 in GDP per capita in PPS

Bulgaria	43 (+7)
Cyprus	1 (-)
Czech Republic	41 (+17)
Estonia	31 (+6)
Hungary	23 (+5)
Latvia	30 (+4)
Lithuania	51 (+13)
Malta	64 (+32)
Poland	81 (+31)
Romania	71 (+16)
Slovakia	28 (+6)
Slovenia	10 (+3)
Turkey	98 (+27)

As in the table above the results show the forecast number of years the candidates will take to reach 75% of the EU-15 average, along with the increased number of years compared to the "base" case above. The different speeds of convergence resulting from "small" differences in growth rates are quite startling. In the case of Malta or Poland, for example, a 0.5% difference in growth rates after accession could affect the time of "75% convergence" with the EU by over 30 years.

Though simplistic, this contains significant policy implications. There have been significant differences in the degree of vigour with which the economies of Central and Eastern Europe have implemented economic reform. The pace and extent of reform has been a key factor in the recovery of output over the 1990s. Advanced reform countries have achieved greater flexibility in re-allocating resources to their most productive use and in general, those economies which have progressed most rapidly in implementing reforms have tended to achieve stronger recoveries in output, and have the most optimistic forecasts for convergence with EU levels.

Current growth rates

To put these calculations into context, the latest growth figures in the Commission's Autumn Forecasts present a very mixed picture for 2002. Whereas the Baltic states weathered the global economic downturn, with robust growth figures of over 4.5%, Poland recorded growth of only 0.8% of GDP. Growth for all ten candidates in 2002 was as follows:

Table 3: Percentage change in GDP at constant prices, 2002

CY	CZ	EE	HU	LV	LT	MT	PL	SK	SI	AC-10
2.2	2.2	4.5	3.4	5.0	5.0	2.5	0.8	3.9	2.6	2.1

Previous enlargements

A clear lesson from previous enlargements is that accession to the EU does not in itself guarantee convergence with EU income levels, as can be seen from the varying records of four previous less prosperous candidates - Ireland, Greece, Spain and Portugal.

Ireland is definitely the star performer of the group. On joining the EU in 1973 its GDP was only 60% of the EU average, by 1990 it had reached around 75% and ten years later Ireland's GDP stood at 120% of the EU average.

Spain and Portugal have also seen some solid improvements since joining the EU. Spain's GDP increased from 71% of the EU average on joining in 1986, to 83% in 2001. Portugal, whose GDP stood at only 56% of the EU average when they joined in the same year as Spain, now has a GDP approaching 75% of the EU average.

But Greece however, who joined 5 years earlier than Portugal and Spain with a GDP of about 60% of the EU average, has seen only a gradual convergence to a current GDP level which is only 72% of the EU average.

3. *Structural Challenges*

If the transitional economies of Central and Eastern Europe are to continue a steady convergence with the GDP levels of the current EU, then just becoming members is, in itself, not a sufficient goal. Without addressing the need for far reaching structural reform policies, not only will the new Member States be disappointed when instant prosperity fails to materialise, but the current Member States will find themselves in an EU with a depressed economic periphery.

The scope of the challenge, which lies before the accession states, is apparent from an analysis of the differences between the accession states and the current EU-15, with respect to overall sectoral composition. In terms of employment, the share of those employed in the agriculture sector is, on average, three times as high in the accession states than in the EU-15 (which is not reflected in a proportionately high share of gross value-added); in some individual cases this rises to four or five times as much.

Graph 3: Sectoral share of employment in 2001 (%)

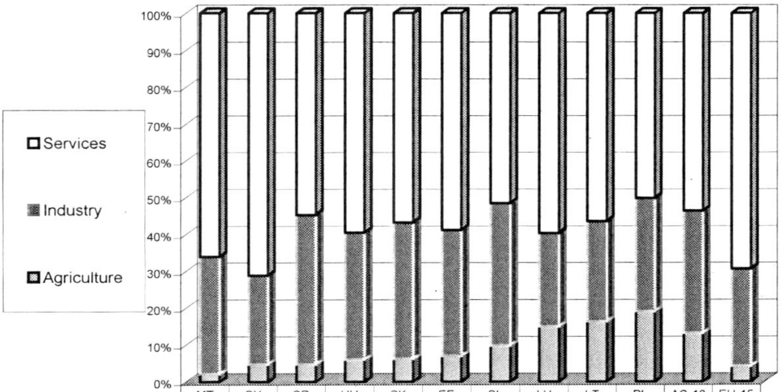

	MT	CY	CR	HU	SK	EE	SL	LV	LT	PL	AC-10	EU-15
Services	66,0	71,1	54,6	59,4	56,7	58,7	51,4	59,6	56,3	50,1	53,6	69,3
Industry	31,8	24,0	40,5	34,5	37,1	34,2	38,6	25,3	27,2	30,7	33,2	26,4
Agriculture	2,2	4,9	4,9	6,1	6,3	7,1	9,9	15,1	16,5	19,2	13,3	4,3

Source: Eurostat

Up to now the candidates have been guided in part by the Copenhagen criteria of *"establishing a functioning market economy and having the capacity to withstand competitive pressure and market forces within the Union"*. Reforms in the Candidate Countries have included privatisation of state-owned companies, trade and price liberalisation and substantial changes to institutional and legal systems that have raised the standards of financial discipline and corporate governance and also allow market mechanisms to operate efficiently.

But substantial challenges lie ahead, as this overview shows. The EPC's Annual Report (2002) on Structural Reforms noted that the *"continuation and acceleration of the structural reform process - interacting with growth and stability orientated macroeconomic policies - is necessary to facilitate economic recovery as well as further improvements in the economic performance of Member States"*. This is no less true, and perhaps more important, for the accession states, who will soon be incorporated into the Lisbon agenda, aiming to make Europe the most competitive and dynamic knowledge-based economy in the world.

Employment

The impact of the ten accession countries joining the EU in 2004 will, on current trends, be very likely to increase unemployment in an enlarged EU, as well as regional disparities in employment. It will also bring about significant changes to the employment profile and labour market structure of the EU. A flexible labour market and continued structural reform will therefore be vital to achieving the strategic Lisbon goal, described above.

But as the following table illustrates, the impact on the overall employment rates (and other Lisbon targets) post-enlargement are not dramatic, due to the fact that the combined working age population of the accession countries is about 20% of the EU's. Nevertheless, across the accession countries, employment rates have decreased and unemployment rates increased, since 1997, and if this trend continues it will place a significant downward drag on the overall strategic goals of an enlarged EU.

Table 4: Employment rates (%) before and after enlargement in the EU in 2001

	Total 15-64	**Women 15-64**	**Older workers 55-64**
EU-15	63.8	54.7	38.2
CC-10	56.8	51.1	31.0
EU-25	62.6	54.1	37.2
2010 Targets	70.0	60.0	50.0

Source: Commission Employment Report (2002)

Unemployment rates across the region are disparate, as shown in the following graph.

Graph 4: Unemployment rates in accession countries, 2001

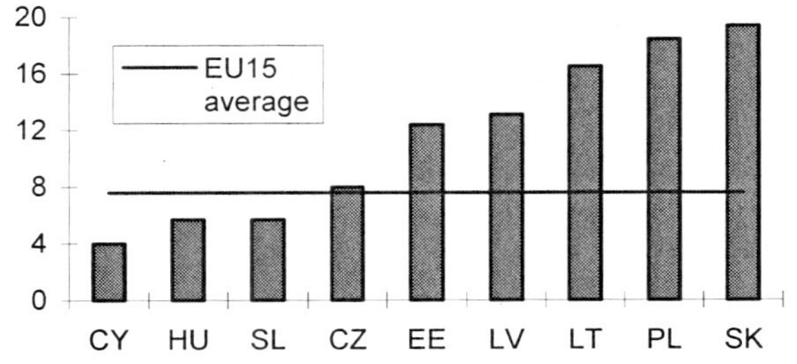

Source: Commission Employment Report (2002)

Poland with the second highest unemployment rate of the accession countries is the significant since it represents over half of the working-age population of the accession states.

Productivity, wage costs and unit labour costs

Though low wages have played a major role in attracting FDI into the candidates in recent years, real wages have been growing rapidly and there is concern that this risks undermining the competitiveness of the accession countries. Obviously the crucial element for investors is unit labour costs, and the candidates will have to ensure that wage growth does not exceed productivity gains. The candidates will therefore need to create a business environment conducive to investment from firms in new technologies, as well as investing in increasing and changing skill levels.

Productivity

Productivity levels currently fall significantly below EU levels, but again there is a wide range across the candidates, with some at the higher range showing a level of productivity, which is twice that of accession states at the lower end of the range.

Graph 5: Labour Productivity, GDP in PPS per person employed, 2002 (EU-15=100)

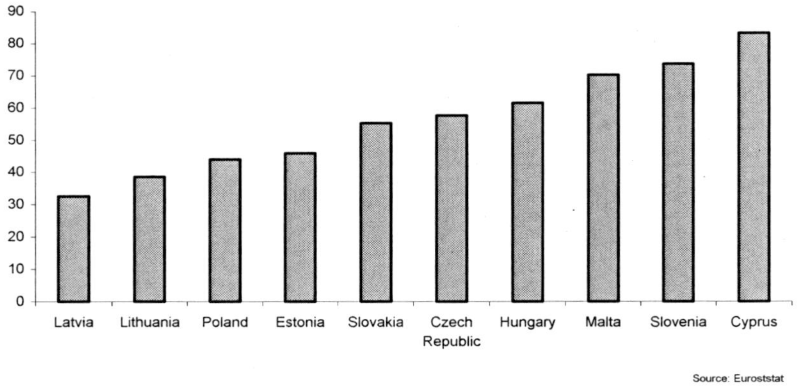

But as mentioned above, unit labour costs depend on productivity *and* wage costs; as the following section shows, wages in the accession states also fall substantially below EU levels.

Wage costs[2]

There are marked differences in the level of labour costs in the accession countries. The level of total hourly labour costs in industry and services, ranges from 2.4 euros in Latvia, to 10.74 euros in Cyprus. This compares to an EU average of 21.5 euros[3], meaning that in most of the accession countries labour costs represent less than ¼ of the EU average.

---

2 All data in this section from Labour Costs Survey 2000, Eurostat *Statistics in Focus 23/2002*

3 1999 figure

Graph 6: Hourly labour costs in industry and services, 2002

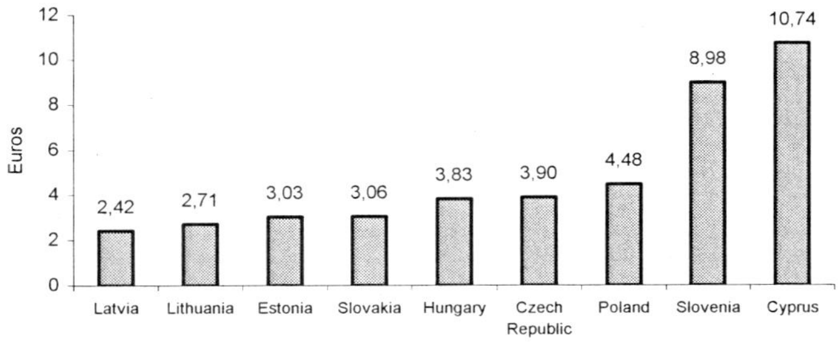

Source: Eurostat

The survey also reveals some interesting information about the structure of costs, breaking down total costs into the three component parts of "wages and salaries", "employers' social contributions" and "other labour costs". Whereas the largest share of costs is the same across all the accession countries, the share of costs accounted for by employers' social contributions is more than double in Hungary (30.3%) compared to those countries with a lower share, such as Slovenia (14.1%) or Cyprus (14.4%).

Graph 7: Structure of labour costs in industry and services, 2001

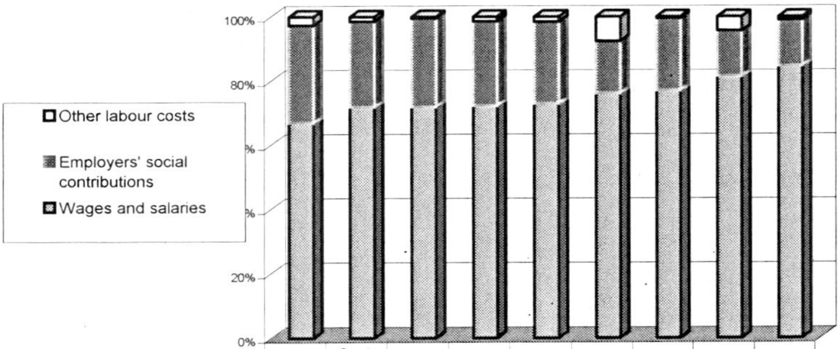

	Hungary	Czech Republic	Lithuania	Slovakia	Estonia	Poland	Latvia	Slovenia	Cyprus
Other labour costs	2,6	1,4	0,4	1,4	1,5	7,6	0,4	4,4	1,0
Employers' social contributions	30,3	26,6	27,5	26,2	25,5	16,2	22,5	14,1	14,4
Wages and salaries	67,1	72,0	72,1	72,4	73,0	76,2	77,1	81,4	84,7

Source: Eurostat

REAL EXCHANGE RATE DEVELOPMENTS IN THE ACCESSION COUNTRIES[1]

PETER PART

1. INTRODUCTION

The Copenhagen economic criteria defined "*the ability of the Candidate Country's economy to withstand competitive pressures and market forces within the Union*" as a pre-condition for joining the EU. The accession process has so far considerably assisted transition countries in achieving substantial progress in structural reforms, and in inducing higher macroeconomic stability. In the medium and long-term, the accession countries will benefit significantly from the adoption of the EU "acquis communautaire" in terms of higher output growth and employment. However, as a consequence of an advancing real convergence process, some major challenges in these economies may appear with regard to competitiveness. Presumed developments of inflation and total factor productivity will exert strong and possibly unpredictable forces.

Hence, in addition to the implementation of stability-oriented macroeconomic policies, a well-designed road map of structural reforms is key for these economies to manage the successful integration into the enlarged EU market. This paper gives an overview on real exchange rate developments and their underlying driving forces during the transition process in the past decade. Secondly, it will also highlight some future perspectives and policy challenges, with a special focus on competitiveness in these economies and implications for structural reforms. The accession countries will have to find appropriate answers to the major policy issue of how to maintain the momentum on both real and nominal convergence without creating severe economic imbalances.

[1] Many thanks for very helpful comments by Wolfgang Nitsche (MoF), Andreas Pregesbauer (MoF), Alfred Katterl (MoF), Helene Schuberth (Austrian National Bank) and Ulrike Magloth (Federal Chancellery).

2. RECENT REAL EXCHANGE RATE DEVELOPMENTS

2.1. (REAL) EXCHANGE RATE DEVELOPMENTS AND EXCHANGE RATE REGIMES

At the outset of the transition from command to market economies, nominal exchange rates were clearly undervalued. Throughout the past decade, we have observed sustained real exchange rate appreciation[2] in the accession countries vis-à-vis the Euro. In the period from 1995 to 2001, real exchange rate appreciation ranged from approximately 10% to a maximum of 100%, with Slovenia, Malta and Cyprus at the lower end, Lithuania and Latvia at the upper margin and the majority of countries within the band of 35% to 60% (see graph 1). This real appreciation has gone hand-in-hand with strong, significantly above EU-15 real GDP growth since the mid-90ies, except for Bulgaria, Romania and the Czech Republic. The latter experienced only moderate or even negative output growth over this period. Nevertheless, despite the rapidly advancing real convergence process in general, output and income levels are still far from approaching EU averages. However, beside these variations in the overall pace of real exchange rate appreciation, the time-profile and the magnitude of fluctuations differed markedly between accession countries. Despite these differences, real exchange rate developments are also driven by a number of common factors. Unit labour costs, and more specifically productivity and real wage developments, play a crucial role when analysing real exchange rates in these economies. Substantial capital flows exert significant impacts on nominal exchange rates, also in the short-run, and thus on external competitiveness.

[2] vis-à-vis the ECU/Euro and in effective terms

Graph 1: Cumulative change in real exchange rates and real GDP (in %)

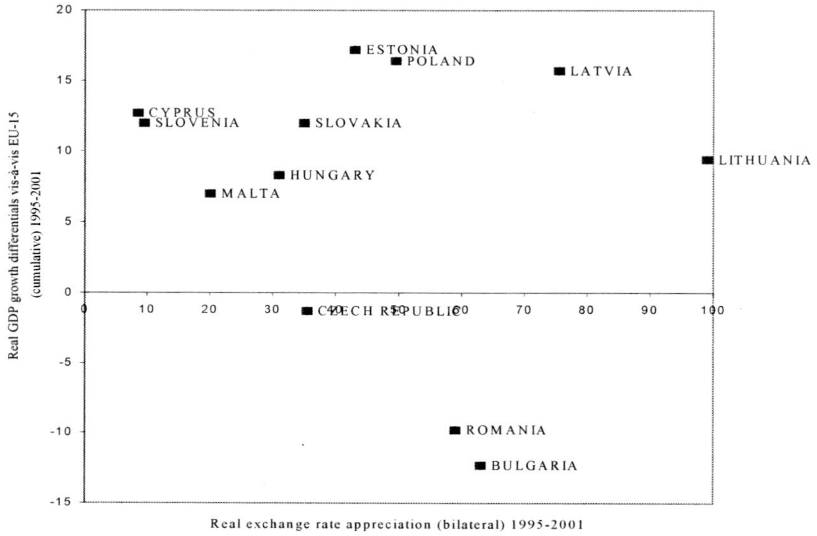

Source: Eurostat, WIIW

The first years of transition were characterised in many countries by abrupt and large (short and longer-term) swings in nominal exchange rates. These were caused by large and possibly disruptive capital flows, external imbalances, output fluctuations, an underdeveloped financial sector, high fiscal deficits, high interest rate differentials and at least double-digit inflation rates. These exchange rate fluctuations consequently distorted investment decisions and trade patterns and to a certain degree dampened consumer confidence. This, together with measures taken to correct these economic imbalances, negatively affected output and employment growth. Many accession countries responded to theses severe economic challenges by visibly altering their exchange rate regimes.

Real appreciation depends crucially on the exchange rate regime. Under a fixed exchange rate regime, with the nominal rate tied to an external anchor, real appreciation is driven by inflation developments only. In a regime of fully flexible rates, such as in Poland to a high degree, real exchange rate developments follow closely the catch-up process in equilibrium. Obviously, however, real developments may deviate substantially from equilibrium trends. Especially in the countries operating flexible regimes, the management of exchange rate strategies may be challenged by large capital flows. In case of large inflows these may bring about excessive currency appreciation, jeopardising a country's competitiveness. In the intermediate regimes, such as a managed float, real exchange rate appreciation could be fully or at least partially caused by nominal trends; here, economic analysis is even much more complex.

Currently, accession countries follow quite divergent exchange rate policy regimes, encompassing currency boards in Bulgaria, Estonia, Lithuania and quasi in Latvia, several pegged exchange rates (in general to the Euro, only in Latvia to the SDR-basket), a managed float in the Czech Republic, Romania, Slovakia and Slovenia and a quasi fully float regime in Poland (see table 1).

Table 1: Current Exchange Rate Regimes in the Accession Balance

	Regime	Peg/Basket	Band	Monetary Policy
Bulgaria	fixed peg	Euro		currency board
Cyprus	fixed peg	Euro	+/- 15% (+ softer inner bands)	
Czech Republic	managed float	main reference: Euro		inflation targeting
Estonia	fixed peg	Euro		currency board
Hungary	central parity	Euro	+/- 15%	implicit inflation targeting
Latvia	fixed peg	SDR	intervention at +/-1%	quasi currency board + monetary aggregates
Lithuania	fixed peg	(formerly to USD) as of 2.2.2002: Euro		currency board
Malta	fixed peg	Trade weighted basket	intervention at +/- 0.25%	
Poland	full float			inflation targeting
Romania	managed float	main reference: USD		monetary aggregates targeting
Slovakia	managed float	main reference: Euro		monetary aggregates targeting
Slovenia	managed float	main reference: Euro		monetary aggregates targeting

Source: European Commission (2002)

With the ultimate goal of joining EMU, ERM-II participation represents an important intermediate step of monetary integration. Whilst, in principle, several exchange rate regimes and different stages of nominal and real convergence are considered to be compatible with the ERM-II system, it is absolutely crucial that a credible and viable exchange rate strategy will be pursued in order to create a favourable environment for coping with economic vulnerabilities associated with the ongoing process of catching-up, enhanced competition and increased market flexibility. However, most of the accession PEPs remained rather vague on concrete paths of monetary integration.

In recent years, with the exception of those countries with currency boards, accession countries have tended to adopt a more flexible policy stance. This move towards more exchange rate flexibility was, in general, motivated by the necessity to better accommodate the surge of (short-term) capital inflows rather than to maintain international competitiveness. Subsequently, nominal exchange rate developments have overall become steadier and less disruptive.

Graph 2: Selected nominal exchange rate developments 1999-2002 (vis-à-vis Euro, Index 1999=100)

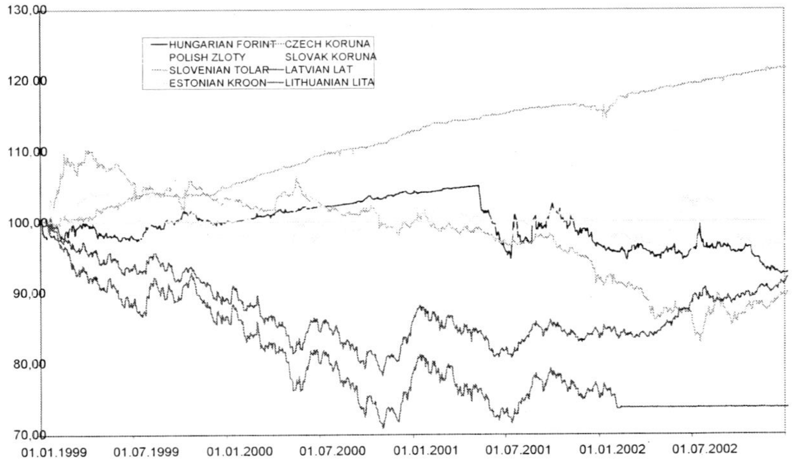

Source: OeNB

Graph 2 shows the more gradual appreciation/depreciation trends in selected accession countries over the period 1999-2002. Whilst, in particular, Romania and Slovenia have been facing nominal depreciation over the last four years, the opposite has mostly been true for many other accession countries, above all for Latvia and Lithuania: the currencies of most accession countries have strengthened against the Euro (see graph 2). Only Poland, and to a minor extent, Hungary, Latvia, Lithuania and the Czech Republic, were exposed to larger shorter-term volatility. In contrast to the more structural driving forces of long-term trends, short-term fluctuations are still driven mainly by the exchange rate regime, capital flows, and inflation and interest rate differentials vis-à-vis their most important trading partners and the degree of financial integration.

2.2. Inflation Developments: The Balassa-Samuelson Effect and Impacts Related to the Transition to Market Economies

Inflation developments are, in particular, driven by wages, productivity and monetary policy. Inflation has been the main factor of real appreciation, as the strengthening of the currencies has been playing a greater role only in recent years. Regarding the monetary policy framework, the accession countries have apparently started to converge to the Euro area monetary policy set-up of independent central banks, pursuing the goal of price stability and the non-bailing-out of the public sector. Together with the initial disinflation programmes based largely on pegs to external anchors, this transformation of monetary policy has successfully assisted in first stabilising and then reducing high and volatile inflation and interest rates. Hence, accession countries have made considerable progress in bringing inflation down from double to single-digit numbers and, thus, closer to EU-15 levels in 2001.

Yet, significant inflation differentials vis-à-vis the Euro inflation rate still exists in several countries. In 2001, CPI inflation rates were within a range from fairly low levels in Lithuania (1.3%) and Cyprus (2.0%), to 9.2% in Hungary, and to the outlier of 30.3% in Romania, compared to 2.3% in EU-15. All accession countries, except for Cyprus, Latvia and Lithuania, envisage a further decline of inflation over the PEPs' time-horizont. In Romania, in light of the very high present CPI inflation, a particularly ambitious fall to single-digit levels is foreseen in 2005. Many accession countries count on structural reforms and liberalisation to reduce inflation, but also on strict low inflation-targeting. The projected declines in inflation rates will require substantial efforts, including sound fiscal policies, far-reaching structural reforms, an appropriate framework of monetary and exchange rate policies and (price) stability oriented wage policies.

Table 2: CPI inflation rates and price levels

	CPI inflation 1996 (in %)	CPI inflation 2001 (in %)	CPI price level 2001 (index, EU-15=100)
Bulgaria	121.6	7.4	31
Cyprus	3.0	2.0	83
Czech Republic	8.8	4.7	46
Estonia	23.1	5.8	47
Hungary	23.6	9.2	46
Latvia	17.6	2.5	54
Lithuania	24.6	1.3	48
Malta	2.0	2.9	88
Poland	19.9	5.5	54
Romania	38.8	30.3	39
Slovakia	5.8	7.1	41
Slovenia	9.9	8.4	67
EU-15	2.4	2.3	100

Source: European Commission, OeNB

In the coming years, inflation differentials may be continuously driven by a catch-up process in product markets. The so-called Balassa-Samuelson effect suggests that transition countries with higher potential growth will also face notably higher inflation rates (or, by putting it in a more forward-looking way, in a catching-up process higher income levels will induce higher relative prices in sheltered sectors). Productivity growth in the exposed sectors will determine wage increases and will also be higher because of higher innovation and technological progress. As wage increases in the sectors with lower productivity growth (sheltered services industries) will roughly follow the same pattern as in the exposed sector, this will lead to higher price increases in the whole economy. While there is more or less consensus on the existence of the Balassa-Samuelson effect, empirical evidence gives no uniform picture of its actual size.

This depends, in particular, on the assumptions of how far product markets are already integrated into the EU internal market, how "perfect" competition is in these countries, and/or in how far it is possible to differentiate between tradeable and non-tradeable products. Moreover, while in many accession countries wages were fairly equalised across sectors in the pre-transition period, a stronger wage differentiation reflects overall market conditions nowadays. Real exchange rate appreciation has, in part, been also the result of raising administered prices, lifting subsidies and other administrative barriers to price competition and changes in indirect taxation. And, finally, in the accession countries productivity growth in the service sector will benefit from new information and communication technologies which have lately helped the more industrially advanced countries to keep inflation down.

Again, graph 1 very clearly demonstrates, in comparing Bulgaria and Romania with other accession countries, that the relationship between real GDP growth and real exchange rate appreciation is not straightforward because of negative growth effects of high inflation and deferred structural adjustments. Inflation differentials vis-à-vis the EU/Euro average could be attributed to initially distorted structures of these economies which, with the introduction of market-based reforms and prices, brought about massive changes in output, employment and (relative) price levels. This real exchange rate appreciation mainly mirrored labour market and relative wage adjustments between the exposed sector, which was heavily subsidised in centrally planned economies, and the sheltered one. Labour shedding, in particular to gain productivity in the traded-sector, was accompanied by price liberalisation. Generally speaking, these effects of the labour reallocation process, with a few exceptions, worked through five year after the actual transition process had been initiated.

Recent empirical studies have attempted to disentangle the Balassa-Samuleson catching-up effect from these structural reforms at the beginning of the transition process. This has consequently led to lower estimates of the former. The European Commission stated in its European Economic Review 2002 that this effect might be smaller than the estimates of 4-5% published some years ago and might have prevailed especially in the more advanced transition economies.

In 2001, price levels in accession countries remained well below EU-15 levels, ranging from 31% of EU average in Bulgaria, over 67% in Slovenia to 83% in Cyprus (see table 2). According to the PEPs, with moderate inflation, low price levels and no sizeable nominal appreciation, the convergence of price levels between accession countries and EU averages is assumed to progress quite moderately until 2005. In this sense, most PEPs have kept fairly silent on the extent the countries expect the still occurring inflation differentials with EU-15 to be related to the Balassa-Samuelson effect one the one hand, or to specific transition factors, such as deregulation, indirect tax harmonisation or relative price changes on the other.

2.3. (Unit) Labour Cost Developments and Real Exchange Rate Appreciation

Initially, the comparative advantage of accession countries, especially in the labour-intensive industries, was a result of low and falling (nominal) wages combined with a highly-qualified labour force and undervalued currencies. After the first period of rapid structural adjustment ending around 1992, cost competitiveness deteriorated markedly in many accession countries, as (real) unit labour costs (converted into Euro/ECU at current exchange rates) rose significantly. However, (real) unit labour cost developments varied quite substantially across countries and sectors throughout the 90ies. In many manufacturing industries cost competitiveness even notably improved. Here, many accession countries have experienced a striking increase in the productivity differential between the tradeable and the non-tradeable sectors, contributing via strong changes of relative prices to real exchange rate appreciation. Nevertheless, until 2000, unit labour costs remained at relatively low levels compared to the advanced countries (see table 3).

Table 3: Nominal and unit labour costs 2000

	Productivity levels[1] (index, Austria=100)	Nominal labour costs[2] (index, Austria=100)	Unit labour costs (index, Austria=100)
Bulgaria	28	4	17
Czech Republic	46	14	49
Estonia	37	10	38
Hungary	72	13	19
Latvia	33	8	37
Lithuania	37	7	30
Poland	52	17	34
Romania	28	5	18
Slovakia	45	11	25
Slovenia	43	31	72

Source: WIIW, 1) compared at purchasing power parity, 2) converted into Euro at current exchange rates

Besides real exchange rate appreciation, this increase in unit labour costs was largely due to considerable wage increases in many countries. Since 1992, nominal and (even more pronounced) real wages went up substantially over the last decade, more than compensating already high labour productivity growth in several accession countries (c.f. up to 15% in manufacturing in Hungary over the period 1993-2000). However, despite these increases, wages in most accession countries are still fairly low compared to EU-15 levels, though wage dispersion among accession countries is definitely also high. The low level, however, applies to average productivity as well, which, together with some existing product quality gaps, will constrain wage cost advantages. While wages were rather equalised in the pre-transformation phase, wage differentiation among industries already turns out to be higher in some accession countries compared to EU-15 nowadays.

2.4. CAPITAL FLOWS AND CURRENT ACCOUNT SUSTAINABILITY

The role of capital flows in triggering exchange rate dynamics is especially associated with current account sustainability. Their effects hinge fundamentally on their nature and structure, whether they finance public or private consumption or investment expenditure, whether financing occurs via FDI or portfolio flows. In recent years, large FDI inflows, with the focus on the private sector and related to large-scale privatisation programmes, have been able to finance a great deal of occurring (high) current account deficits in the accession countries. For instance, in 2001, the current account deficit of the accession countries amounted to 4% of GDP on average, ranging from an almost balanced level of 0.4% of GDP in Slovenia to a medium-term unsustainable one of 8.6% of GDP in Slovakia.

In the short-run, FDI inflows are presumed to still play a dominant role in financing, above all due to further large-scale privatisation plans of many governments. In the future, especially in connection with the gradual phasing-out of massive privatisation, the accession countries are expected to rely much more on (short-term) capital inflows for their domestic financing needs. This might give rise to more disruptive exchange rate movements. Indeed, a main concern is that these large inflows will lead to an overvalued currency, thereby hampering competitiveness and exacerbating already existing current account deficits that may, in turn, lead to the eventual reversal of capital flows.

Moreover, the accession countries may especially face very volatile capital flows in the run-up to EMU participation, due to expected positive (real) interest rate differentials with the Euro area and declining exchange rate volatility at the same time because of expected ERM-II participation. This could be even aggravated by adopting the "acquis communautaire" and in particular, by the forthcoming liberalisation of the capital account. Moreover, in recent years, the privatisation process has often initiated larger cross-border intra-company portfolio flows which are likely to remain in the future, as privatisation plans have not been completed so far. Given the remaining fragility of financial sector, and even if structural reforms are further advanced, large and volatile capital flows could have an unfavourable impact on the economies. For this reason, also taking account of the different stages of progress in structural reform, as well as the discrepancies in market size and market conditions, the optimal strategy and the speed of monetary integration in combination with structural reform will have to differ markedly across accession countries.

3. Conclusions

In the future, accession countries are likely to face further real exchange rate appreciation, as inflation differentials with EU-15 will not, in general, diminish completely due to catching-up price movements, internal market integration in association with low initial price levels and further adjustments in administered prices. When real appreciation cannot be absorbed by productivity gains or by moderate, productivity-related wage developments, this will obviously constrain external competitiveness and could further aggravate the already existing current account deficits. There is vast potential for gains in productivity both through more efficient use of capital, human resources and technologies and through upgrading technology.

A sound macroeconomic policy framework, in particular credible and viable monetary and exchange rate policies in combination with productivity-related wage settlements, is key for lowering macro and financial vulnerabilities and conflicts between low inflation, external stability and output/employment growth. For this reason, accession countries will take these real convergence and other transition effects on prices into account, while committing themselves to credible stability-oriented inflation objectives and to an ambitious disinflation process, respectively. Structural reforms to enhance flexibility on product and labour markets will clearly help to keep inflationary pressures better down.

This should be accompanied by the strengthening of the financial sector, to cope with higher capital flows pursuant to the liberalisation of the capital account and to increase the effectiveness of monetary policy. These ongoing reform efforts will be of particular relevance with the prospect of ERM-II and later of EMU participation. Thus, it will be crucial for the accession countries to find an appropriate policy mix between the speed of monetary integration and enhanced structural reforms.

4. *References*

Capek, A. (2002), "Real convergence and real appreciation - the Czech experience", WIIW Monthly Report 2002/4, Vienna.

EBRD (2002), "Transition Report", London.

European Commission (2002), "European Economic Review 2002", Brussels.

European Commission (2002), "Report on macroeconomic and financial stability in the Candidate Countries", Brussels.

European Commission (2001), "The economic impact of enlargement", Enlargement Papers, Brussels.

European Strategy Paper on progress towards accession (2002), Brussels.

Jazbec, B. (2001), "Determinants of real exchange rates in transition economies", OeNB Focus on Transition 2001/2, Vienna.

Landesmann, M. (2003), "Structural features of economic integration in an enlarged Europe: patterns of catching-up and industrial specialisation", European Economy, January 2003.

Oblath, G., Richter, S. (2002), "Macroeconomic and sectoral aspects of Hungary's international competitiveness and trade performance on EU markets", WIIW Research Report 2002/9.

Pre-Accession Economic Programmes 2002.

WIIW - Vienna Institute for Comparative Economic Studies (2002), "WIIW Structural Report", Vienna.

Assessment of Product Markets in the Candidate Countries[1]

Lars Östling

1. Introduction

This contribution contains a preliminary analysis of the 13 Candidate Countries' product markets and their transition to the knowledge-based economy. The purpose of this paper is to give information for an assessment of how the Candidate Countries can be integrated into the existing surveillance of the structural reform elements of the EU economic policy processes.

A comprehensive analysis of the Candidate Countries' structural reforms has been made in the Commission Regular Reports on the Copenhagen economic accession criteria. A more in-depth description of each Candidate Country's structural reform measures is presented in the Candidate Countries' Pre-Accession Economic Programmes (PEPs). Several other Commission studies have partly dealt with structural reforms in the Candidate Countries. The analysis in this paper draws on this material and different indicators, especially the structural indicators used to measure progress towards the Lisbon Strategy objectives achieved in the present Member States. This facilitates comparisons between the Candidate Countries and the EU.

The paper starts with section 2 describing the general economic environment relevant for the product market performance in the Candidate Countries. Section 3 is concerned with labour productivity and the structure of the economy, stressing the differences between Candidate Coun-

[1] Working document from the European Commission Directorate General for Economic and Financial Affairs submitted to the Economic Policy Committee ad-hoc group on enlargement. The document has been prepared by Lars Östling with the support of Fabienne Ilzkovitz, Adriaan Dierx and Peter Grasmann. The views expressed in this working document can not necessarily be attributed to the European Commission.

tries and EU Member States. The next section deals with market integration. It is assessed to what extent the Candidate Countries' product markets are integrated with the EU economy through trade and investment. Section 5 focuses on issues relevant to the business environment, such as competition policy, state aid, regulatory burden and SMEs. Due to a lack of consistent data in this area it is difficult to make a detailed evaluation. Section 6 is devoted to the knowledge-based economy. It contains a first assessment on how much the Candidate Countries have achieved in their transition to the knowledge-based economy. Finally, in section 7 the main structural reform priorities relating to the product markets in the Candidate Countries are discussed. The paper ends with a summary section.

2. *GENERAL ECONOMIC BACKGROUND*

There has been limited success among Candidate Countries in terms of catching-up with the EU Member States standards of living levels during the second half of the 1990s. The 13 Candidate Countries' weighted average per capita GDP in 1995 PPS terms was 38.5% of the EU average in 2001, compared with 37.8% in 1995. There appears to have been some additional catching-up in 2002. Eight Candidate Countries were relatively better off in 2002 than in 1995, whereas five Candidate Countries, according to available statistics, had a higher GDP per capita relative to that of the EU back in 1995.[2] However, during the last three years the catching-up process seems to have accelerated with a solid majority of Candidate Countries increasing their relative GDP per capita. The dispersion between Candidate Countries is still large ranging from 74% of the EU average in Cyprus to 23% of the EU average in Turkey.

---

[2] A statistical break in the series between 1999 and 2000 affects the comparison between 1995 and 2001 for all Candidate Countries. This especially concerns Cyprus and it is uncertain if GDP per capita in Cyprus really has dropped between 1995 and 2001.

Graph 1: Income level per capita 2002 and 1995 in 1995 PPS with EU average = 100.

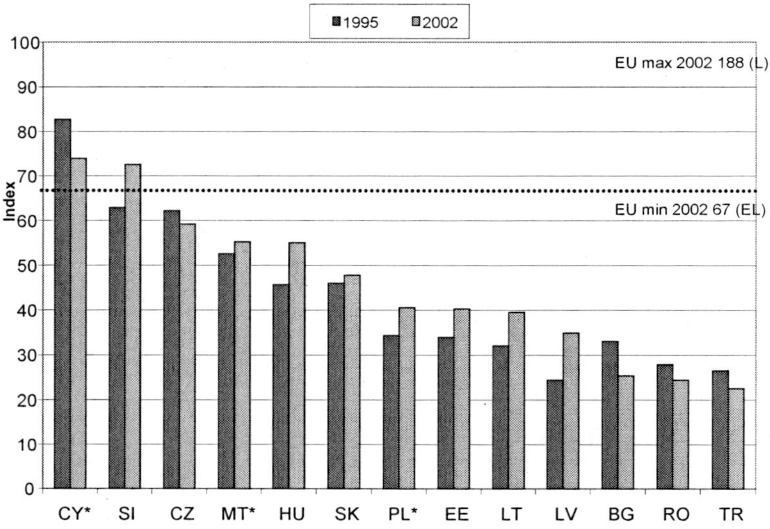

Source: Eurostat * CY provisional data for 2001 instead of 2002, Data for MT 1999 instead of 2002. PL forecast for 2002.

It is evident that the Candidate Countries have a long way to go to achieve the same prosperity as the EU, as illustrated in graph 1. Even with high long-term growth figures, it will take many years before the majority of the Candidate Countries will reach the level of the least prosperous EU Member States. Already now, however, the most prosperous Candidate Countries are at the same level as the least prosperous EU Member States. This points to the large differences between the Candidate Countries, which resemble the differences between EU Member States.

Graph 2: Annual average GDP growth from 1995 to 2002.

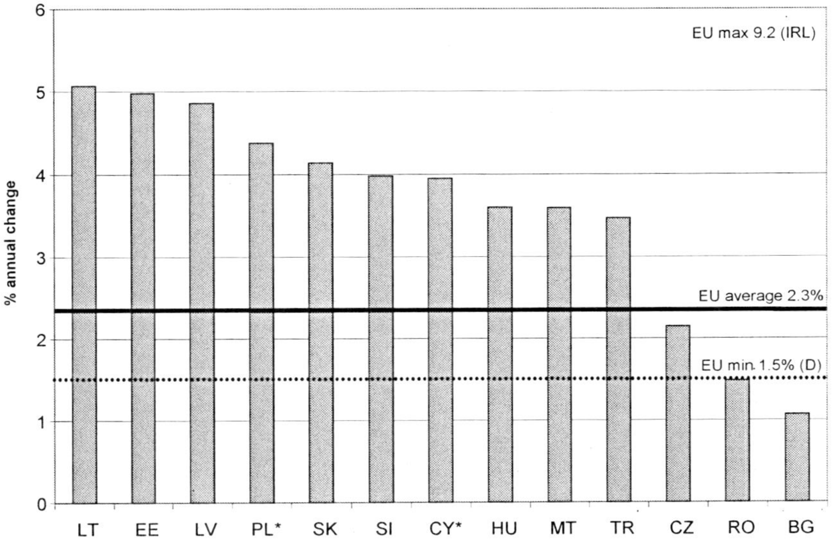

Source: Eurostat * PL estimate for 2002. CY forecast for 2002 and provisional data for 2000-2001.

The gap in income levels between Candidate Countries and EU Member States is substantial, but there is evidence that the Candidate Countries are slowly closing the economic gap to the EU. In 2000, all Candidate Countries posted positive GDP growth for the first time. Five Candidate Countries have had an uninterrupted positive growth record for the 1995 to 2002 period and no Candidate Country has had less than four years of positive growth during the period. Furthermore ten of the Candidate Countries had higher average growth than the EU average growth over the 1995 to 2002 period, with the Czech Republic, Romania and Bulgaria being the exceptions.

The return to growth in all Candidate Countries could indicate the start of a period of sustainable high economic growth. This could be compared with the developments after accession of Ireland, Spain, Portugal and Greece.[3] For these countries it took many years before the full eco-

[3] The Commission paper "*Real convergence in Candidate Countries: past performance and scenar-*

nomic benefits of EU membership materialised. Similarly, after several years of sluggish growth many Candidate Countries can now fully start to reap the fruits of structural reforms and increased economic integration with the EU, which for some of them started ten years ago with the Europe Agreements.

Graph 3: Inflation in 2002 as annual change of HICP.

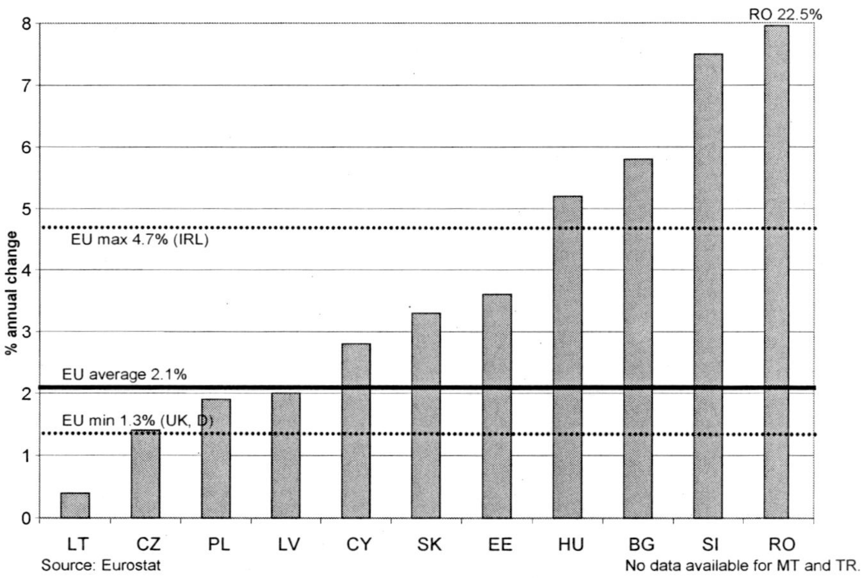

Inflation has come down in most Candidate Countries, but is generally still higher than in the EU as illustrated in graph 3. In 2002, Lithuania, the Czech Republic, Poland and Latvia had inflation levels below the EU average. Four Candidate Countries recorded an inflation rate above 5%, as measured by change in HICP over the previous year, thereby exceeding the highest inflation rate among the EU Member States.

ios in the Pre-Accession Economic Programmes" gives a good overview of the economic performance in PT, IE, ES and GR before and after joining the EU. Another evaluation of the convergence of GR, IE, ES and PT with other EU Member States can be found in Martin, Velazques and Funck *"European integration and income convergence"*, World Bank 2001.

The relatively high inflation may not be too detrimental for the Candidate Countries' competitiveness if it can be attributed to the catching-up process. Various estimates indicate that the so-called Balassa-Samuelson effect accounts for a part of the inflation in Candidate Countries, but there is no consensus on the magnitude of the effect.[4] Thus it is possible that the catching-up can be combined with a relatively low consumer price level, similar to the developments in Portugal, Spain and Greece.

Graph 4: Consumer price levels 2001 in purchasing power standard (PPS) with EU average consumer price level = 100.

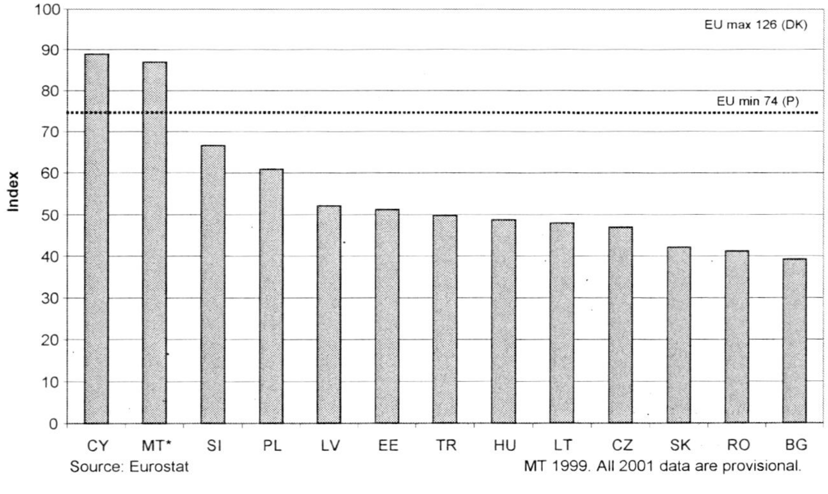

[4] See European Commission 2002 "Balassa-Samuelson effects outside the Euro area" for a comprehensive overview of different estimates.

Consumer price levels are distinctly lower in most Candidate Countries compared with EU consumer price levels, as shown in graph 4. In seven Candidate Countries the relative consumer price level is less than half the EU average. None of the Central or Eastern European Candidate Countries has a consumer price level equal to the EU Member State with the lowest consumer price level. The low consumer price level is partly due to the low levels of GDP per capita and remaining administered prices. The relationship between price levels in Candidate Countries and their income levels needs to be further explored.

Consumer prices in Candidate Countries have risen significantly in the past years and this may continue. The abolishing of price controls are likely to contribute to further increases of consumer price levels in Candidate Countries. A moderating effect on the consumer price level is expected from increased competition through imports and the development of more efficiently functioning domestic product markets. Depending on exchange rate movements, the consumer price level in the Candidate Countries could converge rather rapidly towards the EU level.[5]

[5] Real exchange rate movements are reflected in changes in the purchasing power parities, which will affect the purchasing power standard. See the Eurostat webpage for more information: http://europa.eu.int/comm/eurostat/newcronos/info/notmeth/en/theme1/strind/ecoref.htm

Graph 5: Administered prices in Candidate Countries in 2001 as share of Consumer Price Index (CPI).

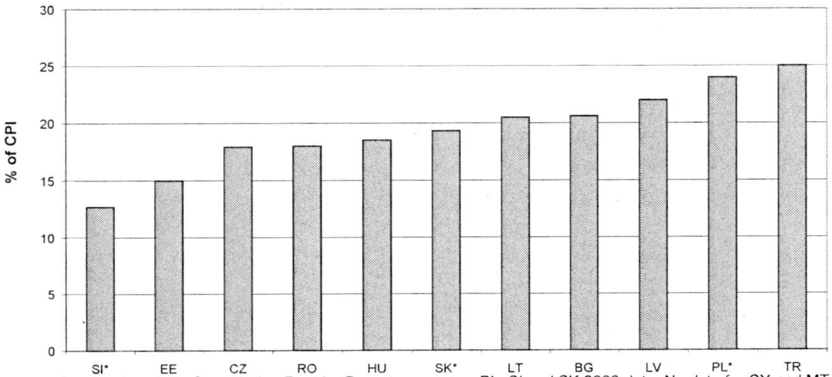

Source: European Commission Regular Reports. PL, SI and SK 2000 data. No data for CY and MT.

One factor contributing to the low consumer price level in Candidate Countries are price regulations. According to data in the European Commission Regular Reports, there are still substantial price controls in the Candidate Countries. Administered prices, e.g. in the energy sector, are common in most Candidate Countries, covering from 13% to 25% of the consumer price index (CPI) in 2001 (see graph 5). In five Candidate Countries, regulated prices comprise more than a fifth of the CPI. Several Candidate Countries are undertaking reforms, which will reduce price controls and open up markets for competition. There is no comparable data available for the EU Member States.[6]

6 There are few examples of price regulations in the EU Member States. Some price controls remain on energy and a few goods.

3. *Productivity and the Structure of the Economy*

In order to increase economic growth and close the gap in GDP per capita to the EU, one main challenge in the Candidate Countries will be to increase labour productivity.

Graph 6: Labour productivity per person employed 2002 with EU average = 100.

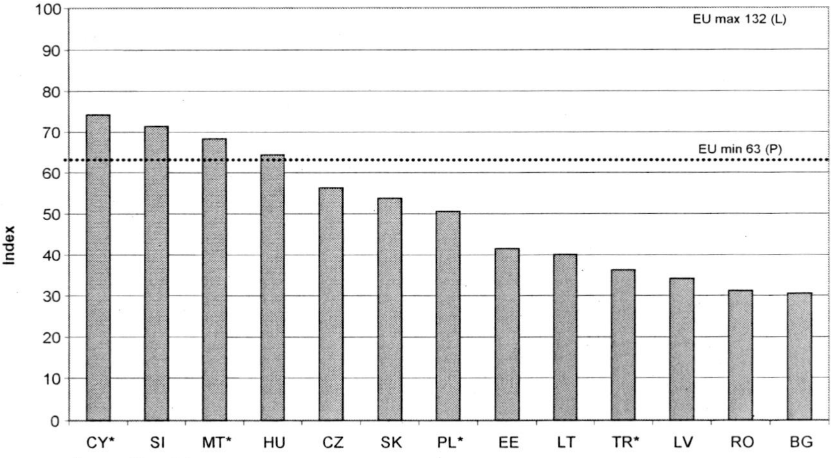

Source: Eurostat

* CY,PL and TR forecast. MT 1999 data.

Labour productivity is relatively low in most Candidate Countries, as illustrated in graph 6. Six Candidate Countries do not reach half the EU average productivity level and only four Candidate Countries have a labour productivity level, which is above the lowest productivity level among the EU Member States. However, labour productivity has increased steadily for most Candidate Countries between 1996 and 2002. The increase in labour productivity has in several Candidate Countries outpaced the EU productivity increase, although labour productivity in some sectors seems to remain low.

Productivity growth in the Candidate Countries could be further boosted in the future, as implemented structural reforms begin to pay off, including a shift in the sectoral composition of the economy to sectors with a higher value added. Improvements of the general business environment and a successful transition to the knowledge-based economy will also contribute to raise productivity and increase living standards.

The sectoral composition in Candidate Countries with a relatively large agricultural sector and the existence of big state-owned manufacturing companies with hidden unemployment contribute to explain the low labour productivity. The sectoral composition of the economy in the Candidate Countries differs from the composition in the current EU Member States. In general, service sectors are less developed than manufacturing industries in the Candidate Countries.

Graph 7: Gross value added in the industry sector in 1991, 1995 and 2001 as % of total value added.

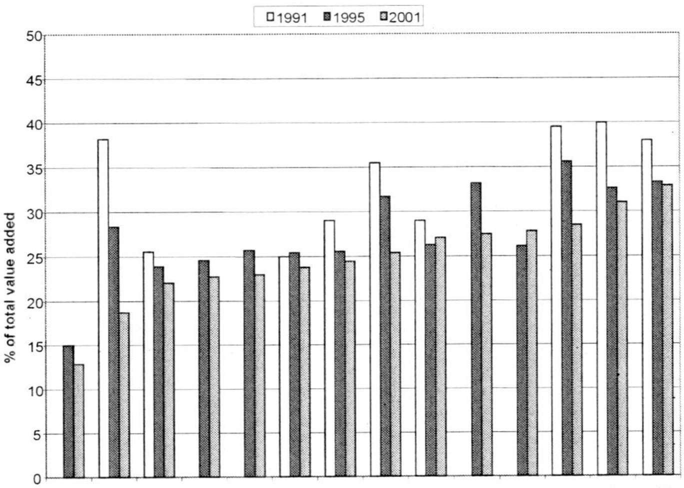

Source: Eurostat
BG 2000 and 1996 data instead of 2001 and 1995. PL 1992 data instead of 1991. No 1991 data available for LT, SK, BG, EE and CY.

Since 1991, the industry share in the economy has decreased in all Candidate Countries, as illustrated in graph 7. In Hungary and Turkey the share of the industry as a percentage of total value added has remained relatively stable, whereas it has dropped significantly in Latvia, Romania, Slovenia and Poland. The share of industry in the Candidate Countries' economies in 2001 ranged from 13% to 33%, and in Cyprus and Latvia the share of industry was below the EU level (22% of total value added).

Whereas the share of manufacturing has declined, the share of the service sector has increased in most Candidate Countries. This is illustrated in graph 8, which shows the development in the service sector of financial intermediation, real estate and business renting activities.[7] However, even though the service sector has increased in Candidate Countries, it is still considerably smaller than in the EU.

Graph 8: Gross value added in the sector financial intermediation, real estate and business-renting activities in 1991, 1995 and 2001 as % of total value added.

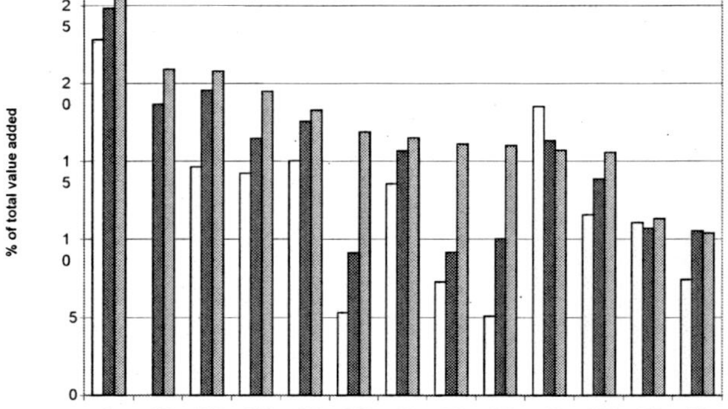

Source: Eurostat SK and EE 1993 data instead of 1991. PL 1992 data instead of 1991. HU and RO 2000 data instead of 2001. CY 1999 data instead of 2001. No data available for BG.

---

[7] This sector was chosen because of data availability.

The contribution to total gross value added from the sector financial intermediation, real estate and business renting activities does not exceed 21% for any Candidate Country, whereas the EU average is 27%. However, it is evident that in a number of Candidate Countries there has been a rapid growth in this sector since 1991, even surpassing the sector's growth in the EU. This indicates a significant resource reallocation in terms of production value in these countries.

One other sector standing out in the Candidate Countries is the agricultural sector. Although the share of the sector in % of GDP has decreased during the last decade, it is still a relatively significant sector in all Candidate Countries. This is illustrated in graph 9, describing the share of the sector agricultural, hunting, forestry and fishing in the Candidate Countries. Agriculture is dominating this sector and hereafter the sector is referred to as the agricultural sector.

Graph 9: Gross value added in the agricultural, hunting, forestry and fishing sector in 1991, 1995 and 2001 as % of total value added.

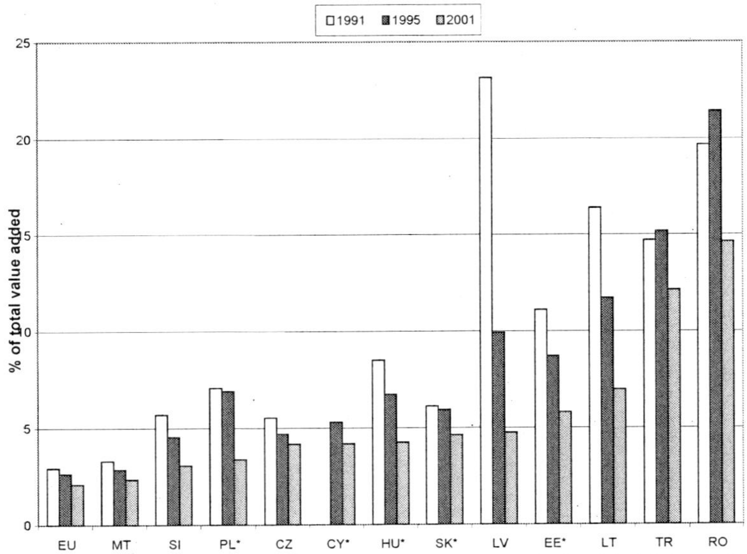

Source: Eurostat PL 1992 data and EE, SK 1993 data instead of 1991. CY 1999 data and HU 2000 data instead of 2001. No data available for CY 1991. No data available for BG.

The agricultural sector was large in many Candidate Countries in 1991. In all Central and Eastern European Candidate Countries it accounted for more than 5% of total value added in 1991, peaking in Latvia, 23%, and Romania, 20%. The sector's share of total value added in the EU in 1991 was less than 3%. Although the sector has decreased in all Candidate Countries it is still relatively large in many of them. In 2001, the agricultural sector accounted for a larger share of the economy in all Candidate Countries than the EU average. In six Candidate Countries, in 2001 the sector still accounted for close to 5% or more of total valued added, which is significantly above the EU average of 2.1%. Even if the agricultural sector continues its relative decline it will take time before the size of the sector comes down to the EU average.

Another difference in the sectoral composition of the economy is that the public sector still is relatively large in several Candidate Countries. This reflects the remaining state ownership of big companies in some Candidate Countries.

Graph 10: Private sector share of GDP in Candidate Countries in 2001.

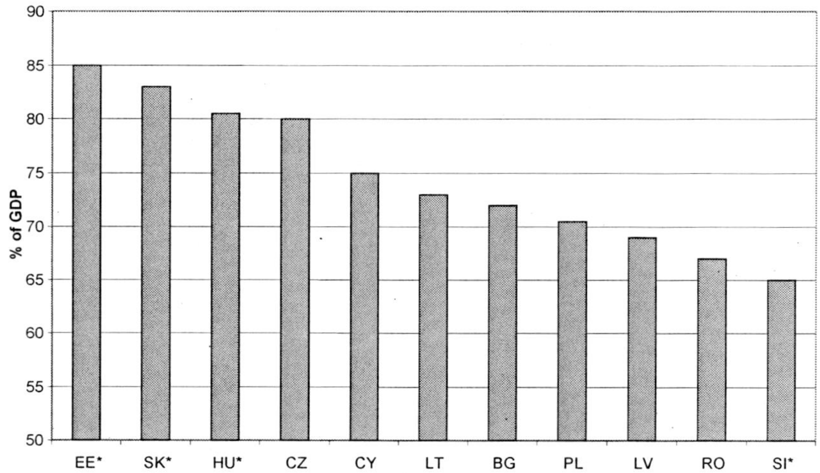

Source: European Commission Regular Reports

No data available for TR and MT. 2000 data for EE, SK, HU and SI.

The private sector has increased significantly in most Candidate Countries over the last decade, but in a number of Candidate Countries the private sector is still relatively small as illustrated in graph 10.[8] In Latvia, Romania and Slovenia the public sector still accounted for one third of GDP or more in 2001 and only in Estonia, the Slovak Republic and Hungary did the private sector produce more than 80% of GDP, which could be higher than in some EU Member States. The relatively small private sector in some Candidate Countries may indicate a lack of competition and ample room for efficiency gains. There is no comparable data available for the EU Member States, but some other data indicates that the private sector on average is larger in the EU Member States. The general government sector accounts for between 8% and 20% of GDP in EU Member States, according to the national accounts.

Privatisation of public assets has been undertaken in Candidate Countries in order to reduce the public sector's influence on the economy and to promote efficient markets. Through privatisation, well needed foreign capital and knowledge can be attracted, increasing the economic efficiency. In graph 11 the revenues from privatisation from 1994 to 1999 are shown.

8 As there is no uniform definition across countries the figures should be interpreted with caution. Data originates from national sources in the Candidate Countries and EBRD.

Graph 11: Privatisation revenues in % of GDP as an annual average between 1994 and 1999 according to World Bank Development Indicators 2001. EU figures are from "OECD in figures - 2000 edition".

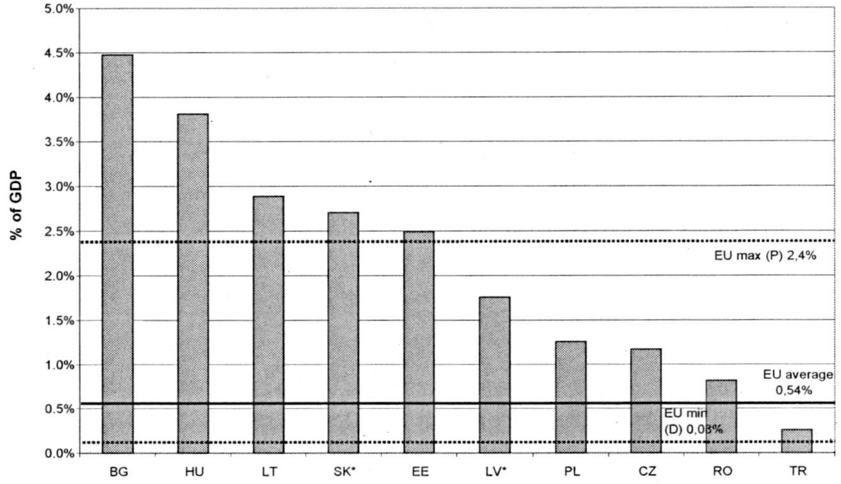

Source: World Bank Development Indicators 2001 and OECD in figures.

LV 1994-1998 data. SK 1994-1997 data. No data avilable for SL, CY and MT.

Privatisation has been one of the main economic reforms in the Central and Eastern European economies and remains high on their structural reform agendas. Annual average privatisation revenues in these Candidate Countries ranged from less than one percentage point of GDP to almost 4.5 percentage points of GDP for the 1994 to 1999 period. For single years and countries the revenues from privatisation have reached double digit figures. In some countries, notably Estonia, the privatisation process has been practically completed. In other Candidate Countries, the proceeds from privatisation are still considerable.

Summarising, labour productivity is low in the Candidate Countries. This indicates that the structural shift to more productive sectors has not yet been completed. For a number of Candidate Countries the private sector is still relatively small and substantial price controls remain. These Candidate Countries have room for further reform in these areas, which could support labour productivity.

4. *ECONOMIC INTEGRATION*

Opening up markets and increasing economic integration with the EU are key measures to improve the functioning of the economies in the Candidate Countries. The two main mechanisms for economic integration with the EU are trade and foreign direct investment (FDI). Trade integration increases competition in the Candidate Countries and FDI contributes to raising the growth potential. Together with other structural reforms this will help the Candidate Countries to catch up with the more prosperous EU Member States.

Graph 12: Total trade in relation to GDP in 2001.

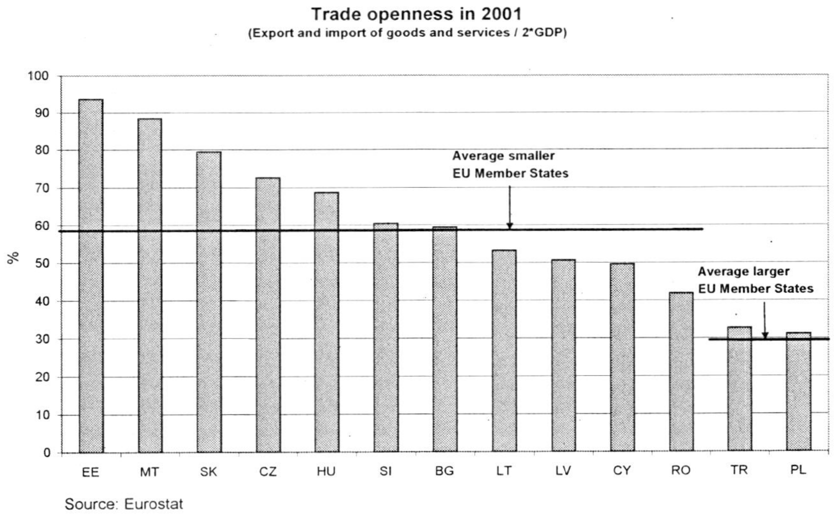

The Candidate Countries are in general open economies. This fact is illustrated in graph 12 where the trade of goods and services as a share of GDP is depicted. Seven of the Candidate Countries have a total trade openness that is higher than the average for smaller EU Member States.[9] All Candidate Countries have higher trade openness than the average for

[9] EU small member states are NL, BE, PT, EL, SE, AT, DK, FI, IE and LU. Large member states are DE, IT, UK, FR, and ES.

large EU Member States. The high trade openness in the Candidate Countries is partly explained by the fact that most of the Candidate Countries are small countries. The three Candidate Countries with the least trade are also the biggest ones: Turkey, Poland and Romania.

The Candidate Countries do not only have open economies, but they are also well integrated with the EU economy. This is manifested both by high export shares to the EU and by substantial FDI from the EU.

Graph 13: Export of goods from the Candidate Countries to the EU in 2001 as share of total goods exports.

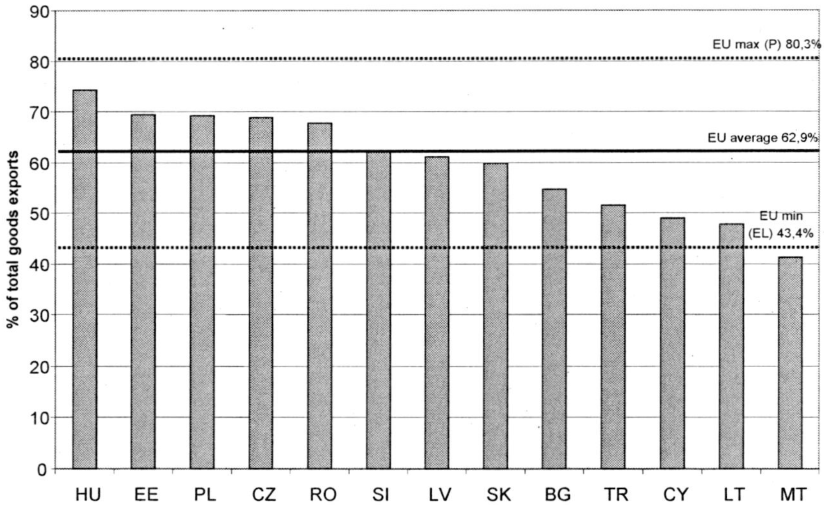

Source: Eurostat from national sources

Most of the Candidate Countries' export of goods go to the EU, as illustrated in graph 13. For all but three Candidate Countries, more than half their export of goods go to the EU. The exceptions are Cyprus, Lithuania and Malta.[10] Five of the Candidate Countries have a higher export share to the EU than the EU average, although they are not yet part of the internal market.[11] Thus, in trade terms the Candidate Countries seem to be as integrated in the EU as current Member States.

In a majority of Candidate Countries, the export share of "machinery and transport equipment" has increased significantly between 1996 and 2000. In these countries the export share for this sector typically exceeds one third of the total value for all exports. On the other hand, export shares for "food and live animals, beverages and tobacco" has decreased in most Candidate Countries and exceeds 10 percent of the total export value only for Cyprus, Turkey and Lithuania.

There are also indications on an increasing degree of intra-industry trade between the Candidate Countries and the EU. Several Candidate Countries have a level of intra-industry trade comparable to EU Member States. However, this applies primarily to the larger Candidate Countries, as the smaller countries seem to have a more specialised production structure, which is reflected in a narrower range of export products.

[10]In Malta, this is explained by one single big manufacturing company, which in 1999 switched from exporting mainly to the EU to exporting to other markets. Cyprus is very well integrated with the EU through the service sector, predominantly tourism, which integration effects is not reflected in the trade of goods. In Lithuania's case, the low export to the EU is partly explained by high energy exports to Belarus and other non-EU countries.

[11]This is even more remarkable as the share of EU exports went down in seven of the Candidate Countries between 2000 and 2001.

Graph 14: High technology export as share of total export of manufacturing goods 2000 according to World Bank development indicators.

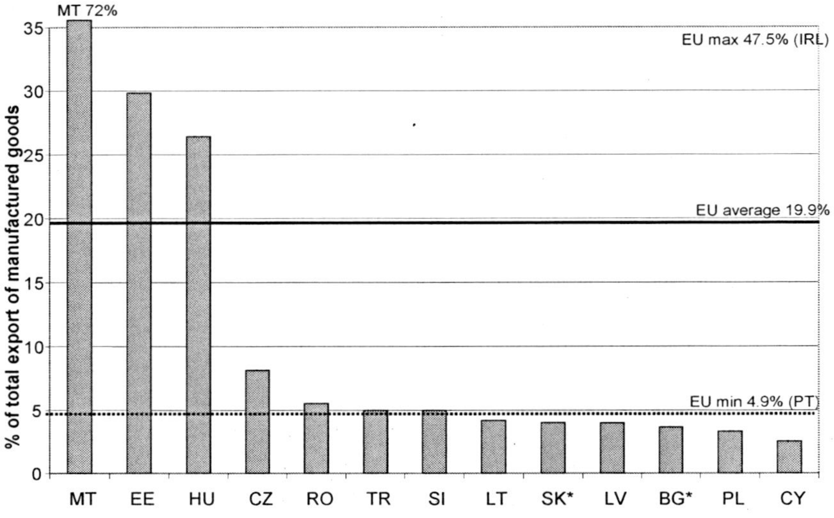

Source: World Bank Development Indicators 2002

* 1997 data for BG and 1999 for SK

As shown in graph 14, most Candidate Countries have considerably less high-technology exports than the EU average. However, in Malta, Estonia and Hungary, high tech exports are well developed, exceeding 25% of total manufactured exports, thereby surpassing the EU average of 20%. In Estonia and Hungary there have been dramatic increases in the share of high technology exports during the period 1995 to 2000, with an average increase of more than 3 percentage points per year. In Malta high technology exports increased by close to 2 percentage points on an annual average for the same period. No other Candidate Country recorded an average annual increase by more than 0.7 percentage points. The EU average annual increase for the same period was 0.9 percentage points.

However, the share of high technology exports has increased in all Candidate Countries for the period 1995 to 2000, with the possible exception of Cyprus, Malta and the Slovak Republic. This would indicate a structural shift at least in some Candidate Countries from the old industrial structure towards a knowledge-based industrial structure. This conclusion is supported by data showing that in recent years the export share of capital- or technology-intensive production has increased in most Candidate Countries.

Graph 15: Foreign direct investment flows to Candidate Countries from EU as % of GDP. Annual average 1996 - 2001.

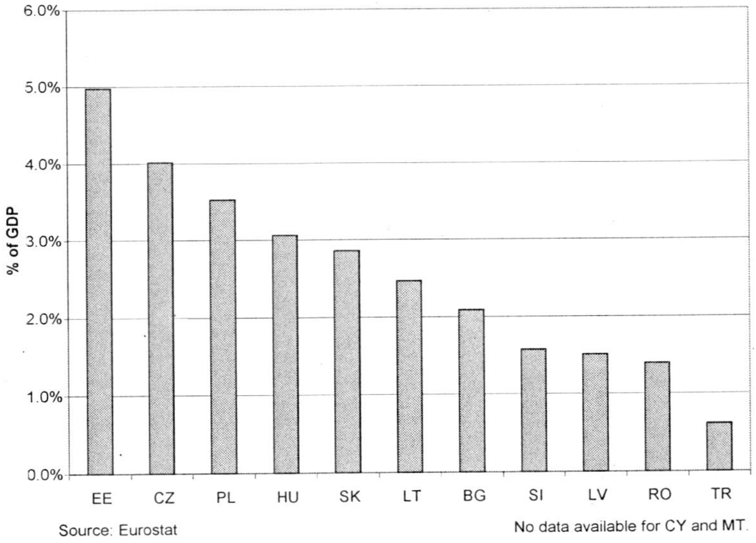

Integration is also driven by foreign direct investment. FDI from EU Member States is high in several Candidate Countries, reflecting high growth prospects and profitable investment opportunities. Graph 15 shows the annual average FDI between 1996 and 2001 from EU Member States to the Candidate Countries.[12] In Estonia, the Czech Republic, Poland and Hungary annual FDI from EU averaged more than 3% of

[12]The annual average was chosen since the annual values are volatile reflecting large privatisations and other temporary effects.

GDP. This is considerable more investment than Slovenia, Latvia, Romania and Turkey managed to attract whose average annual inflow of FDI from EU Member States was below 1.6% of GDP. As comparison, FDI to EU Member States from other EU Member States during these years averaged 3% of GDP. However, FDI in the EU comprises a substantial amount of mergers and acquisitions, which does not necessarily involve investment in new assets. In the Candidate Countries, it is likely that more FDI has been invested in greenfield projects or invested in replacement of old production assets as part of the privatisation and restructuring process.[13] FDI could be particularly important for the Candidate Countries, as this source of investment may not only contribute with capital, but also with technology transfer and management know-how. FDI in the Central and East European Candidate Countries is concentrated in a few sectors. Out of the total FDI stock in these countries more than two thirds was invested in four sectors: "manufacturing", "financial intermediation", "real estate, renting and business activities" and "trade, repair of motor vehicles, etc".[14]

FDI is one important source for investment in the Candidate Countries, but the bulk of the capital for private investment is channelled through other sources. Therefore the total level of business investment is an important additional indicator.

---

[13] It has not yet been possible to obtain reliable data for Candidate Countries on the share of greenfield investments.

[14] Data is taken from the WIIW-WIFO database, which covers the Central and East European Candidate Countries. These FDI data should be used with caution. Even though all these countries follow the established IMF definitions and methodological guidelines, serious differences appears in practice, according to the methodological note in the WIIW-WIFO database.

Graph 16: Business investment, gross fixed capital formation by the private sector as % of GDP in 2001.

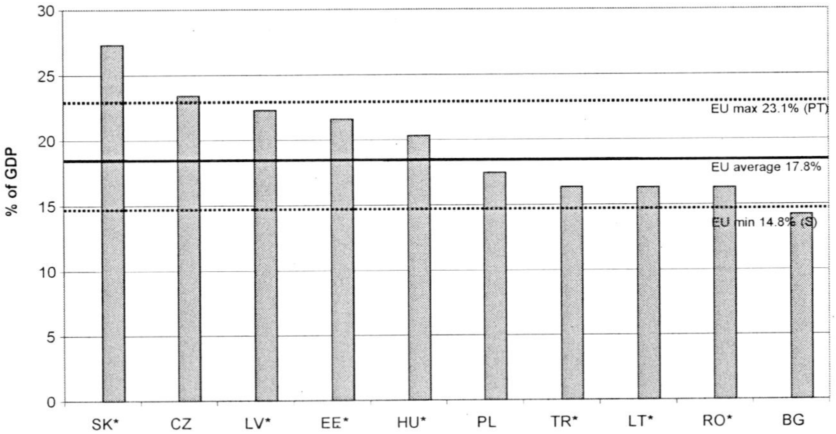

Source: Eurostat

* 1998 data for RO. 1999 data for SK. 2000 data for EE, LT, LV, HU and TR. No data available for SI, CY and MT.

Graph 16 shows business investment in ten Candidate Countries. In five of these Candidate Countries, business investment in 2000 exceeded the EU average of 18% of GDP. However, whereas business investment in most EU Member States has been stable or increasing from 1998 to 2001, the results have been more mixed in the Candidate Countries. In several Candidate Countries business investment has even been falling.

The high trade openness and the high share of export to the EU clearly show that the Candidate Countries already can face competition on the internal market at least in some sectors. Furthermore, the Candidate Countries are generally open for import from EU Member States, which increases competition in the domestic markets. The openness in the Candidate Countries should thus contribute to more efficient markets. However, the high trade openness and the FDI inflows do not automatically facilitate functioning markets across the whole economy. There may still be sectors with a significant impact on the total economy where competition is weak.

5. *BUSINESS ENVIRONMENT*

The starting point for the enterprise sector in the Candidate Countries in the former centrally planned economies of Central and Eastern Europe was not encouraging. Most enterprises were in state ownership and the predominant industry was in most cases heavy manufacturing. Considering this starting point the change in the enterprise structure the last decade has been profound.

Data is still relatively scarce, but available data point at a thriving business sector in most Candidate Countries.[15] SMEs typically account for more than half of total employment[16] and a substantial part of the production in terms of GDP. This development indicates that a relatively favourable climate for entrepreneurship has emerged, which can contribute to higher productivity.

However, at the same time, studies suggest that improvements in the administration and local government are needed to support business in general and SMEs in particular.[17] Anecdotal evidence suggests that barriers to entry and exit remain in some sectors and that administrative burdens are heavy in several Candidate Countries. There may still be a substantial amount of red tape preventing start-ups to thrive and grow. The development of an appropriate administrative capacity, less administrative burden for the business sector and transparent regulatory frameworks have been identified by most of the Candidate Countries in their 2002 PEPs as key measures to promote a dynamic business development.

---

[15] EU Commission "Enlargement papers: progress towards meeting economic criteria for accession: the assessment from the 2001 regular report".

[16] In the EU on average 66% of total employment was in SMEs in 1998, defined as companies with 0 to 249 persons employed. In Italy and Portugal, the member states with the highest share, SMEs contributed with 80% of total employment, whereas the lowest share of employment in SMEs in the EU was found in Ireland, 49%.

[17] EU Commission "European Economy: Evaluation of the 2001 pre-accession economic programmes of Candidate Countries".

The Candidate Countries keep good pace to implement the acquis as part of their preparation for EU membership. In this process they will also have to adopt the EU competition policy framework. Anecdotal evidence suggests that competition policy in the Candidate Countries could improve and that restructuring and further strengthening of competition authorities is necessary. There are no data before accession on implementation of internal market directives or on the share of public procurement published in the Official Journal, because public procurement is not yet published in the Official Journal. When these data become available for the new EU Member States, they will provide some information for an assessment of the opening up of public procurement in these countries.

A major issue in the Candidate Countries is the existence of state subsidies and other obstacles hindering better functioning markets. It is possible that substantial state subsidies exist in some Candidate Countries. This may take the form of soft budget constraints[18] for state owned companies, tax exemptions or other forms as parts of efforts to sustain industrial activities in economically weak regions or within non-competitive sectors. If this is the case, it will be necessary to overhaul state aids in Candidate Countries with the purpose to both reduce total state aid and redirect state aid towards horizontal measures.

[18] The state could have different economic expectations than a private owner seeking to maximise the company market value.

Graph 17: State aid in 2000 as % of GDP, excluding aid to agriculture and fishery.

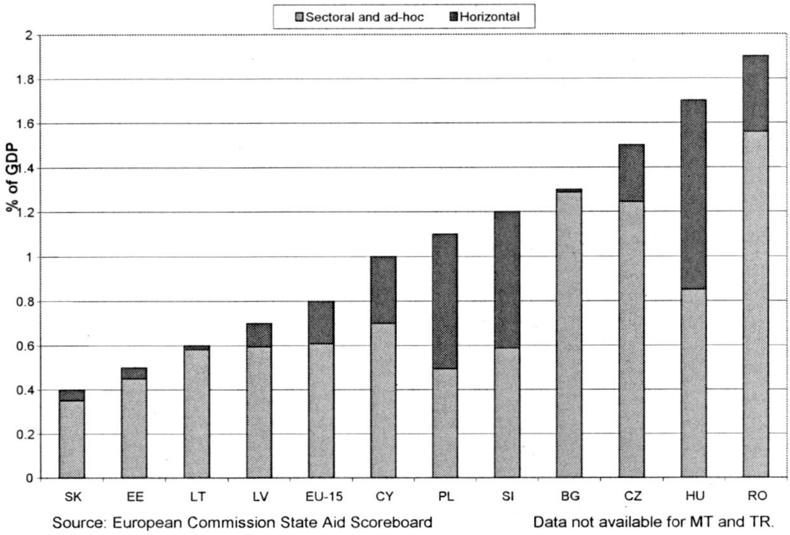

Total state aid in Candidate Countries, excluding aid to agriculture and fishery, ranged from 0.4% of GDP to 1.9% of GDP in 2000 according to the Commission's State Aid Scoreboard (see graph 17). The EU average was 0.8% of GDP. Four Candidate Countries recorded lower total state aid than the EU average, whereas state aid in Hungary and Romania was more than double the EU average. However, in per capita terms, the total state aid in all Candidate Countries, except Hungary, was below the EU average in 2000. In several Candidate Countries, a large share of the aid was sectoral or ad-hoc, e.g. steel and coal, which can have a particularly distorting effect on the economy. This is especially pronounced in Bulgaria, Lithuania and Estonia were horizontal aid correspond to 10% of total aid or less. The data on state aid for Candidate Countries should be used with caution. Due to several factors, such as recent adoption of state aid legislation, classification of state aid and measurement problems, the information on state aid in Candidate Countries could be less complete than for EU Member States. Significant changes in state aid policies after the year 2000 and large annual fluctuations also implies that results for individual Candidate Countries may change significantly over time.

6. *FOSTER A KNOWLEDGE-BASED ECONOMY*

Progress towards the knowledge-based economy is another key element to increase productivity, growth and employment creation. In general, more wealthy countries have a higher degree of maturity in information and communication technologies (ICT) and a larger share of high technology in their economies. Consequently, the Candidate Countries may have special challenges to encounter in this area compared with EU Member States.

Several indicators show that Candidate Countries lag behind EU Member States in the transition to the knowledge-based economy. This could be a hampering factor for the economic catch-up in the Candidate Countries.

Graph 18: Business and other R&D expenditure as % of GDP in 2000.

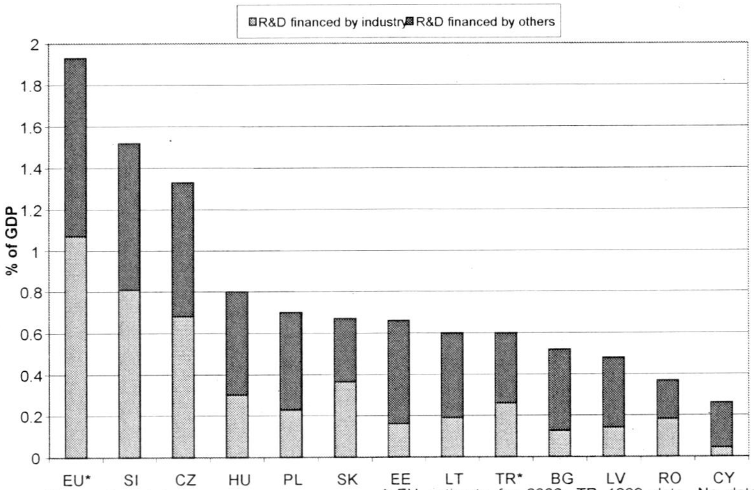

Source: Eurostat

* EU estimate for 2000. TR 1999 data. No data available for MT.

Candidate Countries have a poor record for both total and business R&D as share of GDP, which is illustrated in graph 18. In 2000, the average total R&D expenditure for the Candidate Countries was well below 1% of GDP, compared with almost 2% of GDP for the EU average. Slovenia, 1.5% of GDP, and the Czech Republic, 1.3% of GDP, had the highest R&D expenditures among the Candidate Countries in 2000. Bulgaria, Latvia, Romania and Cyprus invested 0.5% of GDP or less in R&D. This large difference in R&D investment among Candidate Countries is mirrored also among EU Member States, where total R&D expenditure in 1999 ranged from 0.7% in Greece to 3.8% in Sweden. There is not much sign of increasing R&D investment in the Candidate Countries. For half of the Candidate Countries, total R&D investment as % of GDP was lower in 2000 than in 1995. The decrease was most pronounced in the countries with the least R&D.

Also business R&D investments were low in the Candidate Countries in 2000, corresponding to less than 0.4% of GDP, which is not even a third of the EU average. In Bulgaria, Romania, Cyprus, Estonia, Latvia and Lithuania, business R&D investment was less than 0.2% of GDP. Only in Slovenia and the Czech Republic did business R&D investment reach 0.6% of GDP. Moreover, business expenditure on R&D, as a percentage of GDP, increased in only half of the Candidate Countries between 1995 and 2000. There is therefore no sign that the large gap in business R&D expenditures between Candidate Countries and the EU is about to close.

ICT expenditure is another indicator on the emergence of a knowledge-based economy. Investment in ICT could increase the productivity in the economy and promote a structural shift to more value adding industries. The indicator on ICT investment gives a rather mixed picture for the Candidate Countries, as illustrated in graph 19.

Graph 19: ICT expenditure as % of GDP in 2000.

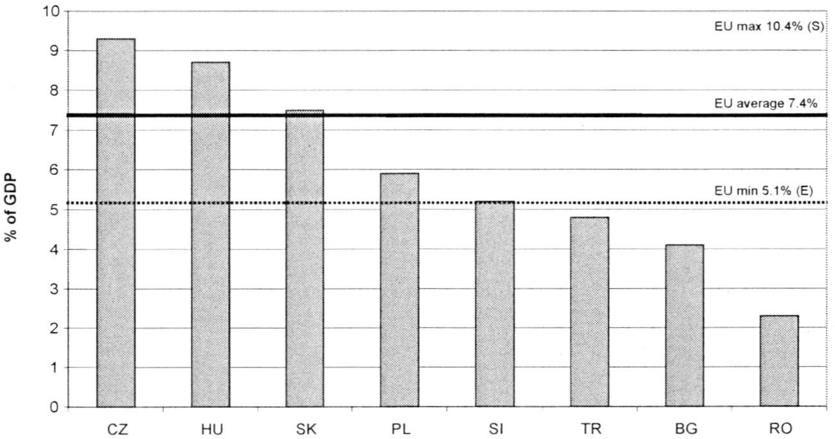

Source: World Bank Development Indicators 2002

No data available for EE, LV, LT, CY and MT.

Three Candidate Countries, the Czech Republic, Hungary and the Slovak Republic, invested more in ICT in 2000 than the EU average.[19] Three other Candidate Countries, Turkey, Bulgaria and Romania, invested less than the least investment prone EU Member State. This points to a large dispersion between Candidate Countries with regard to ICT investment. Several Candidate Countries run the risk of falling further behind. Furthermore, no Candidate Country, except the Czech Republic could match the growth of ICT investments in the EU during the last six years, from 1995 to 2000. This trend points to a further widening of the gap in ICT maturity between the EU Member States and the Candidate Countries.

The internet penetration ratio is one indicator of IT maturity. The consumer internet household penetration for those Candidate Countries where data was available in 2001 ranged from 2% in Latvia to 24% in

[19]Due to limited data availability, it has not been possible to check whether the large ICT-investments are caused by mobile telephone investments. Investments in IT may be considered more productive than some communication investment.

Slovenia.[20] In the EU, the average internet penetration rate in 2001 was 36%, ranging from 12% in Greece to 64% in Sweden.[21] The Candidate Countries are generally lagging the EU Member States also concerning mobile telephone penetration. The gap for mobile phones in 2001 was 38 percentage points (37% for Candidate Countries and 75% for EU Member States).[22]

7. *REFORM PRIORITIES IN THE CANDIDATE COUNTRIES*

Most challenges in product markets seem to be shared by both Candidate Countries and EU Member States. These challenges include reform of network industries, strengthening of competition rules and competition authorities, efforts to make the public sector more efficient and embracing the knowledge-based economy. However, Candidate Countries are facing more severe problems in their reform efforts, especially regarding the transition to the knowledge-based economy.

It is likely that the enlargement in 2004 will further increase the pressure for further structural reforms in the product markets in the Candidate Countries. The Candidate Countries seem to be ready to meet this challenge. In their 2002 Pre-Accession Economic Programmes (PEPs), they have all set priorities for the reforms to be undertaken to further strengthen their product markets and to facilitate the transition to the knowledge-based economy.

The Commission evaluation of the 2002 PEPs from November 2002 concludes that the main emphasis of the planned reforms in Candidate Countries in product markets seems sensible. After attaining macroeconomic stability the focus has rightly shifted to structural reforms to sup-

[20] Data on internet penetration in Candidate Countries is scarce. There is very little data from Eurostat on internet penetration in enterprises and only for seven Candidate Countries regarding household internet penetration (CY, CZ, EE, LT, LV, PL, SI).

[21] Eurostat structural indicators.

[22] IDC "European Telecommunications Services - Monitoring European Telecoms Operators: Final Report", 2002

port sustainable and high economic growth. Strengthening competition, reducing barriers to market entry and promoting productivity enhancing R&D are among the necessary structural reforms on the supply side mentioned in the evaluation.

In the Commission evaluation, it is noted that the main measures to strengthen product markets in the Candidate Countries are largely the same in the 2001 and 2002 PEPs. This is logical reflecting the long-term nature of structural reforms. Although the PEPs are reflecting specific circumstances in each Candidate Country, there are several broad categories of measures figuring in most PEPs, which is illustrated in table 1. A majority of Candidate Countries emphasised both in their 2001 and 2002 PEPs that privatisation and restructuring of industries is a high priority. Several Candidate Countries also stressed the importance of deregulation, support for SMEs and the general business environment, improvement of regulations and development of competition policies. If the Candidate Countries are able to carry out the reforms envisaged in their PEPs, they are likely to make good progress to catch up with the EU Member States and close the gap in income levels.

Table 1: Product market measures identified by Candidate Countries in their 2002 Pre-Accession Economic Programmes.

Candidate Country	Main product market measures in the 2002 PEPs
Bulgaria	- Privatise infrastructure industries - Liberalisation of prices - Deregulation of monopolies
Cyprus	- Liberalise utilities - Rationalise public intervention in the economy
Czech Republic	- Restructuring of industries - SME - Export promotion
Estonia	- Further develop entrepreneurship - Competition and market supervision
Hungary	- Increase competitiveness of SMEs - Regulation of public utilities - Privatisation - Laying foundation for knowledge-based economy
Latvia	- Complete privatisation - Deregulation of utilities - Develop entrepreneurship - Export promotion
Lithuania	- Restructuring and privatisation - SME
Malta	- Restructuring and privatisation - Liberalise utilities - Abolish price controls
Poland	- Conclude privatisation - Restructure several industries - Develop entrepreneurship - Develop infrastructure
Romania	- Accelerate privatisation and restructuring - Strengthen SMEs - Improve competition policy
Slovak Republic	- Restructuring and privatisation - Improve entrepreneurial environment - Export promotion
Slovenia	- Privatisation and restructuring - Reduce administrative barriers - Liberalise telecom and utilities
Turkey	- Privatisation - Establish regulatory authorities

8. SUMMARY

Summarising, it seems that most challenges in product markets are shared by both Candidate Countries and EU Member States. However, Candidate Countries are facing more severe problems in their reform efforts, especially regarding the transition to the knowledge-based economy. It is also likely that some product market issues which are already tackled in existing EU processes, such as privatisation, administered prices and the sectoral composition of the economy, need to be discussed more intensively than is currently the case for the existing Member States.

Furthermore, it is likely that accession will increase the pressure for further structural reforms in the product markets for the ten Candidate Countries in the first accession wave. The Candidate Countries concerned seem to be ready to meet these challenges. In their 2002 Pre-Accession Economic Programmes (PEPs) they have all set priorities for the reforms to be undertaken to further strengthen their product markets and to facilitate the transition to the knowledge-based economy. These structural reforms should contribute to high economic growth and increasing living standards in Candidate Countries.

9. REFERENCES

Centre for European Policy Studies (2003), "The Euro at 25".

Federal Ministry for Economic Affairs and Labour (2000), "Eastern enlargement: the sooner, the better?", European Academy of Excellence, Vienna, Austria.

European Bank for Reconstruction and Development (2000), "Ten years after: what is special about transition countries".

European Bank for Reconstruction an Development (2000), "Defying the odds: initial conditions, reforms and growth in the first decade of transition".

European Commission (2002), "State Aid Scoreboard - Special edition on the Candidate Countries".

European Commission (2002), "Statistical Yearbook on Candidate and south-east European Countries".

European Commission (2002), "Progress towards meeting economic criteria for accession: the assessment from the 2002 regular report".

European Commission (2002), "Structural reforms in Candidate Countries - trends, challenges and the Lisbon strategy".

European Commission (2002), "Balassa-Samuelson effects outside the Euro area".

European Commission (2002), "Towards the enlarged union - Strategy paper and report of the European Commission on the progress towards accession by each of the Candidate Countries".

European Commission (2002), "Information note on the main findings of a report on macroeconomic and financial sector stability developments in Candidate Countries".

European Commission (2002), "Report on macroeconomic and financial sector stability developments in Candidate Countries".

European Commission (2001), "Enlargement of the European Union: costs and benefits for present Member States - case studies for Germany, Austria, Italy and Denmark".

European Commission (2001), "Real convergence in Candidate Countries - past performance and scenarios in the Pre-Accession Economic Programmes".

European Commission (2001), "Evaluation of the 2001 Pre-Accession Economic Programmes of Candidate Countries".

European Commission (2001), "Progress towards meeting economic criteria for accession: the assessment from the 2001 regular report".

European Commission (2001), "Report on Candidate Countries' measures to promote entrepreneurship and competitiveness".

European Commission (2001), "The economic impact of enlargement".

European Economy Group (2001), "The trade impact of the integration of the Central and Eastern European Countries on the European Union".

Eurostat New Cronos database http://www.cc.cec/newcronos/
IDC (2002), "European Telecommunications Services - Monitoring European Telecoms Operators: Final Report".
Oesterreichische Nationalbank (2002), "Price dynamics in Central and Eastern European EU accession countries", Working Paper 61.
Oesterreichische Nationalbank (2001), "Focus on transition".
World Bank (2002), "World Development Indicators 2002", CD-ROM.
World Bank (2002), "Transition the first ten years".
World Bank (2001), "European integration and income convergence".
World Bank (2001), "World Development Indicators 2001", CD-ROM.

AGRICULTURE IN CANDIDATE COUNTRIES

CHRISTOPHE BLANC

In spite of the downward trend, the agriculture share in GDP and employment in most Central Eastern European Countries remains considerably higher than in the present European Union. In many of those countries, agriculture needs restructuring. Very small subsistence farms play an important role. Labour productivity is very low in such farms which are partly excluded from agri-food market channels. Eastern European agriculture also appears ill prepared to face Western European competition after enlargement. Agri-food production in many of those countries is for instance still far from meeting quality requirements of EU markets.

Despite recent stabilisation, in most countries agricultural production remains lower than pre-transition levels.

Graph 1: Gross agricultural production (1989=100)

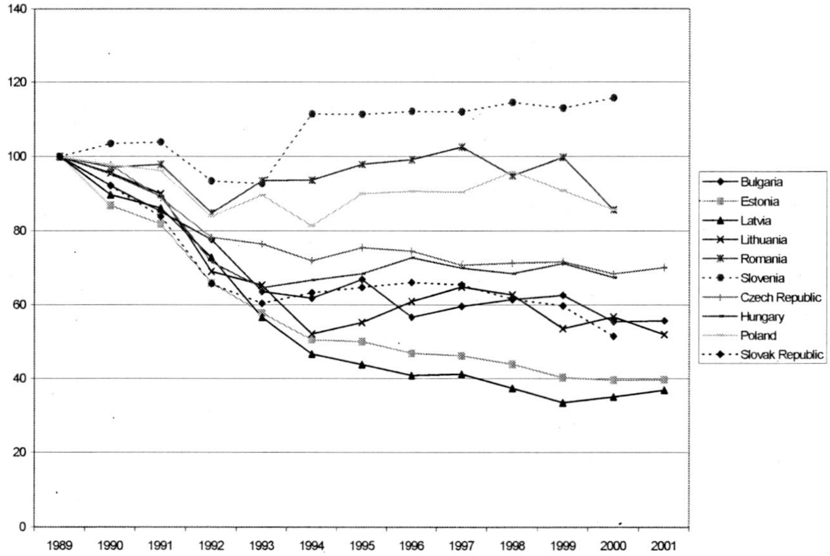

Source: OECD

Despite stabilisation since the mid 90s, agricultural output remains in most countries considerably lower than pre-accession levels (see Graph 1). Resumption of macro economic growth since the mid 90s did not transmit to the agricultural sector. Only in Slovenia is production now higher than its pre-transition levels. In some Baltic states and Bulgaria, agricultural production stabilised at less than 40% of its pre-transition level. It has been stagnating for several years at less than 60% of the 1989 level in Bulgaria, Lithuania and Slovakia.

Production decrease was lower for crops. Crop production growth is resuming in some countries but farmers lack financial resources to buy necessary inputs (fertilisers, pesticides). Production development potential is nevertheless rather good in some CEECs[1] such as Hungary. Livestock production growth is hindered by lack of capital and difficulties to respect European sanitary and quality standards, but low labour costs could favour investments and future production growth. This would not entail higher exports since growing meat consumption with increasing living standards would easily absorb domestic production growth.

Agricultural trade balance of Eastern European deteriorated during transition. This resulted from low competitiveness of Eastern European agriculture.

Resumption of macro-economic growth in CEECs did not result in growing demand for national food products. Thus imports grew to satisfy growing demand. As a consequence, agro-food trade balance deteriorated in most countries. Only Hungary and Bulgaria still enjoy agro-food surplus. The Czech Republic and the Baltic states that recorded agro-food surpluses before transition, now record deficits.

In fact, CEECs imports of processed products grew rapidly whereas their exports consisted mainly in raw products. This reflected a deterioration of CEECs agricultural competitiveness. Development of agro-

[1] Central Eastern European Countries

food exports to the European Union was hindered by the low quality of agro-food production and its difficulties to meet European quality standards. That lack of competitiveness is reflected by the fact that those countries encountered difficulties filling their reduced duty export quotas to the EU.

Thus lower prices in Eastern Europe did not result from higher competitiveness but from lower quality standards. With the gradual introduction of European regulations, production costs are rising. Prices of most agricultural commodities are thus gradually rising and approaching European levels, even exceeding them for some commodities. Rising real exchange rates (due to the Balassa Samuelson effect) will probably accentuate that phenomenon.

In most Candidate Countries farm support remains lower than in the European Union.

Eastern European agriculture enjoys lower support than European agriculture. Economic transition at the beginning of the 90s brought about a lowering of support for CEECs agriculture. Disruption of storage and transportation systems made prices fall to levels lower than world prices in some places. Prices gradually rose in the late 90s with production costs increases and direct payments were gradually introduced in some countries. Thus producer support recovered, but remains in most countries lower than its pre-transition level.

With the exception of Slovenia PSE[2] are a lot lower than in the present European Union (see Table 1). Contrary to the European Union, price support represents in those countries the main source of transfers to farmers. The recent introduction and increase of area and headage assis-

[2] Producer support estimate (PSE) is derived from the following calculation: The difference between production valued at domestic prices and production valued at world prices is added to direct payments to farmers. Subsidised inputs are also taken into account. PSE is thus an indicator of the value of transfers from consumers and taxpayers to producers. The nominal value of PSE can, for purpose of international comparison, be compared with the value of agricultural output.

tance did not alter that fact with the exception of Slovenia. In spite of increased lobbying of farmers, the lack of financial resources, prevented those countries from developing policies involving levels of support similar to the European Union. The gradual introduction of direct payments in new Member States will entail an increase of PSE but PSE will remain lower than in the European Union, direct payments being only gradually phased in .

Subsistence farming developed during transition and will probably slow Eastern European agriculture modernisation.

In most CEECs collective farms were broken up and land was either returned to former owners or distributed to employees. But those farms still play an important role in the Czech Republic, Slovakia and Bulgaria (see Table 2). In these countries, many collective farms were not totally dismantled. Most became private co-operatives or companies but their title deeds were dispersed among numerous owners. Those owners therefore do not directly manage these farms. Employees often collectively manage them. But employees are more concerned with employment protection than with economic performance. They do not consider profitability and productivity improvement as a priority. Therefore these farms cannot easily be considered as the backbone of future agricultural development.

This ratio (PSE as a percentage of agricultural output value) is presented in Table 1.

Table 1: Producer support estimate in Candidate Countries (as a percentage of output value)

	1991	1992	1993	1994	1995	1996	1997	1998	1999	2000	2001
Bulgaria	-40	-45	-4	-27	-25	-55	-10	2	-2	1	3
Estonia	59	-89	-32	-10	0	7	6	20	6	7	13
Latvia	70	-143	-40	7	5	3	5	20	22	15	16
Lithuania	-262	-124	-37	-15	0	1	4	16	16	6	11
Romania	15	8	16	19	10	12	3	30	20	19	24
Slovenia	N.C.	32	25	29	35	27	32	42	49	39	40
Czech Rep.	53	32	29	21	20	19	6	23	24	16	17
Hungary	12	18	20	22	13	10	6	19	23	20	12
Poland	-1	1	11	17	11	13	12	22	19	7	10
Slovakia	41	30	40	29	14	2	11	31	25	23	11
EU-15	44	38	37	35	35	32	32	36	39	34	35

Source: OECD

Table 2: Land distribution among different farm categories (percentage of agricultural land and average area)

	Family farms		Co-operatives		State Farms		Companies	
	% land	Av. area (ha)	% land	Av. area (ha)	% land	Av. area (ha)	% land	Av. area (ha)
Poland	83	6.9	3	222	2	1832	12	415
Hungary	60	3	24	833			16	204
Czech Republic	38	37	29	1493			33	1004
Slovenia	96	4,8			4	371		
Estonia	64	10					36	564
Slovakia	5	7,7	60	1509	15	3056	20	1191
Romania	69	2,4	16	301	15			
Bulgaria	52	1,5	42	637	6	735		
Lithuania	67	4,2			33	372		
Latvia	95	12			1	340	4	309

Source: Pouliquen (2001).

Land privatisation also resulted in the development of very small subsistence family farms. Rising unemployment prevented people from leaving the farming sector in spite of low earnings and high modernisation potential. As a consequence, agriculture became a social safety net for a population which had to deal with a massive rise of unemployment. Thus, agricultural employment decreased very slowly and even grew in some countries such as Romania.

That latter phenomenon entailed the development of very small subsistence farms. Family farms are thus in Eastern Europe considerably smaller than in the European Union. Farms bigger than 50ha account for less than 30% of agricultural land in CEECs compared with more than 60% in the European Union. In those subsistence farms marketable production account for only a small share of total production, the bulk of which is consumed by farm households, thus household income does not derive from the sale of agricultural products but from welfare payments (pensions...). Those farms enjoy low labour costs but lack of financial resources prevents them from investing and increasing production. They are not integrated in product collection network and cannot meet European quality and sanitary requirements. Bigger family farms would probably more easily overcome Western European competition but are developing very slowly. Lack of financial resources and poorly functioning land markets prevent them from expanding.

The emergence of a competitive agricultural sector after enlargement will be slow.

Subsistence farming thus plays an important role in most of those countries with the notable exception of Slovakia, the Czech Republic. Resistance of subsistence farmers will slow the necessary restructuration of the sector. As was previously outlined, modernisation of farms and entailing decrease of agricultural employment is hindered by lack of employment opportunities in other sectors. That problem seems less acute in Hungary and Slovenia and the Czech Republic that enjoy smaller unemployment rates. But even in those countries, adequacy between present farmers qualifications and new urban jobs qualifications requirements could be problematic.

Agriculture modernisation is also hindered by inadequate access to credit and lack of capital. Direct payments will increase farmers' financial resources. It could enable them to modernise their farms. More financial resources for input purchases would be available. Productions of cereals and oilseeds could thus increase, especially in countries with high potential such as Hungary. Increase in animal productions such as meat and dairy products, for which quality and sanitary requirements are harder to meet, would be slower. Direct payments will also entail an increase in subsistence farmers' income. This could reinforce subsistence farming and slow agriculture modernisation.

ANNEX

Table 3: Share of agriculture in GDP and employment in Eastern European Countries (2000)

	Share in employed civilian working population (%)	Share of agriculture in GDP (%)
European Union (15)	4.3	1.7
Central Eastern European Countries	21.5	5.1
Bulgaria	27.0	15.8
Czech Republic	5.3	3.4
Estonia	7.0	5.7
Hungary	7.2	3.9
Latvia	14.4	3.9
Lithuania	18.4	7.9
Poland	18.7	3.3
Romania	45.2	11.4
Slovakia	7.5	2.7
Slovenia	9.6	4.3

Source: European Commission

REFERENCES

Pouliquen (2001), "Competitiveness and farm incomes in the CEECs agri-food sectors", Study for the European Commission.

OECD (2002), "Agricultural Policies in Transition Economies", Trends in Policies and Support.

EBRD (2002), "Transition report".

FINANCIAL SECTORS IN EU ACCEDING COUNTRIES - STYLIZED FACTS AND CHALLENGES

REINER MARTIN, GIACOMO CAVIGLIA AND CHRISTIAN FEHLKER [1]

1. INTRODUCTION[2]

Acceding countries (ACs) have made major achievements over the past decade in establishing overall sound and stable banking sectors and in developing many other segments of their financial markets.[3] Progress has been particularly significant in restructuring and consolidating the banking sector of the transition economies. This has been mainly accomplished through the privatisation of state-owned banks and the extensive opening-up to foreign ownership. Despite these considerable achievements, some issues remain as to whether, at the current stage, all features of their financial sectors already fully meet the challenges entailed in the EU integration process as well as in the countries' process of real and nominal convergence.

[1] European Central Bank. Views expressed in this paper are exclusively those of the authors and do not necessarily correspond to those of the ECB. Valuable research assistance by Stefan Wredenborg is gratefully acknowledged.

[2] For a more detailed overview see ECB (2002), "Financial Sectors in EU Accession Countries", Frankfurt.

[3] The acceding countries have departed from highly diverse economic environments, as not all countries (in particular Cyprus and Malta) had to go through a process of transforming their economies.

This contribution reviews briefly the link between financial and economic development and outlines some key features of ACs' financial sectors[4]. The description of the key features of ACs' financial sectors focuses in particular on the efficiency of the system and its level of integration with the EU. This is followed by a short overview of the regulatory systems for the financial sectors in ACs. The final section looks at challenges for the adjustment of ACs' financial sectors and their infrastructure due to EU integration.

Financial Development and Real Convergence

Financial development has increasingly been found by economic research to be linked to the economic development and growth performance of an economy.[5] In particular, financial sector development in ACs may stimulate the real convergence process via several channels. One channel refers to the mobilisation of savings, which is vital as these countries have high investment needs to modernise the capital stock necessary for catching-up growth. By providing safe depository facilities, by offering key trade financing services and by diversifying financial risks and pooling liquidity, national savings and investments are likely to be fostered. As a side effect, more efficient domestic financial intermediation may alleviate recourse on foreign savings, which in most transition acceding countries led to current account deficits that at times have threatened external sustainability.

Strengthening the monitoring function of financial markets in ACs is seen as crucial in enforcing corporate performance. Sound corporate governance structures require the existence and, equally important, the implementation of property and creditor rights, contract law and bankruptcy regulation as well as the use of proper accounting standards. Ex-

---

[4] This contribution focuses mostly on the eight transition economies among the EU acceding countries. Cyprus and Malta present a financial sector whose structures are more closely in line with that of the EU.

[5] However, the importance of financial markets for growth is not uncontested and counter-examples of solidly growing economies without a highly developed financial system exist.

ercising effective corporate control on a sound legal basis fosters market-driven restructuring processes, leading to enhanced productivity of existing input factors and the accumulation of new factors of production. Almost all ACs appear to display some potential to foster financial market development by strengthening the legal framework and especially by enforcing the existing rules and standards.[6]

Turning the attention to some empirical findings, a positive relationship between financial and economic development can indeed be observed for ACs (Graph 1). Analysing along the dimensions of GDP per capita and domestic credit in relation to GDP, all euro area member countries clearly lie ahead of the acceding countries in transition with regard to both financial and economic development. Therefore, further convergence may be expected to go hand in hand with financial development. However, the time series for ACs under consideration might be too short to assess whether the relationship is a strong one and whether causality flows indeed from financial development to growth or vice versa.

[6] See for example European Commission (2002), "Regular Report on AC's Progress towards Accession", Brussels. These reports are published separately for each country on an annual basis. See also European Bank for Reconstruction and Development (2002), "Transition Report", London. This publication is also annually published.

Graph 1: Financial vs. economic development
Domestic credit as % of GDP (2001)

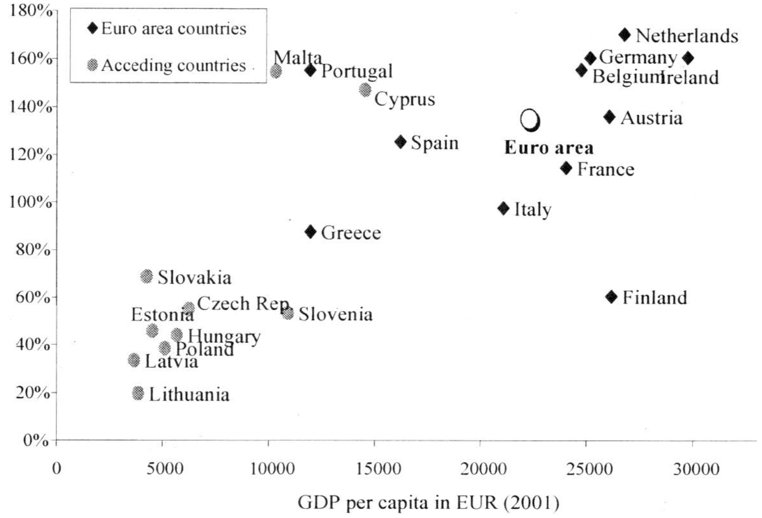

Source: European Commission and IFS.

The dispersion of financial sector size increases for higher income countries, reflecting that different models of financial sector size are compatible with a given stage of development. Still, even the - relatively small - Austrian financial sector is about three times the size of the average financial sector in acceding countries, indicating the enormous potential for financial sector growth in these countries.

Key Features of the Financial Sector in acceding countries

The financial sector of the Central and Eastern European ACs has undergone major changes since the beginning of transition. The former so-called monobanks have been broken up into a two-tier structure of central banking and commercial banking and after several rounds of banking crises and an initial period of transition-related recession a broadly stable and functioning banking sector has been established in all countries. At present, the financial sector is characterised by the strong dominance of an overall well-capitalised banking sector over capital markets, a still relatively low level of financial intermediation and a relatively low degree of liquidity in many market segments. Furthermore, a high degree of foreign involvement can be observed in almost all financial market segments of ACs.

2. *KEY FEATURES OF AC FINANCIAL SECTORS AFFECTING EFFICIENCY*

The financial systems in ACs are largely bank-based, and the dominance of the banking sector over capital markets is even more pronounced than in some euro area countries that are known for their bank-based systems (Graph 2). The average stock market capitalisation of ACs amounts to around 18% of GDP at the end of 2001 (euro area: around 72% of GDP), while domestic credit represents to 47% of GDP (euro area: close to 135% of GDP). Of all acceding countries, only the non-transition countries Cyprus and Malta have a domestic financial intermediation mechanism that broadly mirrors the financial intermediation mechanism of euro area Member States.

Although recent studies have revived the discussion about the respective merits of bank-based versus market-based financial systems, there is no clear evidence as to the general appropriateness of any of the two systems. The importance seems to lie more on the establishment of a proper legal and regulatory framework for financial services - i.e. establishing international accounting standards, reinforcing minority shareholder rights and property rights etc. - than on considerations whether markets or banks are better suited to support economic development.[7]

[7] Levine R., "Financial Development and Economic Growth: Views and Agenda," Journal of Economic Literature 35 (1997), pp. 688 - 726.

Graph 2: Banking sector vs. stockmarket

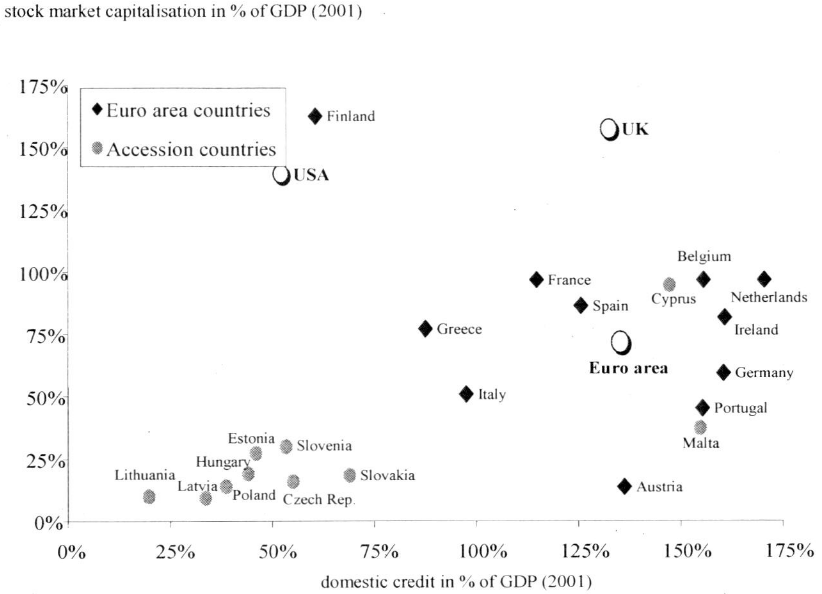

Source: ECB, IMF's International Financial Statistics, International Federation of Stock Exchanges and Accession Countries'

National Central Banks and Stock Exchanges (Luxembourg is not displayed but included in the euro area average).

Overall, the banking sector in ACs seems to be well-capitalised, with the risk-weighted capital ratio exceeding the Basle recommendation of 8% in all countries, often by a large margin. The share of non-performing loans has been substantially reduced in countries that have faced severe banking crises a few years ago, while it actually somewhat increased in other ACs as a consequence of high real interest rates and/or decelerating growth.

The level of financial intermediation still remains relatively low. This is mainly reflected in the ratio of bank assets to GDP in transition countries, which is only about one-quarter of that in the euro area, and in the ratio of domestic credit to GDP, which is only about one-third of that in the euro area. For stock and bond markets, the level of market capitalisation broadly corresponds to one-fifth and one-fourth, respectively, of that in the euro area. However, access to bank financing and capital markets abroad is somewhat alleviating domestic financing constraints.

Access of individuals to capital represents one of the fastest growing areas of the banking system's operations in most ACs but starting from a low level. The strong current rise in lending to households (Table 1), which is expected to continue over the coming years, largely reflects a catching-up phenomenon, as the share of household lending in overall bank credit as well as the households' level of indebtedness (i.e. the ratio of household financial liabilities to disposable income) is still very low. In Hungary, for example, the level of indebtedness of individuals - in 2002 at around 7% of disposable income falls far short of the above 50% rate seen in the EU member countries. The availability of financial services varies across the regions within ACs with rural areas clearly lagging behind. Innovative distribution channels such as internet banking have also become available although they are still less developed than in euro area countries.

Table 1: Commercial bank lendig to households* (% of total at year end)

	1998	**2000**	**2001**
Czech Republic	6	9	12
Estonia		20	22
Hungary		8	12
Latvia	10	15	15
Lithuania	11	10	11
Poland		24	27
Slovakia	8	14	21
Slovenia	22	30	27
Bulgaria	10	7	8
Romania		4	4
Euro area*	42	43	42

Source: National data, IFS, ECB staff calculations.
Note: * As % of total loans of euro-area residents excluding MFI.

Loans with a maturity of over one-year are predominant in this market segment, accounting for nearly 80-90% of total lending to households, while consumer credit represents the largest share of household lending by credit institution.

The availability of risk capital and low cost debt finance for small and medium-sized firms (SMEs), especially at the earliest stages of their life cycle, is important for funding innovation and development. Although some progress has been made here, it remains inadequate and risk capital is - by and large - too expensive. The Risk Capital Action Plan that was adopted in 1998 deserves particular attention in this context as it aims to eliminate remaining barriers, which impair the full development of risk capital markets in Europe. A recent communication on its implementation explicitly refers to the significant contraction of the venture capital industry in the ACs being still new and relatively underdeveloped.[8]

Liquidity levels in some segments of acceding countries' financial markets - including foreign exchange, money, bond and stock markets - are relatively low. Stock market turnover - as a rough proxy for liquidity - is particularly low in absolute terms, given the small size of the markets. For example, the annual turnover of the three largest stock exchanges in ACs (Poland, Hungary and the Czech Republic) is each equivalent to 2-5 days of turnover at the stock exchange in Frankfurt. However, it should be noted that also in the euro area a large variation in market size and liquidity exists.[9]

---

[8] European Commission (2002), "Communication from the Commission to the Council and the European Parliament on Implementation of the Risk Capital Action Plan", COM(2002) 563 FINAL.

[9] In 2000, the Warsaw stock market has reached a capitalisation and turnover level roughly comparable to that of Vienna, the smallest stock market in the EU with a capitalisation of only 13% of GDP (euro area: 84% of GDP).

3. INTEGRATION OF AC FINANCIAL SECTORS

Ownership in AC banks has been largely converted from public to private and from domestic to foreign. This can be seen as a result of transition, numerous banking crises and extensive opening of the domestic system to foreign direct investment. Except in a few countries, the privatisation process can be regarded as largely completed, due to major efforts and funds by public authorities to restructure and recapitalise the banking system. Notable exceptions to private ownership in banks are Poland, where the government controls the largest bank and Slovenia, where government controls the second largest bank and holds a significant share in the largest bank. Moreover, ACs have in individual cases retained interests in the privatised banks by guaranteeing for future losses.

Virtually all large banks in ACs are majority owned by EU banks. EU banks both act as strategic investors and as portfolio investors, thus assuming no managerial role. For almost all large AC banks an EU bank with controlling interest is identifiable and US firms hold few significant stakes mainly in Czech and Polish banks. Rating agencies frequently refer to these ownership structures when assigning a rating grade to AC banks and express the expectation that the owner will provide additional support in case of need.

Geographic proximity apparently plays a role in the investment decisions of EU banks in the ACs. Furthermore, investment is concentrated with a few and large EU banks. For Sweden and Finland, the Baltic states are the most important investment targets while Greece is linked to Cyprus. Poland, Hungary and the Czech Republic have rather diversified links to banks from Belgium, the Netherlands, France, Germany, Italy and Austria.

In addition to direct ownership, EU banks also have significant cross-border exposure to ACs. While Germany shows by far the largest exposure in absolute terms, Belgium ranks second and is followed by France and the Netherlands. The main recipient countries are Poland, the Czech Republic and Hungary. Foreign participants coin much of the activity on financial markets, including foreign exchange, stock and bond markets. Furthermore, a large share of financing of domestic enterprises ultimately takes place via banks abroad and foreign capital markets.

The structure of bank's assets and income in the ACs approaches EU figures but remains diverse. This divergence could give rise to individual paths of integration in the future. As a common feature, most AC banks appear to be adequately capitalised and approach cost/income ratios that are also found with EU banks. Interest income remains the dominant source of revenue while profitability of banks is quite dispersed across banks with no clear picture at country level emerging. Some EU banks have benefited in the recent past from their investment in ACs, which bolstered their profitability. The structure of banks' activities differs across banks and countries if measured by the relative importance of loans versus more liquid assets and the size of off-balance sheet items, the latter reaching a multiple of asset values in the most extreme cases.

Regulatory systems for the financial sectors in ACs

Economic policy has to establish a supervisory framework, which ensures that financial intermediaries operate in a safe and sound manner. Both, a sound legal basis and prudent implementation are crucial in maintaining public confidence in the stability of financial sectors. Moreover, maintaining the level playing field across institutions in an enlarged EU will also be crucial for current EU members with a view to overall financial stability in the EU and in order to avoid a supervisory "race to the bottom" by lowering supervisory standards.

The achieved progress in establishing a sound legal fundament in ACs is overall rather advanced but progress remains uneven across countries and across different sectoral frameworks. The most significant progress was achieved in those countries that started relatively early and in the sector that is most relevant for financial intermediation, namely banking supervision. From a historical perspective, laws on banking have generally been established at an early stage of the transition process but underwent frequent reforms that extended the scope and sophistication of requirements. Laws addressing the insurance and securities sectors also frequently date back to that stage but developments in the regulatory framework for these sectors appear to be more gradual.

All ACs have aligned their regulatory frameworks with EU legislation to a sufficient extent that enables them to join the EU. The formal context, in which financial regulation is incorporated into the accession process, is the Copenhagen Criteria. More, specifically, the acquis communautaire relates to financial sector regulation in its Chapter 3 "Freedom to provide services", which in turn is closely linked with Chapter 4 "Free movement of capital". A number of transitional arrangements and exemptions were concluded, namely as regards deposit insurance schemes. These may become relevant from the point of view of consumer protection.

Further challenges remain for the ACs particularly after having joined the EU. These challenges also stem from the fact that a substantial part of the relevant legislation is currently under review and new legislative procedures, namely the Lamfalussy Procedure, are being introduced. The transposition and implementation of the substantial reform process within the EU that has started in 1999 under the Financial Services Action Plan (FSAP) presents an additional challenge for ACs. Whereas many ACs have already addressed a few issues that are also dealt with under the FSAP such as supervising capital based pension funds, substantial challenges remain.

The institutional structure in financial sector supervision and the allocation of resources to supervisory authorities differs significantly across

ACs. As regards the allocation of responsibilities, most ACs have separated supervisory competencies in line with sectoral borders while others have recently established a single supervisory authority. Even in these latter cases the central bank remains involved in supervision in various forms while in case of a sectoral separation, banking supervision is mostly allocated with the central bank. As regards the availability of resources, competent authorities in ACs have significantly increased the number of staff mainly in banking supervision. Also, EU Member States and ACs have already established various bilateral memoranda of understanding mostly on supervisory co-operation and information sharing.

Challenges of EU Integration

Looking ahead, EU accession represents an important structural change for both the banking and the non-banking sector. As for market developments, integration is seen as accelerating concentration, raising pressure for efficiency, promoting the extension of service availability in segments such as mortgages, consumer credit and SME finance and strengthening the competition both for deposit taking and lending activities. This trend is already prevalent in most ACs and entails a number of challenges for the development and functioning of the banking system and the non-banking system as well as financial stability. As for banks, EU integration is seen as accelerating a trend towards transforming the subsidiaries of foreign banks in ACs into branches, in order to reduce costs and avoid the subsidiaries' narrower constraints on exposure limits.

As for structural and policy developments, integration can be expected to advance further liberalisation, especially through the chapters on the free movement of capital and services, fostering better regulation and providing a momentum especially for retail banking. Furthermore, integration will foster the centralisation of activities in head offices outside acceding countries, making a closer co-operation between national and foreign supervisors important. The enforcement of the Basle II Capital

Accord will provide another challenge for banks.

The adjustment process of ACs market infrastructure seems particular challenging against the background of a continuously evolving market infrastructure of the euro area. These changes are particularly relevant for payment systems and may also affect other market infrastructure elements. Hence, ACs need to establish modern and efficient infrastructures, but they also have to make sure that these investments are compatible with a future participation in the EU and the euro area and take ongoing changes in the euro area's market infrastructure into account. Thus, the need for co-operation among the competent monetary and supervisory authorities will likely increase in the future.

Labour Markets, Labour Market Policies and Challenges in the Candidate Countries

Christina Burger[1]

1. *Introduction*

1.1. Evolution of labour market challenges in the transition period

The labour markets of the former centrally planned economies on the eve of transition were characterised by full employment (i.e. no open unemployment) and excess of labour demand over supply. Labour hoarding was present in many sectors contributing to low levels of labour productivity. "Full employment" was achieved at the cost of low wages with a "demotivating effect on workers". Job security was ensured and a large amount of hidden unemployment was created through soft budget constraints. Firms rarely laid off workers and, as open unemployment was virtually zero, an unemployment security system was redundant and hence non-existent. Overstaffing, i.e. hidden unemployment, is estimated to have been as high as 30 percent. Where the structural division of labour is concerned, employment was concentrated in heavy industries, usually in large conglomerations, and in the public sector. In Estonia, for example, 80% of the workforce were employed in the state sector and the rest in co-operatives in 1989. Strong SMEs, as well as self-employment, were lacking, with private initiative only being tolerated in the agricultural sector, which in general recorded employment shares larger than in countries with comparable levels of GDP.

[1] Working document from the European Commission, Directorate General for Economic and Financial Affairs submitted to the Economic Policy Committee ad-hoc group on enlargement. The document has been prepared by Christina Burger with the support of Björn Döhring, David Young, Mary McCarthy, Jan-Host Schmidt and Heinz Handler. The views expressed in this working document can not necessarily be attributed to the European Commission.

Little wage variation was allowed by centrally determined wages. Non-cash benefits played an important role and were probably less equally distributed than monetary wages. The work force tended to be well educated and the female labour force participation rate was high.

Most candidate economies experienced substantial falls in GDP and wages as well as a pronounced decrease of employment at the initial stage of transition, with smaller declines in labour productivity. Stagnant unemployment accompanying the restructuring of the economies was another key feature of the transition process. There are, however, a few exceptions to this pattern: The Czech Republic experienced an exceptionally long period of low unemployment and Estonia achieved significant labour reallocation from the beginning of the transition process.

The **transition period** was/is characterised by job shedding in the public sector and with some delay, job creation in the private sector - with an increased incidence of temporary (frictional) unemployment and a significant level of structural unemployment. The temporary mismatch between labour demand and supply was/is due to the length of time taken to develop new private enterprises and the process of privatisation of enterprises. Privatisation agreements have typically included employment guarantees, thereby slowing down the transition in the labour market. Employment losses were transformed to a large extent into economic inactivity which concerned, in particular, less productive workers. Outflows to inactivity even exceeded outflows to unemployment. In order to acquire the new skills needed in the labour market, increased participation in higher education can now be observed, contributing also to a decline in employment participation rates. Nevertheless, older and younger workers, in particular, have difficulties in finding a job - the former because of a lack of new skills and the later because of a lack of experience and because vocational training is insufficiently responsive to market demands.[2]

1.2. EU-REQUIREMENTS CONCERNING THE LABOUR MARKET

The European co-ordination on employment[3] is part of the acquis communautaire which has to be transposed into national employment policies by the accession countries. This strategy (with all its targets, instruments and evaluation), which is currently under revision, must therefore be implemented in the accession countries as soon as they are members.

EU guidelines and directives with respect to labour law focus on four areas:

- Equal opportunities for men and women: Equal access to employment, training and promotion as well as to social security, occupational security schemes and self-employment activities must be assured. This could require changes in legislation of the accession countries.
- Co-ordination of social security schemes: Although no harmonisation is envisaged, technical changes to national legislation will have to be made.
- Health and safety at work: In this respect not only legal changes but also the establishment of a certain infrastructure (effective labour inspectorates and worker training) will be required.
- Labour law and working conditions: EU regulation concentrates on protecting employees of insolvent enterprises, conditions on collective redundancies, transfers of undertakings and protection of young people. Concerning these aspects, accession countries are exposed to a change in legislation.

2 For an overview of the evolution of labour market challenges see Boeri - Terrell, 2002; IMF, 2001a; Nesporova, 2002.

3 Since the Amsterdam Treaty, which came into force on May 1 1999, incorporates an employment Title which outlines the Luxembourg process.

In addition to the acquis communautaire, conditions for membership in the EU were set out by the Copenhagen European Council in 1993. The economic criterion is defined as "*the existence of a functioning market economy as well as the capacity to cope with competitive pressure and market forces within the European Union*".

The Essen European Council, at the end of 1994, defined a pre-accession strategy to prepare the countries of central Europe for EU membership. This strategy was based on the implementation of the Europe Agreement, the Phare Program of financial assistance and participation in different EU programmes opened to accession countries, and, finally, a "structured dialogue" bringing all Member States and Candidate Countries together to discuss issues of common interest. The latter is founded on the so called "Accession Partnership".

The **"Accession Partnership"** provides an assessment of the priority areas in which the Candidate Country has to make progress in order to be ready for accession. In accordance with the Accession Partnership, the Commission and the governments of the accession countries have carried out bilateral employment policy reviews. The objective of these reviews is to examine the extent to which the countries have made progress in adapting the labour market functioning and policy so as to be able to implement the European Employment Strategy upon accession. The starting point in the Employment Policy Review is a Joint Assessment Paper (JAP) by the European Commission and the national government. The Joint Assessment of Employment Priorities is one element of the attempt to a more systematic employment-policy development. In addition, several accession countries have already developed employment strategy plans organised along the pillars (of the old guidelines) of the Luxembourg strategy which should be a good preparation for their future incorporation in the employment process.

The Accession partnership has also led to the establishment of Pre-Accession Economic Programmes (PEPs) which take into account the requirements for economic and monetary union and concentrate mainly on public finance. These programmes are relevant for the analysis of employment in the accession countries in so far as they cover topics such as tax structures and benefit systems, which in turn are important for creating incentives for employment.

The principle underlying the labour market reforms in the pre-accession periods is that labour markets in the accession countries have to be flexible and solve the problems on their own, because the role of mobility to ease these problems (especially concerning unemployment) can be restricted by long transition periods imposed concerning the free movement of workers. The free movement of workers is completely suspended for the first two years after accession in some EU Member States, especially those along the border to the accession countries. Thereafter, one of the existing Member States can request an extension of this transition period for its territory, if this is deemed necessary, for three years initially and subsequently for two further years.

1.3. WHERE DO THEY STAND AND WHERE ARE THEY GOING: THE LISBON STRATEGY

The European Council in Lisbon set an overall goal for the European Economy "*to become the most competitive and dynamic knowledge-based economy in the world, capable of sustainable economic growth with more and better jobs and greater social cohesion.*"
Moreover, it has set goals concerning the participation in the labour market:

- to raise the employment rate to 70% by 2010 and
- to increase the number of women in employment to more than 60% by 2010.

In Stockholm, intermediate targets have been agreed on:

- to raise the employment rate to 67% by 2005 and
- to increase the number of women in employment to 57% by 2005.

Finally, a goal for the participation of older workers was introduced at the meeting of the European Council in Stockholm:

- to increase the employment rate among older women and men (55-64) to 50% by 2010.

The current employment rates of the Candidate Countries and the EU average are listed in the following table:

Table 1: Employment rates 2001

	total	female	older
Accession countries	56.7	51.0	30.2
Bulgaria	49.6	46.8	23.9
Cyprus*	65.9	53.2	49.2
Czech Republic	65.1	57.0	37.1
Estonia	61.3	57.3	48.4
Hungary	56.5	49.8	24.1
Lithuania*	60.1	58.5	41.6
Latvia	58.7	55.7	36.9
Malta	54.2	31.6	31.0
Poland*	55.0	48.9	28.4
Romania	62.4	57.1	48.2
Slovenia	63.8	58.8	25.5
Slovak Republic	56.8	51.8	22.4
EU			
Average	64.1	55.0	38.8
Maximum	76.2 DK	72.0 DK	66.8 SE
Minimum	54.9 IT	40.9 EL	25.1 BE

Source: Eurostat, 2003a

No Candidate Country reaches the Lisbon or Stockholm goal for the EU **overall employment rate**. In Cyprus and the Czech Republic, the employment rate is higher than the EU average; in all other countries it is lower than this. Only Bulgaria and Malta face a lower total employment rate than Italy, which has the lowest level within the EU. Concerning the target for the female employment rate, the Czech Republic, Estonia, Lithuania, Romania and Slovenia reach or exceed the Stockholm goal, whereas no country reaches the Lisbon goal. All Candidate Countries, with the exception of Malta, have higher female employment rates than the lowest EU rate. In Bulgaria, Cyprus, Hungary, Poland and the Slovak Republic the employment rate of women is lower than the EU average. Finally, no accession country reaches the Stockholm goal for older workers. In the Slovak Republic, Hungary and Bulgaria, fewer older people participate in the labour market than in Belgium, where the employment rate of the older workers is the lowest in the EU. Cyprus, Estonia, Lithuania and Romania have values above the EU average. Thus, a lot would have to be done in the Candidate Countries to reach the goals set in Lisbon and Stockholm. But this is true for some EU Member States as well.

Table 2 shows the total **unemployment rates** from 1997 (where available) to 2002 as well as the development of long-term unemployment. The highest (total and long-term) unemployment rates in the Candidate Countries exceed the upper bounds for the EU countries. Moreover, in contrast to the EU countries, unemployment seems to have risen in many Candidate Countries since mid 1990s. This is even more true for long-term unemployment. One can probably conclude that the structural problems in the labour market are more pervasive in the Candidate Countries than in the current EU Member States.

Table 2: Evolution of unemployment

	Total unemployment						Long-term unemployment rates				
	1997	**1998**	**1999**	**2000**	**2001**	**2002**	**1997**	**1998**	**1999**	**2000**	**2001**
Acc. Count.	-	-	-	13.6	14.5	14.8				6.6	7.6
Bulgaria	-	-	-	16.4	19.2	18.1	-	-	-	9.6	12.6
Cyprus	-	-	-	5.2	4.4	3.8	-	-	-	1.2	-
Czech Rep.	-	6.4	8.6	8.7	8.0	7.3	1.4	2.0	3.2	4.2	4.3
Estonia	9.6	9.2	11.3	12.5	11.8	9.1	4.5	4.8	5.5	6.3	6.2
Hungary	9.0	8.4	6.9	6.3	5.6	5.6	4.5	4.3	3.4	3.1	2.6
Lithuania	-	11.8	11.2	15.7	16.1	13.1	-	7.4	5.0	8.1	-
Latvia	-	14.3	14.0	13.7	12.8	12.8	-	7.8	7.5	8.2	7.4
Malta	-	-	-	7.0	6.7	7.4	-	-	-	-	2.9
Poland	10.9	10.2	13.4	16.4	18.5	19.9	-	-	-	7.4	-
Romania	5.3	5.4	6.2	6.8	6.6	7.0	2.7	2.6	3.1	3.7	3.3
Slovenia	6.9	7.4	7.2	6.6	5.8	6.0	3.5	3.3	3.3	4.1	3.7
Slovak Rep.	-	-	16.7	18.7	19.4	18.6	-	-	7.7	10.1	11.3
EU											
Average	10.0	9.4	8.7	7.8	7.4	7.7	4.9	4.5	4.0	3.5	3.5
Maximum	17.0 ES	15.2 ES	12.8 ES	11.3 ES	10.6 ES	11.3 ES	8.1 ES	7.0 ES	6.9 IT	6.5 IT	5.8 IT
Minimum	2.7 LU	2.7 LU	2.4 LU	2.3 LU	2.1 LU	2.8 LU	0.9 LU	0.8 LU	0.7 LU	0.5 LU	0.5 LU

Source: Eurostat, 2003a

Unemployment in general and long-term unemployment in particular are higher among low educated and low skilled persons in the Candidate Countries. The same is true for ethnic minorities and younger persons.

In more than half of the Candidate Countries, unemployment rates of women are lower than for men as shown in table 3. In general, the trends seem, however, to be the same for male and female unemployment. Women, however, suffer more from long-term unemployment than men.

Table 3: Evolution of unemployment by gender

	Unemployment men						Unemployment women					
	1997	**1998**	**1999**	**2000**	**2001**	**2002**	**1997**	**1998**	**1999**	**2000**	**2001**	**2002**
Acc. Countr				12.6	13.7	14.2				14.8	15.5	15.6
Bulgaria	-	-	-	16.7	20.0	18.7	-	-	-	16.2	18.4	17.4
Cyprus	-	-	-	3.2	2.9	2.9	-	-	-	7.8	6.4	5.0
Czech Rep.	-	5.0	7.2	7.3	6.7	5.9	-	8.1	10.3	10.3	9.7	9.0
Estonia	10.3	9.9	12.5	13.4	11.5	9.8	8.9	8.3	10.1	11.5	12.0	8.4
Hungary	9.7	9.0	7.4	6.8	6.1	6.0	8.1	7.8	6.3	5.6	4.9	5.1
Lithuania	-	13.1	12.3	17.9	18.4	13.3	-	10.4	10.0	13.4	13.8	13.0
Latvia	-	15.0	14.3	14.4	14.1	13.7	-	13.6	13.6	12.9	11.6	11.8
Malta	-	-	-	6.6	6.1	6.4	-	-	-	7.8	8.0	9.8
Poland	9.1	8.5	11.8	14.6	17.1	19.1	13.0	12.2	15.3	18.6	20.2	20.9
Romania	5.0	5.5	6.8	7.2	6.9	7.3	5.7	5.3	5.6	6.3	6.2	6.6
Slovenia	6.8	7.3	7.0	6.4	5.5	5.7	7.1	7.5	7.4	6.8	6.2	6.4
Slovak Rep.	-	-	16.6	18.9	19.8	18.4	-	-	16.9	18.5	18.9	18.8
EU												
Average	8.9	8.2	7.5	6.7	6.5	6.9	11.6	11.1	10.2	9.2	8.6	8.7
Max.	13.1 ES	11.2 ES	9.8 FI	9.1 FI	8.6 FI	9.1 FI	23.4 ES	21.8 ES	18.7 ES	16.7 EL. ES	15.5 EL	16.4 ES
Min.	2.0 LU	1.9 LU	1.8 LU	1.8 LU	1.7 LU	2.1 LU	3.9 LU	4.0 LU	3.3 LU	3.1 LU	2.7 LU	3.0 NL

Source: Eurostat, 2003a

Finally, **unemployment rates of young persons,** as shown in table 4, by far exceed the corresponding unemployment rates in the EU Member States.

Table 4: Evolution of youth unemployment

	Youth unemployment					
	1996	**1997**	**1998**	**1999**	**2000**	**2001**
Bulgaria	-	-	-	-	10.2	13.6
Cyprus	-	-	-		4.0	3.5
Czech Rep.	-	3.2	5.0	7.6	7.5	6.7
Estonia	-	8.3	6.1	8.3	8.5	8.8
Hungary	6.6	5.8	6.0	4.9	4.6	3.7
Lithuania	-	-	10.6	9.1	10.1	10.2
Latvia	-	-	11.2	10.2	8.2	8.6
Malta						
Poland	-	8.2	7.5	10.2	13.4	15.2
Romania	-	8.0	7.5	7.4	7.4	7.0
Slovenia	7.1	7.5	7.7	7.5	6.1	5.7
Slovak Rep.	-	-	-	14.7	16.5	17.6
EU						
Average	10.2	9.2	9.3	8.5	7.8	7.1
Maximum	17.3 ES	13.2 ES	12.8 IT	12.6 EL	11.7 IT	10.3 FI
Minimum	3.7 LU	2.9 LU	2.5 LU	2.3 LU	2.5 LU	2.7 LU

Source: Employment in Europe, 2001 and 2002

Where **sectoral developments** are concerned, most countries experienced a fall in the still-dominant agricultural sector and in the industrial sector. In Romania, for instance, agriculture accounts for about two fifths of employment, where much of the farming is subsistence in nature. Although a more or less pronounced rise in employment in the services sector has been observed, the services sector is still viewed as the most likely source of new jobs. Most self-employment is concentrated in agriculture and in the services sector. SMEs are still to be developed and are seen as an important job motor. 50 to 60% of all employees in Candidate Countries work for small enterprises with less than 50 employees. In Slovakia, this is true for more than 97% of workers and 80% among them work in an enterprise with less than 10 employees.

2. KEY ISSUES IN EMPLOYMENT POLICY

The European Council in Brussels, in March 2003, listed the following areas on which Member States should focus in their employment policy, which are also likely to become priorities for the accession countries, once they are members:

- *"reforms in tax and benefit systems and their interaction, so that they promote participation in the labour force and tackle poverty and unemployment traps, and increase labour demand and participation, in particular of those with low earning prospects;*
- *improving wage formation systems, so that they take into account the relationship between wages, price stability, productivity, training levels and labour market conditions, and modernising employment legislation taking account of the need for both flexibility and security, inter alia, by relaxing overly restrictive elements that affect labour market dynamics, while respecting the roles of social partners in accordance with national practice;*
- *improving the effectiveness of active labour market programmes, by better follow-up and monitoring; improving labour mobility, over occupations, sectors, regions and across borders, for example by improving transparency and recognition between systems of vocational education;*
- *increasing labour supply particularly amongst older people, women, immigrants and young people; encouraging active ageing, by discouraging early retirement incentives; and reducing barriers and disincentives for female labour force participation, including through better child care facilities."*

The following overview concentrates mainly on these priorities insofar as data are available for the Candidate Countries. It also touches on some other issues which have been highlighted in the BEPGs and discussed in the EPC, e.g. efficiency of the active labour market policies and investment in human capital. While the corresponding situation in EU Member States is used as a comparison point, this is not intended to provide a "benchmark", as many Member States still have ground to make up if the Lisbon EU-wide targets are to be achieved.

2.1. TAX-BENEFIT-SYSTEMS

The high incidence of job shedding in the transition period has led to the introduction of an unemployment insurance system in all of the Candidate Countries. The design of the tax-benefit system, comprising also social assistance and early retirement schemes, is of crucial importance and a review of such systems is urged in the Commission recommendation for the BEPGs 2002 "*to make work pay and encourage the search for jobs*".

Expenditures on social benefits

Public expenditures on social benefits in the accession countries, where data are available, seem to be in line with the shares of GDP spent in the EU countries, with Poland showing a relatively high ratio in % of GDP. The same seems to be true for total government disbursements and total tax revenue. One can conclude that social benefits do not seem to play a completely different role in accession compared to the EU countries.

Table 5: Expenditures for social benefits and their role in public finances

	Social Benefits paid by Government	Government total Disbursements	Total tax revenue
		% of GDP, 2000	
Czech Rep.	13.6	46.1	39.5
Hungary	-	47.5	38.7
Poland*	18.9	43.7	35.2
Slovak Rep.	12.1	52.2	35.8
EU-rates:			
Median	14.2	43.3	42.0
Maximum	18.8 DE	52.2 SE	53.3 SE
Minimum	8.1 IE	29.2 IE	31.5 IE

*: Tax revenue 1999 Source: OECD Database

Net replacement ratios and incentives

Net replacement ratios compare the various (cash) benefits made available to those without work (net of taxes) with potential in-work income and hence are a good indicator of incentives to take up work that are embedded in tax-benefit systems. Net replacement ratios are currently only available for those countries which are members of the OECD - where accession countries are concerned, only the Czech Republic, Hungary, Poland and the Slovak Republic.

Table 6: Net replacement ratios (in the 1st month of unempl., after a waiting period)

	APW wage level				66.7% of APW wage level			
	single	**Married couple**	**Couple 2 kids**	**Lone parent 2 kids**	**single**	**Married couple**	**Couple 2 kids**	**Lone parent 2 kids**
Czech Rep.	49	67	70	71	66	69	70	72
Hungary	48	48	60	61	65	65	75	76
Poland	36	43	46	47	53	62	58	67
Slovak Rep.	79	77	78	80	77	75	77	79
EU-rates:								
Median	64	63	73	73	78	76	82	80
Max.	82 LU, NL	89 NL	89 NL	87 LU, FI	89 DK	89 DK	95 DK	96 DK
Min.	31 IE	44 IE, IT	44 EL	47 EL	39 IT	40 IT	46 EL	47 IT

Source: OECD, 2002a.

The variation in net replacement ratios is very high across the EU with a spread of between 40 and more than 50%-points. As regards the accession countries, the lowest net replacement ratios are recorded in Poland and the highest in the Slovak Republic, where the ratios exceed the median value for the EU countries for average wage earners. The presence of children and/or spouses tends to increase the net replacement ratios in the Czech Republic, Hungary and Poland. This is not the case in the Slovak Republic. The additional benefits granted for an unemployed person's family tend to increase the net replacement ratios more than in

EU countries. The difference in net replacement ratios between single workers earning the average production worker wage and those earning only two thirds of the average wage seems to be greater in the accession countries than in the EU.

Table 7 shows the net replacement ratios for the same groups of countries and family types for long-term benefit recipients.

Table 7: Net replacement ratios for long-term benefit recipients

	APW wage level				66.7% of APW wage level			
	Single	Married couple	Couple 2 kids	Lone parent 2 kids	Single	Married couple	Couple 2 kids	Lone parent 2 kids
Czech Rep.	37	60	80	74	54	84	100	96
Hungary	28	28	38	40	28	28	39	41
Poland	33	50	74	56	48	72	93	81
Slovak Rep.	38	62	80	60	54	90	100	100
EU-rates:								
Median	49	57	68	68	63	80	84	71
Max.	60 NL, DK	71 FI, SE	89 FI	79 DK	85 DK	102 SE	110 SE	97 DK
Min.	0 IT	4 IT	10 EL	11 EL	0 IT	5 IT	11 EL	12 EL

Source: OECD, 2002a.

Net replacement ratios for those unemployed with children are higher for long-term benefit recipients than for persons in the first month of unemployment in the Czech and the Slovak Republics and in Poland. This might be problematic in so far as incentives for long-term unemployed to seek a job should be stronger, whereas at the start of an unemployment spell, benefits could be more generous. In order to increase the efficiency of the allocation of labour resources and to improve the match of labour demand and supply, some frictional unemployment may be deemed beneficial.

Although no comparable data are available, it can be stated that in Malta a relatively small gap between minimum wage and the unemployment benefit exists, in particular for large families. This raises problems concerning low wage earners which have few incentives to take up work. Net replacement ratios for skilled industrial workers with three dependants amount to 78% in Cyprus. In Lithuania, a value of 70% of the average wage is recorded for one adult and two children. The Polish unemployment insurance system grants a flat rate amounting to 29% of the net average wage and 78% of the minimum wage. Compared to that, the Polish social assistance payment is rather generous: A single person receives 70% of the net minimum wage and a married couple with two children 198%. In comparison with EU Member States, the situation in the accession countries is not outstanding. In the Netherlands e.g., unemployment benefit replacement rates for wages at the minimum wage level are between 74 and 94% depending on the family situation. In Greece, the level of daily unemployment benefit amounts to about half the minimum wage.

Net replacement ratios are particularly high in some countries, e.g. as recorded in certain cases in the Czech and the Slovak Republics, where they amount to 100% for some family types. But in a few EU Member States, in some cases the ratios exceed even the 100% threshold; thus the situation in the accession countries is not extraordinary. A comparison of the development of net replacement ratios between 1995 and 1999 for average wage earners gives a divergent picture: the net replacement ratios decreased in Hungary and in the Czech Republic for single workers; they increased for persons with children in Poland. The development of the median value, the highest and the lowest net replacement ratios of the EU Member States show no clear trends either (see graphs on last page).

Design of tax-benefit systems

At the start of transition when **unemployment benefit systems** were newly introduced, they were designed to be relatively generous both in terms of the amount paid and in terms of duration. As unemployment increased, the systems had to be revised in order to remain sustainable and to allow them to activate jobseekers. In Poland, initially no end date for the payment period was fixed, but it was later shortened to one year. Maximum duration was halved in the former Czechoslovakia and Hungary and the level of the benefit had to be reduced in Bulgaria, the former Czechoslovakia and Poland.

Concerning the employment conditions governing eligibility for unemployment benefits, the requirement concerning previous employment duration varies a great deal in the EU countries as well as in the accession countries. The conditionality in the Czech Republic is the same as that of Germany. The Slovak Republic seems to be more restrictive with a requirement of 24 months of employment in 3 years. A waiting period does not exist in half of the EU Member States and, in the others, it ranges between 3 and 8 days, with the accession countries being in the same range.

The payment rate (% of previous gross/net income) in the EU lies between 40 and 90% with a median value of 70%. Unemployment systems in the accession countries tend to be less generous on average than in the EU. Poland is a particular case in point, having a flat rate, like Ireland and the UK. Finally, the unemployment benefit in the EU is granted for periods between 6 months in the UK and Italy and 60 months in France, the Netherlands and Denmark. The median value of duration amounts to 12 months with three countries granting the benefit for 60 months. The accession countries tend to be much less generous than the EU countries, where duration of benefits is concerned, with the shortest duration of 4 months in Bulgaria and the longest in Poland of 18 months.

Table 8: Main characteristics of the unemployment benefit system

	Employment conditions	Waiting period	Payment rate %*	Duration (months)
Bulgaria	9 months in last 15 months	-	60%	4 to 12 depending on length of previous employment
Cyprus	26 weeks	3 days	60%	156 working days
Czech Republic	12 months in 3 years	7 days	50% 40 after 3 months	6
Estonia	12 in 24 months	7 days	50% for first 100 days 40% thereafter	180 days, longer in case of long insurance
Hungary	12 months in 4 years	-	65	12
Latvia	9 months in 12 months	?	50 for 6 months then depending on employment and duration	9 months
Lithuania	24 months in 3 years	7 days	19-34%	6 months in 12 months
Malta	?	?	Flat rate	150 days
Poland	365 days in 18 months	1 day	Flat rate	18 max (lower in areas with low unemployment)
Romania	12 months during last 24	-	75% of gross national minimum wage	6/9/12 months depending on length of previous employment
Slovenia	12 in last 18 months	?	70% of average wage in last 12 months for 3 months, 60% afterwards	3-24 months depending on length of employment history
Slovak Republic	24 months in 3 years	-	50% 45 after 3 months	6 or 9 months depending on length of employment history

* previous gross income, in CZ and LT previous net income.
Source: OECD (2002a) for CZ, PL, IMF (2001) for LV; JAPs of BG, CY, EE, LT, RO; GVG (2003) for EE, HU, MT, SK; Homepage of the Ministry for Labour for SI

Generally speaking, the unemployment benefit systems in the accession countries do not deviate too much from the EU systems, bearing in mind the strong degree of heterogeneity in both groups of countries.

As for **other benefit systems**, social assistance and/or unemployment assistance schemes exist in most accession countries. Mostly, unemployed persons are eligible to participate in such schemes after termination of unemployment benefits or in cases where they are not at all entitled to receive unemployment benefits. A recent change in the Bulgarian system reduced the period in which unemployment assistance is paid to six months in order to encourage job search. The social allowance system in the Czech Republic provides several benefits simultaneously thereby creating a poverty trap in particular for large families. A similar situation can be observed in Lithuania where social security recipients receive benefits from different resources and can accumulate an income from benefits which exceeds the minimum wage. In the Slovak Republic, payments from the social assistance system for a family with two children are at the level of the average net wage and thus give rise to significant employment disincentives. In Hungary, however, reforms were designed explicitly to reduce poverty traps. In most accession as well as EU countries, unemployment assistance (paid when unemployment insurance is exhausted) and social assistance are given without a limit on duration. Exceptions to this trend include Hungary, the Netherlands, Portugal, Spain and Sweden. A subsistence allowance increases the disposable income to the "subsistence level" in Estonia, which under certain circumstances has lead to an income level above the unemployment benefit. The system of public assistance allowances seems to be rather restrictive in Cyprus, where only just over 1% of the long-term unemployed are entitled to receive this type of benefit. The social assistance benefit for a single person in 1998 amounted to 10% of the average wage in Romania, about 15% in the Baltic countries, over 20% in Hungary, about 33% in the Czech and Slovak Republic. These ratios were exceeded by the values of Belgium and the UK (about 40%) and Finland, the Netherlands and Sweden (about 60%).

The accession countries devote more resources to non-employment benefits than the EU countries. Generous non-employment benefits decrease the incentives for low productivity workers to search and accept a job by increasing their reservation wage.

Early retirement schemes are sometimes used as response to the decline in employment. This is particularly true for the Czech Republic. In Poland 12% of the registered unemployed receive pre-retirement benefits and the share is on an upward trend. The system was introduced in order to release jobs for young people and is rather generous, providing between 120 and 160% of the unemployment benefit. No early retirement system exists in the Slovak Republic and Malta. In some countries, e.g. the Czech Republic, disability benefits provide a more generous alternative to social allowance, particularly for older workers, and are used as an alternative to early retirement, as in Malta.

Unfortunately, no systematic data on the participation in early retirement programmes are available. Some tentative conclusions can be drawn from the table below which shows public expenditure on old age pensions and early retirement as a percent of GDP.

Table 9: Expenditure on pensions

	Old age pension	**Early retirement programmes**
	Public expenditure, % GDP, 2000	
Czech Republic	7.8	1.8
Hungary	6.0	1.2
Poland	10.8	1.4
EU-rates:		
Median	9.0	2.2
Maximum	14.2 IT	4.0 DK
Minimum	4.3 UK	1.1 BE

Source: OECD, 2002c

Expenditure on old age pensions seems to be in line with the EU countries, whereas expenditure on early retirement programmes tends to be less generous. Early retirement schemes were reduced during the transition period as they overburdened public finances when unemployment and economic inactivity rose. Some accession countries have made efforts to increase the retirement ages (the statutory retirement age was raised to 62 in Hungary and Latvia; 63 in Estonia; 65 in Cyprus; 63/men, 60/men in Bulgaria, 62/men, 61/women in the Czech Republic; 60/men, 62.5/women in Lithuania).

The **tax burden** on labour and the general tax burden are rather high in most accession countries. Thus, they share one of the main problems with EU Member States. Tax rates on low wage earners show pronounced differences in this tax burden, ranging from a tax rate of 43.6% in Slovenia to 17% in Cyprus in 2001. Only in four countries was the tax rate on low wage earners lower than the EU average. Nevertheless, between 2000 and 2001, only about half of the acceding countries reduced the tax rate on low wage earners, as a measure to encourage job creation.

Graph 1: Tax rates of low wage earners 2002

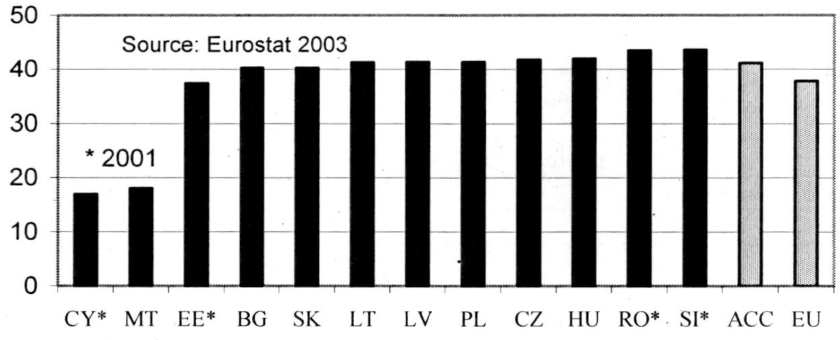

The tax wedge does not exceed the highest EU values. Neverthless, the accession countries share the problem of a high tax burden with the EU-MS. Cyprus is an exception, which has a relatively low overall tax burden. The tax wedge for an average production worker wage earner amounts to 23.2%, for a person earning two thirds of the average wage to just over 17%. This is extremely low compared to Lithuania with tax wedges of 42 and 45% and the Slovak Republic with tax wedges amounting to 40 and 41%.

Table 10: Tax burden - Average personal income tax and social security contribution rates on gross labour income 2001

	% average production worker wage			
	67%	**100%**	**133%**	**167%**
Czech Republic	41.6	43.0	44.3	45.3
Hungary	49.7	52.6	56.4	57.7
Poland	41.8	42.9	43.5	43.9
Slovak Republic	41.0	42.1	44.0	45.5
EU-rates				
Median	38.5	44.2	47.2	49.9
Max	49.2 BE	55.6 BE	59.0 BE	61.4 BE
Min	17.4 IE	25.8 IE	31.6 IE	32.9 UK

Source: OECD, Tax data base, 2000-02

Employer and employee contributions to all forms of social security amount to about 60% of wages in the typical case in Romania; this is more than most other countries, such as Hungary and Slovakia (50% each), France (47%), Germany (about 40%) and Latvia (37%).

High tax rates not only create disincentives for the take up of work, but also contribute to the already high and increasing **informal sector** in the Candidate Countries. Another reason for the increase in the size of the shadow economy is poor law enforcement and the large decline in incomes following market liberalisation.

Table 11: Shadow Economy (Labour Force as a % of Working Age Population 1998/99)

Bulgaria	30.4	**Lithuania**	20.3
Czech Republic	12.6	**Poland**	20.9
Estonia	33.4	**Romania**	24.3
Hungary	20.9	**Slovak Republic**	16.3
Latvia	29.6	**Slovenia**	21.6

Source: Schneider, 2002

Conclusions

Policy concerning tax-benefit systems in the accession countries seems grosso modo to resemble the policy approaches in the EU Member States. Unemployment benefit systems do not seem to be more generous or to provide less appropriate incentives for seeking and taking up work - apart from some problematic cases than in EU Member States. Disincentives appear to come more often from the social assistance schemes and early retirement systems than from the unemployment benefit systems. Reforms assessed in terms of the development of net replacement ratios, mostly go in the right direction in accordance with the requirements of the BEPGs and the Luxembourg Strategy according to which "*Particular attention should be given to promoting incentives for unemployed or inactive people to seek and take up work,...*". As in the case of Member States, more precise conclusions await the analysis of marginal effective tax schedules, which are currently being estimated for the existing Member States and the four OECD countries which are Candidate Countries. The high tax burden on labour is a common problem shared between most EU and accession countries, which needs to be further tackled by both groups of countries.

2.2. WAGE BARGAINING SYSTEMS

The Broad Economic Policy Guidelines 2002 include a recommendation concerning wages "*Wage developments ... should reflect different economic and employment situations. Governments should promote the right framework conditions for wage negotiations by social partners. For wage developments to contribute to an employment-friendly policy-mix, social partners should continue to pursue a responsible course and conclude wage agreements ... in line with the general principles set out in the Broad Economic Policy Guidelines.*" Although this recommendation is only given to EU Member States, it can of course be applied to accession countries, too.

Minimum wages

Minimum wages can be seen from a social point of view of guaranteeing a certain minimum standard of living to the working population. From an economic point of view, minimum wages may guarantee a certain intensity of effort which workers are willing to undertake. On the other hand, the minimum wage may act as a barrier to the labour market entry of low-productivity workers whose productivity falls short of what would correspond to the minimum wage. Of course with the minimum wage, what matters is whether the level is prohibitively high in countries where the unemployment rate is high. Legally binding minimum wages exist in all accession countries. Their influence on the labour market varies however, as does the ratio of the minimum wage to the average wage. In Estonia, Hungary and Romania, the comparably **low minimum wage,** in combination with rather low unemployment benefits, does not appear to be a barrier for hiring additional employees. About 5% of the employees are paid around the minimum wage in Hungary, about 4% in Romania and about 3% in Poland. In Malta, which has a very **high minimum wage** in comparison to the average wage, the lowest wage exceeds the legal minimum by 8%. Involvement of the social partners in one way or another (be it consultation, a recommendation by the social partners or tripartite negotiations) is common in most accession countries. Several countries use an indexation system (e.g. the Slovak Republic and Slovenia) or base the increase of the minimum wage on forecasts of inflation and wage increases (e.g. Poland and the Slovak Republic).

At the start of the transition, almost all countries introduced legally binding minimum wages at levels similar to this in western countries (about 45 to 50% of the average wage). As nominal minimum wages remained unchanged for several years despite high inflation, the ratio of the minimum wage to the average wage fell. Table 12 provides an overview of the latest available data on the minimum wage in relation to the average wage. Moreover, data on the monthly minimum wage in Euro and in Purchasing Power Parities are provided. In January 2003, Slovenia and Malta had national minimum wages which exceeded the lowest minimum wage in the EU (i.e. Portugal). The differences in the levels of the minimum wages are considerably reduced when Purchasing Power Parities are used for the calculation of comparable minimum wages.

Table 12: Minimum wages

	Minimum wage as % of average wage	**Year**	**Monthly minimum wage, January 2003**	
			in €	**in PPP**
Bulgaria	35.0	2001	56	139
Czech Republic	34.0	2001	199	389
Estonia	28.2	1999	138	264
Hungary	40.0	2001	212	384
Lithuania	40.0	2001	125	252
Latvia	40.0	2000	116	239
Malta	74.0*	2001	535	752
Poland	38.0	2000	201	351
Romania	34.0	2002	73	194
Slovak Republic	38.5	2000	118	265
Slovenia	58.0	target value	451	668
EU Member States	45.0 - 50.0		Min: 416 PT	Min: 543 PT

* in % of average net wages

Sources: OECD (2001) for CZ; IMF (2001) for EE, OECD (2002b) for HU, others: JAPs; for the last two columns: Eurostat, 2003b.

For the most part, **no regional variation** of the minimum wage is provided for, which seems to increase regional divergence in the labour market. This is especially true for Poland, where the generally high minimum wage seems to harm job creation especially in certain regions. In Lithuania, however, a new law allows the government to set different minimum wages for individual branches, employee groups or regions.

Box 1: Regional unemployment and labour mobility

Regional unemployment is rather high in most accession countries with Slovakia and Bulgaria showing the widest gap between regions. Table 13 lists the regions with the lowest and highest unemployment rates in 2001. They vary between 2.0 and 32.8%, a range quite similar to that concerning EU NUTS level 2 regions.

Table 13: Regional unemployment in the accession countries 2001

Region	Unemployment rate
Közep-Magyarország (HU)	2.0
Praha (CZ)	3.0
Nyugat-Dunántúl (HU)	3.2
Bucuresti (RO)	4.1
Közép-Dunántúl (HU)	4.3
Nord-Vest (RO)	4.8
Jihozápad (CZ)	5.7
Slovenija	5.7
Yugoiztochen (BG)	22.9
Severen Tsentralen (BG)	23.3
Lubuskie (PL)	23.6
Východné Slovensko (SK)	23.9
Dolno´slaskie (PL)	24.1
Severoiztochen (BG)	26.5
Severozapaden (BG)	32.8

Source: Eurostat, 2002

So far, **labour mobility** has not contributed to reducing this problem. Mobility in central planned economies was restricted by the resident permit system and housing restrictions. Moreover, there was an attempt to stabilise the territorial distribution of the population by moving jobs to people. In the course of the transition, the closing of large enterprises in "one company towns" and the decline in agriculture have led to high unemployment rates in some areas. Labour mobility seems generally to be low, caused partially by high prices for new housing and a low housing stock and turnover in urban areas. The low degree of wage dispersion in regional respects is another factor to explain low labour mobility. In several countries (esp. in the Czech Republic and Romania), commuting is common; however, relocation is not. In others (Hungary, Poland), the poor roadway systems are found to hinder internal migration. People face problems in selling or renting their houses. The attitude during communism, under which people had a job for life, has also contributes to low movement across regions within a country, despite relatively large regional economic differences. Fostering mobility is not only important from the point of view of regional development, but also in order to reduce the mismatch in the labour market. Labour mobility after transition has been found to be more pronounced in terms of occupational than in terms of regional mobility (Svejnar, 2002).

Policies in the Candidate Countries try to cope with the impediments to mobility through mobility grants for unemployed or persons with low income (Bulgaria, Czech Republic, Hungary, Poland, Slovenia, Slovak Republic), regional employment (Bulgaria) and education (Latvia) programmes, training services for businesses in slowly developing areas (Hungary), support for SMEs (Slovakia), reimbursement of recruitment costs for firms recruiting labour in a region with high unemployment (Hungary), temporary foreign employment (Cyprus), the improvement of the transport system (Hungary) and subsidies for the construction of houses (Hungary and Slovakia). These measures cover the main European approaches to enhance mobility and tackle the special problems (such as those incorporated in the transport system) of the accession countries.

Wage bargaining mechanisms and institutions

The discussion of how wage bargaining structures affect wage developments has to a large extent been shaped by the Calmfors and Driffill hypothesis. It predicts an "inverted U" relationship between unemployment and the degree of centralisation of wage bargaining. Fully centralised and fully decentralised bargaining both favour the employment situation: the first, because it can better take into account the economy wide consequences of the wage bargaining; the latter, because it can better reflect the productivity in the firm.

In the communist area, tripartite bargaining was well developed in contrast to the bilateral discussions between employers and employees. In this respect, one has to bear in mind that private employers did not really exist in the planned economies. **Wage negotiations** have gradually been developed in all accession countries.[4] There are, however, still important differences. In Lithuania and Bulgaria, for instance, bipartite discussion and collective bargaining lags clearly behind the tripartite co-operation. In some countries (e.g. Czech Republic, Slovak Republic), work councils have to be established which have to be involved in important business decisions. Usually, collective agreements cover not only wages, but also regulations concerning overtime or rules for dismissals. In Latvia and Romania, agreements on the sectoral level or on the enterprise level are automatically binding for all workers, regardless whether they are members of a trade union or not. In the Czech and the Slovak Republics, the government may decide to extend the collective agreements to non-organised workers. In some countries, wage negotiations are urged to take into account special characteristics of the work performed by the individual workers, such as hazardous working conditions, work at night, or demand and supply conditions for a special pro-

[4] For further details see Annex 1 on wage development and wage bargaining.

fession (in Lithuania) or a guideline annual rate negotiated at the national level (in Poland). Table 14 indicates the degree of centralisation of wage negotiations. The dominant level for wage bargaining in the accession countries seems to be the enterprise level.

Table 14: Degree of (de)centralisation of wage negotiations

	national	sectoral	enterprise
Bulgaria	x		
Cyprus		x	x
Czech Rep.			x
Estonia			x
Hungary			x
Latvia			x
Lithuania			x
Malta			x
Poland			x
Romania			x
Slovak Rep.	x	x	
Slovenia		x	x

Sources: JAPs

Membership of **trade unions** plays a crucial role in most wage bargaining systems. It has obviously decreased from the 100% coverage of the work force registered at the beginning of economic transition. By the end of the year 2000, the degree of trade unionisation was below 30% of the labour force. The fall was particularly strong in Estonia, now amounting to 18% as well as in Poland and Hungary (now 20% each). In Lithuania, union coverage fell from 85% of the labour force in 1989 to about 13% in 1996. The role played by trade unions has changed from an "ideological" one to active participation in wage bargaining. Employer organisations represent on average 30-40% of industrial enterprises, or between 2 and 5% of the total number of enterprises (see EC 2002b). The strength of the trade unions varies a lot between different countries: from Poland at one end of a possible scale where firms are characterised by strong insider power of trade unions to Estonia at the other end of the scale, where employees have no right to demand negotiations.

Even in the **public sector**, wage bargaining between the government and trade unions is becoming more and more common. Wages differentiate between different grades, positions and administrational branches. Partly, earnings of civil servants are set as multiples of a base amount (in Poland) or the minimum wage (in Lithuania). Wages in the state-owned enterprises are more and more linked to the financial performance of the companies. Especially in Romania and Bulgaria, co-operations that were until recently state owned had a soft budget constraint and wage increases did not at all reflect changes of productivity. Within the framework of the IMF agreements, this has changed and wage increases are now subject to strict conditions (profit, absence of state subsidies and debts duly paid).

Wage dispersion

Wages seem to cover a wide range both within and between the accession countries. The average wage level in the sector with the lowest wages amounts to 33% of the average wage in the sector with the highest wage in Bulgaria and to 61.9% in Slovenia. This has implications not on the acquisition of general and specific education and training by workers, but also for the efficient allocation of productive human resources.

Table 15: Wage differences in the accession countries 1997

	Bulgaria	Czech Republic	Hungary	Latvia	Poland	Romania	Slovak Republic	Slovenia
Wage dispersion*	33.5	61.4	51.3	47.5	42.2	46.7	55.7	61.9
Sector with lowest wage	other services	agriculture	agriculture	trade and catering	trade and catering	trade and catering	agriculture	manufacturing
Sector with highest wage	power and water	financial services and real estate	financial services and real estate	transport and communication	mining	mining	financial services and real estate	public administration

* Wage in sector with lowest wage as a % of wage in sector with highest wage
Source: OECD Data base

Income distribution has grown more unequal during transition, although it is still comparable to EU levels. The position of low wage earners has deteriorated, while that of highly paid workers has improved. Returns to education were low under central planning but this situation has changed dramatically in the course of the transition period. Differences in educational attainment account for one third of the explained variation in earnings. Inter-industry wage differentials are the second most important factor explaining earnings inequality. Gender is the third important factor, contributing very little to the differences, although it seems that gender gaps have increased in recent years In contrast to returns to education, returns to work experience have not increased during the transition period. Quite the reverse, in most accession countries work experience is now less rewarded than previously (see Rutkowski, 2001, and Boeri - Terrell, 2002).

A comparison between the private and the public sectors does not lead to a uniform picture: Wages are higher in the public sector than in the private sector in Bulgaria and Slovenia. The opposite is true for e.g. in Hungary, Malta and Poland, the latter faces difficulties in attracting highly productive staff in the budgetary sector.

The decentralisation of the wage setting process has had a stronger impact on the wage structure than the speed of privatisation or other reforms. However, wages should not be used to draw conclusions about household poverty: Low-paid workers are often secondary earners (young people, women) whose earnings complement other family member's income. In Bulgaria, for example, families with a low-paid household member are less often poor than families without a low-paid worker (see Rashid - Rutkowski, 2001).

Labour costs

Labour costs per working hour including non-wage labour costs are much lower than in all EU countries, with the exception of Slovenia. Slovenian labour costs exceed those in Portugal where the lowest value within the EU can be observed.

Table 16: Labour costs per working hour 2001 in Euro

Bulgaria	1.41
Czech Republic	3.53
Hungary	3.65
Poland*	4.60
Romania	1.45
Slovak Republic	2.91
Slovenia	6.89
EU	19.77
Max	22.12 BE
Min	5.49 PT

*: 2000, Source: Guger, 2002

2.3. Labour Market Regulation

Labour market flexibility is a prerequisite for the successful transition of the formerly planned economies. This concerns not only wage flexibility, but also the regulations on hiring and dismissals, working time and other non-standard forms of employment. These topics are covered within the Employment Guidelines, under the heading "modernisation of the organisation of work". Flexible working arrangements and an appropriate balance between flexibility and security are especially stressed - also in the BEPGs and the Barcelona Council Conclusions.

The Estonian labour market has been judged as the most flexible by various authors (see e.g. Rashid - Rutkowsky, 2001, Cazes - Nesporova, 2001) - job destruction and creation rates are even higher than the EU-average. Latvia, on the other hand, has very strict regulations. Although labour law lays down only the minimum requirements, the social partners have the right to develop more detailed provisions concerning mutual rights and obligations. Strict regulation can be observed in the Slovak Republic compared to other transition countries, but they are far less strict than in Italy, Spain or Portugal. Detailed provisions for performing over 360 narrowly defined occupations have a negative impact on labour mobility in Slovenia. In Poland, job turnover is similar to that in relatively regulated labour markets (such as Germany), but substantially lower than in flexible ones such as the UK or USA, due to the strict employment protection legislation and the presence of strong trade unions.

2.3.1. Employment Protection Legislation

Regulations concerning the hiring and dismissals of employers can make it easy or difficult for firms to adjust their workforce. High costs of dismissals and strict rules concerning hiring (e.g. quotas for special groups) may smooth out employment dynamics over the economic cycle. However, this may be achieved at the cost of misallocation of human resources, to the extent that it encourages employees to reduce turnover costs by hoarding labour. For employees strict labour regulation provides secure jobs and may be viewed as part of quality in work which may increase their motivation. Employees may be willing to pay a premium for having secure employment in form of lower wages. On the other hand, the job security provided by employment protection legislation could also lead employees to reduce their work effort. Labour protection improves the situation of insiders compared to outsiders. Thus, low productive outsiders in particular may face even more difficulties in finding a job.[5] Employment protection legislation in accession countries has been found to result in lower job turnover, lower flows into unemployment and longer unemployment spells, but not to longer job tenure (see Nesporova, 2002).

Accession countries tend to be most restrictive concerning collective dismissals and least restrictive concerning temporary employment as can be seen from table 17 which depicts indicators of the strictness of employment protection legislation in some accession and EU countries. In comparison to some EU members, regulation seems to be in line with the more restrictive countries (such as Germany, Italy, France and Portugal) concerning regular employment, but less restrictive, close to less regulated countries such as the United Kingdom, where temporary employment is concerned. On collective dismissals, the accession countries can only be compared to Italy and Portugal.

---

5 For a general discussion of employment protection legislation, see EC, 2001a.

Table 17: Strictness of Employment Protection Legislation, Late 1990s[1]

	Regular Employment	**Temporary Employment**	**Collective Dismissals**	**Overall EPL strictness Index'[2]**
Czech Rep.	2.8	0.5	4.3	2.1
Estonia	3.1	1.4	4.1	2.6
Hungary	2.1	0.6	3.4	1.7
Poland	2.2	1.0	3.9	2.0
Slovak Rep.	2.6	1.4	4.4	2.4
Slovenia	3.4	3.1	4.8	3.5
UK	0.8	0.3	2.9	0.9
Germany	2.8	2.3	3.1	2.6
France	2.3	3.6	2.1	2.8
Italy	2.8	3.8	4.1	3.4
Portugal	4.3	3.0	3.6	3.7

Source: Knogler 2002 and Worldbank, 2002.
Notes: 1) Indicators range from 0 to 4 according to degree of strictness. 2) Weighted average of indicators for regular contracts, temporary contracts, and collective dismissals. 3) Rankings increase with strictness of employment legislation.

The termination of a contract is usually connected with costs for the employer which can be divided in two groups: first, the severance benefits paid directly to the employee, and second, costs imposed from outside on the employer, such as information procedures or negotiations with trade unions.

The notice period for the termination of a contract (two months on average) tends to be much longer in accession countries than the EU average (12.3 days). The **grounds for terminating** a contract are limited. Usually termination is prohibited during justified periods of absence and for pregnant women. Disabled individuals tend also to have special regulations concerning dismissal. In Estonia, women raising a child under 3 years are protected by the prohibition of being dismissed. In Poland, periods of excused absence during which termination is prohibited can last up to 9 months. Special security is provided to older persons for whom termination of a work contract is prohibited within two years before pension entitlement. Hiring and dismissal procedures have already been simplified in Slovenia, where the dismissal regulation was previously were strict.

When an employee is dismissed, **notification** to a third party (labour office and/or trade union) is generally required without the necessity of receiving permission from this third party. This is broadly in line with EU practice. In Bulgaria, notification of the relevant territorial body for tripartite co-operation, the municipal administration and the territorial unit of the labour office is required. Difficult co-ordination with trade unions is costly and usually takes much time. The local trade union and the local labour office have to be informed about dismissals by Czech firms. Similarly, the national labour organisation and the trade union must be informed in the Slovak Republic. Firms in Lithuania have to give notice to the labour office and the municipality. The latter has a formal possibility of stopping dismissals. Finally, in Poland the enterprise trade union to which the employee belongs or the union, which would represent the employee's interest, has to be informed. If this union raises objections against the dismissal, the employer is obliged to apply to a supra-enterprise trade union. In the case of mass layoffs, notice must be given to the enterprise level union and the district labour office.

Laws about **severance pay** tend to play the greatest role in countries where unemployment benefits are low. These countries require formal sector employers to pay benefits when permanent employees are dismissed. The typical amounts often correspond to between six and twelve monthly wages for tenured workers. Both the severance pay and the notice period tend to increase stepwise with the length of the employment period in the firm.

In some countries, **support for job search** must be given by the dismissing enterprise. If a person is dismissed in the Czech Republic for reasons on the employer's side, the employer is obliged to actively assist in finding other suitable employment in co-operation with the state authority. In Poland, the employer is obliged to provide employees with 2 or 3 days off, if the reason for the termination is on the employer's side. Dismissed persons have a right of entitlement to compensatory pay if they take up a new job at a lower wage. The new employer is obliged to pay a compensation for the difference in earnings for a period of six months. The costs of these payments are incurred by the Labour Fund.

Table 18: Regulation concerning dismissals

	Notice period (individual)	Notice period (Mass layoff)	Legal provisions for severance pay
Bulgaria	30 days	60 days	1 month wage, 2 months for persons who acquired the right to pension, 6 months if employee has worked with the same employer for the last 10 years, negotiations with trade unions often lead to higher compensation
Czech Republic	2 months	30 days	2 months wage, collective agreements can negotiate additional months
Estonia	2 months, 0 if bankruptcy (IMF 2001) 2 weeks to 4 months (Arro, 2001)		1-4 months wage 1 month in case of unsuitability of worker 4 months if employee has worked with the same employer for the last 10 years
Latvia			No mandatory severance pay
Lithuania	n.a.	60 days	
Poland	2 weeks if employee was employed for less than 6 months 1 month if employed for at least 6 mo. 3 months if employed for at least 3 years	45 days	1 months wage for employees with employment shorter than 10 years, 2 month if duration 10-19 years, 3 months if 20 or more years,

Table 18 (continued): Regulation concerning dismissals

	Notice period (individual)	Notice period (Mass layoff)	Legal provisions for severance pay
Romania	15 days agreements at sectoral level may stipulate longer periods		6-15 months wages, depending on length of service in case a company's restructuring plan cost was born by government and world bank
Slovak Rep.	2 months 3 months in case of closure or relocation	1 month	2 months wage

Sources: Arro (2001) for EE, Beleva-Tzanov (2001) for BG; IMF (2001), for EE, LT, LV; Kwiatkowski (2001) for PL, OECD (2000) for RO, OECD (2002d) for SK; Vecernik (2001) for CZ

Regulations aimed at the integration of and providing job chances for **disadvantaged groups** often achieve the opposite results: Enterprises may choose between a special quota of disabled workers or a levy in Poland. Most enterprises vote for the latter. Latvia imposes quotas on employers concerning women re-entering the labour market, for labour market entrants, ex-convicts and workers less than five years from retirement age. All together this touches around one third of the labour force. In Lithuania, a legal employment guarantee is given to persons younger than 18 years, single parents with a child under 14, persons within five years of reaching the pension age, newly released prisoners and disabled persons. Quotas for employment of persons from these groups can be legally enforced. Disabled persons must account for at least 3% at firms with 20 or more employees and severely disabled persons for 0.2% in the Slovak Republic.

2.3.2. WORKING TIME

Working time flexibility is one way to decrease labour costs, especially if overtime is considered. From the employee's point of view, working time flexibility may lead to welfare gains resulting from a better match of actual working time and preferences. The availability of part time and fixed term contracts may induce more people to enter the labour market (in particular those who have to care for children or elderly persons) and may induce employers to increase labour demand. Moreover, these forms of work provide a way for new labour force entrants to achieve experience. Their advantage lies in the greater flexibility in organising production schedules and in the more advanced possibilities for reacting to variations in demand.

The degree of **working time flexibility** is varied across the accession countries. Low flexibility can be observed in Bulgaria and in Lithuania. In most countries, a shift away from regular full-time wage employment, which is still the most prevalent form, to irregular time-limited and flexible employment arrangements, including self employment, has been taking place and is still on-going. Normal working time normally corresponds to a 40-hours working week and shorter working periods for certain sectors (e.g. 37 hours in mining and around-the clock-operations in the Czech Republic). Overtime is usually restricted and an additional premium has to be paid. Special restrictions are applied to certain groups, such as young persons, pregnant women or minors.

Table 19: Regulations concerning overtime

	Overtime Time restrictions	Overtime pay	
Bulgaria	3 hours day/2 hours night work per day 30 hours day/20 hours night work per month	50% 75% 100%	on working days on holidays on official holidays
Czech Republic	150 hours p.a. if involuntary 416 hours p.a. if voluntary	n.a.	
Estonia	200 hours p.a. 4 hours per day	50% 60% 70% 150%	or additional time off; for evening work (6-10) for night work (10-6) work on public holidays
Poland		50% 100%	for first 4 hours, for hours at night, Sunday or other days of rest
Romania	8 hours per week	n.a.	
Slovak Rep.	8 hours per week 150 days per year	25%	

Sources: Arro (2001) for ES; Beleva-Tzanov (2001) for BG; OECD (2000) for RO; OECD (2001) for CZ; OECD (2002c) for PL; OECD (2002d) for SK.

Non-standard employment as a % of total employment is characterised by a wider spread in the accession countries than in the EU. **Part-time employment** is more pronounced in Estonia than in the Netherlands, the EU country with the highest part-time share, and is less pronounced in the Slovak Republic than in Greece, the EU country with the lowest part-time share. Several accession countries (e.g. Cyprus, Lithuania, Malta, Romania) have only recently changed legislation in order to increase incentives for and provide flexible forms of part-time work.

Table 20: Non-standard employment as a % of total employment **2001**

	Part-time	Fixed-term
Bulgaria	3.4	5.7
Cyprus	8.1	8.1
Czech Republic	4.3	6.9
Estonia	6.9	2.6
Hungary	3.3	6.4
Latvia	10.0	6.0
Lithuania	8.2	5.3
Poland	9.5	8.6
Romania	16.8	1.6
Slovak Republic	2.3	4.6
Slovenia	6.1	10.8
EU	17.9	13.4
Maximum	42.2 NL	31.7 ES
Minimum	4.0 EL	3.1 IE

Source: European Commission, 2002d

The incidence of **fixed-term contracts** is clearly below the lowest EU value in Poland, the Slovak Republic, Lithuania and Romania. Several European countries limit the use of fixed-term contracts to certain maximum periods, and fixed-term agreements are limited in about one-third of collective agreements in Bulgaria, Czech Republic, Hungary and the Slovak Republic and in almost half in Poland, thereby strengthening the position of insiders at the cost of outsiders.

Table 21: Regulations concerning fixed-term contracts

Bulgaria	Only 2 successive jobs
Czech Rep.	No limits for adults, not even disabled no temporary contracts for school graduates from secondary vocational education, apprentices under 18 - only if they ask for it
Estonia	Maximum duration is 5 years
Hungary	Regulated
Poland	Can only be renewed twice before being automatically transformed into contract of indefinite duration
Romania	Max. 24 months, allowed if parties agree to them in writing
Slovak Rep.	Restricted to 3 years (does not apply to firms with less than 20 employees)
Slovenia	Limited

Sources: Arro (2001) for EE; Cazes - Nesperova (2001) for CZ; IMF (2001), for BG; OECD (2000) for RO; OECD (2002d) for SK; Vecernik (2001) for CZ; Worldbank (2001b) for PL; JAPs for HU and SI

In Bulgaria, the proportion of fixed-term contracts amounted to 1/3 of all contracts in mid-2000 according to trade unions. Due to the application of the seniority principle, fixed-term contracts are characterised by lower wages. Such contracts seem to be widespread for unskilled workers in some sectors (e.g. forestry and tourism) in Romania. Increasing reliance on alternative forms of labour contracts is observed in Poland, particularly in sectors that account for most of the growth in employment over the last few years (30% of jobs in services in the private sector are self-employed or part time). These alternative forms are, however, not new - private, temporary labour contracts were already concluded under central planning in the 1980s.

2.3.3. SELF EMPLOYMENT

In the Candidate Countries, self employment as an other form of "non-standard" employment is not a strategy for the unskilled, but rather a labour market choice that brings high rewards. Enterpreneurs are consequently one group of winners of the transition. In all Candidate Countries, the self-employed account for the largest share of individuals in the top consumption group. The share of self employment in the Candidate Countries is similar to the (range of) ratios in the Member States (EBRD, 2000).

Table 22: Self employment in % of total employment, 2001

Bulgaria	13.7
Cyprus	20.6
Czech Republic	14.6
Estonia	6.7
Hungary	13.9
Latvia	10.3
Lithuania	15.9
Poland	22.5
Romania	25.7
Slovak Republic	8.4
Slovenia	11.8
EU	14.8
Maximum	43.3 GE
Minimum	5.0 SE

Source: European Commission, 2002d

2.3.4. FEMALE LABOUR PARTICIPATION AND EMPLOYMENT RATES

The high participation rates of women in the labour market during communism has continuously declined during the transition period, although employment rates of women in the transition countries are still high compared to many EU countries.[6] This is mainly due to a lack of possibilities to combine work and family life based, inter alia, on restrictive labour law.

[6] Equal treatment of men and women has to be guaranteed by law in order to fulfil the acquis communautaire.

Currently, women are over-represented in lower paid sectors and under-represented in the higher paid sectors in accession countries. The choice of study programmes is often determined by traditional patterns, although women have a higher level of education on average in many accession countries.

Measures to increase the participation of women in the labour market have covered several fields: Awareness raising, information and gender education is often used in order to address the different problems facing women. Many accession countries face problems due to lack of **flexible working patterns,** which are currently being addressed by national policies. In general, special provisions for parents including parental leave, reduced and flexible working hours, are made in the public service. Quotas for women returning to the labour force after maternity leave have to be fulfilled in Latvia. Parental leave was introduced as a new right for fathers in Estonia. The Polish labour code does not make any provision for substitute employees and hence creates problems for employers who have to find temporary replacement for workers on leave. As a number of laws provide privileges for women with children, which do not apply for men with or persons without children, gender discrimination in recruitment has been observed in Lithuania (see JAP Lithuania, 2002). The government now envisages a refinement of the legal provisions.

Access to affordable **childcare facilities** deteriorated in most accession countries during transition. The need to develop such facilities is particularly acute in Cyprus and Malta, where no public childcare facilities exist. Lithuanian parents face special difficulties in access to pre-school childcare.

2.4. EDUCATION AND SKILLS

Appropriate education and skills are a prerequisite for a competitive economy and there is a need to ensure that the skills acquired are suited to the needs of the economy. Job opportunities and wages tend to increase with skills. The virtue of lifelong learning is considered to go beyond economic competitiveness and job creation, by enabling people to cope with new challenges. One difficulty, especially faced in connection with education in the accession countries, is insufficient preparation for the transition from school to work. The hiring of school leavers often requires additional on-the-job training. Ethnic minorities seem to face special problems in all accession countries in acquiring appropriate skills.

2.4.1. SCHOOL EDUCATION

Public expenditures on education in the accession countries seem to be within the range of the GDP shares in EU countries. Public expenditure on education amounts to between 3.1% of GDP in Romania and 6.9% in Estonia.

Table 23: Public expenditure on education as % of GDP 2001

Accession countries**	5.0
Cyprus	5.9
Czech Republic	4.3
Estonia	6.9
Hungary	4.5
Lithuania	6.0
Latvia	5.9
Malta	5.0
Poland**	5.2
Romania	3.1
Slovak Republic	4.2
EU*	4.9
Max*	8.4 DK
Min	3.5 EL

Source: Eurostat, 2003a. *: 2000; **: 1999

As to indicators concerning school education, all accession countries with the exception of Slovenia achieve a higher score than the EU average in terms of average years of education. The variation of class size in the accession countries is substantial, but nevertheless in line with variation within the EU. Latvia has e.g. an average class size comparable to Austria and Belgium. In Poland, it is larger, but still comparable to that in Spain.[7]

Table 24: Basic school enrolment ratio % 1998

Bulgaria	94.3
Czech Rep.	97.6
Estonia	95.0
Hungary	99.2
Latvia	90.9
Lithuania	96.1
Poland	98.1
Romania	97.0
Slovak Rep.	93.9
Slovenia	98.2

Source: EBRD, 2001

Those leaving the educational system without sufficient skills for the workplace are also at risk for poverty and social exclusion. In 2002, the share of early school leavers was very divergent in the acceding countries. In general, male students suffered more from early drop-outs than female. Compared to the EU, however, the accession countries came off rather well.

[7] See Gundlach, (2002) and Knogler (2002).

Graph 2: Early school leavers not in further education and training, 2002

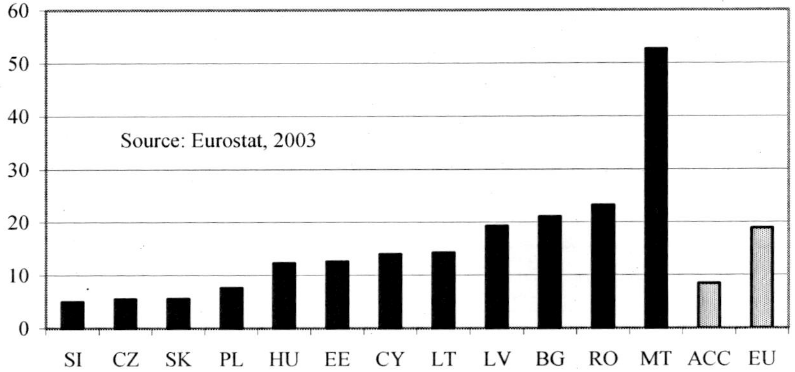

As to the number of tertiary graduates in science and technology, an indicator which tries to highlight the ability of a country to cope with the technical and scientific challenges in the knowledge society, the accession countries are within the range of the European countries. Lithuania has recorded an outstandingly high value for this indicator, which exceeds that of more than two third of European countries.

Table 25: Tertiary graduates in science and technology per 1000 inhabitants aged 20-29, 2001

Accession countries*	6.3
Bulgaria	7.9
Czech Republic	5.6
Estonia	7.3
Hungary*	3.7
Lithuania	13.1
Latvia	7.6
Malta	3.3
Poland	7.4
Romania	4.9
Slovenia	8.2
Slovak Republic	7.4
EU	
Median*	9.8
Max*	23.2 IE
Min*	1.8 LU

Source: Eurostat, 2003a.

Education seems to have concentrated too much on encyclopedic learning and less on the application of knowledge. Vocational training systems are now being developed and improved. They already existed in former times but were characterised by weak links between education and enterprises and in-depth specialisation. People in the accession countries do not yet perceive learning as lifelong process. Coherent strategies for lifelong learning are still lacking. Systems of continuing training are currently being set up, although a large number of providers already exist in Bulgaria, Poland and Latvia. Adult participation in lifelong learning in 2002 ranged from 1.1% in Romania to 9% in the Slovak Republic, which was the only country which exceeded the EU average. The direction of change was, however, not uniform, with some countries showing an increase and others a decrease in 2002.

Graph 3: Adult participation in lifelong learning 2002

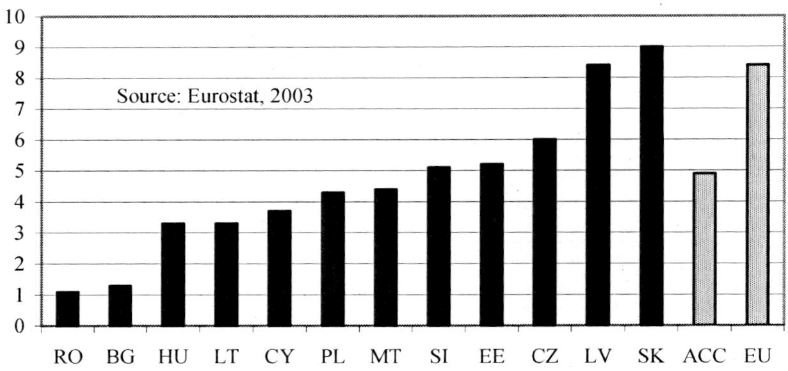

2.4.2. SKILLS

Workers in centrally planned economies tended to have received extensive technical education, but foreign investors have perceived a lack of adaptability and flexibility. They have complained especially about deficiencies at the level of managerial and skilled employment. The literacy scores of the adult working population in a number of central European countries were, however, very close to those in other OECD countries. Table 26 shows the latest results from the OECD PISA study which concentrates on 15 year olds. The countries are ranked on a scale with an average score of 500 points and a standard deviation of 100. Results are given for reading, mathematical and scientific literacy. Reading skills are not only important per se but also as a crucial prerequisite for lifelong learning. In this category, all Candidate Countries rank significantly below the OECD average, although some EU countries have a worse ranking. Mathematical literacy is considered to be important for analytical skills, logic skills and reasoning. The results for the Czech Republic do not differ significantly from the OECD average, but those for the others fall significantly below it. Finally, scientific literacy points to the capability to think scientifically, to understand scientific concepts, to use scientific knowledge, to identify questions and to draw conclusions. The accession countries come out best in this category. The Czech Republic significantly exceeds the OECD average. The figure for Hungary lies approximately at the OECD average and the others achieve results below the OECD average.

Table 26: PISA literacy scores 2000

	reading literacy	mathematical literacy	scientific literacy
Czech Republic	492	498	511
Hungary	480	488	496
Poland	479	470	483
Latvia	458	463	460
EU			
Max	546 FI	536 FI	538 FI
Min	441 LU	446 LU	443 LU

Source: EC, 2002c.

2.4.3. ACTIVE LABOUR MARKET POLICY

Activation plays a crucial role in the Emloyment Strategy and the Broad Economic Policy Guidelines. Member States are requested to intensify their efforts to develop preventive and employability-oriented strategies in order to be able to offer a new start (training, retraining, work practice, a job, guidance or counseling) to every unemployed adult within a year and to every unemployed young person within six months. In most accession countries, as in the EU, a shift from passive to active labour market policy can be observed during the last years. The shares of GDP spent on active labour market policies still tend to be rather low compared to EU countries, as can be seen in table 21.

Table 27: Expenditures on active labour market policy

	ALMP % of GDP	Year
Bulgaria	0.35	2001
Czech Republic	0.17	2000
Estonia	0.08	1999
Hungary	0.47	2000
Latvia	0.16	2000
Lithuania	0.09	2000
Malta	0.08	1999
Poland	0.20	2000
Romania	0.15	2001
Slovak Republic	0.18	2000
Slovenia	0.40 1.00	1998 target for 2006
EU		
Median	1.15	2000
Maximum	1.74 UK	2000
Minimum	0.46 EL	2000

Source: OECD (2002) for EU countries; OECD (2001a) for CZ, Worldbank (2001b) for PL; others: JAP.

As to the special **programmes**, active labour market policies include measures which are also used in EU countries. Each country has, however, a particular focus. Bulgaria puts great emphasis on temporary job schemes, especially in the public sector, as do Latvia, Lithuania, Poland, Slovenia and the Slovak Republic. Recruitment subsidies play a very modest role in Estonia and an important role in Bulgaria, Hungary, Lithuania, Poland and Slovenia. Support for self employment is granted in most countries. Training and re-training play a very important role in a wide range of countries (such as Cyprus, the Czech Republic, Estonia, Latvia, Poland, Romania, Slovenia) and a minor role in Bulgaria and the Slovak Republic. In the latter, training is usually provided to meet the needs of a specific employer. Romanian labour market policy puts great stress on support for small businesses in form of counselling and loans.

Disabled persons belong to **special target groups** in Cyprus, the Czech Republic, Estonia, Latvia and Slovenia. Special focus is placed on young unemployed persons in the Czech Republic, Romania and Estonia. The integration of non-Estonian-speakers is another important goal in Estonia. In Estonia and Poland, long-term unemployed receive special attention. Moreover, in Poland several special target groups are defined, such as women, lone parents, jobless households, school graduates, persons released from prisons, persons released from military service and miners losing employment in hard coal collieries. In Latvia, special job-seekers clubs for social-psychological rehabilitation have been introduced. Convicted persons and those released from prison are another important target group.

As **women** tend to suffer from longer unemployment spells than men, training programs for unemployed women and for women returning to the labour market after a long break are offered in most accession countries. In Poland, women make up the majority of participants in several active labour market programmes and special programmes are devoted to them. As women apparently face special problems in becoming self-employed, they receive special support in Estonia and Slovakia.

Concerning the **effectiveness** of active labour market policies, there is some evidence in the Czech Republic that these policies have lowered the length of unemployment for persons who would tend to have longer unemployment spells without this measure. Only 25% of the participants in Latvia found a job in 1997. The proportion increased to just over 50% in 2000. In Poland, the employment rate is higher and the unemployment spell shorter for those who have undertaken training. Temporary job schemes in Bulgaria seem to function more as an income support than as activation measures. A certain degree of cream skimming can be observed in the Slovak Republic. Women, low skilled and older unemployed face a lower chance of being accepted into such programmes (see EBRD, 2000).

3. Conclusions and Summary

During the transition period, job shedding took place in the public sector and in state-owned enterprises. Employment creation in the private sector has been and is clearly lagging behind. Unemployment and economic inactivity are both important problems in the labour market.

While challenges in the labour market of the accession countries do not differ fundamentally in nature from those in the EU Member States, the problems are often more severe. Low employment rates and high unemployment rates remain serious problems. This poor labour market performance may be attributed for the most part to the break down in economic activity and the restructuring of the economy. The types of labour market policies used do, however, not deviate much from that in the EU. Each of the accession countries has its own special problems (e.g. high net replacement ratio in the tax benefit system or strict employment protection legislation), but the same can be said from the EU countries as well. Some problems, such as a high tax burden and the labour market implications of an ageing society, are shared between current and future EU members.

Concerning the Lisbon and Stockholm targets, there is still a long way to go for the accession countries. In this respect, special emphasis must be put on increasing the employment rate of older workers and the overall employment rate.

4. References

Arro, R., Eamets, R., Järve, J., Kallaste, E., Philips, K. (2001), "Labour Market Flexibility and Employment Security - Estonia", ILO, Employment Paper, 25/2001.

Belena, I., Tzanov, V. (2001), "Labour Market Flexibility and Employment Security - Bulgaria", ILO, Employment Paper, 30/2001.

Boeri, T., Terrell, K. (2002), "Institutional Determinants of Labour Reallocation in Transition", Journal of Economic Perspectives - Volume 16, Number 1 Winter 2002, p. 51-76.

Bosworth, D., Dawkins, P., Stromback, T. (1996), "The Economics of the Labour Market", Addison Wesley Longman Ltd, Essex, 1996.

Cazes, S., Nesporova, A. (2001), "Towards excessive job insecurity in transition economies?" ILO, Employment Paper, 23/2001.

Corcoran, T. (2001), "Labour market trends, policies and institutions in the Candidate Countries", paper prepared for the Seminar on the Impact of Enlargement on the EU Labour Markets, Thursday 15 March 2001, Brussels.

Employment Service of Slovenia (ESS), "Annual Report 2001".

European Bank for Reconstruction and Development (2000), "Transition Report", London.

European Bank for Reconstruction and Development (2001), "Transition Report", London.

European Commission, Directorate General for Economic and Financial Affairs (2001a), "Employment protection legislation", Note to the Economic Policy Committee, D(2001) ECFIN /02/003, January 2001.

European Commission, Directorate General for Education and Culture, Directorate General for Employment and Social Affairs (2001b), "Summary and Analysis of the Feedback from the Candidate Countries as Part of the Consultation on the Commission's Memorandum on Lifelong Learning - Supporting Document to the Communication from the Commission Making a European Area of Lifelong Learning a Reality", prepared by the European Training Foundation (ETF), November 2001.

European Commission, Directorate General for Economic and Financial Affairs (2002a), "Evaluation of the 2001 Pre-Accession Economic Programmes of Candidate Countries", European Economy - Enlargement Papers, January 2002.

European Commission (2002b), "Industrial Relations in Europe 2002, Directorate General for Employment & Social Affairs, 2002.

European Commission, Directorate General for Education and Culture

(2002c), "European Report on Quality Indicators of Lifelong Learning - Fifteen Quality Indicators, Report based on the work of the Working Group on Quality Indicators", Brussels, June 2002.

European Commission, Directorate General for Employment & Social Affairs (2002d), "Employment in Europe", 2002.

European Commission (2003), "Progress on the implementation of the Joint Assessment Papers on employment policies in Candidate Countries", Communication from the Commission to the Council, the European Parliament, the European Economic and Social Committee and the Committee of the Regions, COM (2003), 37 final, Brussels, 30.1.2003.

Eurostat (2001), "Employment and Labour market in Central Europe", 2/2001.

Eurostat (2002), "Regional unemployment rates in the Central European Candidate Countries 2001", General Statistics, 6/2002.

Eurostat (2003a), "Structural Indicators", http://europa.eu.int/comm/eurostat/Public/datashop/print-product/EN?catalogue=Eurostat&product=1-structur-EN&mode=download, June 2003.

Eurostat (2003b), "Minimum Wages - EU Member States and Candidate Countries", Statistics in Focus, Theme 3 - 10/2003, January 2003.

Franz, W. (1996), "Arbeitsmarktökonomik", SpringerVerlag, Berlin et al.

Garibaldi, P., Makovec, M., Stoyanova, G. (2001), "From Transition to EU Accession - The Bulgarian Labor Market During the 1990s", World Bank Technical Paper No. 494, May 2001.

Guger, A. (2002), "Internationale Lohnstückkostenposition 2001 unverändert", WIFO-Monatsberichte, 9/2002.

Gesellschaft für Versicherungswissenschaft und -gestaltung e.v. (GVG) (2003), "Study on the Social Protection Systems in the 13 accession countries", Study financed by the European Commission - Employment and Social Affairs DG, January 2003.

Gundlach, E. (2002), "Human Capital Formation: What Pre-Accession Countries Can Learn from the EU Experience", The IPTS Report,

No. 65, June 2002.

IMF (2001), "Labour Markets in Hard-Peg Accession Countries: The Baltics and Bulgaria", IMF Country Report No. 01/100, 2001.

Joint Assessment of Employment Priorities In Poland, Jan 2001.

Joint Assessment of Employment Priorities of the Czech Republic, May 2000.

Joint Assessment of Employment Priorities of Slovenia, July 2000.

Joint Assessment of Employment Priorities in Estonia, March 2001.

Joint Assessment of Employment Priorities of Malta, October 2001.

Joint Assessment of Employment Priorities of Hungary, November 2001.

Joint Assessment of Employment Priorities in the Slovak Republic, November 2001.

Joint Assessment of Employment Priorities in Cyprus, December 2001.

Joint Assessment of Employment Priorities in Lithuania, February 2002.

Keane, M.P., Prasad, E.S. (2002), "Changes in the Structure of Earnings During the Polish Transition", IZA, Discussion Paper No. 496, May 2002.

Knogler, M. (2001), "Die Arbeitsmärkte der Beitrittskandidaten vor dem Hintergrund der EU-Osterweiterung", Working Paper Nr. 228, Osteuropa-Institut München, Februar 2001.

Knogler, M. (2002), "Arbeitsmarkpolitische Herausforderungen in den Ländern der EU-Beitrittskandidaten", Working Paper Nr. 235, Osteuropa-Institut München, Februar 2002.

Kwiatkowski, E., Socha, M.W., Szanderska, U. (2001), "Labour Market Flexibility and Employment Security - Poland", ILO, Employment Paper, 28/2001.

Mortensen, J., Richter, S. (2000), "Measurement of Costs and Benefits of Accession of the European Union for Selected Countries in Central and Eastern Europe", The Vienna Institute for International Economic Studies, January 2000.

Nesporova, A. (2002), "Unemployment in the transition economies", Paper prepared for the ECE Spring Seminar 2002; Employment Strategy Department, ILO.

OECD (2000), "Labour Market and Social Policies in Romania".

OECD (2001), "Economic Surveys: Czech Republic".

OECD (2002a), "Benefits and Wages - OECD Indicators".

OECD (2002b), "Economic Surveys: Hungary".

OECD (2002c), "Economic Surveys: Poland".

OECD (2002d), "Economic Surveys: Slovac Republic".

OECD (2002e), "Economic Surveys: The Netherlands 2001/2002", Volume 2002, Issue 3.

OECD (2002f), "Economic Surveys: Greece 2001/2002", Volume 2002, Issue 13.

OECD (2002g), "Employment Outlook", July 2002.

Rashid, M., Rutkowski, J.J. (2001), "Labor Markets in Transition Economies: Recent Developments and Future Challenges", SP Discussion Paper No. 0111, Social Protection, World Bank, April 2001.

Rutkowski, J.J. (2001), "Earnings Inequality in Transition Economies of Central Europe - Trends and Patterns During the 1990s", SP Discussion Paper No. 0117, Social Protection, World Bank, July 2001.

Schneider, F. (2002), "The Size and Development of the Shadow Economies of 22 Transition and 21 OECD Countries, IZA, Discussion Paper No. 514, June 2002.

Svejnar, J. (2002), "Transition Economies: Performance and Challenges", Journal of Economic Perspectives - Volume 16, Number 1 Winter 2002, p. 3-28.

Vecernik, J. (2001), "Labour Market Flexibility and Employment Security - Czech Republic", ILO, Employment Paper, 27/2001.

Worldbank (1999), "Slovenia: Economic Transformation and EU Accession, Main report".

Worldbank (2001a), "Bulgaria - The Dual Challenge of Transition and Accession", A World Bank Country Study, May 2001.

Worldbank (2001b), "Poland's Labor Market - The Challenge of Job Creation", A World Bank Country Study, October 2001.

Worldbank (2002), "Slovak Republic - Living Standards, Employment, and Labour Market Study", A World Bank Country Study, February 2002.

5. *ANNEX: DETERMINATION OF WAGES*

Minimum wage determination in Candidate Countries

The minimum wage is determined by the **government after consulting the social partners** in Bulgaria, Hungary - where it was previously set by a tripartite council - and Lithuania. The minimum wage in Bulgaria can be re-negotiated at the branch or regional level, but it may not be lower than the nationally set minimum wage. In Poland, the Minister for Labour and Social Policy sets the minimum wage in a regulation based on a recommendation of the **tripartite commission**, which itself bases its recommendation on forecasts of inflation and wage increase and an analysis of household budget surveys. For young workers covered by special vocational training contracts a special minimum wage exists. In Romania, **collective framework agreements** are negotiated each year at the national level for each sector which set the minimum gross wage for an unqualified worker. At the local level social partners determine an enterprise-specific minimum wage at least as high as the minimum wage agreed nationally and qualification coefficients which determine, when multiplied by the enterprise minimum wage, the basic wage for each job. A law establishes the minimum wage in Estonia. In Latvia the minimum wage is subject to revision based on an agreement among the **social partners**. An indexation mechanism with direct involvement of the social partners is used in the Slovak Republic, thereby taking into account the evolution of the average wage and changes in the official subsistence minimum income. In Slovenia, the minimum wage was introduced in 1995 and has since then been increased at the same rate as the basic wage from the collective agreement, which compensates for 85% of the inflation in the previous year. Up to the point where it reaches 58% of the average wage in the manufacturing sector, an additional increase based on the growth of GDP in the previous year is taken into account.

The **evolution** of minimum wages has differed a lot among the accession countries. E.g. in the Czech Republic, the minimum wage was not adjusted for a long period thereby allowing it to be overtaken by the level of social benefits. A stepwise adjustment was subsequently agreed. The monthly statutory wage almost doubled in two years in Hungary in 2001 and 2002. Consequently, the proportion of wage earners receiving the statutory minimum wage increased from 10% in the business sector two years ago to one third in 2002. The finally-imposed wage level was partly paid by the enterprises "under the table" even before the increase of the minimum wage. The increase hurt especially the low labour cost industries such as agriculture, tourism and textiles. As a reaction, increased use of part time work was observed. Moreover, labour subsidies were paid to the sectors most affected by the minimum wage. In Bulgaria, the minimum wage amounted to 54% of the average wage at the beginning of the 90s; it decreased to 27% in 1997 and again increased thereafter to 35% in 2001.

Wage bargaining mechanisms and institutions

Tri-partite co-operation-councils exist in Bulgaria at national, industry and local levels. Until recently, anticipated inflation was a more important factor in wage bargaining than productivity trends. In Cyprus, most bargaining takes place at the industrial and enterprise levels. A **mixed system** of wage formation at industry and firm levels is applied in the Czech Republic. The Czech government makes a decision on whether or not to impose the increases agreed in some firms on employees and employers in other firms. In 2000 the Minister for Labour and Social Affairs ordered 1900 non-unionised firms in the construction sector to implement the agreement reached in unionised firms. More or less the same rights are given to the Slovakian minister, who can set collective agreements as binding for employers who are not members of the organisation in the same sector and with similar economic and social conditions. Collective bargaining between employers and trade unions takes place at sectoral and national levels in the Slovak Republic. In Slovenia, the responsibility for wage bargaining at the sector and enterprise levels remains with the social partners. A law ensures that wage growth lags behind productivity growth. In Malta, the government has a mediation role in wage disputes in the private sector.

Wage bargaining at the enterprise level is predominant in Estonia. The same is true for Hungary, where around 45% of the workforce in enterprises with up to five employees are covered by collective agreements concluded at the enterprise level. **Decentralised wage bargaining** has contributed in Hungary to a more flexible wage structure where education and skills are better reflected. In Latvia, the tripartite social dialogue is well developed, but the bipartite discussion and collective bargaining lacks clearly behind. Employers organisations and trade unions cover a relatively small share of all employers and employees. Nevertheless, collective agreements on wages and labour conditions are settled in more than half of the enterprises where a trade union is represented. Bipartite collective bargaining is currently developing at the sectoral level. The new labour law states that a sectoral agreement, which covers at least 60% of the workforce in a sector, will be binding for all employers and employees in this sector. In Lithuania, wages are also a matter for free bargaining between employers and employees. The law states, however, that wages should reflect supply of and demand for the profession, the amount and quality of the work and requests additional payment for hazardous working conditions, overtime and work at night or during holidays. Wages in Poland are negotiated at the enterprise level, taking into account the guideline annual rate determined by the national tripartite commission for social and economic matters, which is mostly seen as a minimum rate. In Romania, the government lays down the institutional framework for the wage negotiations, which are mostly carried out at the enterprise level. Only relatively large trade unions and employer associations are allowed to participate in the collective bargaining. The law permits only one collective agreement in each enterprise, which is binding for all workers regardless of whether they are members of a trade union or not. A trade union in an enterprise may only negotiate if it represents 50% of the workers or belongs to an association, which has been found to be representative at the national level.

Degree of corporatism

In Cyprus, the **collective agreements** cover wages, pay systems, overtime and sickness pay, holidays, and rules for recruitment and dismissals. Employers from non-unionised firms in the Czech Republic are required to organise **work councils** if so requested by employees. Employees elected to these councils are paid even if they do not carry out their normal work. Employers must engage in lengthy consultations with these councils when important business decisions are to be made (e.g. lay-offs, technical change, health and safety). If the workers fail to elect a work council, the employer must negotiate with each worker individually. The new labour code in Slovakia provides for the establishment of employees' councils representing all employees in firms where no trade unions operate. In Estonia, the employer is **not obliged to initiate negotiations** nor to conclude a collective agreement; the employees have no right to demand the initiation of negotiations or the conclusion of an agreement. Agreements may be concluded at enterprise, branch or state level and may be bilateral or tripartite. The agreement is extended to the members of the workers' organisation that concluded the agreement. In practice, it is generally extended to all workers of the enterprise. If an agreement is concluded at the branch level, it might also become effective in enterprises where the trade union has no members, but the employer is represented in the employer's union. However, a representative of a branch trade union may not ask for the conclusion of an agreement from an enterprise that has no union. Not only trade unions, but also workers' representatives representing non-members may conclude a collective agreement. In fact, the number of collective agreements concluded is small and strikes are rare. This may be partly explained by the fact that there are simply no effective trade unions.

Some **special features** concerning wage systems can be observed in several countries: In Bulgaria bonuses still play an important role in the earnings. In the Czech Republic, the government has to pay the outstanding wages of former employees of bankrupt firms. This creates an incentive for firms to leave wages unpaid. Real wage moderation and productivity improvements in Romania have been led more by product market competition than by the labour market situation. Private firms pay lower average wages than state-owned firms and tend to have a more unequal wage distribution.

The Quality of Public Finances in the Acceding Countries

Kari Varis and Lauri Taro

1. Introduction

At the moment, most acceding countries (ACs) are running fiscal deficits. Although fiscal adjustment has been part of the stabilisation policy, deficits have remained high and are perhaps facing additional upward pressure due to e.g. weakened economic growth and rising expenditure needs. Public debt levels are in general relatively low but it is noteworthy that in several countries debt levels have been increasing somewhat in recent years. Table 1 presents the deficit and graph 1 the debt developments in the ACs.

Table 1: General government balance (% of GDP)

	1998*	1999	2000	2001	2002	2003p
Czech Republic	-4.5	-3.7	-4.0	-5.5	3.9	5.8
Estonia	-0.4	-4.0	-0.4	0.2	1.3	-0.3
Hungary	-8.0	-5.6	-3.0	-4.7	-9.2	-4.5
Latvia	-0.7	-5.3	-2.7	-1.6	-3.0	-3.1
Lithuania	-3.1	-5.7	-2.6	-2.2	-2.0	-2.1
Poland	-2.3	-1.5	-1.8	-3.0	-4.1	-4.0
Slovak Republic	-4.7	-6.4	-10.4	-7.3	-7.2	-4.9
Slovenia	-2.3	-2.2	-3.3	-2.8	-2.6	-1.4

Source: Fiscal notifications 2003, * Fiscal notifications 2002; p planned.

The ACs are going to meet considerable challenges, as they improve their basic infrastructure and develop their welfare systems. The main avenue in promoting the quality of public finances should be redirecting public funds so that these challenges will be met and public finances can better support economic growth and other Lisbon goals.

Once EU members, the ACs will enter the EU economic policy coordination framework. In the 2002 Council recommendation for the Broad Economic Policy Guidelines (BEPGs), it was noted that to maximise the contribution of public finances to growth and employment and the achievement of the goals agreed in Lisbon and Stockholm, all Member States must achieve and sustain sound budgetary positions. An appropriate balance and sequencing have to be drawn between running down public debt, cutting taxes and continuing to finance public investment in key areas. According to the 2002 BEPGs, the Member States should:

i. *pursue efforts to make tax and benefit systems more employment friendly;*
ii. *promote the quality of public expenditure by redirecting funds towards physical and human capital accumulation and research and development;*
iii. *enhance the efficiency of public spending by institutional and structural reforms;*
iv. *improve the long-term sustainability of public finances by pursuing the comprehensive three-pronged strategy, of raising employment rates, reducing public debt and adapting pension systems;*
v. *reform pension policies so as to secure the long-term financial sustainability, to safeguard the adequacy of pensions and meet changing societal needs; and*
vi. *pursue tax co-ordination further.*

Graph 1: General government debt (% of GDP)

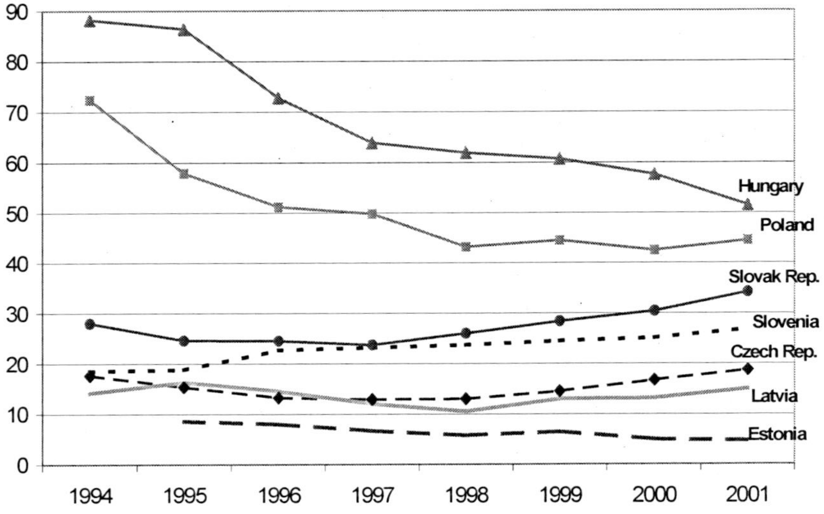

Source: EBRD.

This paper attempts to raise some preliminary thoughts as to what the current and future challenges and risks facing the ACs in the area of public finances are. Pension questions are dealt with separately.

2. *THE STRUCTURE OF PUBLIC FINANCES*

The overall level and composition of revenues and expenditures in the acceding countries resembles that of the present Member States, although significant differences for individual countries can be found.

The ratio of public expenditure to GDP remains relatively high in most of the ACs, at above 40% in 2001. However, total government expenditure declined by several percentage points of GDP in the late 1990s in those countries that were in transition. Activities carried out by the government were reduced, state-owned enterprises privatised to a varying degree and complex systems of taxes and subsidies meant to equalise incomes across different enterprises and sectors reformed or dismantled.

In the 2002 PEPs, most ACs envisaged lower deficits and a continued decline in GDP ratios for both public expenditures and revenues in the medium-term. This kind of a scenario is, nevertheless, challenged by the present weakness in the global and in the European economy and the mounting expenditure pressures rising from e.g. EU and NATO membership.

Table 2: General government finances (% of GDP)

	Revenue		Expenditure		Balance		Primary balance	
	2001	2005	2001	2005	2001	2005	2001	2005
Cyprus	40.5	42.2	43.5	42.5	-3.0	-0.3	2.6	4.8
Czech Rep.	42.1	41.3	47.1	46.8	-5.0	-5.5	-3.8	-3.6
Estonia	38.6	38.4	38.4	38.4	0.2	0.0	0.5	0.3
Hungary	46.1	42.5	50.2	45.0	-4.1	-2.5	0.2	0.7
Latvia	41.4	38.6	43.0	40.6	-1.6	-2.0	-1.0	-1.1
Lithuania	34.2	36.1	36.1	37.6	-1.9	-1.5	-0.2	0.0
Malta	37.4	35.8	44.4	38.8	-7.0	-3.1	-3.4	0.2
Poland	41.8	42.2	45.3	44.5	-3.5	-2.2	-0.6	1.5
Slovak Rep.	41.2	39.8	46.6	41.8	-5.4	-2.6	-2.0	0.4
Slovenia	43.1	42.5	45.6	43.3	-2.5	-0.8	-0.5	0.9
EU	46.4	-	47.2	-	-0.8	-	2.9	-

Source: PEPs 2002.

On the revenue side, total tax income in the ACs averaged about 35% of GDP in 2000. Privatisation of state assets has played an important role as an additional source of income in many of the countries. The cumulative amount of privatisation receipts varies considerably from country to country, between 3 and 30% of GDP, which reflects both the approaches chosen in large-scale privatisation as well as the attractiveness of the assets on offer. Privatisation of the corporate sector is for a large part completed in the most advanced countries.

Table 3: Structure of general government revenue in 2000 (% of GDP)

	Czech Rep.	Es-tonia	Hungary	Lat-via	Lithuania	Po-land	Slovak Rep.	Slove-nia	Euro-zone
Current revenue	39.2	38.7	41.8	36.8	30.4	41.6	36.6	41.5	45.0
Tax revenue	36.7	35.8	36.2	31.3	28.5	39.9	34.1	39.2	44.9
Personal income tax	5	7.8	7.2	6	7.8	4.6	4.6	7.6	9.9
Corpo-rate income tax	3.9	1.0	2.2	1.7	0.7	2	3	-	3
Social security contri-butions	14.7	12.4	9.8	10.7	7.1	8.7	13	13.6	15.9
Prop-erty tax	0.5	0.4	0.9	1	0.6	-	-	2.3	1.5
Indirect tax	12.6	14.2	16	11.9	11.7	11.4	13.5	15.7	13.6
Totoal public revenue	40.6	-	44.5	-	-	41.6	46.1	-	-

Sources: IMF/EU, OECD, Finmin of Poland

Financing the scale of public expenditure - not much different from that of the present Member States - lays a heavy burden on the tax base, which is narrower in the ACs. Social security contributions take a large share of total labour costs.

Nominal tax rates for labour and capital incomes are rather high, while many exemptions and tax evasion reduce effective rates. The distortions caused by high rates of taxation on labour are a serious impediment to a job-intensive growth strategy, according to the IMF and the EU Commission. There is a general intention in the tax policies, as laid out in the 2002 PEPs, to gradually shift the tax burden from labour and capital towards consumption. As the nominal VAT rates are already close to or at EU rates, boosting effective consumption tax income should take place mainly through a broadening of the tax base and by higher excise duties. Furthermore, there is a need to improve tax administration and the effectiveness of tax collection. A significant lowering of company taxation is planned according to the PEPs.

Table 4: Value Added Tax and Corporate Income Tax rates in 2002

	VAT	Corporate income tax
Cyprus	10	23/28
Czech Republic	22	31
Estonia	18	0*/26
Hungary	25	18
Latvia	18	25
Lithuania	18	15
Malta	15	35
Poland	22	28
Slovak Republic	23	25
Slovenia	20	25
EU min.	15	-

Source: International Bureau of Fiscal Documentation, EU Commission; * reinvested profit;

As for the expenditure side of budgets, spending on public services and social transfers as a percentage of GDP is at comparable levels with that of the present Member States. Some ACs appear to spend more on services and less on transfers, while others do the opposite. Also needs differ, for example poverty rates are high in some ACs, but low in others. In most cases, it takes time before pension and health insurance schemes adopted by the ACs are mature and can fully contribute to social security.

The World Bank estimates that up to 80% of government expenditures in these countries is rigid in the sense that it is determined by rules outside the budget bill process. These are mainly expenditures in the areas of defence, old age and disability pensions and transfers to local governments. Such rigidity is often compounded by indexation clauses for pensions and public sector wages.

Public investment levels are higher in the ACs than in the present Member States, due to the poor state of infrastructure. Old networks and utilities of the transition countries from the period of heavily subsidised energy, housing and transport prices are ill-suited for the needs and standards of a market economy. For example, rail networks are extensive and heavily staffed, while road networks remain inadequate. Telecommunications services are still vastly undersupplied, especially for households. The ACs face considerable challenges in replacing old technology and building new infrastructure networks. In the 2002 PEPs, investment expenditure is foreseen to be maintained at a level of 3% of GDP, on average.

Table 5: Structure of general government expenditure as a share of GDP in 2000

	Czech Rep.	Estonia	Hungary	Latvia	Lithuania	Poland *	Slovak Rep.	Slovenia	Eurozone
Current expenditure	38.4	36.3	39.9	36.6	30.4	-	38.2	39.2	43.8
Government consumption	8.7	24.6	14.4	16.1	16.6	15	17.6	17.6	19.8
Interest payments	1.1	0.3	6.1	1.1	1.7	3	2.7	1.5	3.7
Subsides and current transfers	28.6	11.4	19.4	18.9	12.1	-	17.9	20.1	19.8
Subsides	8.1	0.8	2.8	5	0.2	-	4	1.5	1.4
Current transfers	20.5	10.6	16.6	13.9	11.9	-	13.9	17.9	18.4
Capital expenditure	5.9	3.2	7.1	4	1.9	2.8	3.9	4.1	1
Total public expenditure	46.1	40.1	47.5	40.6	32.3	45.5	52.2	43.3	44.8

Sources: IMF/EU, OECD, Finmin of Poland; * 2001

3. MACRO-ECONOMIC STABILITY OF PUBLIC FINANCE

Accession countries will enter the EU as Member States with a derogation. They will assume the EMU framework including adherence to the provisions of the Stability and Growth Pact. They are expected to join the exchange rate mechanism ERM II, although not necessarily immediately after accession, and eventually to adopt the euro. Before adopting the euro, their macro-economic stability will be assessed with the help of the Maastricht nominal convergence criteria. Fulfilment of these criteria requires simultaneous price, fiscal and exchange rate stability.

Many of the ACs have fiscal deficits and rapid growth rates of public expenditure, which can be contained only under rapid real and nominal economic growth. These policies may, however, turn out to be unsustainable under periods of slower GDP growth and inflation. Presently, several ACs are, in fact, facing this kind of a situation, as they are under increasing pressure to bring about a consolidation of their public finances in the coming years.

The gross public debt situations are influenced by privatisation incomes and other transitional phenomena, which mask the underlying trends. Some countries also had the advantage of starting from a low level of indebtedness[1], while others have debt levels closer to those of the old Member States. Without corrective measures the presently quite manageable debt positions may deteriorate quickly in the countries currently running large deficits.

International disinflation and ACs' strive for the fulfilment of the convergence criteria are rewarded in the form of lower interest rates for government bonds. On the other hand, for most ACs fulfilment of the criteria would require substantial fiscal (or monetary) tightening, which could slow down real convergence or postpone it further in future.

---

[1] E.g. the Baltic countries, as Russia inherited all of Soviet Union debt.

Structural change and transitional costs due to the EU membership make fiscal stability assessment particularly difficult. Deficiencies in the quality of data complicate it further. There are good reasons to tread carefully in drawing any strong conclusions on the basis of partial information.

Sustainable convergence should be the ultimate goal for the new Member States. To achieve that, they need to maintain a judicious macroeconomic policy mix which allows their economies to catch up, while maintaining public finances in good balance. Sustainability also requires that long-term challenges deriving from unfavourable age structure of population are addressed duly. It would appear evident that some of the new member countries would be ready for joining ERM II at an earlier date than others. Differences among the new Member States and the nature of the procedure imply that decisions are taken on a case-by-case basis.

Table 6: EMU Convergence

	Price stability, avg. of period, %yoy			General gov. balance % of GDP			General gov. debt % of GDP		
	2001	**2002**	**2003**	**2001**	**2002**	**2003**	**2001**	**2002**	**2003**
Ref. value	3.6	3	2.8	-3	-3	-3	60	60	60
Cyprus	2	2.8	4.3	-3	-3.5	-4	54.6	-	-
Czech Rep.	4.7	1.4	1.5	-5.5	-6.5	-6.3	19.4	23.3	26.3
Estonia	5,8	3.6	3.5	0.5	1.3	-0.5	5.4	5.1	4.8
Hungary	9.2	5.3	5	-4.2	-9.1	-4.9	51.8	53.3	54.8
Latvia	2.5	1.9	2.5	-1.9	-2.5	-2.9	13.8	13.9	14
Lithuania	1.3	0.3	1	-2.3	-1.8	-1.9	29.1	28.4	28.6
Malta	2.9	2.2	2.7	-7	-6.1	-5.2	65.4	66.6	65.6
Poland	5.5	1.9	1.1	-3.1	-4.2	-4.2	42.9	48	46.1
Slovak Rep.	7.3	3.3	8.8	-5.4	-7.7	-5.3	42.7	34.5	34.1
Slovenia	8.5	7.5	6	-2.5	-1.8	-1.5	28.4	31	32.4

Sources: European Commission Forecast spring 2003, Deutsche Bank Research 2003, Ameco 2003. f = forecast

Credit ratings for sovereign bonds measure investor confidence in a broader sense. Not only the rate of indebtedness, but also confidence in economic policies and institutions more generally together with the quality of assets and the extent of contingent liabilities, among other things, influence the rating. Credit ratings for the ACs are presented in Table 7.

Table 7: Credit ratings in May 2003 (local currency debt / foreign currency debt)

	Moody's	S&P	Fitch
Slovenia	Aa3/Aa3	AA/A+	AA/A+
Cyprus	A2/A2	AA-/A	AA/A+
Hungary	A1/A1	A/A-	A+/A-
Estonia	A1/A1	A-/A-	A+/A-
Malta	A3/A3	AA-/A	AA-/A
Czech Rep.	A1/A1	A+/A-	A/BBB+
Poland	A2/A2	A/BBB+	A+/BBB+
Latvia	A2/A2	A-/BBB+	A/BBB
Slovak Rep.	A3/A3	A-/BBB	A-/BBB
Lithuania	Baa1/Baa1	A-/BBB+	A-/BBB

Source: Bloomberg. Scale used by Moody's, Standard & Poor's and Fitch Group: Aaa/AAA, Aa1/AA+, Aa2/AA, Aa3/AA-, A1/A+, A2/A, A3/A-, Baa1/BBB+, Baa2/BBB, Baa3/BBB- etc.

4. *PRELIMINARY FINDINGS*

The acceding countries face several medium-term risks and challenges, which may not have been fully addressed in the 2002 PEP budget projections. Here are some preliminary observations:

1. It is vital that the availability and quality of public sector data for Candidate Countries be improved to allow a more detailed assessment.

2. For most ACs the present economic slowdown has increased deficits from those presented in the latest PEPs, thus increasing the need for budgetary consolidation.

3. Privatisation has significantly supported state budgets, but now its role is declining. The possibilities for expenditure savings by transferring costly activities from public to private sector have largely been exhausted. This may influence the public finance developments in the future.

4. A large part of the FDI inflows has been attracted by the opportunities offered by privatisation. Now that these opportunities are decreasing, FDI inflows may diminish, unless stronger incentives for new private sector investment are introduced. The possibly resulting lower nominal and effective corporate tax rates would add to the pressures to broaden the tax base and avoid too much tax burden remaining on labour income; especially when taking into account the simultaneously intensifying tax competition.

5. On the expenditure side, spending pressures abound. Part of the expenditure increase is automatic or obligatory. EU membership will raise income, but also augments public spending. There will be costs due to new institutions, more administration as well as higher standards and requirements. In many ACs, military spending requirements will rise with NATO membership.

6. The need for public investment expenditure will remain high in the foreseeable future. High level of investment is necessary for a rapid real convergence by the acceding countries. In their PEPs, all ACs seem to design their policies in a way to maximise the use of EU structural funds, which could lead to the risks that (a) this kind of prioritisation will lead to a sub-optimal investment structure; and (b) the attractiveness of EU funding will lead to a too high level of investment and public investment expenditure due to additionality.

7. Social indicators (male life-expectancy, poverty rates) reveal a need for economic reform, but also for better social and health services in many countries and regions. This keeps up public expenditure pres-

sure. Education expenditure should also be a priority in these countries to enable them to catch up with the present Member States. Moreover, it is to be expected that prices and wages converge gradually towards the EU-level also in the public sector. To cope with the twin challenge of the rapidly increasing public expenditure pressures and fulfilment of the higher EU standards on the public services, the ACs need to put special emphasis on improving the efficiency of their public services.

5. *References*

IMF (2002), "Into the EU, Policy Frameworks in Central Europe".

Deutsche Bank Research (2003), "EU Enlargement Monitor No. 10".

EBRD (2002), "Transition report", London.

European Commission (2002), "Public Finances in EMU 2002", European Economy No3/2002.

European Commission (2003), "Ameco database".

European Commission (2003), "Economic Forecasts for the Candidate Countries", Spring 2003.

International Bureau of Fiscal Documentation (2002), "Taxation & Investment in Central and East European Countries".

Ministries of Finance of the Candidate Countries (2002), "The Pre-Accession Economic Programme 2002".

Ministries of Finance of the Candidate Countries (2002), "The Fiscal Notification 2002".

OECD (2002); "Economic Outlook 2002".

Demographic Outlook and Pension Reform Challenges in the Accession Countries

Micheline Lambrecht, Felix Lowinski, Dominique Simonis, Patrick van Brusselen[1]

1. Aim

The population of the present EU Member States will undergo substantial changes in size and age profile in the coming decades which may have profound implications for the long-term sustainability of public finances, as shown in the EPC report of October 2001 on budgetary challenges posed by ageing populations.[2]

In the accession countries, against the backdrop of public spending on pensions equivalent to between 4% and 13% of national income in 2000 and a demographic outlook for most countries similar to that for the present Member States, the long-term sustainability of public finances is an issue that deserves increased attention, even if debt ratios at present in many cases are lower than in the present Member States.

In line with the goal of the Lisbon strategy to ensure that public finances contribute to growth and employment, the relevance of the sustainability of public finances arises from the direct economic and financial implications of ageing, but also from possible crowding-out effects relative to other urgent categories of government spending. The present note presents a very first and preliminary analysis of the issue only.

---

[1] The paper benefited from comments by Henri Bogaert, the chairman of the Ageing Working Group of the EU's Economic Policy Committee, and Heinz Scherrer from the secretariat of the Economic Policy Committee.

[2] EPC/ECFIN/655/01 of 24 October 2001.

2. THE DEMOGRAPHIC OUTLOOK

At present, there are no Eurostat demographic projections available for the Candidate Countries. Recent UN population forecasts show that in most Candidate Countries the working age population (aged between 20 and 64), the number of elderly persons aged 65 or over, and the old-age dependency ratio would follow broadly similar trends as in the present Member States but actually surpassing EU levels by around 2040 (see Graph 1 and the Table on the old-age dependency ratio in Annex 1; Slovenia and the Czech Republic would surpass EU dependency ratio levels even earlier).

Graph 1: Old-age dependency ratio, 2000-50

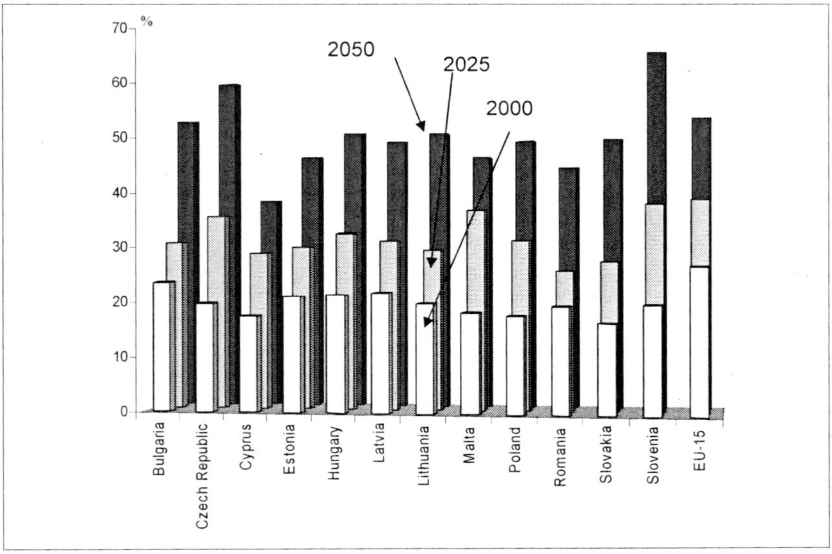

Source: UN population projections 2002 (EU-15: Eurostat population projections 1995 - baseline scenario). Note: The old-age dependency ratio is defined as persons aged 65 or over as a percentage of the working-age population (aged 15-64).

The demographic outlook in the Candidate Countries is as follows (see Tables 1-3 and Annex 1):

- **Total population**: The aggregate population of the twelve accession countries (i.e. not including Turkey) decreases under the influence of negative natural and migration balances, while the still positive natural and migration balances of the EU-15 will help to keep those of the EU-27 positive. In the long run (2050), according to the UN population forecast, the total population of the EU-27 would decrease further by 6.8%, as compared with 3% for the EU-15.

- **Fertility and life expectancy**: With the exception of Cyprus and Malta, which have fertility and mortality parameters similar to those of the present EU Member States, the accession countries have very low fertility and lower life expectancies (LE) at birth than the present Member States. This leads to negative natural balances.

- **Migration**: With the exception of Cyprus and Malta and the notable positive migration balance of Hungary, most of the accession countries have a strong negative migration balance, especially Bulgaria (the estimation for Bulgaria must though be treated with care).

Table 1: Demographic parameters in 2001 (mostly estimations)

	Total fertility rate	LE at birth - men	LE at birth - women
Bulgaria	1.2	68.2	75.3
Czech Rep.	1.14	72.1	78.5
Cyprus	1.79	75.3	80.4
Estonia	1.34	65.1	76
Hungary	1.32	67.7	75.7
Latvia	1.24	64.5	75.6
Lithuania	1.25	67.5	77.7
Malta	1.51	75.1	79.3
Poland	1.29	70.2	78.4
Romania	1.2	67.7	74.8
Slovakia	1.21	69.1	77.2
Slovenia	1.22	72.3	79.7
EU-15	1.47	75.3	81.4
maximum	Ireland = 1.98	Sweden = 77.5	France = 83
minimum	Italy = 1.24	Ireland = 73	Ireland = 78.5

Source: Eurostat

Table 2: Population change in 2001 (mostly estimations; in '000)

	Natural balance[1]	Migration balance	Change in population
Bulgaria	-44.2	-23.9	-68.1
Czech Rep.	-17.0	-8.6	-25.6
Cyprus	3.3	3.1	6.4
Estonia	-5.9	0.2	-5.7
Hungary	-35.0	14.0	-21.0
Latvia	-13.3	-1.4	-14.7
Lithuania	-8.9	-2.6	-11.5
Malta	0.9	2.3	3.2
Poland	5.0	-16.7	-11.7
Romania	-39.2	-4.9	-44.1
Slovakia	-0.8	1	0.2
Slovenia	-0.8	4.7	3.9
AC-12	-155.9	-32.8	-188.7
EU-14	403.7	1160.3	1564.0
EU-27	247.8	1127.5	1375.3

[1] Birth-deaths

Source: Eurostat (migration balance for Bulgaria adjusted)

Table 3: Evolution of the population 2000-2050 (in '000 000)

			Change	
	2000	**2050**	**Absolute**	**%**
Bulgaria	7,9	4,5	-3,4	-43,0
Czech Rep.	10,3	8,4	-1,8	-17,9
Cyprus	0,8	0,9	0,1	16,1
Estonia	1,4	0,8	-0,6	-46,1
Hungary	10,0	7,5	-2,5	-24,9
Latvia	2,4	1,7	-0,7	-27,9
Lithuania	3,7	3,0	-0,7	-19,1
Malta	0,4	0,4	0,0	2,5
Poland	38,6	33,4	-5,2	-13,6
Romania	22,4	18,1	-4,3	-19,1
Slovakia	5,4	4,7	-0,7	-13,4
Slovenia	2,0	1,5	-0,5	-23,2
EU-15	376,4	364,2	-12,2	-3,2
EU-27	481,7	449,2	-32,5	-6,8

Source: UN Population forecasts 2002

Overall, demographic changes of this magnitude, as in the EU Member States, will have substantial economic implications, e.g. via the labour supply. A decline in the size of the active labour force will lead to a lower rate of economic growth unless offset by increases in factor productivity. This development may make it more difficult to finance the impact on public spending on pensions caused by ageing population and will pose a challenge in the light of the Lisbon objectives.

3. *MACROĖCONOMIC CONTEXT*

3.1. GROWTH PERFORMANCE

The Candidate Countries experienced differing growth paths during the transition in the 1990s (Table 4). By 2001, only half of them surpassed their pre-1990 levels of real GDP. In general, GDP bottomed out between 1991 and 1993. Poland's GDP reached its trough in 1991, the Czech Republic, Slovakia and Slovenia in 1992, and Hungary in 1993.

In the Baltic states, Latvia reached its low point in 1993 and Estonia and Lithuania in 1994. A high growth period ensued between 1995 and 2002. Despite the consequences of the economic crisis in Russia, which were mostly felt in Lithuania, bringing about a 3.9 percent decline of GDP, and in Estonia to a lesser extent, overall growth over the 1995-2002 period reached an average rate of 4.9 percent, 5.6 percent and 3.9 percent, respectively in Estonia, Latvia and Lithuania. Both Romania and Bulgaria went through severe economic recession in the early 1990s. Then economic recovery started in 1993 and 1994, respectively. However, episodes of severe economic and financial crises occurred in both countries (in 1996 in Bulgaria and in 1997 in Romania) and the economic situation improved only recently. Average annual GDP growth rates for the two countries are below one percent over the period 1991-2002.

Table 4: Real GDP growth 1991-2002 (% of change)

	1991	1992	1993	1994	1995	1996	1997	1998	1999	2000	2001	2002	2002//1995	2002//1991
BG	na	-7.3	-1.5	1.8	2.9	-9.4	-5.6	4.0	2.3	5.4	4.0	4.0	0.5	-0.1
CZ	-11.6	-0.5	0.1	2.2	5.9	4.3	-0.8	-1.0	0.5	3.3	3.3	2.2	1.7	1.7
HU	-11.9	-2.1	-0.6	2.9	1.5	1.3	4.6	4.9	4.2	5.2	3.7	3.4	3.9	2.6
PL	-7.0	2.5	3.7	5.2	7.0	6.0	6.8	4.8	4.1	4.0	1.1	0.8	3.9	4.2
RO	-13.1	-8.7	1.5	3.9	7.1	3.9	-6.1	-4.8	-1.2	1.8	5.3	4.2	0.4	0.5
SK	na	na	6.2	5.2	6.5	5.8	5.6	4.0	1.3	2.2	3.3	3.9	3.7	na
SI	-8.9	-5.5	2.8	5.3	4.1	3.5	4.6	3.8	5.2	4.6	3.0	2.6	3.9	3.1
EE	na	na	na	-2.0	4.3	3.9	9.8	4.6	-0.6	7.1	5.0	4.5	4.9	na
LV	-10.4	-34.9	-14.9	0.6	-1.6	3.7	8.4	4.8	2.8	6.8	7.7	5.0	5.6	-2.0
LT	-5.7	-21.3	-16.2	-9.8	3.3	4.7	7.3	5.1	-3.9	3.8	5.9	5.0	3.9	-2.0
CY	0.7	9.7	0.7	5.9	6.2	1.9	2.4	5.0	4.6	5.1	4.0	2.2	3.6	4.3
MT	na	4.7	4.5	5.7	6.2	4.0	4.9	3.4	4.1	4.8	-0.4	2.8	3.3	4.0
EUR-12	na	1.5	-0.8	2.4	2.2	1.4	2.3	2.9	2.8	3.5	1.5	0.8	2.2	1.9
EU-15	na	1.1	-0.4	2.8	2.4	1.6	2.5	2.9	2.8	3.4	1.5	1.0	2.2	2.0

Source: AMECO, European Commission, November 2002. Note: (//) Average growth rate

Employment dropped markedly in response to the severe contractions in output in the early stages of the transition period. However, the transition-induced fall in the Central and Eastern European Countries GDP in the early 1990s was not met by an immediate and proportional drop in employment, due to initial labour hoarding. Then, over the following years, structural change brought massive layoffs, new job opportunities limited in number and oriented toward the higher skilled/educated, with substantial reductions in the labour force. Though GDP recovered in Poland as of 1992, employment rose only moderately between 1994 and 1998, and dropped once again thereafter. In Hungary, though renewed GDP growth appeared in 1994, employment rose only modestly between 1998 and 2001. Over the 1995-2002 period, important job losses were also noted in Latvia, Lithuania, Bulgaria and Romania, with only Cyprus and Slovenia exhibiting small positive annual average rates of job growth over the period.

This evolution of GDP and employment lead to important and sustained gains in labour productivity over the 1995-2002 period, particularly in Poland, the three Baltic states, Slovakia and Slovenia (Table 5). With the exception of Cyprus and Malta, only the Czech Republic, Bulgaria and Romania had average annual labour productivity growth rates below three percent over the period 1995-2002, while EU labour productivity grew at approximately one percent over the same period.

Table 5: Implicit labour productivity 1991-2002 (growth rate)

	1991	1992	1993	1994	1995	1996	1997	1998	1999	2000	2001	2002	2002//1995	2002//1991
BG	na	1.0	0.1	1.2	1.6	-9.5	-1.8	4.2	4.4	10.6	8.8	3.5	2.7	2.1
CZ	na	na	6.0	5.0	3.5	2.2	4.6	3.4	1.1	4.2	3.4	3.6	2.3	na
HU	na	na	0.3	1.1	5.2	4.1	-0.1	0.4	2.6	4.0	2.9	2.3	3.2	na
PL	na	na	6.2	4.2	5.1	4.0	3.9	2.4	6.9	6.4	3.0	2.3	4.1	na
RO	-12.6	-5.9	5.5	4.5	13.0	5.2	-2.3	-2.5	3.5	-0.7	5.9	3.9	1.8	2.6
SK	na	na	na	na	4.3	2.4	6.8	2.4	4.7	4.9	2.3	3.7	3.9	na
SI	-3.6	-1.0	4.8	5.7	3.0	4.5	5.1	3.8	3.9	3.5	2.3	2.6	3.7	3.5
EE	na	na	na	1.4	11.1	6.5	9.7	6.7	3.9	8.5	4.2	3.1	6.1	na
LV	-9.6	-29.7	-8.6	12.0	1.9	6.5	6.4	4.1	3.4	6.8	7.8	5.5	5.8	0.8
LT	-7.9	-19.5	-12.6	-4.2	5.3	3.7	6.6	5.9	-3.4	7.8	10.4	5.0	5.1	0.0
CY	na	na	na	na	1.6	0.9	2.7	3.9	3.2	2.2	2.1	1.6	2.4	na
MT	na	na	na	na	na	na	na	2.9	4.5	2.5	-0.7	2.7	na	na
EUR-12	na	2.4	0.8	2.7	1.7	0.9	1.6	1.0	1.0	1.4	0.1	0.4	0.9	1.3
EU-15	na	2.5	1.2	2.9	1.7	1.0	1.6	1.1	1.1	1.5	0.3	0.6	1.0	1.4

Source: AMECO, European Commission, November 2002. Note: (//) Average growth rate

Table 6: Gross investment, in constant prices 1991-2002 (growth rate)

	1991	1992	1993	1994	1995	1996	1997	1998	1999	2000	2001	2002	2002//1995	2002//1991
BG	na	-7.3	-17.5	1.1	16.1	-21.2	-23.9	32.9	25.3	8.2	19.9	8.0	4.9	2.1
CZ	-27.3	16.5	0.2	9.1	19.8	8.2	-2.9	0.7	-1.0	5.3	7.2	3.0	2.9	5.8
HU	-10.4	-2.6	2.0	12.5	-4.3	6.7	9.2	13.3	5.9	7.7	3.5	6.5	7.5	5.3
PL	-4.5	2.4	2.9	9.2	16.5	19.7	21.7	14.2	6.5	2.7	-9.8	-6.5	6.3	6.8
RO	-31.6	11.0	8.3	20.7	6.9	5.7	1.7	-5.7	-4.2	5.5	6.6	7.0	2.2	5.6
SK	na	na	-3.1	-2.5	1.8	30.9	14.3	11.0	-18.5	1.2	9.6	0.9	6.1	na
SI	-11.5	-12.9	10.7	14.1	16.8	8.9	11.6	11.3	19.1	0.2	-1.9	2.5	7.2	6.9
EE	na	na	na	6.3	4.1	11.4	17.6	11.3	-14.8	13.3	9.1	16.0	8.6	na
LV	-63.9	-28.7	-15.8	0.8	8.7	22.3	20.7	44.0	-4.0	20.0	17.0	4.5	17.0	6.3
LT	na	na	na	na	na	17.6	22.0	9.9	-6.3	-3.9	8.7	15.0	8.6	na
CY	na	na	na	na	-1.7	7.4	-4.5	2.4	-0.1	7.0	1.4	6.0	2.7	na
EUR-12	na	0.1	-6.3	2.3	2.5	1.3	2.5	5.3	6.0	4.9	-0.3	-1.9	2.5	1.4
EU-15	na	-0.4	-5.8	2.7	2.8	1.8	3.0	6.5	5.2	4.6	-0.2	-2.1	2.7	1.6

Source: AMECO, European Commission, November 2002. Note: (//) Average growth rate

At the same time, there was a marked increase in investment (Table 6), particularly over the period 1996-2002, when large inflows of foreign capital were registered. While Hungary attracted foreign investment at an early stage of transition, Poland, Latvia, Bulgaria and Romania started out with very low ratios of investment to GDP during the first half of the 1990s. As of 1996, investment rates increased sharply, more than doubling in Latvia, and rising substantially above the EU average investment rates in all Central and Eastern European Countries but Bulgaria. Investment picked up significantly in Bulgaria as from 1998, and to a lesser extent in Romania from 2000, but current investment ratios remain the lowest of all the countries under review (with the exception of Cyprus and Malta).

3.2. BREAKDOWN OF GROWTH INTO ITS VARIOUS COMPONENTS

To analyse the sources of growth in the countries under review, recent empirical studies[3] have put output developments in a longer-run perspective, linking the initial transition years with the last two central planning decades, and provide a decomposition of GDP growth in order to identify the contributions of factor accumulation and productivity changes to overall economic growth. A characteristic of the planned economies is that, until the beginning of the 1960s, economic growth has been mainly driven by investment in capital and shifts in production from agriculture to industry. Then, growth has slowed down inexorably under the influence of external constraint and the lack of TFP growth.

The growth decomposition data in Campos and Coricelli (2002) show that, over the 1991-1995/7 period, average output growth (a 1.1 percent

[3] Campos N., Coricelli F. (2002), "Growth Transition: What We Know, What We Don't and What We Should", Journal of Economic Literature, vol. XL, September, pp. 793-836. Doyle P., Kuijs L., Jiang G. (2001), "Real Convergence to EU Income Levels: Central Europe from 1990 to the Long-Term", IMF Working Paper, N°146. De Broeck M., Koen V. (2000), "The Great Contractions in Russia, the Baltics and the Other Countries of the Former Soviet Union: A View from the Supply Side", IMF Working Paper, N°32.

decline) in the Central and Eastern European Countries[4] is essentially due to the 1.2 percent decline in overall (TFP) productivity, while production factor growth (+0.1 percent) contributes positively to change in output (Table 7). At the country level, differences are striking. Hungary and Slovenia experienced relatively high TFP-driven output growth contrary to Poland where factor growth represents the main contribution to growth. The Czech Republic, Slovakia, Bulgaria and Romania experienced negative average output growth rates, which were also driven by steep declines in TFP. In Bulgaria, the output fall was reinforced by the negative contribution of factor growth. On the whole, it appears that output has been influenced more by changes in TFP than in changes in the quantity of inputs used. In the Baltic States, negative average output growth rates in Estonia, Latvia and Lithuania were both driven by steep declines in TFP and by the negative contribution of factor growth.

Table 7: Contributions to growth rates for the accession countries over the period 1991-97 (average)

	Output growth	TFP growth	Factor growth
BG	-8.8	-6.2	-2.6
CZ	-4.2	-5.1	0.9
HU	1.9	1.6	0.3
PL	1.8	0.1	1.7
RO	-2.4	-2.4	0
SK	-1.6	-2.3	0.7
SI	8.9	7.9	1
EE	-3.4	-2.2	-1.2
LV	-8.6	-5.3	-3.4
LT	-6.3	-4.5	-1.8

Source: Campos N. and Coricelli F. (2002), op.cit., pp.798-800.

[4] This average is calculated for Bulgaria, Croatia, the Czech Republic, Hungary, Poland, Romania, Slovakia, and Slovenia.

In a study by Doyle, et. al. (2001), which allows for a distinction between capital and employment contributions to overall output growth, in five Central European countries[5], the growth decomposition data show that the cumulative output growth over the 1991-1999 period benefited from relatively high TFP growth in Hungary, Poland, and Slovenia (Table 8). The higher cumulative output growth in Poland was due to the higher contribution of capital to growth. The contribution of employment was negative in the countries under review, except in Slovakia.

Table 8: Cumulative output growth in Central European countries 1991-99 (in percent)

		Contribution of		
	Cumulative GDP growth	**TFP growth**	**Employment**	**Capital**
CZ	9.1	4.6	-4.3	9.0
HU	16.6	20.2	-11.1	9.2
PL	47.9	20.9	-1.6	24.3
SK	21.8	2.0	6.2	12.4
SI	25.6	21.0	-6.4	10.9

Source: Doyle P., Kuijs L., and Jiang G. (2001), op.cit., p.31.

Investment rates for the second half of the 1990s would suggest a strong growth of the productive capital stock. However, one must take into account that a significant part of the accession countries' capital stock must have been made obsolete at the beginning of the transition process, replaced by new imported capital equipment. This would imply that the strong post-transition growth in such countries as Latvia, Estonia, Hungary, Lithuania and Slovenia are not so much due to capital deepening as to increases in total factor productivity. Only in the case of Poland, both total factor productivity growth and capital deepening contribute strongly to GDP growth.

[5] The data cover the Czech Republic, Hungary, Poland, Slovakia, and Slovenia.

This is a finding of recent empirical studies[6] that use growth accounting techniques to evaluate and decompose the growth performance of the Central and Eastern European Countries. It should be noted as a health warning, though, that the production function approach to growth accounting for transition economies poses the problem of the plausible representation of these economies by the Cobb-Douglas production function, with assumed weights of capital and labour. First, the estimation of this type of function with the sum of factor elasticities equal to unity implies "long run" constant returns to scale, and unity-negative own-price elasticities. This raises the question whether such theoretical, steady-state properties, are characteristic of the transition economies over the last decade. At the steady-state, the capital output ratio remains constant. With increasing capital output ratio, the countries could achieve faster than steady-state growth and would also converge more rapidly on EU income levels. Moreover, there is an implicit assumption that the quality of labour and capital is unchanged over the time period under review. This is a particularly strong assumption in the context of the transition from a planned to a market economy, accompanied by a significant opening of the economy through trade and investment.

The production function approach also brings forth practical questions, bearing on the production factor data used for estimation. The shortcomings of employment data expressed in thousands of units, in the context of transition economies subject to supply, demand and institutional shocks has been largely commented upon. The questions posed by such an approach are also numerous, and maybe even more complex, when one turns to the data on productive capital stock. Building capital stock series in each country requires assumptions on the rate of depreciation and on the portion of each country's capital stock rendered obsolete at the beginning of the transition process.

---

[6] See footnote 2.

3.3. RECENT GROWTH PERFORMANCE

With the exception of Bulgaria, Romania and the Czech Republic, the annual average growth rates of GDP of the Central and Eastern European Countries (CEECs) exceeded 3 percent between 1995 and 2002, and were in general significantly above EU-15 levels (see Table 4). After the years of exceptionally high world growth in 1999-2000 which benefited the CEECs as a whole, there was a deceleration in the pace of growth in many countries over the last two to three years, although it accelerated in a few others. Overall, the CEECs have so far avoided the immediate negative effects of the global economic downturn and the weak economic performance of Western Europe, owing to the combination of various factors, of which the continuing recovery in their domestic demand, the contribution of the ongoing expansion of FDI to fixed investment, the diversion of sales from traditional to new markets[7]. The sensitivity to the deteriorating external environment also varies across industries, which can explain that overall slowdown in industrial production is less pronounced in some countries, according to their particular specialisation[8]. However, it is unlikely that these economies will be able to remain unaffected by external factors, due to their strong dependence on trade, in particular with the European Union.

Poland stands out among the accession countries in transition and the recent slowdown is particularly noteworthy. Following several years of strong growth, with growth rates above 4 percent between 1994 and 2000, the economy dropped to a state of near stagnation, with growth rates to around one percent in 2001 and 2002. This evolution of growth in Poland can be attributed to both external and internal conditions[9].

7 UN/ECE (2002), ECE/UN, "Economic Survey of Europe", 2002 No. 2, p.11.

8 There is a strong differentiation across the CEECs in terms of structures and trade specialisation. See Landesmann M. (2003), "Structural features of economic integration in an Enlarged Europe: patterns of catching-up and industrial specialisation", Economic Papers, n°181, European Commission.

9 OECD (2002), "Economic Survey of Poland", June 2002, pp.16-35. UN/ECE (2002), ECE/UN, Economic Survey of Europe, 2002 No. 1, pp.63-69.

With respect to external conditions, Poland suffers from the recent weak performance in the economies of its main trading partners, the EU, and particularly Germany. With respect to internal conditions, the economic slowdown in Poland can be attributed to a cyclical downturn in investment, both from domestic and foreign firms[10], accompanied by declining private consumption, employment, and productivity. The economic slowdown results in a further deterioration of the persistently high unemployment rate. While employment had grown over the 1994-1998 period, substantial new net job losses have arisen starting in 1999, and continue through 2002. At the same time, we note a marked decline in labour productivity growth, which dropped from 6.9 percent in 1999 to an estimated 2.3 percent in 2002. Finally, gross investment growth rates dropped from 6.5 percent in 1999 to -9.8 percent in 2001 and an estimated -6.5 percent in 2002, due to excess productive capacity, gloomy prospects for growth in sales, declining profitability, and high real interest rates. This drop in gross investment pushes the investment to GDP ratio from a high of 26.7 percent in 1999 down to 21.8 percent in 2002.

Although remaining high in comparison with EU GDP growth, Hungarian growth rates, after reaching 5.2 percent in 2000, slowed down to 3.7 percent in 2001, and an estimated 3.4 percent in 2002. Growth in Slovenia also dropped from 5.2 percent in 1999 to an estimated 2.6 percent in 2002. The three Baltic states continued to experience particularly high growth between 2000 and 2002, with rates of up to 7.7 percent for Latvia in 2001, 5.9 percent for Lithuania in 2001, and 7.1 percent for Estonia in 2000. Growth also picked up in Slovakia, from 1.3 percent in 1999 to an estimated 3.9 percent in 2002. In Romania, growth accelerated from 1.8 percent in 2000 to 5.3 percent in 2001 and 4.2 percent in 2002. Finally, growth rates reached and stayed above 4 percent in Bulgaria between 2000 and 2002.

---

[10]Foreign direct investment inflows in 2001 were 25 per cent lower than in 2000 (See OECD (2002), "Economic Survey of Poland", June 2002, p.30).

According to official forecasts, all the economies of the CEECs expect an acceleration of growth in 2003 (Table 9). The most significant upturn is awaited in Poland. However, taking into account the uncertainties surrounding the global economic outlook, short-term prospects for growth are likely to be moderate.

Table 9: Real GDP growth 2002-2004 (% of change)

	2002*	2003*	2004*
BG	4.0	5.0	5.5
CZ	2.2	3.2	3.8
HU	3.4	4.5	4.9
PL	0.8	3.2	3.9
RO	4.2	4.6	4.7
SK	3.9	3.9	4.8
SI	2.6	3.6	4.0
EE	4.5	4.7	5.1
LV	5.0	5.5	6.0
LT	5.0	3.5	4.5
CY	2.2	3.5	4.1
MT	2.8	3.4	3.6
EU-15	1.0	2.0	2.6

Source: * Official forecast by the European Commission Autumn 2002 forecast for the Candidate Countries (Nov. 2002)

3.4. Labour Markets: Participation and Employment Rates

In the Lisbon agenda, the goal of higher factor productivity goes hand-in-hand with one of higher participation and employment. The overall labour market participation rates[11] (for persons aged 15 to 64) in the 1990s were lower in the accession countries than in the EU, with the exception of Cyprus. They were relatively stable, except in the Baltic countries, where they declined (Annex 2). By contrast, the participation rate of older persons aged 55 to 64 was high (albeit with a decreasing tendency) in the Baltic countries, the Czech Republic and Romania. In

[11] Ratio of labour force to working-age population (15-64).

Hungary it rose significantly from 28.8 in 1996 to 36.3 in 2001. The changes in participation rates reveal considerable scope for narrowing the current gap.

For the employment rate, the Lisbon Council agreed a specific target for the EU as a whole of 70% by 2010, and an interim target of 67% by 2005. With the exception of Cyprus and the Czech Republic, the overall employment rates[12] (for persons aged 15 to 64) in the Candidate Countries, especially Bulgaria and Poland, are lower than in the EU (50.7% for Bulgaria and 53.8% for Poland, compared with 63.9% for the EU-15 in 2001; see Table 10). The Stockholm Council set an additional target for the female employment rate of more than 60 per cent by 2010 (with an interim target of 57 per cent by 2005, of which several accession countries fall short). Employment among older workers also comes under the Lisbon spotlight, the Stockholm Council having agreed a 50 per cent employment target for 2010. The employment rates of older persons aged 55 to 64 are generally lower than in the European Union, except in Cyprus and in the Baltic states, where they are significantly higher.

[12] Ratio of employment to working-age population (15-64), i.e. the percentage of the working age population actually in work.

Table 10: Employment rates in the accession countries (as % of age-specific groups)

	Male											
	15-64						55-64					
	1996	1997	1998	1999	2000	2001	1996	1997	1998	1999	2000	2001
Bulgaria	--	--	--	--	56.1	53.6	--	--	--	--	34.9	34.2
Czech R.	--	77.1	76.1	74	73.1	73.2	--	38.5	37.5	37.6	36.1	36.9
Cyprus	--	--	--	78.7	78.9	79.7	--	--	--	66.3	67.1	67.9
Estonia	--	69.7	70.3	66.3	64.3	65.6	--	59.6	60.9	59.2	50.2	57.1
Hungary	59.4	59.6	60	62.4	62.7	63.3	27.1	27.1	26.3	29.3	33	35
Latvia	--	--	63.5	65.2	62.3	61.9	--	--	49.2	50.2	48.3	44.8
Lithuania	--	--	67.6	68.9	61.8	59.8			57	56.7	52.2	48.6
Malta	--	--	--	--	--	--	--	--	--	--	--	--
Poland	--	66.2	66.3	63.6	61.2	59.2	--	44.5	42.7	41.8	37.4	38.3
Romania	--	73.4	71.9	70.4	69.5	68.6	--	62.8	61.9	59.4	57.4	56
Slovakia	--	--	--	64	61.6	61.8	--	--	--	36.4	35.2	37.7
Slovenia	66	67.1	67.5	66.8	66.7	68.5	28.1	29.8	32.8	32.2	31	33
EU-15	70.1	70.3	71	71.7	72.5	73	47.2	47.1	47.3	47.5	48	48.6

	Female											
	15-64						55-64					
	1996	1997	1998	1999	2000	2001	1996	1997	1998	1999	2000	2001
Bulgaria	--	--	--	--	47.2	47.9	--	--	--	--	11.2	11.4
Czech R.	--	60.2	58.9	57.4	56.8	57	--	24	23.2	23.6	22.1	23
Cyprus	--	--	--	50.2	52.5	56.5	--	--	--	28.8	31.9	32.6
Estonia	--	60.6	60.7	58	57.1	56.9	--	40.5	42	39.3	37.5	41.9
Hungary	45.1	44.8	46.8	48.8	49.4	49.6	10.2	10.7	9.3	11.1	13	14.6
Latvia	--	--	54.2	54.1	53.5	56.1	--	--	28.1	26.4	25.9	30.1
Lithuania	--	--	58.5	61.4	58.5	57.4	--	--	27.4	31.8	34.5	31.8
Malta	--	--	--	--	--	--	--	--	--	--	--	--
Poland	--	51.6	52.2	51.6	49.3	48.4	--	27.7	25.2	24.5	21.8	23.8
Romania	--	61.1	60.1	59.7	59	58.2	--	48.2	48.4	47.3	47.3	45.8
Slovakia	--	--	--	52.1	51.1	51.8	--	--	--	10.6	10.2	10
Slovenia	57.5	58.4	59.5	58.1	58.5	58.6	12.9	16.4	19.4	14.9	14.3	14.4
EU-15	50.1	50.6	51.5	52.8	54	54.9	25.8	26.1	26.3	27.1	27.9	28.8

	Male and female women											
	15-64						55-64					
	1996	1997	1998	1999	2000	2001	1996	1997	1998	1999	2000	2001
Bulgaria	--	--	--	--	51.5	50.7	--	--	--	--	22.1	23.9
Czech R.	--	68.6	67.5	65.6	64.9	65	--	54.8	53.4	53.2	51.6	52.4
Cyprus	--	--	--	64.2	65.5	67.9	--	--	--	47	49	49.8
Estonia	--	64.9	65.3	62	60.6	61.1	--	48.9	50.2	47.9	43	48.6
Hungary	52	52	53.2	55.4	55.9	56.3	17.6	17.9	16.7	19.1	21.9	23.7
Latvia	--	--	58.6	59.4	57.7	58.9	--	--	37	36.6	35.4	36.4
Lithuania	--	--	62.9	65	60.1	58.6	--	--	40.2	42.6	42.2	39.1
Malta	--	--	--	--	--	--	--	--	--	--	--	--
Poland	--	58.8	59.2	57.5	55.1	53.8	--	35.5	33.3	32.5	29	30.5
Romania		67.2	65.9	65	64.2	63.3	--	55	54.7	52.9	52	50.5
Slovakia	--	--	--	58	56.3	56.7	--	--	--	22.2	21.4	22.5
Slovenia	61.7	62.8	63.5	62.5	62.7	63.6	19.9	22.7	25.9	23.4	22.3	23.4
EU-15	60.1	60.5	61.2	62.3	63.2	63.9	36.2	36.3	36.6	37.1	37.8	38.5

Source: Employment in Europe 2002 - European Commission and EPC Ageing Working Group 2001.

3.5. ECONOMIC DEPENDENCY RATIOS

Table 11 below presents three dependency ratios:

- the old-age dependency ratio, which expresses the number of people aged 65 or over as a percentage of the population aged 15 to 64 (elderly as a percentage of the working-age population);
- the potential economic dependency ratio, which expresses the population aged 15 or over not in the labour force as a percentage of the number of persons in the labour force (number of potentially inactive persons as a percentage of the total labour force);
- the effective economic dependency ratio, which expresses the population aged 15 and over not employed as a percentage of the number of persons employed (effective balance of inactive persons and unemployed versus economically active).

Even if available for the years 1995 to 1999 only, the results for the accession countries underline the finding of the critical importance of increasing employment rates as a means of meeting the economic and budgetary challenges of ageing populations in the EPC's report for the Member States. Higher employment rates, especially amongst women and older workers, can help mitigate the challenges of ageing populations. In the accession countries, with the exception of Bulgaria, the demographic old-age dependency ratio is lower than in the EU (for long-term projections of the old-age dependency ratio, see Annex 1). By contrast, because of lower participation rates especially among men, the potential economic dependency ratios are significantly higher than in the EU. The difficult employment conditions reinforce this trend, which is reflected in the effective economic dependency ratio. Additional efforts will be required by the accession countries to increase employment rates.

Table 11: Economic dependency ratios

a) Old-age dependency ratio (%)

	1990	1991	1992	1993	1994	1995	1996	1997	1998	1999	2000
Bulgaria	20	20	21	21	22	22	23	23	23	24	24
Czech R.	19	19	19	19	19	19	19	20	20	20	20
Cyprus	17	17	17	17	17	17	17	17	17	17	18
Estonia	18	18	18	19	20	20	20	21	21	21	21
Hungary	20	20	20	21	21	21	21	21	21	21	21
Latvia	18	18	19	19	20	20	21	21	21	21	22
Lithuania	16	17	17	17	18	18	18	19	19	20	20
Malta	16	16	16	17	17	17	17	18	18	18	18
Poland	16	16	16	16	17	17	17	17	17	18	18
Romania	16	16	17	17	17	18	18	18	19	19	19
Slovakia	17	17	17	17	17	18	18	18	19	19	20
Slovenia	16	16	16	16	16	16	16	16	16	16	16
EU-15	**--**	**22**	**22**	**23**	**23**	**23**	**23**	**24**	**24**	**24**	**--**

b) Potential economic dependency ratio

	1992	1993	1994	1995	1996	1997	1998	1999	2000
Bulgaria	--	--	--	89	89	90	92	92	91
Czech R.	64	63	62	63	63	64	64	64	66
Cyprus	--	--	--	--	--	90	91	91	90
Estonia	--	--	--	--	69	69	72	75	74
Hungary	84	92	99	105	107	108	106	102	101
Latvia	--	--	--	65	66	63	64	66	68
Lithuania	--	--	--	--	--	--	58	60	59
Malta	--	--	--	--	--	119	120	122	120
Poland	70	74	73	74	74	75	75	75	74
Romania	--	--	--	69	78	87	92	99	94
Slovakia	--	--	--	70	68	70	67	67	68
Slovenia	--	--	--	82	85	87	87	87	86
EU-15	**75**	**77**	**77**	**77**	**77**	**77**	**75**	**75**	**--**

c) Effective economic dependency ratio

	1990	1991	1992	1993	1994	1995	1996	1997	1998	1999	2000
Bulgaria	69	94	111	114	113	110	109	116	115	118	128
Czech R.	--	--	68	70	70	69	70	72	75	80	81
Cyprus	--	--	--	--	100	95	97	100	102	102	99
Estonia	47	50	59	71	75	85	88	87	90	98	99
Hungary	--	--	103	118	123	127	129	129	125	118	115
Latvia	49	49	60	69	86	91	95	92	91	92	93
Lithuania	55	52	56	63	73	77	76	75	78	80	88
Malta	--	--	--	--	--	--	--	130	131	135	132
Poland	--	--	98	104	104	102	100	97	94	101	108
Romania	64	65	71	78	80	90	93	101	107	117	113
Slovakia	--	--	--	--	95	93	89	93	92	100	107
Slovenia	68	80	90	95	98	97	100	103	104	102	101
EU-15	**--**	**87**	**91**	**95**	**96**	**96**	**96**	**95**	**92**	**90**	**--**

Sources: Population = UN for the CC, AMECO for EU; Labour force and employment = AMECO and own calculations

4. *MAIN CHARACTERISTICS OF PENSION SYSTEMS*

Tables 12-15 provide an overview of some basic characteristics of the pension systems in the accession countries. As in the EU-15, there are substantial differences amongst those countries that result in diverging reform needs regarding the financial sustainability of the pension systems. As for first-pillar pensions, five accession countries (Cyprus, Estonia, Hungary, Latvia and Malta) offer universal state pension schemes (Table 15). Means testing, however, is applied only in a minority of the Candidate Countries. A majority offer labour-market-based public pension schemes. All of them are mandatory for workers in the private and public sectors and for most of the self-employed. The schemes for the private sector and the self-employed are usually almost identical as far as the financing arrangements are concerned. They usually represent pay-as-you-go (PAYG) schemes, sometimes with state budget financing.

There are notable differences in regard to the size of current public spending on public pensions (Table 12). In several countries, public pension expenditure is close to or above 10 per cent of GDP (Bulgaria, Cyprus, Latvia, Poland, Slovenia). Long-term projections, where available, point to a sharply rising trajectory for public pension expenditure due to ageing populations. Ageing populations could lead to a substantial increase in public expenditures in many accession countries.

Table 12: Public pension expenditures in 2000-50 (% of GDP)

	2000	2030	2050	Change 2000-50
Cyprus	8	11.9	14.8	+6.8
Czech Republic	7.8[5]	-	14.6[5]	+6.8
Estonia	6.9 [2,4]	-	-	
Hungary	6.0[5]	-	7.2[5]	+1.2
Latvia	9.8 [4]	-	-	
Lithuania	5.3	6	7	+1.7
Malta	5.4 [2,4]	-	-	
Poland	10.8	9.6	9.7	-0.9
Slovakia	7.9 [4]	-	-	
Slovenia	13.2	19.7	18.1	+4.9
Bulgaria	9.1 [2,4]	-	-	
Romania	6.4	7.8	8.2	+1.8
EU-15	10.4	13.0	13.3	+2.9

Sources: If not explicitly indicated, data are based on the 2002 Pre-Accession Economic Programmes.
Notes: -: not available; [1)]2002; [2)]2001; [3)] 2000; [4)] According to Gesellschaft für Versicherungswissenschaft und -gestaltung e.V. (which in turn draws on national statistics). [5] OECD. Since definitions of public pension expenditures are not identical for each country, caution is warranted when making comparisons.

In several acceding countries, funded schemes within the publicly financed pension systems have gradually become more prominent in recent years. Cyprus, Estonia, Hungary, Latvia and Poland have introduced a three-pillar pension system (compulsory and non-funded/compulsory and funded/voluntary and funded) and Lithuania and Slovakia are planning to do so in the near future. The projected development of pension fund assets is shown in table 13. Those projections might be uncertain and may not necessarily realise. However, it should be recognised that if funding is to make a meaningful contribution towards financing age-related expenditures, then very considerable resources will need to be devoted. Future updates of the Pre-Accession Economic Programmes, and notably the first Convergence Programmes in 2004 for the acceding countries would benefit from a more extensive description of reforms underway, including the precise role of funding and the pace of asset accumulation. For many accession countries, the section of the PEPs on the long-term sustainability of public finances should be more comprehensive.

Table 13: Pension fund assets (% of GDP)

	2000	2020
Bulgaria	-	-
Czech Republic	-	-
Cyprus	39.0	25.2
Estonia	-	20 [1]
Hungary	-	31 [1]
Latvia	-	20 [1]
Lithuania	-	-
Malta	-	-
Poland	2.54	46.5
Romania	-	30 [1]
Slovakia	-	-
Slovenia	-	-
EU-15	44	

Sources: 2002 PEPs; [1]) according to Gesellschaft für Versicherungswissenschaft und -gestaltung e.V.

Challenges facing pension systems in the accession countries, quite similar to those facing EU Member States, may for instance include the relatively low effective retirement age (even if some countries have made efforts to increase the retirement age the proportion of older workers in the work force has fallen dramatically since the early 1990s), the dynamics of early retirement arrangements (in some countries those have been used as a response to the decline in employment, e.g. in the Czech Republic or Poland), expenditure pressures due to indexation rules (in some countries pensions are indexed to wages, in others to prices, and in some they are adjusted on an ad hoc basis), and finding the right balance between contribution rates and the level of benefits paid out (for some key determinants of activity of the elderly and benefits of public pensions, see Table 14).

Table 14: Determinants of activity of the elderly and benefits of public pensions in the accession countries

	Statutory retirement age		Pension regime	Indexation rules (P = prices; W = wages)	Taxation rules
	Men	Women			
Bulgaria	63	60	E-R	P/W	Not taxed
Czech R.	62	59	E-R	P/W	Not taxed
Cyprus	63	63	E-R	W	-
Estonia	63	58,5	E-R	P/ [3)]	Taxed as income [iii)]
Hungary	62	57 [2]	E-R	P/W	Not taxed [iv)]
Latvia	62	58,5 [1]	E-R	P/W [4)]	Taxed as income [ii)]
Lithuania	62	58	E-R	-	Not taxed
Malta	61	60	E-R	W	-
Poland	65	60	E-R	P/W	Taxed as other income
Romania	60 [1]	55 [1]	E-R	P	Not taxed [iv)]
Slovakia	60	57	E-R	P/W	10% on second-pillar benefits
Slovenia	64	59,5	E-R	-	Not taxed [i)]

Notes: [1)] 2001; [2)] 2000; [3)] Increase is determined equally by rise of CPI and by rise in social security contributions. [4)] Partly indexed to contribution to GDP growth. E-R means earnings-related systems, where pensions are related to past earnings. It should be noted though that in some accession countries the earnings-related systems come very close to flat-rate systems which provide a basic income irrespective of wages earned or contributions made (e.g. in Latvia or Lithuania). [i)] For personal income tax purposes, net pensions are notionally grossed up by the average personal income tax rate, and a personal income tax schedule is applied. If the computed amount of tax is greater than the amount represented by "gross" pension minus net pension, then the person pays tax. In effect, this means that only high-income pensioners pay, albeit very little, income tax.[ii)] Pensions granted before 1 January 1996 are not subject to taxation. Pensions granted or recalculated after that date are subject to taxation. The annual tax exemption limit is LVL 12 000.[iii)] However, pensions less than three times the non-taxable minimum (EEK 36 000 a year, EEK 3 000 a month), which make up the overwhelming majority of cases, are not subject to taxation.[iv)] After 2013, the pension base will be shifted from net to gross earnings and will be made subject to taxation. [v)] Taxation of only those pensions which are higher than twice the national average gross salary.

Table 15: Overview of first- and second-pillar pensions in the accession countries

First-pillar	**BG**	**CY**	**CR**	**EE**	**H**	**LV**	**LIT**	**MT**	**PL**	**RO**	**SK**	**SL**
General												
Universal	No	Yes	No	Yes	Yes	Yes	No	Yes	No	No	No	No
Means-tested	Yes	-	No	-	No	No	Yes	No	No	-	No	Yes
Labour-market-based	Yes	Yes	Yes	Yes	Yes	Yes	Yes	-	-	-	-	Yes
Private sector												
Mandatory	Yes	Yes	Yes	Yes	Yes	Yes	Yes	Yes	Yes	Yes	Yes	Yes
PAYG/FF/SF	PAYG	PAYG/SF	PAYG/SF	PAYG	PAYG[+]	PAYG	PAYG	PAYG/SF	PAYG/SF	PAYG/SF	PAYG	PAYG
Public sector												
Mandatory	Yes	Yes	Yes	Yes	Yes	Yes	Yes	Yes	Yes	Yes	Yes	Yes
PAYG/FF/SF	PAYG	PAYG/SF	PAYG/SF	PAYG	PAYG[+]	PAYG	SF	PAYG/SF	SF	PAYG/SF	PAYG	PAYG
Self-employed												
Mandatory	Yes	Yes	Yes	Yes		Yes		Yes	Yes	Yes		Yes
PAYG FF/SF	PAYG	PAYG/SF	PAYG/SF	PAYG	PAYG[+]	PAYG	PAYG	PAYG/SF	PAYG/SF	PAYG/SF		PAYG
Second-pillar												
Private sector												
Mandatory	Yes	Yes[**]	No	Yes[***]	Yes[***]	Yes	No[*]	-	Yes	-	No	No
Public sector												
Mandatory	Yes	Yes[**]	No	Yes[***]	Yes[***]	Yes	No[*]	-	Yes	-	No	No

Notes: -: Not applicable; PAYG (pay-as-you-go); FF (fully funded); SF (financed by state budget); [*] Second pillar yet to be established; [**] Partial; [***] For new entrants; voluntary for others; [+] Any deficits are financed from the state budget.

Annex 3 provides an overview of recent reforms of public pension systems in the Candidate Countries, as laid out in the 2002 PEPs. Common features of those reforms include:

- **A gradual increase of the retirement age.** To date, the retirement age in most accession countries is relatively low. In the long run, many countries also aim at equalising the retirement ages of men and women. The eligibility for early retirement and disability schemes is tightened.
- **A shift in the indexation of pension benefits.** Some countries shift from wage indexation, or ad-hoc price adjustments, to price indexation, or to hybrid price and wage indices.
- **An increase in contributions.** The reform agendas often include some increase in the overall pension contributions, mostly in response to budgetary pressures.
- **Incentives for increased funding.** In most countries reforms have been accompanied by a strengthening of occupational and private pension schemes, e.g. via tax incentives.
- **A move towards more actuarial systems.** While some countries reemphasised the distributive character of their pension system, others moved towards a closer link between contributions paid in during active working life and benefits paid out during retirement (however, in some cases with very long phasing-in periods).

5. *MEDIUM TO LONG-TERM GROWTH PROSPECTS AND IMPLICATIONS WITH RESPECT TO THE SUSTAINABILITY OF PUBLIC PENSION SCHEMES*

The transition from planned to market economies brought about severe economic recession in many of the Central and Eastern European Countries. More than a decade after the beginning of the reform process, it is of particular interest to attempt to determine how much catching-up, or real convergence, has actually occurred with respect to the Western European economies.

Recent evidence[13] based on 1993-2001 quarterly data for eight CEECs, (using statistical correlation analysis and VAR modelling techniques for output and price impulse response functions) indicates that there are significant similarities between the CEECs and the Western European economies. These similarities can be seen in the relatively clear and positive correlation of output and price fluctuations, but also in the nature and speed of responses of the two groups of countries to supply and demand shocks. Significant differences seem to exist among the CEECs, with respect to correlation and shock responses, with either the EU taken as a whole, or with certain specific EU countries. This would indicate that the basic features and mechanisms of market economies now exist and function in a large number of CEECs, and that the main convergence issue is now one of catching-up to Western European income levels or, to put it otherwise, of high and sustained GDP growth.

Though numerous and sometimes deep differences subsist between them, Doyle et al (2001) show that the CEECs as a group currently seem to be in a position where future GDP growth should be driven mainly by increases in TFP. The labour force is expected to continue to decline in a number of CEECs or, at best, rise only modestly. Demographic trends cannot be counted upon to support high future output growth rates. Educational standards, measured by the average number of years of education, are fairly similar to EU standards, though the quality and nature of schooling is sometimes different. Thus, future growth should not be massively supported by demographic or labour market developments, and one should in line with the Lisbon targets aim at increasing "employability" through increasing educational levels and reducing labour market imbalances.

---

[13]Frenkel M., Nickel Ch. (2002), "How symmetric Are the Shocks and the Shock Adjustment Dynamics Between the Euro Area and Central and Eastern European Countries?", IMF Working Paper, n°222.

It has also been suggested that there is currently only a limited potential for increases in domestic saving, thus limiting investment growth rates in the absence of significant external borrowing. Efforts should be pursued in developing the institutions and regulatory frameworks that reinforce sound domestic financial markets and are conducive to higher domestic savings rates.

Overall, future GDP growth appears to be linked more to increases in TFP and sound institutional and regulatory frameworks than to future increases in factor intensities. However, in the medium term, high and sustained TFP-driven GDP growth rates should also lead to rising employment, even in the face of increased labour productivity. Labour productivity developments should allow for increases in real wages. The increases in employment and real wages would then generate a larger (taxable) wage base, on which one could more easily base the financing of public pension schemes even in light of sharply increasing dependency ratios. It should also be kept in mind that at the moment significant parts of the workforce do not pay taxes and social security contributions, or do so a reduced rates or for only part of their incomes.

6. *CONCLUSIONS*

While a case-by-case analysis is warranted on the impact of population ageing on public finances in the accession countries, the results of the preliminary analysis above suggest that demographic developments in a number of countries may soon result in additional pressures on public pension expenditure. The objectives for the reform of pension systems, agreed at the EU level, have been defined by:

- the Stockholm European Council, which agreed to set an EU target for increasing the average EU employment rate among older workers (aged 55-64) to 50% by 2010; and
- the Barcelona European Council, which called for an increase in the effective average retirement age in the EU of some five years by 2010.

In line with those objectives, the following points seem important for the accession countries:

Unless offset by increases in total factor productivity, a decline in the size of the active labour force may dampen growth expectations and thereby slow down the catching-up process. High and sustained total factor productivity-driven GDP growth rates including labour productivity are key to reach a larger taxable wage base on which one could more easily base the financing of public pension schemes in the light of the demographic challenges.

Many accession countries have already introduced a wide range of pension reforms. However, in order to counter longer-term spending trends, in line with the EU's three-pronged strategy for tackling the budgetary implications of ageing populations in several countries further reforms seem needed before the projected decline in the size of the active labour force fully materialises (the window of opportunity for pension reform before this happens is not much different relative to present Member States). In view of low employment rates, such reforms need to focus on raising the employment rate of older workers and the effective retirement age. The pension system and/or other transfers such as early retirement, disability or unemployment benefits should provide better incentives for older workers to remain in the workforce.

In a number of accession countries far reaching reforms aimed at increasing funding have been introduced. However, in some countries reform of pension systems will still have to include measures for reducing the cost of existing public pension systems. Moreover, if funding is to make a meaningful contribution towards financing age-related expenditures, then very considerable resources will need to be devoted.

Scope for further improvements is to be found in reforming pension systems in the direction of better financial sustainability. Several accession countries have introduced, or are contemplating to introduce notionally defined-contribution systems in which while the PAYG character of the system is preserved, individual pension benefits are computed actuarially and are based on effective working-life contributions. The introduction of such actuarially neutral systems, which link the replacement rate to the life expectancy of each age cohort, and strenghten the link between contributions and benefits at the individual level is best practice also among current Member States. Appropriate reforms aimed at combining flexibility regarding the retirement age and actuarial neutrality are to be encouraged.

Increased funding of pensions may have notable effects on the structure, liquidity and effectiveness of national financial markets. Increased private funding should be accompanied by appropriate supervision and regulation of private funds so as to safeguard the funds managed on behalf of contributors.

Data availability in the field of pension reform is rather poor for most of the countries concerned. More information seems to be needed, in particular on:

- long-term projections for pension expenditures;
- effective retirement ages;
- contribution (and replacement) rates.

Future updates of the Pre-Accession Economic Programmes, and notably the first Convergence Programmes for the acceding countries in 2004 would benefit from a more extensive description of reforms underway, including available long-term projections for pension expenditures as well as the precise role of funding and the pace of asset accumulation. For many accession countries, the section of the PEPs on the long-term sustainability of public finances should be more comprehensive.

So as to produce comparable long-term projections for pension expenditures for the first Convergence Programmes, it is suggested to include the accession countries in the next round of common projections for public spending on pensions, health and long-term care for the elderly by the Economic Policy Committee's Ageing Working Group in 2004/5.

7. ANNEX

Annex 1: Demographic assumptions - UN population projections 2002

	Fertility rate			
	2000-05	2020-25	2045-50	change
Bulgaria	1,1	1,4	1,9	0,8
Czech R.	1,2	1,4	2,0	0,8
Cyprus	1,9	1,9	1,9	0,0
Estonia	1,2	1,5	2,0	0,8
Hungary	1,2	1,5	2,0	0,8
Latvia	1,1	1,5	2,0	0,9
Lithuania	1,2	1,5	2,0	0,8
Malta	1,8	1,8	1,8	0,1
Poland	1,3	1,6	2,1	0,8
Romania	1,3	1,6	2,1	0,7
Slovakia	1,3	1,4	1,7	0,4
Slovenia	1,1	1,4	1,8	0,7
EU-15	1,5	1,6	1,7	0,2
EU-27	1,3	1,5	1,9	0,6

	Male life expectancy			
	2000-05	2025-30	2045-50	change
Bulgaria	67,1	71,9	75,3	8,2
Czech R.	72,1	76,6	78,4	6,3
Cyprus	76	78,3	79,9	3,9
Estonia	65,8	71,3	74,7	8,9
Hungary	67,8	73,2	76,1	8,3
Latvia	65,7	71,2	74,6	8,9
Lithuania	67,6	73,2	76,1	8,5
Malta	75,9	80	82	6,1
Poland	69,8	74,6	76,9	7,1
Romania	66,5	71,6	74,2	7,7
Slovakia	69,8	74	76,6	6,8
Slovenia	72,3	76,8	78,6	6,3
EU-15	75,0	78,7	80,0	5,0
EU-27	70,1	74,7	77,2	7,1

	Female life expentancy			
	2000-05	2025-30	2045-50	change
Bulgaria	74,8	78,5	81,1	6,3
Czech R.	78,7	82,8	84,4	5,7
Cyprus	80,5	82,9	84,5	4
Estonia	76,4	79,5	81,5	5,1
Hungary	76,1	80,5	82,5	6,4
Latvia	76,2	79,3	81,3	5,1
Lithuania	77,7	81,1	83	5,3
Malta	81	84,1	86,1	5,1
Poland	78	81,4	83,3	5,3
Romania	73,3	77,7	79,7	6,4
Slovakia	77,6	80,4	82,4	4,8
Slovenia	79,6	83,4	85	5,4
EU-15	81,3	84,3	85,5	4,2
EU-27	77,8	81,2	83,1	5,3

	Total population			
			Change	
	2000	2050	Absolute	%
Bulgaria	7,9	4,5	-3,4	-43,0
Czech R.	10,3	8,4	-1,8	-17,9
Cyprus	0,8	0,9	0,1	16,1
Estonia	1,4	0,8	-0,6	-46,1
Hungary	10,0	7,5	-2,5	-24,9
Latvia	2,4	1,7	-0,7	-27,9
Lithuania	3,7	3,0	-0,7	-19,1
Malta	0,4	0,4	0,0	2,5
Poland	38,6	33,4	-5,2	-13,6
Romania	22,4	18,1	-4,3	-19,1
Slovakia	5,4	4,7	-0,7	-13,4
Slovenia	2,0	1,5	-0,5	-23,2
EU-15	376,4	364,2	-12,2	-3,2
EU-27	481,7	449,2	-32,5	-6,8

	Share of older persons in the working-age population.			
			Change	
	2000	2050	Absolute	%
Bulgaria	16,6	28,2	11,6	69,4
Czech R.	15,3	26,8	11,6	75,7
Cyprus	14,3	22,2	7,9	54,9
Estonia	16,2	27,1	10,9	67,2
Hungary	16,1	25,7	9,5	59,0
Latvia	17,5	29,2	11,7	66,9
Lithuania	15,8	28,2	12,4	78,3
Malta	15,0	22,5	7,5	50,1
Poland	12,5	25,7	13,1	104,8
Romania	15,0	24,5	9,5	63,8
Slovakia	15,4	26,8	11,5	74,7
Slovenia	12,7	26,4	13,7	108,4
EU-15	16,4	18,1	1,6	10,0
EU-27	15,3	25,5	10,2	66,6

Pop. aged 55-64 as % of pop. aged 15-64

	Very old as a % of elderly			
			Change	
	2000	2050	Absolute	%
Bulgaria	13,1	24,4	11,4	87,0
Czech R.	16,9	29,0	12,1	71,3
Cyprus	22,8	32,5	9,7	42,6
Estonia	17,2	27,0	9,8	56,8
Hungary	16,9	26,6	9,7	57,5
Latvia	18,2	29,0	10,8	59,4
Lithuania	18,0	32,5	14,5	80,4
Malta	19,4	33,4	14,0	72,2
Poland	16,2	26,6	10,4	64,3
Romania	13,5	23,4	9,9	73,1
Slovakia	16,0	25,6	9,5	59,4
Slovenia	15,8	34,0	18,2	114,8
EU-15	22,6	37,0	14,4	63,7
EU-27	17,4	29,3	11,9	68,1

Pop. aged 80+ as % of pop. aged 65+

Total population (millions)

	2000	2005	2010	2015	2020	2025	2030	2035	2040	2045	2050
Bulgaria	7,949	7,570	7,185	6,816	6,467	6,125	5,787	5,458	5,143	4,835	4,531
Czech R.	10,272	10,218	10,138	10,028	9,895	9,727	9,509	9,253	8,981	8,706	8,429
Cyprus	0,784	0,815	0,841	0,864	0,885	0,899	0,907	0,911	0,913	0,913	0,910
Estonia	1,393	1,316	1,253	1,190	1,127	1,062	0,995	0,931	0,870	0,811	0,752
Hungary	9,968	9,721	9,489	9,254	9,021	8,783	8,532	8,261	7,990	7,735	7,486
Latvia	2,421	2,353	2,288	2,225	2,161	2,090	2,015	1,941	1,874	1,810	1,744
Lithuania	3,696	3,653	3,594	3,538	3,483	3,418	3,341	3,255	3,168	3,082	2,989
Malta	0,390	0,398	0,405	0,411	0,416	0,418	0,417	0,414	0,409	0,404	0,400
Poland	38,605	38,427	38,253	38,035	37,741	37,254	36,577	35,795	34,967	34,170	33,370
Romania	22,438	22,150	21,819	21,437	21,026	20,585	20,130	19,662	19,186	18,688	18,150
Slovakia	5,399	5,419	5,430	5,420	5,384	5,317	5,224	5,108	4,978	4,834	4,674
Slovenia	1,988	1,976	1,955	1,926	1,890	1,847	1,794	1,733	1,667	1,598	1,527

Working-age population aged 15-64 (millions)

	2000	2005	2010	2015	2020	2025	2030	2035	2040	2045	2050
Bulgaria	5,41482	5,29941	5,11353	4,76479	4,42635	4,11046	3,81213	3,52004	3,18718	2,83302	2,54023
Czech R.	7,16405	7,27303	7,20308	6,86697	6,5482	6,30011	6,04481	5,7654	5,32223	4,84374	4,53113
Cyprus	0,51229	0,54513	0,56532	0,56981	0,56978	0,56695	0,56758	0,56814	0,56794	0,56046	0,54745
Estonia	0,94645	0,91792	0,88331	0,82513	0,76332	0,70261	0,64757	0,59633	0,5411	0,48655	0,43179
Hungary	6,81896	6,74594	6,64054	6,41286	6,04963	5,75662	5,55323	5,28145	4,91563	4,50165	4,23811
Latvia	1,64188	1,64248	1,617	1,5491	1,47116	1,38331	1,30241	1,23256	1,15715	1,08138	0,99047
Lithuania	2,48228	2,52573	2,53044	2,49088	2,40634	2,28252	2,14375	2,03313	1,91804	1,81167	1,68952
Malta	0,26284	0,2709	0,27388	0,26701	0,2615	0,25488	0,25175	0,25172	0,24723	0,23923	0,23084
Poland	26,52451	27,2044	27,63354	26,87044	25,52605	24,25542	23,50695	22,8985	21,85006	20,39044	18,80527
Romania	15,35665	15,49714	15,39623	15,04818	14,5341	14,01859	13,71502	12,91791	12,11833	11,20133	10,55783
Slovakia	3,72945	3,86237	3,92692	3,86728	3,72958	3,59669	3,47688	3,36078	3,17272	2,93009	2,70918
Slovenia	1,39515	1,39836	1,38075	1,33839	1,26289	1,18597	1,10887	1,03533	0,96184	0,87913	0,80608

Elderly population aged 65 or over (millions)

	2000	2005	2010	2015	2020	2025	2030	2035	2040	2045	2050
Bulgaria	1,28225	1,24395	1,19175	1,2208	1,25187	1,2678	1,27035	1,26943	1,30454	1,35849	1,36373
Czech R.	1,42094	1,45342	1,60702	1,87952	2,11965	2,24407	2,31913	2,37078	2,54567	2,73382	2,75537
Cyprus	0,08998	0,09897	0,11241	0,12808	0,14502	0,16386	0,17794	0,18801	0,19273	0,19989	0,21065
Estonia	0,20014	0,20727	0,20068	0,20138	0,20543	0,21026	0,21114	0,20802	0,2061	0,2026	0,20218
Hungary	1,45943	1,46971	1,52412	1,61395	1,78597	1,87056	1,8516	1,88654	2,00517	2,16467	2,1691
Latvia	0,35734	0,38716	0,394	0,39635	0,40654	0,42959	0,45012	0,46021	0,46858	0,47156	0,49137
Lithuania	0,49422	0,53825	0,57112	0,58691	0,6183	0,67193	0,74336	0,78755	0,82569	0,84121	0,8619
Malta	0,04815	0,05329	0,0604	0,07424	0,08409	0,09362	0,09811	0,09762	0,09959	0,10357	0,10736
Poland	4,68508	4,95325	4,96615	5,62261	6,63708	7,54216	7,84356	7,88793	8,15327	8,68053	9,30912
Romania	2,98571	3,17053	3,07146	3,12736	3,3721	3,59558	3,56134	3,94267	4,24866	4,62299	4,71394
Slovakia	0,61481	0,63468	0,66766	0,74415	0,87285	0,98159	1,05551	1,09359	1,1714	1,27697	1,34875
Slovenia	0,27663	0,3039	0,32662	0,3565	0,40633	0,44829	0,48134	0,50242	0,51454	0,52886	0,53093

Very elderly population aged 80 or over (millions)

	2000	2005	2010	2015	2020	2025	2030	2035	2040	2045	2050
Bulgaria	0,16743	0,21299	0,23674	0,25108	0,24174	0,24138	0,27967	0,30732	0,3201	0,32471	0,33296
Czech R.	0,24084	0,32132	0,37749	0,40694	0,42501	0,51736	0,66563	0,76486	0,77865	0,7808	0,79985
Cyprus	0,0205	0,02342	0,02599	0,02884	0,03256	0,03897	0,04608	0,05315	0,0609	0,06552	0,06842
Estonia	0,03451	0,03914	0,04679	0,04923	0,05214	0,04808	0,04972	0,05325	0,05628	0,0564	0,05467
Hungary	0,24651	0,30689	0,34859	0,36897	0,37987	0,41482	0,46787	0,55411	0,5794	0,55105	0,57689
Latvia	0,06492	0,07778	0,09452	0,10164	0,11128	0,1105	0,11069	0,11735	0,13029	0,13983	0,14228
Lithuania	0,08906	0,10429	0,13248	0,15599	0,17223	0,18158	0,18459	0,2002	0,22975	0,26609	0,28012
Malta	0,00933	0,01175	0,0139	0,01639	0,01878	0,02227	0,02954	0,03336	0,03682	0,0374	0,03583
Poland	0,75993	0,96426	1,19165	1,345	1,42063	1,3861	1,73917	2,24334	2,60089	2,58253	2,48046
Romania	0,4029	0,50982	0,60805	0,66982	0,71894	0,67021	0,73702	0,87894	0,96905	0,91278	1,10128
Slovakia	0,09866	0,13096	0,15089	0,16121	0,16523	0,17968	0,21886	0,27901	0,32011	0,33875	0,34492
Slovenia	0,04382	0,05804	0,07573	0,09026	0,09935	0,10727	0,12151	0,14701	0,16433	0,17548	0,18064

Old-age dependency ratio (%)

	2000	2005	2010	2015	2020	2025	2030	2035	2040	2045	2050
Bulgaria	23,7	23,5	23,3	25,6	28,3	30,8	33,3	36,1	40,9	48,0	53,7
Czech R.	19,8	20,0	22,3	27,4	32,4	35,6	38,4	41,1	47,8	56,4	60,8
Cyprus	17,6	18,2	19,9	22,5	25,5	28,9	31,4	33,1	33,9	35,7	38,5
Estonia	21,1	22,6	22,7	24,4	26,9	29,9	32,6	34,9	38,1	41,6	46,8
Hungary	21,4	21,8	23,0	25,2	29,5	32,5	33,3	35,7	40,8	48,1	51,2
Latvia	21,8	23,6	24,4	25,6	27,6	31,1	34,6	37,3	40,5	43,6	49,6
Lithuania	19,9	21,3	22,6	23,6	25,7	29,4	34,7	38,7	43,0	46,4	51,0
Malta	18,3	19,7	22,1	27,8	32,2	36,7	39,0	38,8	40,3	43,3	46,5
Poland	17,7	18,2	18,0	20,9	26,0	31,1	33,4	34,4	37,3	42,6	49,5
Romania	19,4	20,5	19,9	20,8	23,2	25,6	26,0	30,5	35,1	41,3	44,6
Slovakia	16,5	16,4	17,0	19,2	23,4	27,3	30,4	32,5	36,9	43,6	49,8
Slovenia	19,8	21,7	23,7	26,6	32,2	37,8	43,4	48,5	53,5	60,2	65,9

Population aged 65+ as % of population aged 15-64

Share of the very elderly in total elderly population (%)

	2000	2005	2010	2015	2020	2025	2030	2035	2040	2045	2050
Bulgaria	13,1	17,1	19,9	20,6	19,3	19,0	22,0	24,2	24,5	23,9	24,4
Czech R.	16,9	22,1	23,5	21,7	20,1	23,1	28,7	32,3	30,6	28,6	29,0
Cyprus	22,8	23,7	23,1	22,5	22,5	23,8	25,9	28,3	31,6	32,8	32,5
Estonia	17,2	18,9	23,3	24,4	25,4	22,9	23,5	25,6	27,3	27,8	27,0
Hungary	16,9	20,9	22,9	22,9	21,3	22,2	25,3	29,4	28,9	25,5	26,6
Latvia	18,2	20,1	24,0	25,6	27,4	25,7	24,6	25,5	27,8	29,7	29,0
Lithuania	18,0	19,4	23,2	26,6	27,9	27,0	24,8	25,4	27,8	31,6	32,5
Malta	19,4	22,0	23,0	22,1	22,3	23,8	30,1	34,2	37,0	36,1	33,4
Poland	16,2	19,5	24,0	23,9	21,4	18,4	22,2	28,4	31,9	29,8	26,6
Romania	13,5	16,1	19,8	21,4	21,3	18,6	20,7	22,3	22,8	19,7	23,4
Slovakia	16,0	20,6	22,6	21,7	18,9	18,3	20,7	25,5	27,3	26,5	25,6
Slovenia	15,8	19,1	23,2	25,3	24,5	23,9	25,2	29,3	31,9	33,2	34,0

Population aged 80+ as % of population aged 65

Annex 2: Labour market participation rates (as % of age-specific groups)

	Male											
	15-64						55-64					
	1996	**1997**	**1998**	**1999**	**2000**	**2001**	**1996**	**1997**	**1998**	**1999**	**2000**	**2001**
Bulgaria	--	--	--	--	67.4	67.8	--	--	--	--	39.9	41.8
Czech R.	--	80	79.8	79.7	79	78.5	--	56.8	55.4	55.9	54.5	54.7
Cyprus	--	--	--	--	81.6	81.9	--	--	--	--	69.3	77
Estonia	--	78.8	78.7	76.2	75.6	74.5	--	63.9	65.5	64.3	56.7	61.5
Hungary	66.6	66	66.3	67.5	67.6	67.6	28.8	28.9	27.8	30.3	34.3	36.3
Latvia	--	--	75.1	76	73.6	72.7	--	--	57.6	54.1	53.9	52.3
Lithuania	--	--	78.9	77.7	75.5	74.5	--	--	60.1	60.6	59.5	59.4
Malta	--	--	--	--	--	--	--	--	--	--	--	--
Poland	--	73.1	72.5	72.1	71.8	71.6	--	47	45.2	45.7	41.1	43.3
Romania	--	77.7	76.7	76.1	75.7	74.3	--	63.6	62.6	60.2	58.4	57.7
Slovakia	--	--	--	78.3	76.5	77.4	--	--	--	41.2	41	43
Slovenia	71.1	71.8	73	72.2	71.7	72.5	29.1	31	33.7	33.9	33.5	34.8
EU-15	77.7	77.7	77.9	78.1	78.1	78.1	--	--	--	--	52.6	--

	Female											
	15-64						55-64					
	1996	**1997**	**1998**	**1999**	**2000**	**2001**	**1996**	**1997**	**1998**	**1999**	**2000**	**2001**
Bulgaria	--	--	--	--	56.1	59.1	--	--	--	--	12.5	18.3
Czech R.	--	63.4	63.7	63.9	63.5	63	--	25.1	24.3	24.8	23.3	24.2
Cyprus	--	--	--	--	56.7	60	--	--	--	--	33.3	35.3
Estonia	--	67.1	66.5	64.8	64.8	65.6	--	42.3	43.5	41	39.3	46.6
Hungary	49.5	48.6	50.8	52	52.5	52.2	10.8	11.1	10	11.3	13.2	14.8
Latvia	--	--	62.9	62.6	61.9	63.6	--	--	29.8	29.2	28.1	33
Lithuania	--	--	65.7	67.7	67.6	66.5	--	--	29.1	32	36.5	35
Malta	--	--	--	--	--	--	--	--	--	--	--	--
Poland	--	59.5	59.4	59.6	60.5	60.8	--	29.2	26.6	25.9	24.4	26
Romania	--	65.4	64	63.7	63.6	62.4	--	48.4	48.4	47.5	47.5	46
Slovakia	--	--	--	62	62.8	63.6	--	--	--	11.3	11.1	11.1
Slovenia	61.5	62.9	64.4	63	63.1	62.5	13.2	16.8	19.7	15.1	14.8	15
EU-15	57.3	57.8	58.4	59.2	59.8	60.2	--	--	--	--	29.9	--

	Male and female											
	15-64						55-64					
	1996	**1997**	**1998**	**1999**	**2000**	**2001**	**1996**	**1997**	**1998**	**1999**	**2000**	**2001**
Bulgaria	--	--	--	--	61.6	63.3	--	--	--	--	25.1	29.3
Czech R.	--	71.7	71.7	71.8	71.2	70.7	--	40	38.9	39.5	38.1	38.7
Cyprus	--	--	--	--	69	70.8	--	--	--	--	50.8	52.6
Estonia	--	72.7	72.4	70.3	70	69.9	--	51.7	53	51	46.8	53.1
Hungary	57.8	57.1	58.4	59.6	59.9	59.7	18.7	19	17.8	19.6	22.6	24.4
Latvia	--	--	68.7	69.1	67.5	68	--	--	41.5	39.9	39.1	41.3
Lithuania	--	--	72.1	72.6	71.5	70.4	--	--	42.5	44.4	46.5	45.6
Malta	--	--	--	--	--	--	--	--	--	--	--	--
Poland	--	66.2	65.9	65.8	66.1	66.1	--	37.4	35.2	35	32.1	33.9
Romania	--	71.5	70.3	69.8	69.6	68.3	--	55.5	55	53.4	52.5	51.4
Slovakia	--	--	--	69	69.6	70.4	--	--	--	24.8	24.5	25.4
Slovenia	66.3	67.4	68.8	67.6	67.4	67.5	20.6	23.5	26.5	24.3	23.7	24.6
EU-15	67.4	67.7	68.1	68.6	69	69.2	--	--	--	--	--	--

Source: Employment in Europe 2002 - European Commission and EPC Ageing Working Group 2001.

Notes: Four Candidate Countries have also undertaken long-term projections in their Pre-Accession Economic Programme Reports 2002 (total participation rates, as % of 15-64 age group, change 2001-50): Czech Rep.: + 8,6; Cyprus: +10,6; Lithuania: +15,2; Slovenia: +16,7.

Annex 3: Reform of public pension systems in the accession countries (outlined in the 2002 PEPs)

BG	A **three-pillar pension system** has been established in Bulgaria. Mandatory public social security based on the PAYG scheme is the first pillar. Mandatory supplementary and voluntary pension insurance in private pension funds form the second and third fully capitalised pillars. The budget of public social security (the first pillar) is generating deficits as a result of the combined impact of several factors: the unfavorable system-dependency ratio (almost 1:1) due to the ageing of the population, outmigration and high unemployment, low contribution compliance before 2001, unreported incomes and employment, financial instability of many of the big insurers, **early retirement eligibility**, and the gradual diversion of contributions to the second pillar. A major step to increase contribution compliance was taken in 2001. In 2002 high contribution compliance of about 98-99% is expected. In 2003 a variety of supplementary social insurance laws will be adopted to develop the second and third pillars further.
CY	The government is currently examining the following reform options: a gradual **increase in the normal retirement age from 63 at present to 65** over the period 2004-11; the indexing of lower-band pensions based on a **price index**, instead of the wage index, as is currently the case; an increase in the rate of return on investment by investing part of the reserves in non-government assets. There will also be a gradual increase in **contribution rates** based on predetermined rules. In more specific terms, the policy option under consideration is to increase contribution rates automatically if the reserves of the fund fall below one year of coverage of pension payments. A gradual increase until 2050 in the contribution rate from the present level of 14.2% of earnings to above 20% is considered necessary to neutralize the effects of the maturing pension

	scheme and population ageing on public finances and to safeguard proper financing of the pension scheme over the long-term.
CR	The Czech pension system consists of a two-pillar scheme. In addition to a public PAYG first pillar, a voluntary individual second pillar supported by government incentives figures prominently. Contribution rates for the first pillar are 6.5% of contributory income for employees, 19.5% for employers and 26% for the self-employed. By 2007 the **statutory retirement age** of 60 for men will be raised to 62 and that for women from 57 to 59 (depending on the number of children). In 2001 the government proposed a reform package that was, however, subsequently rejected by the Chamber of Deputies of the Czech Parliament. A new approach would be launched only after the 2002 elections. According to the government proposal, the pension system should consist of **three pillars**. The first pillar will continue as a mandatory, continually financed pension scheme. The second pillar contemplates the introduction of a collective voluntary pension insurance scheme. The third pillar will continue to develop additional pension schemes with state contribution. Other forms of individual provision for old age (such as life insurance) are also considered to form an integral part of the third pillar. The future first pillar of the mandatory pension schemes (as proposed by the government) meets the following principles: the system will continue to be continuously financed and **a transition is proposed to a notional defined contribution system;** the system will be uniform, without substantial differences for various groups of insured parties (armed forces, civil service employees, etc.); it will reinforce the insurance principle.

EE	The reform process transforms the current PAYG system into a **three-pillar pension scheme**. On 1 June 2002 participants started paying into the second-pillar funds, which are compulsory pension savings schemes. In April 2002 the first-pillar pensions were indexed for the first time. This procedure will be carried out annually in line with the growth of social security contributions and the **Consumer Price Index**. In addition to the first and second pillars, the government introduced a third pillar that makes individual pension savings possible, either by acquiring pension fund shares or by entering into a pension contract with an insurance company.
H	Changes to the newly (1998) established two-pillar system will be on the reform agenda. The pension calculation rules that strengthen the insurance character of the first pillar (PAYG) are being amended**. Beyond 2013** this pillar will be restructured and turned into more of **a defined notional contribution system**. Also from 2013 a new benefit formula will be used to calculate the pensions by which the relatively generous public pension benefits are to be pared down and the degree of equivalence strengthened. The second pillar operates through pension funds established as non-profit institutions. There is also a third pillar that is provided mainly by banks. The **contribution rate to private pension funds** will be raised to 8% in 2002. Further reform steps depend on a comprehensive review exercise for the private pension fund system scheduled for 2003/04.
LV	The pension reform concept (started in 1995) featured the establishment of a three-pillar system. Back-up legislation is now finalised. The first pillar is in the nature of a compulsory non-funded pension scheme

	(PAYG). The second pillar is a public mandatory funded pension scheme (2001). The third pillar establishes a market for private pension funds. The contribution rate to the **second pillar started at 2% of pay and will be increased to 10%** by 2010, while the contribution rate to the first pillar will be reduced accordingly.
LIT	The pension system is currently based on the PAYG principle, with pension insurance contributions equivalent to 25% of wages. Regarding future demographic challenges (2025: 7 pensioners per 10 contributors, 2050: 9 pensioners per 10 contributors), the government submitted a draft law on pension reform to parliament that would introduce a **mandatory privately funded pension scheme** on 1 January 2004. **5% of the participant's income** will be reallocated from the PAYG contributions to the privately funded system. However, the **draft was rejected** by parliament as requiring further improvements.
MT	Malta operates a PAYG system administered by the government. There is no second-pillar pension system, by which workers would contribute towards a retirement fund. Likewise, there are no occupational pension schemes, as such funds were wound up in 1979, with a lump sum being then paid to contributors. A National Commission for Welfare Reform was set up in 1999 to examine the extent of these problems and suggest solutions. Lack of consensus among the social partners is holding up publication of the final report, which is known to suggest a number of parametric reforms to the present system together with the introduction of a funded pillar.
PL	Pension system reform started in 1999 with the dual aim of stabilising the pension system's expenditures in the light of an ageing population and limiting the implicit debt. Implementation of the reform has taken place

	according to schedule. The new pension system contains two obligatory elements. The first pillar (PAYG) operates according to the principle of **notional defined contribution** and is serviced by the Social Security Office; the second pillar is a funded one, and the obligatory pension contributions are transferred to the **Open Pension Funds** (OFE). The third pillar is voluntary. Since July 2001 pension contributions have been **registered in accounts**, and since June 2002 a full servicing of accounts, including transferring pension contributions to the open pension funds, has been operating as a mature sophisticated system. In the coming years the planned activities under the reform of the pension system will **incorporate the relevant legislative and administrative aspects**. Work is under way on legislation finalising the package of laws on the pension reform: law on annuities, law on bridging pensions and law on a national actuary. In the long run, amendments are planned to **equalize the situation of men and women within the pension system**. The law on the social insurance system and the law on organization and operation of pension funds will be amended so as to simplify the existing system of information exchange and to strengthen the role and increase allocations of OFE members. As regards pension contributions, in 2004 the beneficiaries will receive initial information on the balance of their pension accounts within the first pillar. Completion of implementation of the computer system should allow increased efficiency in transferring current pension contributions to pension funds, as well as for a gradual reduction in delays. Work is under way on calculating initial capital for individuals insured prior to implementation of the pension reform.
RO	Romania has introduced a three-pillar system. The first pillar consists of a compulsory redistributive component that is publicly managed. The second pillar has a compulsory capitalisation-based component, that is

	privately managed. According to the government programme, this component will be adopted when a reliable source for covering the deficit exists (should have been adopted by the end of 2002). The third pillar features an optional capitalisation-based component which is also privately managed and designed for people who have an income higher than the ceiling established in the public system. The following reforms are also under consideration: setting-up of a **supervisory institution for pension companies**, and establishment of rules to avoid moral hazard for pension companies.
SK	The pension system reforms constitute a gradual shift from continuous pension financing to the new form of pension insurance. The pension system in force is based exclusively on continuous financing. Maintaining public finance stability requires a **shift to a mixed-finance insurance system**. Therefore, a three-pillar system will be established, introducing a second-pillar compulsory pension insurance scheme and a third-pillar private supplementary scheme. In the short term, the pension system is also influenced by a high unemployment rate, a reduction in the number of people paying social security contributions and a declining collection rate for premiums caused mainly by high corporate insolvency. A new Social Insurance Law was adopted in May 2002, and will enter into force on 1 July 2003. It regulates basic social insurance consisting of sickness (health) insurance, pension insurance and accident insurance. It lays down **more stringent conditions of eligibility for benefits**, non-systematic benefits being excluded from the material scope of the pension insurance benefits. It provides a new way of calculating benefits, an **indexation mechanism** and an **amended definition of disablement** and unifies the conditions of eligibility for widower's and widow's pensions. It **equalizes the pension age for men and women** in 2003-19 (60).

SL	The Slovenian pension system has three pillars: The first pillar is a mandatory public pension scheme, while the second pillar is a collective and individual pension scheme (since 2000) that has strong tax incentives. The third pillar is for voluntary individual savings for old-age (e.g. life insurance). The government promotes this pillar by granting **tax reliefs for premiums**/annuities (cap at 3% for premiums). Upcoming changes in the system of mandatory pension insurance are designed for the most part to abolish certain difficulties or uncertain aspects that arose during implementation of the reform and to amend a law with provisions that were implemented subsequently. Changes to a system of voluntary pension insurance may lead to an increase in the number of participants in the system. Further changes also relate to a **mixed system of indexation** of pensions where pensions are adjusted annually in accordance with the change in average wages per employee. The upper limit on the rise in pensions is set by the increase in the average salary per employee in the past year, while the lower limit is set by price increases in the past year.

EDUCATION AND TRAINING IN ACCEDING COUNTRIES

ANA MARTINEZ AND ESTHER GORDO

1. CHALLENGES FOR EDUCATION AND TRAINING SYSTEMS IN THE EU: THE LISBON TARGETS

Human capital is a key element in the Lisbon strategy, which sets an ambitious goal: to obtain a substantial increase in per capita investment in human resources; and to halve the number of 18 to 24 year-olds with only lower-secondary education who are not in further education and training.

Educational systems face similar challenges in current EU Members and in acceding countries: to raise quality of educational systems, improving performance and to ensure population is given adequate skills adapted to the needs of working life and market requirements. In addition, if Lisbon targets are to be met, more resources, and more efficiently invested, will have to be devoted to investment in education, to ensure that overall investment in human resources is conducive to economic growth. However, acceding countries must tackle with more severe problems in terms of mismatch of skills and adaptability of labour force, low participation at tertiary education and inefficiencies.

Efficient investment in education should be a high priority as a part of a policy strategy designed to promote growth and social cohesion, since education is a key growth input, particularly in an increasingly knowledge-based economy, and an important lever of social cohesion policy.

2. *The Economics of Education*

Education could be considered as a key component of human capital, as it encompasses knowledge and skills embodied in humans that are acquired through schooling, training and experience and are useful in the production of goods, services and further knowledge.

Investment in human capital contributes directly to economic performance, at the individual level and for the whole economy. More skilled workers will be more productive with any given technology and they can learn faster, i.e. improve existing production processes or adapt to new technologies faster, and develop new ones more easily. The importance of human capital rises as production processes become increasingly knowledge-intensive.

At individual level, school attainment is a primary determinant of individual income and labour market status (labour force participation rates and employment probabilities). Recent research suggests that an additional year of schooling increases wages at the individual level by around 6.5% in the EU. The link between human capital and individual wages becomes stronger in times of rapid technological change. Given these links between education and earnings and labour market status, education is a key tool of social cohesion policy.

From a macroeconomic point of view, human capital is linked to economic growth through two non-mutually exclusive mechanisms: one the hand, the **level effects**, by which human capital can increase productivity directly (it enters the production function as an additional input); and on the other, the **rate effects** i.e. human capital facilitates the creation or absorption of knowledge (it enters the technical progress function). As important as quantity of human capital is its quality for growth (Lee and Lee (1995) and Hanusek and Kimko (2000)). Some estimates (De la Fuente and Ciccone, 2002) show that an additional year of average school attainment increases the level of aggregate productivity by around 5% on impact and by further 5% in the long run. This second effect reflects the contribution of human capital to technological progress (the rate effects).

Externalities may be important, i.e. that some of the benefits of educational investment will leak out and will be captured by other parties. This would justify public corrective action.

2.1. Policy implications

Policy action in education is based on market failures which lead to sub optimal results from a social point of view, such as capital market failures, risk and uncertainty; asymmetric information; spill over effects; monopsony power and poaching. Social returns from investment in human capital could exceed the private returns to individuals and firms. Thus, investment may be sub-optimal from the social perspective. This justifies corrective measures such as education subsidies and compulsory schooling laws. In addition, there are other arguments in favour of intervention, resting on its redistributive effects, considering education as an instrument of social cohesion.

The education system is key for the development of the knowledge-based society. It should perform four roles with respect to knowledge: it should provide the broad basic education that makes a populace literate, imparting both everyday skills and intellectual abilities needed for an informed citizenship. Secondly, it should stimulate interest and prepare adequate numbers of young people to pursue careers in science and technology. Thirdly, it should educate a diverse labour force and develop skills at various levels of sophistication, including skills needed to navigate in the knowledge economy. Finally, it should conduct research and advanced training that creates the highly trained specialists needed to advance the frontiers of knowledge and its application. A complex nexus of institutions and actors makes up national higher education systems.

A country knowledge economy strategy would explicitly address how knowledge production moves form universities to users. Significant emphasis would be given to institutions whose purpose extends to training and production of knowledge as a public good. It would propose reforms needed to allow these institutions to develop both the research base, and the skilled people, needed for a knowledge economy to flourish. Distance learning, lifelong learning, and policy stimulus for greater mobility of students and teachers would be part of the education strategy needed to support the knowledge economy. Preparing workers to take decisions, to learn, to deal with non-routine problems would be integral to reformed education systems.

To meet these objectives, educational systems should be ensured adequate resources that must be invested efficiently and improve quality and performance. Studies show that the impact of education systems does not necessarily depend on the level of public spending, but as much on the intra-sectoral allocation and the composition of spending. Education policies first must ensure that the available resources are adequately allocated within the sector among education levels: tertiary education programmes should not absorb excessively large shares of the education budget at the expense of primary and secondary education. Also, resources in some cases must be shifted away from the public preschool systems that traditionally have been large in size and scope. Second, the delivery cost of education services can be lowered in many areas, and the quality of spending can be improved through changes in the school curriculum and by ensuring that textbooks and other essential teaching materials are provided.

3. *EDUCATION IN CANDIDATE COUNTRIES*

3.1. OVERVIEW[1]

Education systems in accession countries have gone through major reforms in recent years, as the development of a market economy has raised new needs to be met by the educational systems.

In terms of resources, education spending in the transition economies has been high but somehow inefficient: some structural failures such as over-staffing, duplication of facilities and overemphasis on non-essential services have inflated spending in this sector in certain countries.

Overall, the populations of the accession countries have a **high literacy** rate and the **educational infrastructure** is **well developed.** However, educational attainment **does not fully meet the needs of the private sector** in terms of the **knowledge being produced and the adaptability of the workforce.** There are two important issues facing most accession countries: first, available data show that **an excessively large proportion of their workers are not prepared for knowledge-based jobs**, which is in large part a failure of the education system. Secondly, related to the above, **gross enrolment rates in tertiary education are very low in most accession countries**. Accordingly, efforts should be made to improve performance of educational systems in order to produce skills and qualifications needed in a knowledge society and to raise education expenditure efficiency (reducing cost per person educated).

A review of current education reform plans in accession countries suggests considerable awareness of these issues, although progress in reforms in the education sector varies across accession countries:

---

1 Data for EU and Candidates Countries come from Eurostat, Labour Force Survey, European Report of Quality Indicators of Lifelong Learning and the Unesco.

Estonia has a comprehensive education reform programme connected to labour market needs and to R&D needs. The Estonian Education Strategy focuses on vocational education and higher education. In higher education, priority is given to engineering, technology and teacher training. Adult re-training is also included.

Latvia is connecting all state libraries and schools to the Internet, and providing universal information literacy through its schools.

Lithuania has an education reform programme focused on the quality of higher education, and including reform of curricula (more science based), distance education, adult training and greater international contacts.

Slovakia and Slovenia have announced education reforms. In Slovenia, an expanded proportion of the government budget will go to education.

Hungary is currently implementing a comprehensive higher education reform (1996-2001). The overall objective is to increase responsiveness to social and economic needs; improve the operating efficiency of the system; mobilise private finance; improve equity in higher education finance. As a result of the reform, during the period 1995/1996 and 2000/2001, the gross tertiary level enrolment rate increased from 18% to 30%. During the period 1995/1996 and 1999/2000, the total spending per student as a percent of per capita GDP decreased from 121% to 70%. Private finance in higher education has grown significantly. Within the framework of the reform, programs are currently implemented to adjust national R&D efforts more to private sector demand.

3.2. RESOURCES ALLOCATED TO EDUCATION: PUBLIC EXPENDITURE ON EDUCATION[2]

Graph 1: Public Expenditure on Education, % GDP (2000)

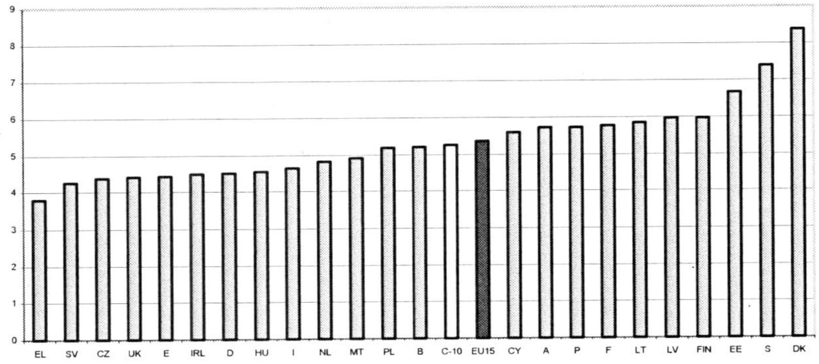

Source: Eurostat, New Cronos

Across EU countries, there is a wide range of variation on the volume of public spending assigned to education, from the highest at 8.1% in Denmark to the lowest at 3.6% in Greece. **Public funding of education** in acceding countries is on average somewhat lower than the EU average of 5.3% of GDP. Two groups among acceding countries can be differentiated: The Baltic states (Estonia, Latvia and Lithuania) with expenditure levels above 6% of GDP, higher than the EU average and ranking among the EU countries with the highest levels; and the Czech Republic and Slovenia with the lowest ratios of public expenditure, not only relative to the EU-15 average but also in an EU with 25 members.
In some Candidate Countries public spending on education has registered a marked drop during the nineties. This is the case of Poland, the Czech Republic and Slovakia. In contrast, public spending has risen

2 It should be noted, though, that these figures are difficult to compare, as they are not controlled for differences in demographic developments. Data comparability may be further impeded by differences in the efficiency of resource input.

steadily in Estonia, Slovenia, Lithuania and Cyprus.

The **share of public spending allocated to education in the public budget,** an indicator of the priority given to education in public spending, varies considerably among EU Members ranging from 14.5% (Denmark) to 6.4% (Greece), with an EU average of 11.2%. For those accession countries for which data is available, they suggest that education absorbs a high percentage of public spending.

The Czech Republic spends 7.8% of its overall public expenditure budget on education, well below the EU average, and exceeds only Greece among the EU countries. Slovakia with 13.9% report figures higher than most EU countries while Cyprus has the highest share with 15.6%.

Concerning **private funding**, there is little information but estimates signal that private expenditure on education is much lower in accession countries than in EU Member States. Families and companies devote fewer resources to education in accession countries.

Graph 2: Total education budget as a share of total public expenditure (1999)

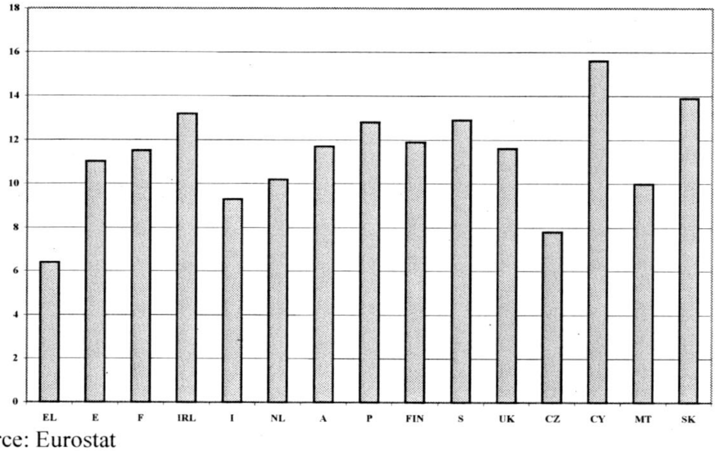

Source: Eurostat

Graph 3: Public Financing as % GDP, by levels of education

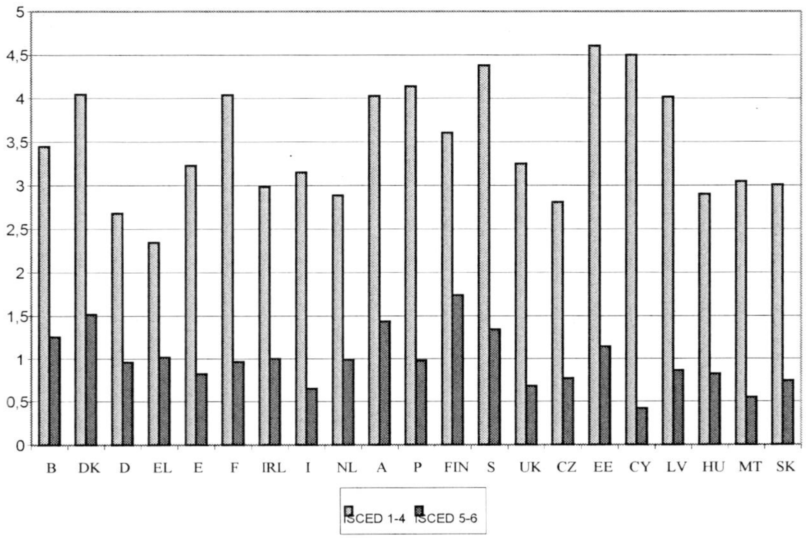

Source: Eurostat

By levels of education, graph 3 shows that in the EU public financing is especially important for primary and secondary education, which receive a much larger proportion of public spending than tertiary education. On average, the EU spends 3.5% of GDP in primary and secondary education. Four countries spend less than the average (2-3%) and five (Denmark, France, Austria, Portugal and Sweden) more than 4%. For the tertiary level, the EU average is 1.1%. Eight Member States spend from 0.65 to 0.99% in tertiary education, below EU average.

Accession countries show a similar pattern. A larger proportion of public spending is allocated to primary and secondary education, ranging from 4.6% in Estonia to 2.7% in Cyprus. Overall, the average among the accession countries is not much lower than in the EU. The difference is much more marked for tertiary education, with higher homogeneity among accession countries but lower average spending than EU members.

3.3. STRUCTURAL ISSUES

Expenditure on education must be complemented with **indicators on efficiency** in the use of those resources. Apparently, there are some concerns on this issue. In many countries the ratio of pupils per teacher and the class size are very low and the number of teachers as part of the active population is quite high in some accession countries compared to EU Member States. In addition in some countries, equipment is outdated and funding for renewing is often scarce. Some accession countries have encouraged the schools to provide services to the market, aiming at compensating the lack of sufficient resources. Big efforts are being made to supply computers, ICT and Internet access, in part thanks to funding of EU programs, and the number of schools connected to the Internet are growing fast, with 95% of Slovenian schools connected in 2000, 75% in Estonia and 40% in Lithuania.

These features of educational system can explain the rise in costs observed in accession countries and the priority given to optimisation of resources in policy agenda.

One major issue is the situation of teachers, which has deteriorated in most accession countries. In general average teacher's salary has grown less than the average salary. In addition, there is a need to update and improve teachers training to deal with the requirements of new curricula, new pedagogies and methodologies and the development of ICT and learning. And available data show a large gap between EU Member States and accession countries on teacher training. This discourages the best qualified from entering the system to prepare for the replacement of older staff and prevents teachers from being adequately retrained.

3.4. Output and Quality of Educational systems

There is a series of indicators, namely **educational attainment** of the population and **participation** in education and training that provide an overview of the output and quality of educational systems of countries concerned.

3.4.1. Educational attainment

Despite the fact that some figures could lead to rather optimistic conclusions and although qualitative information is missing for a number of countries, there is in general for the accession countries a **clear gap in qualifications of the adult population** in quantitative terms, in particular at tertiary level, and in qualitative terms. Recent reforms aiming at improving quality and contents of lower-secondary and general education will change these results.

There are **different indicators** to assess educational attainment: on the quantitative side, the percentage of 25-64 year-olds having completed at least upper-secondary level (International Standard Classification of Education (ISCED) level 3); and the percentage of 25-64 year-olds having completed tertiary education (ISCED 5 and 6). Qualitative information is given by international surveys such the IALS and the PISA study. These indicators have to be complemented with information on the labour market results by level of education.

A. Adult population with at least upper-secondary education

The data obtained from the Eurostat Labour Force Survey show that accession countries are in better position than EU countries. However, these figures must be interpreted with caution. First, attainment has nothing to do with quality of the education provided and do not differentiate between the old communist qualifications and the new qualifications needed for the developing knowledge-based economies.

As the following figure shows, accession countries have a larger proportion of population aged 25-64 having completed at least upper secondary level than the EU. The average in the Candidate Countries is 77.40% of adult population, well above the EU average of 63.80% and the three worst EU performers. The Czech Republic, Estonia, Slovakia and Lithuania score higher than the top EU countries (Germany, 83% and the UK 81%).

These differences remain when considering the younger group of population. Accession countries have, on average, a higher percentage of 22 years olds having completed at least upper secondary education than the EU countries, where the rate is 75%. In the Czech Republic, Poland and Slovakia the figure exceeds 90%. Conversely, Portugal has the lowest percentage (45%) in the EU.

Educational levels improve in younger generations, both in the EU and in acceding countries. In the EU more than 60% of 55-64 year olds had not completed upper secondary education against 29% of 25-34 year olds. In acceding countries, percentages are lower in all age groups and differences are less marked.

Graph 4: Population aged 25-64 completed at least secondary education (2001)

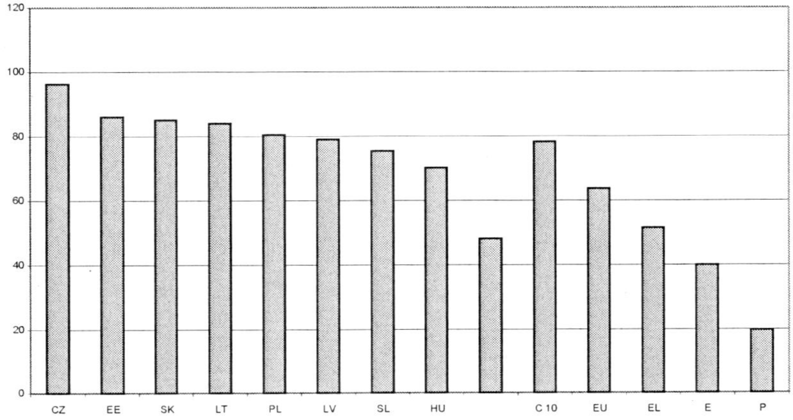

Source: Eurostat

Graph 5: % of population by age group who do not have completed secondary education (2000)

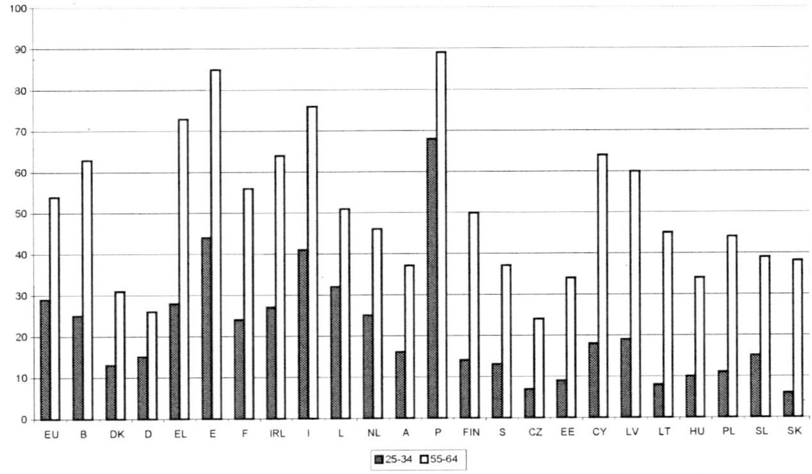

Source: Eurostat

B. Adult population who have completed tertiary education

On average, 22% of 25-64 year-olds have completed tertiary education in the EU, whereas in acceding countries that figure is only 14%. Only Lithuania, Estonia and Cyprus are above the EU average. The majority of acceding countries reach less than 15%, above the two bottom EU countries (Italy and Portugal).

Tertiary levels are higher among the youngest in the EU. Whereas 23% of the EU population aged between 35 and 39 have a tertiary education qualification, the proportion for those aged 55-59 is only 16%. This trend is particularly strong in Greece and Spain, where the proportion of those with tertiary education qualifications is at least twice as high in the 35-39 age group as in the 55-59 age group. In other countries, the age-based differences are less marked since the percentage of people with tertiary education qualifications in the 55-59 age group is relatively high (19% or more in Belgium, Denmark, Germany, the Netherlands, Finland, Sweden, the United Kingdom). In Italy and Portugal the proportions of those with tertiary level qualifications are relatively small across all the age groups considered.

In the acceding countries, there is less disparity in the educational attainment levels between generations. In the majority of these countries the proportion of those with tertiary education qualifications is fairly stable across different age groups, excepting Cyprus where the proportion of those with tertiary education qualifications is at least twice as high in the 35-39 age group as in the 55-59 age group. In Estonia and Lithuania the age-based differences are less marked since the percentage of people with tertiary education qualifications in the 55-59 age group is relatively high. In Poland, and Slovakia the proportions of those with tertiary level qualifications are relatively small across all the age groups considered.

Graph 6: aged 25-64 with tertiary education (2001)

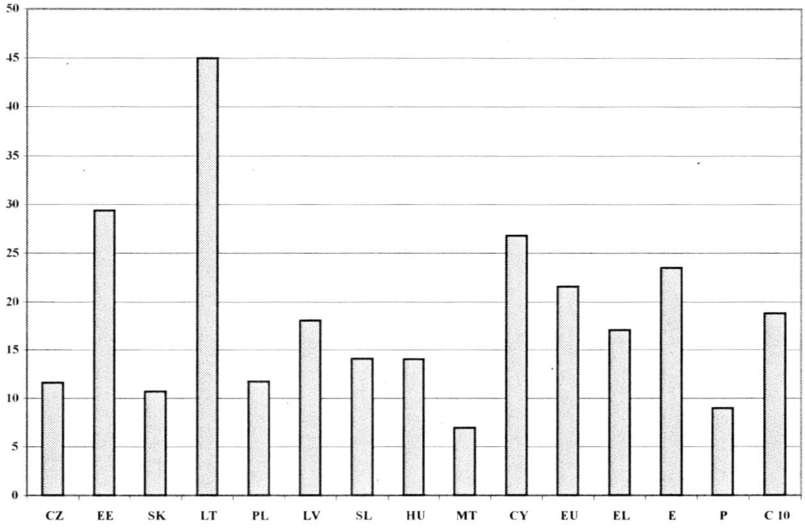

Source: Eurostat

However, figures of educational attainment must be interpreted with caution. Curricula reforms recently undertaken in Candidate Countries are difficult to put in place and in some cases old and outdated curricula are still used. In addition, these aggregate levels are broad categories, which aggregate different qualifications, which do not correspond to the same level in all countries. Finally, there are indicators that some of the candidates showing the highest rates of educational attainment at tertiary level (Lithuania, Estonia) are those that show the highest rate of unemployment and the lowest rate of employment for highly skilled workers (markedly higher and lower than the respective EU rates).

Graph 7: Group age tertiary education 2001

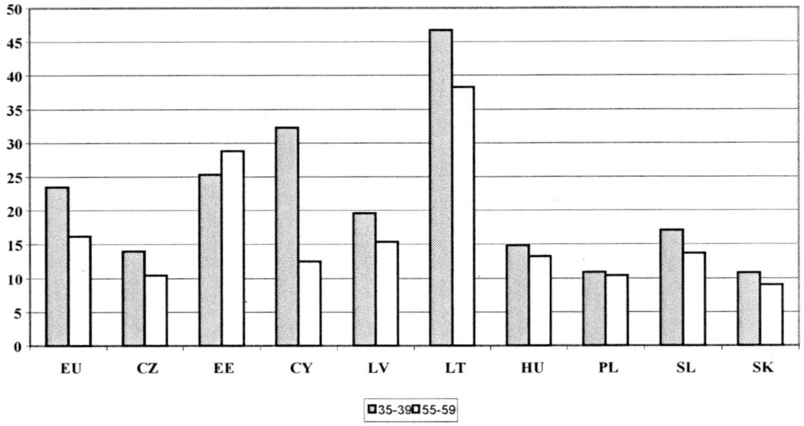

Source: Eurostat

Graph 8: Unemployment rates by level of education (2000)

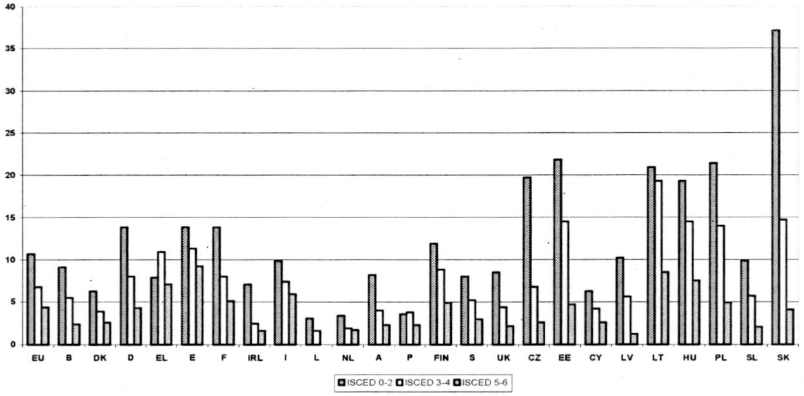

Source: Eurostat

As the graph shows, there is a positive relationship between employment and the level of education attained. In principle, higher education implies better status in the labour market. When comparing figures for the EU and Candidate Countries some features have to be highlighted:

acceding countries have a larger proportion of adult population with at least upper secondary education than the EU. However, unemployment rates for this group are much higher than in current Member States reflecting a mismatch between the educational system and skills provided and the labour market requirements.

In acceding countries, the situation of low skilled workers is especially serious. They are in a much more disadvantaged situation compared to their high-skilled counterparts and even more so when compared to the EU. While unemployment rates of the high skilled workers in Candidate Countries are comparable to the EU (differences reflect mainly higher unemployment rates), the situation of the low skilled is rather different. Unemployment rates are higher than in any EU country and the gap between high and low skilled is wider, reflecting a somewhat stronger segmented labour market. This conclusion is reinforced when taking into account the extremely low employment rates for the low skilled.

C. Qualitative analysis

Qualitative analysis is provided by two studies carried out by the OECD: the International Adult Literacy Survey, conducted between 1994 and 1998, including Poland, the Czech Republic, Hungary and Slovenia; and the PISA (OECD, 2000) study including Poland, the Czech Republic, Hungary and Latvia.

The IALS survey considered the performance of adults (15-65 years) in three literacy fields: prose, document and quantitative literacy. The survey covered 22 countries. Hungary, Poland and Slovenia were placed at the bottom pf the group, except Hungary in quantitative literacy and the Czech Republic, which scored high in the three fields.

Table 1

PROSE	DOCUMENT	QUANTITATIVE
SE 301.30	SE 305.60	SE 305.90
FI 288.60	DK 293.80	DK 298.40
NL 282.70	FI 289.20	CZ 298.10
DE 275.90	NL 286.90	DE 293.30
DK 275	DE 285.10	NL 287.70
BE 271.80	CZ 282.90	FI 286.10
CZ 269.40	BE 278.20	BE 282.00
UK 266.70	UK 267.50	HU 269.90
IE 265.70	IE 259.30	UK 267.20
HU 242.40	HU 249.00	IE 264.60
Sl 229.70	Sl 231.90	Sl 242.80
PL 229.50	PL 223.90	PL 234.90
PT 22.60	PT 220.40	PT 231.40

Source: OECD, International Adult Literacy Survey (1994-1998)

The PISA study confirmed the previous results. Countries are ranked on a scale with an average score of 500 points. It concentrates on 15-years-olds. In the table the European countries are shown, which participated at the survey. The Czech Republic is slightly under the average in reading literacy. The other three, place at the last quarter. In mathematics literacy, the results for the four candidates are better with all of them placing in the second half. In scientific literacy, the results are mixed. The Czech Republic is above the average and Hungary, Poland and Latvia in the last third.

Table 2

Reading	Mathematics	Scientific
FI 546	FI 536	FI 546
IE 527	UK 529	UK 532
UK 523	BE 520	AT 519
SE 516	FR 517	IE 513
AT 507	AT 515	SE 512
BE 507	DK 514	CZ 511
FR 505	SE 510	FR 500
DK 497	IE 503	HU 496
ES 493	CZ 498	BE 496
CZ 492	DE 490	ES 491
IT 487	HU 488	DE 487
DE 484	ES 476	PL 483
HU 480	PL 470	DK 481
PL 479	LV 463	IT 478
EL 474	IT 457	EL 461
PT 470	PT 454	LV 460
LV 458	EL 447	PT 459
LU 441	LU 446	LU 443

Source: OECD, Programme for international student assessment: European Commission, European Report on Quality Indicators of lifelong learning, 2002

3.4.2. PARTICIPATION AT EDUCATION

A. Duration of compulsory education

Compulsory education in accession countries is lower than in the EU: 10 years on average against 12 in the current Member States, with ranges from 9 years to 13 years. On average, students start later and finish earlier their compulsory education in Candidate Countries than in EU members. Duration of primary and secondary education in Candidate Countries is similar to the EU.

Table 3: Duration of primary, lower and upper secondary education (2000)

	BG	CY	CZ	EE	HU	LV	LT	MT	PL	RO	SK	SI
Primary	4	6	5	6	4	4	4	6	6	4	4	4
Lower secondary	4	3	4	3	4	5	5	5	2	4	5	4
Upper secondary	3	3	4	2	4	3	3	2	4	4	4	4

	AT	BE	DK	DE	EL	ES	FR	IE	LU	FI	PT	SE	UK	NL
Primary	4	6	6	4	6	6	5	6	6	6	6	6	6	6
Lower secondary	4	2	3	6	3	4	4	3	3	3	3	3	3	3
Upper secondary	4	4	3	3	3	2	3	2	4	3	3	3	4	3

B. School life expectancy

This indicator (UNESCO, database on Education) measures the probability for children to spend more years in education and overall retention within the education system. Data must be interpreted with caution because neither the length of the school year nor the quality of education is necessarily the same in each country. And it does not take into account the effects of repetition.

The average school expectancy in the EU is 52,60%, with marked differences between Finland and Luxembourg (the top and the bottom countries). Most accession countries for which data is available show lower average school expectancy than the EU, with Slovenia and Estonia reporting the highest values, close to EU average. This suggests that the retention capacity of educational systems is low, with a low probability for a child to spend more years in education.

Graph 9: School expectancy (1999-2000)

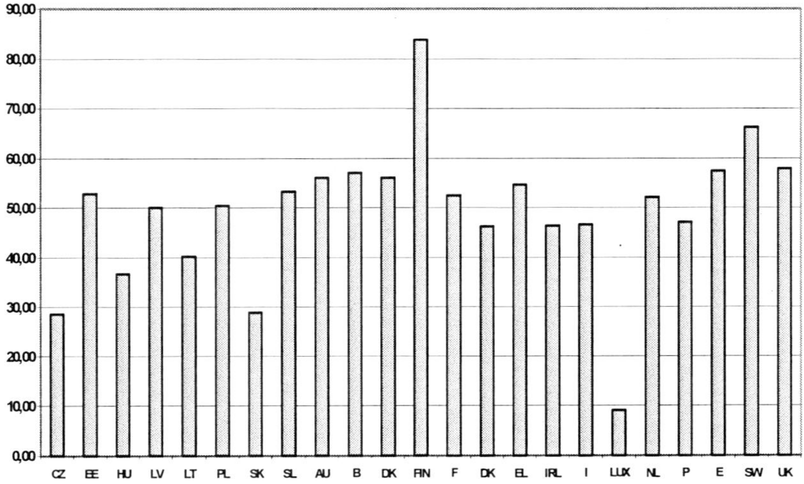

Source: UNESCO

C. Participation at Education

Gross enrolment ratio (GER) is defined as total enrolment in a specific level of education, regardless of age, expressed as a percentage of the eligible official school-age population corresponding to the same level of education in a given school year. It indicates the **capacity of the education system to enrol students of a particular age group.** The indicator includes over-aged and under-aged students because of early or late entrants, and grade repetition. Thus a rigorous interpretation requires additional information on the extent of repetition, late entrants, etc.

According to data from UNESCO, accession countries show lower GER than current EU Members for **secondary education**. In Lithuania, Poland and Slovenia GER exceeds 90% indicating the system is approaching to universal access, if one can expect the under-aged and over-aged enrolments to decline in the future to free places for pupils from the expected age group. Estonia has a GER of more than 100 per cent, which indicates that it is, in principle, able to accommodate all of its school-âge population.

Graph 10: Gross enrolment ratio at secondary education (1999-2000)

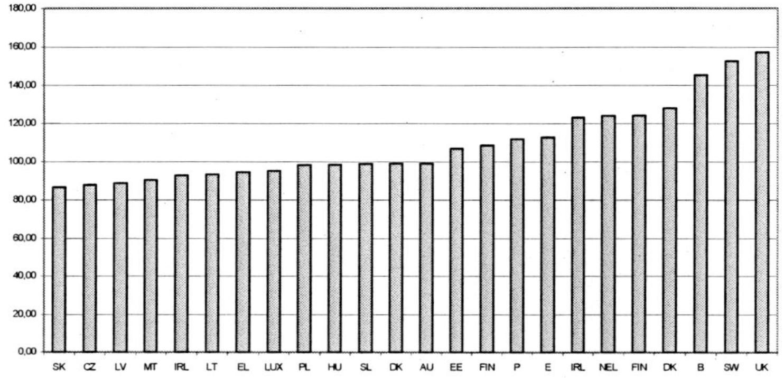

Source: UNESCO

Graph 11: Participation at the end of compulsory education (2000)

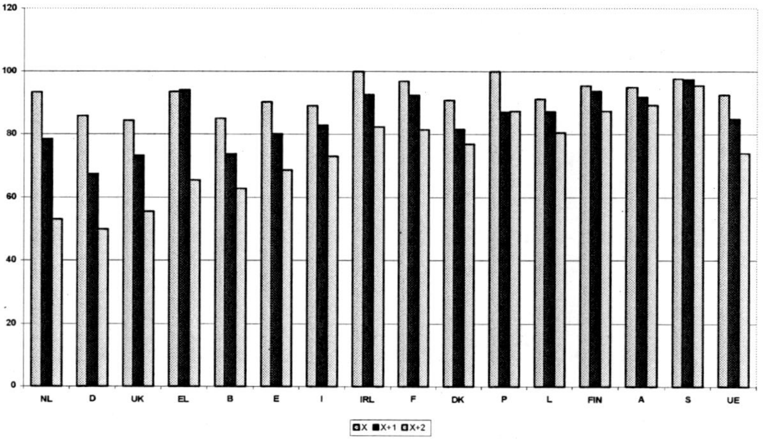

Source: Eurostat

Compulsory education usually ends with completion of the lower secondary level or during the upper secondary education level. Compulsory education end varies from a country to another. The following graphs compare participation at the end of compulsory education age (x) and the following years in accession countries and the EU. At the end of compulsory education, there are no marked differences between accession countries and EU members. With the exception of Malta, participation in education is very high in Candidate Countries, exceeding most EU countries. The Czech Republic, Slovenia, Lithuania and Estonia have the highest participation rates. Only two EU members, Portugal and Ireland, have comparables rates. The average participation rate in the EU is 93%, roughly the same as in the accession countries. Two years after the end of compulsory education, those rates fall to 73% in accession countries and 74% in the EU.

Graph 12: Participation at the end of compulsory education

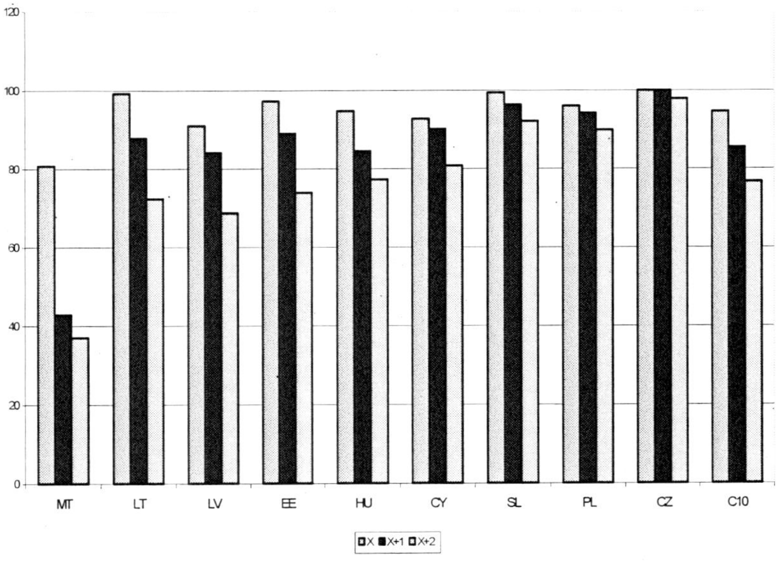

Source: Eurostat

As a result of active policies aimed at raising the educational attainment of the population and of individual choices, participation at upper secondary level has increased significantly in recent years in accession countries.

Participation in vocational education and training is slightly higher than in the EU, and show the same variations. It is particularly high in Central Europe ranging from 70-80% in Czech Republic, Slovakia and Slovenia, while it is lower than 40% in the Baltic states and Cyprus.

An important shift has taken place in Candidate Countries. As a result of the priority given to the development of higher and post-secondary education, as well as to the choices made by students and their families there has been a **shift from the vocational or apprenticeship schemas** which do not provide access to the Maturita and therefore neither to tertiary education to the technical **streams aimed at delivering qualifications at ISCED level 3** as well as the Maturita and access to universities.

Graph 13: Distribution of students in general and vocational upper secondary education (1999-2000)

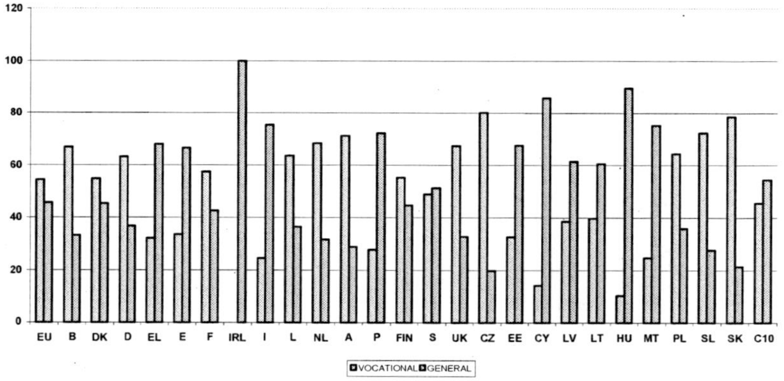

Source: Eurostat

D. Tertiary education

Graph 14: Gross enrolment rates at tertiary education

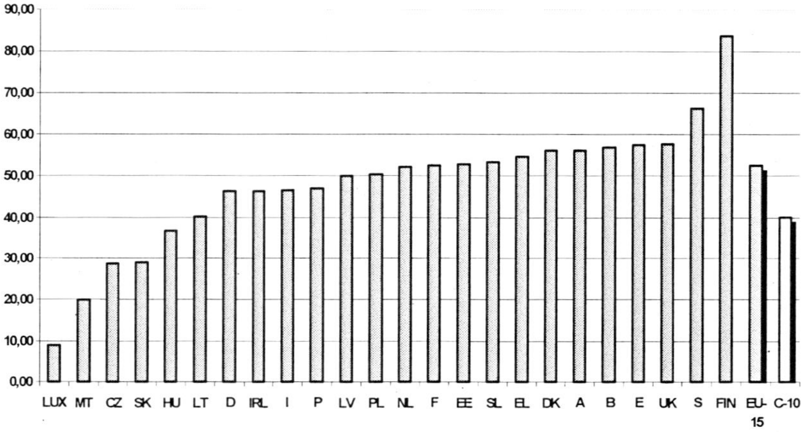

Source: UNESCO

Concerning participation in tertiary education, differences between EU members and Candidate Countries are rather pronounced, according to 99/00 data (UNESCO) on gross enrolment ratio at tertiary level. The average gross enrolment ratio in the EU is 48.9, ranging from less than 10% in Luxembourg to 84% in Finland. Only four Candidate Countries (Poland, Latvia, Estonia and Slovenia) score above the EU average gross enrolment ratio. There are significant differences among Candidate Countries themselves, since gross enrolment range from 19.8 in Malta to 53,3 in Slovenia.

The proportion of students in tertiary education, as a percentage of all pupils and students, is relatively high in Slovenia and low in Malta. It is needed to take into account the structure of the educational system (the length of compulsory education and tertiary education), number of places available in tertiary educational institutions, possible restrictions on admissions and demographic changes. Only Latvia, Poland and Slovenia exceed the average proportion of tertiary students in the EU, 15%, the rest of Candidate Countries are below the EU average. The average for Candidate Countries is 13%, with Cyprus and Malta, reporting the lowest percentages (7% both) respectively). As observed there are sharp differences among accession countries themselves.

Graph 15: % of students in tertiary education

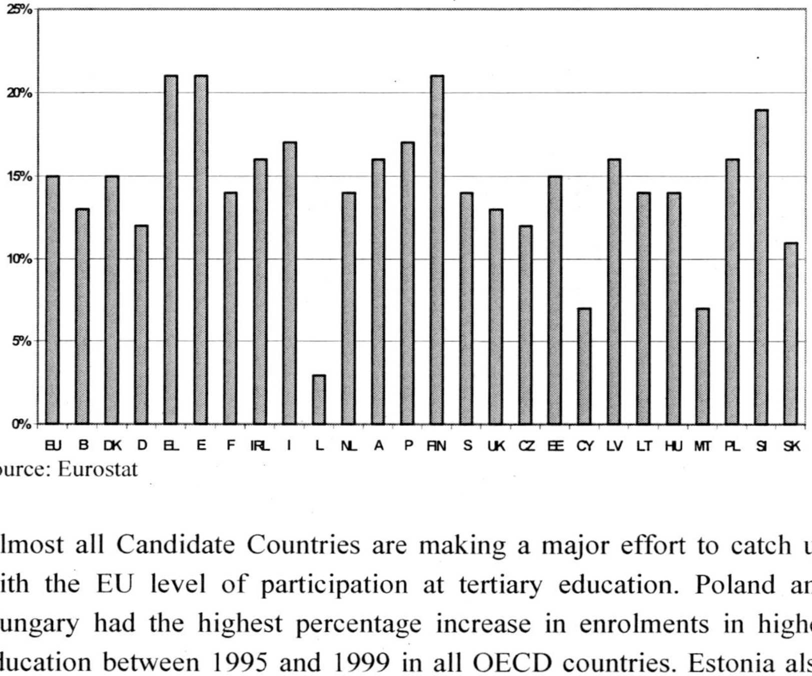

Source: Eurostat

Almost all Candidate Countries are making a major effort to catch up with the EU level of participation at tertiary education. Poland and Hungary had the highest percentage increase in enrolments in higher education between 1995 and 1999 in all OECD countries. Estonia also shows a significant increase (above 80%). Other countries also had substantial increases although to a slower pace.

The level of students in science, mathematics and computing and engineering manufacturing and construction as a proportion of all tertiary students is slightly lower in accession countries than in the EU, where on average the percentage is 27%. Marked differences among accession themselves are also noted, since the percentage range from 11.5% of Malta to the 31.7% of the Czech Republic.

According to data of the European Report on Quality Indicators of Life-long Learning, the proportion of tertiary graduates in **science and technology** in the accession countries, with the exception of Lithuania, is substantially lower than in EU Member States, although it has considerable increased in Estonia, Lithuania and Poland. The figures range from 3.8% in Malta to 12.1% in Lithuania. These figures provide an indicator of the skills produced which are relevant for the development of a knowledge-based economy.

A low proportion of graduates in these fields represent a challenge for the education system and the needs of the market economy. In the EU, the proportion of graduates in sciences, mathematics and engineering accounts for 22%, although this figure conceals substantial differences among Member States.

Graph 16: Tertiary level students in Science, Mathematics and computing and Engineering, manufacturing and construction as % of total tertiary students

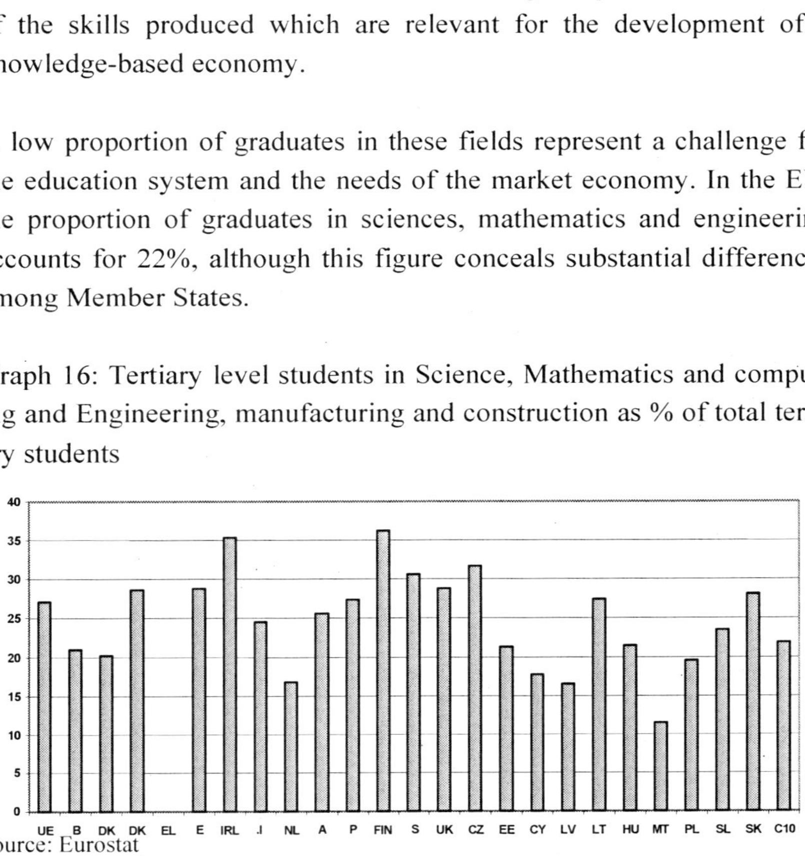

Source: Eurostat

Another indicator of output of the educational system is the number of **drop-outs and early leavers**. Both rates have substantially increased in accession countries, mainly as a result of social problems and the difficulties faced by accession countries in adapting the school system to the needs of the labour market and the individual. However, the early school leaver rate is lower than in the EU countries. This rate amounts to 19.3% for the EU, compared to 12.9% for the average rate in Candidate Countries in 2001. Drop-outs remain an important problem, especially in a number of vocational education and training schools.

Graph 17: % graduates per field of education and training (2000)

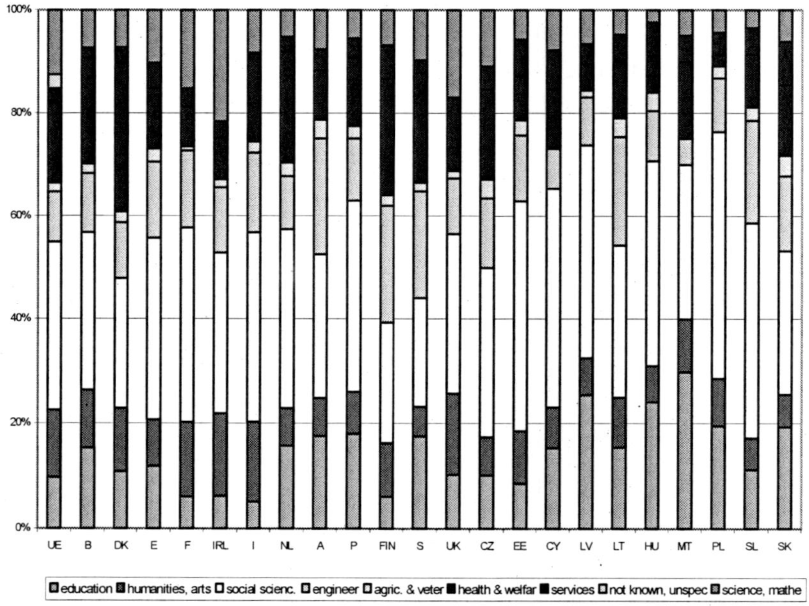

Source: Eurostat

The early school leaver rate must be compared to participation in training to assess whether this is an alternative to higher education to obtain the skills needed to enter the labour market. Data from the Labour Force Survey show large disparities between Candidate Countries and EU countries in terms of participation in continuing vocational training in general for the 25-64 years-olds. On average in Candidate Countries that participation is 3.6% against 8.4% on average for the EU.

Graph 18: Early schoolleavers (aged 18-24) 2000

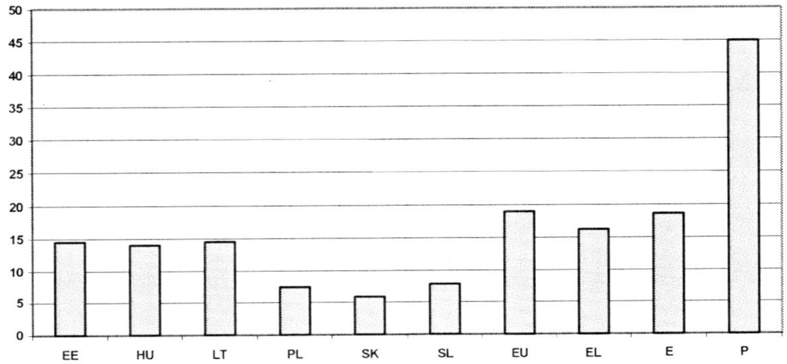

Source: Eurostat

4. *Conclusions*

The Lisbon strategy set two strategic goals in education and training: substantially increase investment in education and halve the proportion of adult population who does not have at least secondary education.

Accession countries have made a big effort to reform their educational systems and to adapt them to the challenges posed by a market economy. Nevertheless when compared to EU Member States and the progress to be made to meet Lisbon objectives, some challenges emerge from the previous analysis.

Concerning resources assigned to education, public investment is on average slightly lower than in the EU, despite accounting for a larger proportion of budgets. In addition some cost-inefficiencies exist related to structural weaknesses (low proportion of pupils per teacher, high proportion of teachers in the active population, class size, equipment, etc).

Participation at education is high in Candidate Countries, especially in secondary education. Compulsory education is shorter than in the EU, although duration of primary and secondary education is similar to the EU. School expectancy is lower. But a gap remains in terms of qualifications of adult population. Although the proportion of adult population having completed at least upper secondary education is larger than in the EU, the opposite is true for tertiary education, where in addition participation rates are lower than in the EU. Furthermore, the number of graduates in science and technology and the results in international tests are lower than in Member States. Recent reforms reveal growing awareness of these issues and as a result of reforms of curricula and other aspects of higher education, participation at tertiary education is rising and a shift has produced from vocational secondary programmes to general programs that provide access to tertiary education.

The gap in qualifications of the adult population represents an important challenge to be addressed, as it is reflected in the labour market status of workers by level of education, suggesting the existence of a much more pronounced dual labour market than in the EU between high skilled and lower skilled workers.

5. *References*

Barro, R.J., Jong-Wha L. (2000), "International Data on Educational Attainment: Updates and Implications", CID Working Paper No 42. Centre for International Development. Harvard University.

Carreiro, P., Heckman, J. (2003), "Human Capital Policy", NBER Working Paper 9495.

Cleaver, K. (2002). "A Preliminary Strategy to Develop a Knowledge Economy in European Union Accession Countries", The World Bank Working Papers.

De la Fuente, A., Ciccone, A. (2002), "Human Capital in a Global and Knowledge-based Economy", Final Report for the DG Employment and Social Affairs, European Commission.

European Commission (2001), "Making a European Area of Lifelong Learning a Reality", COM (2001) 678 final.

European Commission (2002), "Educación y Formación en Europa: Sistemas diversos, objetivos compartidos para 2010. Programa de Trabajo sobre los futuros objetivos de los sistemas de educación y formación", DG de Educación y Cultura.

European Commission (2002), "Employment in Europe 2002. Recent Trends and Prospects", DG for Employment and Social Affairs.

European Commission (2002), "European Report on Quality Indicators of Lifelong Learning", DG for Education and Culture.

European Commission (2002), "Regular Reports on Candidate Countries' Progress towards Accession".

European Commission (2002), "Summary Sheets on Education Systems in Europe: Slovakia, Slovenia, Estonia, Lithuania, Latvia, Malta, Poland, Czech Republic, Romania, Cyprus, Bulgaria", EURYDICE.

European Commission (2003), "Key Data on Education in Europe 2002", EURYDICE, Education and Culture, EUROSTAT.

European Training Foundation (2001), "Cross Country Report. The consultation on the Memorandum on Lifelong Learning in the Candidate Countries".

European Training Foundation (2002), "Key Indicators on vocational education and training".

European Training Foundation (2002), "Preparation by Candidate Countries for involvement in the EU lifelong learning policy: achievements, gaps and challenges. Synthesis of the Monographs exercise Interim Report".

European Training Foundation, Statistics database.

Eurostat, Data on Education Sector.

High Level Task Force on Skills and Mobility (2001), "Final Report"

Hirsch, D. (2002), "How good is our global education? The PISA Survey", OECD Observer, Centre for Educational Research and Innovation.

Keller, C., Heller, P (2001), "Social Sector Reform in Transition Countries", Finance and Development, IMF, September 2001.

Kessler, A., Lülfesmann, C. (2001), "The Theory of Human Capital Revisited: On the Interaction of General and Specific Investments",

Mimeo, University of Bonn.

Newcronos Statistics Database

OECD (2001), "Does Human Capital Matter for Growth in OECD Countries? Evidence from Pooled Mean-Group Estimates", OECD Economic Department Working Paper No282.

OECD (2002), "Education at a Glance 2002", OECD.

OECD (2002), "Investment in Human Capital Through Post- Compulsory Education and Training: Selected Efficiency and Equity Aspects", OECD Economic Department Working Paper No333.

Pleskovic, B., Aslund, A., Bader, W., Campbell, R. (2002), "Capacity Building in Economics: Education and Research in Transition Economies", Policy Research Working Paper 2763, The World Bank.

Sianesi, B., Reene, J. V. (2002), "The Returns to Education: a review of the Empirical Macro-Economic Literature", The Institute For Fiscal Studies WP02/05.

Temple, J. (2001), "Growth Effects of Education and Social Capital in the OECD Countries", Department of Economics, University of Bristol.

World Bank (2000), "Hidden Challenges to Education Systems in Transition Economies", World Bank, Europe and Central Asia Regïon, Human Development Sector.

UNESCO (2002), "Education Sector", UNESCO Institute For Statistics.

UNESCO (2000), "Educación para Todos. Balance hasta el año 2000", Documento Estadístico.

UNESCO Institute for Statistics, "Education Indicators. Technical Guidelines", UNESCO.

R&D AND INNOVATION

HELGE SIGURD NAESS-SCHMIDT

The theme of R&D and innovation is central to any economic policy aiming at fostering higher living standards but is difficult to handle in an operational manner in terms of analytical content and policy recommendations. At worst, it tends at the analytical level to degenerate into listing of a number of input indicators supplemented with patents applied for and obtained.

It is worth bearing in mind that in this area, there is probably much less of a consensus both within the EPC and indeed, in the wider academic/political community, as to what are the main prerequisites for innovation and particular what are the weights to be attached to different factors when explaining differences between Member States. Moreover, policies aiming for higher innovation, particular in terms of higher public subsidies, have both budgetary and social costs, and hence imply trade-offs.

Thus the ongoing discussion on boosting innovation, in particular when going beyond very broad improvement of framework conditions, is by no means finished and have much more open-ended questions compared to inter alia labour markets or liberalisation of telecommunications.

Notwithstanding these qualifications, the EPCs report on the subject and recent work from the OECD may be good starting points for benchmarking the Candidate Countries with focus on the following key areas as the main drivers of innovation (R&D being an input):

- Well educated work force
- Fierce competition in product markets
- Strong climate for entrepreneurship
- Easy access to risk capital and favourable financial conditions as a whole
- Macro-stability

- Infrastructure of research network and co-operation between private and public sector
- Broad brush indicators of innovation

In doing this analysis, it may also be worth bearing in mind, that while the present EU-15 countries are increasingly homogenous in terms of output per worker, the ten countries now ready for membership are substantially less rich (cf. graph 1). Indeed, the richest of the new countries has an income level below the 25 per cent fractile of the new.

Graph 1: Relative living standards, new and old EU-countries, GDP in PPS per person employed relative to EU-15)

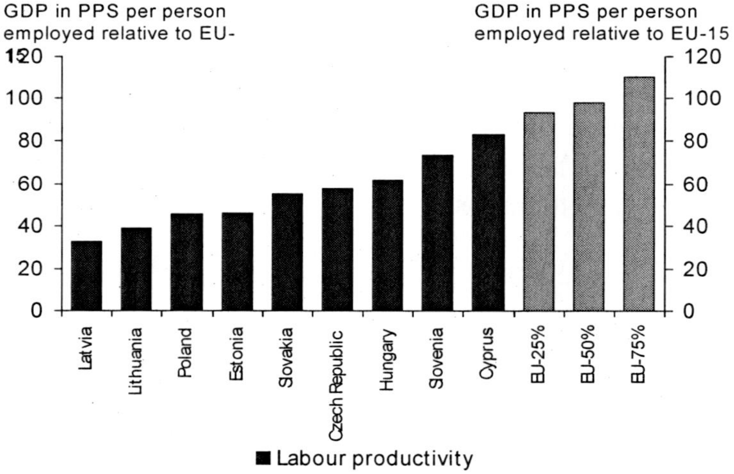

Source: Eurostat

It may thus be useful when going through the various sub-themes to note whether an observed difference essentially can be explained in terms of being a less affluent society or rather more specific characteristics eventually the result of the very changing external and internal political conditions these countries have been facing.

1. *WELL EDUCATED WORK FORCE*

Overall educational attainment is relative impressive. Using the OECD PISA study as the benchmark, the larger of the new member countries score relatively well on reading, mathematical and scientific literacy despite considerable lower income levels (cf. table 2).

Table 1: Literacy impressive, proficiency of 15 olds

	Reading literacy		Mathematical literacy		Scientific literacy	
Country	**Mean**	**Standard deviation**	**Mean**	**Standard deviation**	**Mean**	**Standard deviation**
Czech Republic	492	96	498	-	511	-
Latvia	458	102	463	-	460	-
Hungary	480	94	488	-	496	-
Poland	479	100	470	-	483	-
EU-25%	479	91.5	455.5	-	469.5	-
EU-50%	497	94	503	-	491	-
EU-75%	511.5	99	516	-	512.5	-

Source: OECD, Education at a glance 2002

Moreover, enrolment rates - the percentage of a certain age group joining formal education - is pretty much at par with EU-countries as a whole with relative little variation (graph 2).

Graph 2: Basic school enrolment ratio, 2000

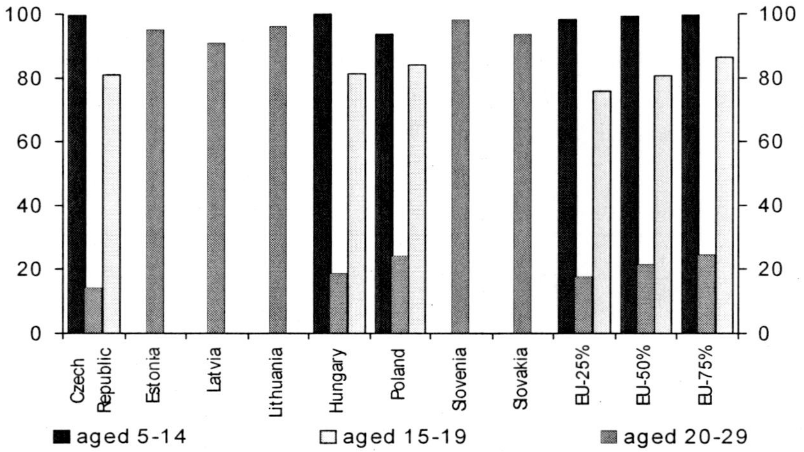

Source: OECD, "Education at a Glance" and European Commission, "Note on Stocktaking of Structural Reforms in Candidate Countries".
Note: Estonia, Latvia, Lithuania, Slovenia and Slovakia refer to 1998.

Commission reports have some qualifications in terms of teaching over-emphasising old-style root learning. While this may be true, one should reflect that quite a few of the present Member States tend to believe that they have gone to far in the other direction. Life long learning seems to receive too little attention.

Public spending on education is very high relative to GDP, in fact with four new Member States above the 75 per cent fractile (graph 3).

Graph 3: Public spending on expenditure in terms of share of GDP at the higher end of the scale, 1999

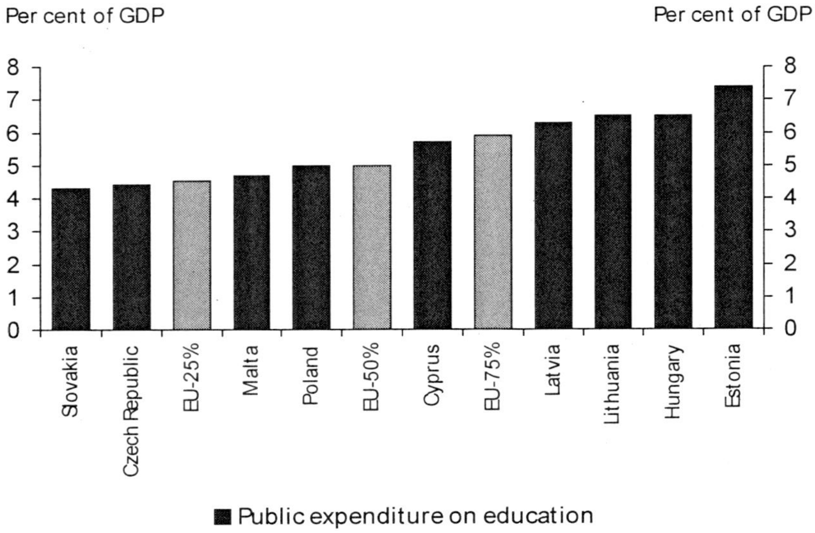

Source: European Report on Quality Indicators of Lifelong Learning

Finally, and perhaps reflecting a more hard-core oriented education policy, the new EU-members appear to have a higher concentration of tertiary degrees in natural sciences etc, which should be helpful in terms of innovation policies. Impressively, the number of graduates per 1000 habitants exceeds the 25 old Member State fractile in all new Member States.

Graph 4: Tertiary graduates in science and technology aged 20-29, 2000.

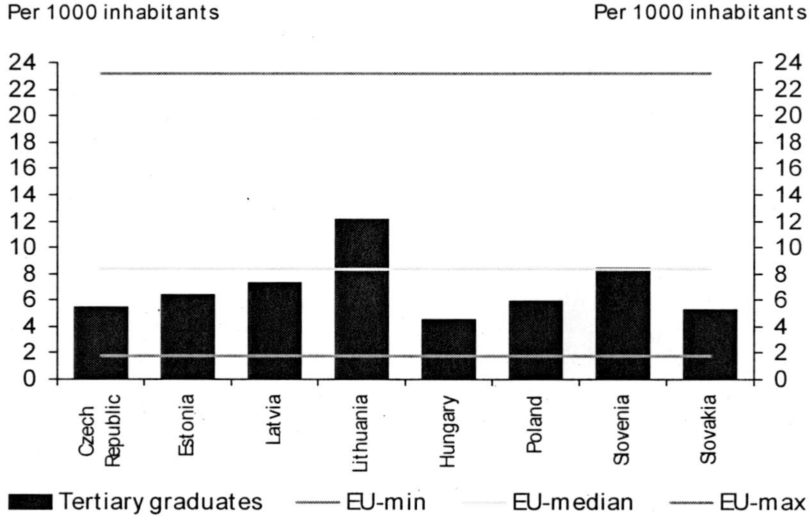

Source: European Commission - Note on Stocktaking of Structural Reforms in Candidate Countries
Note: Slovenia refers to 1999

2. ENTREPRENEURSHIP

A number of the PEPs suggest that entrepreneurship is considered an important subject and is given considerable attention. It is not only to further innovation but also seen as an element in job creation not the least at the regional level.

Typically, public policy in this area focus on two areas: 1) cutting red tape and regulatory compliance costs and 2) providing services to start-ups in terms of business advice, low cost rent facilities etc.

Bearing in mind the Commission reports, anecdotic evidence and the fact that the countries to a large extent have been forced to develop completely new administrative systems, there are good reasons to believe that there is considerable scope for improvement on administrative simplification and low compliances cost.

3. Fierce competition

Studies of innovation, inter alia OECDs, suggest that strong competition is essential. It requires the proper legislative framework backed up by regulatory power and appropriate division of work between relevant agencies. State aid should be minimised and directed to areas with either significant social gains in addition to private or temporary aiming to assist firms and workers to adjust to changed market conditions.

The bottom line is that weakly performing firms should exit, i.e. wind down their business or sell it to better performing competitors, and new firms with bright ideas should not be stopped by barriers to entry that keep alive ailing incumbents.

While the ten new countries have demonstrated enormous progress in this area, the cautious language in the various Commission documents suggests that in terms of implementation continued close surveillance is highly called for.

4. Financial sector conditions

The available evidence suggest that the financial sector in the new Member States are heavily bank based with share markets still being in their infancy and not providing much capital to finance new firms or risky investments in research and development.

However, there is no evidence that a well functioning banking sector could not - at this stage in the development of these countries - provide the instruments for financing innovation.

5. MACRO STABILITY

Recent years have shown marked improvement in macro stability in terms of lower inflation and less pronounced pick up of growth rates (graph 5). Growth rates tend to exceed old Member States (but not in recent years with a large margin). Lower and more stable inflation is helpful, bearing in mind that there is a substantial body of literature that suggests that high and unstable inflation - usually these observations tend to be twinned - creates uncertainty, risk premia and discourages investment in long-term real projects and research. It is very important that progress is sustained, which indeed will be a central part of the work of the EFC in the coming years.

Graph 5: Increased macro stability and growth

a. Annual GDP-growth

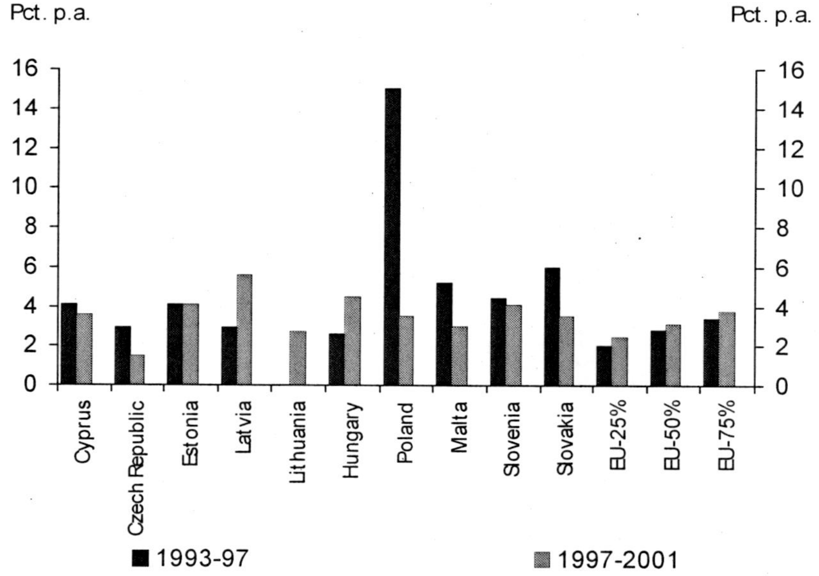

b. Annual inflation rate

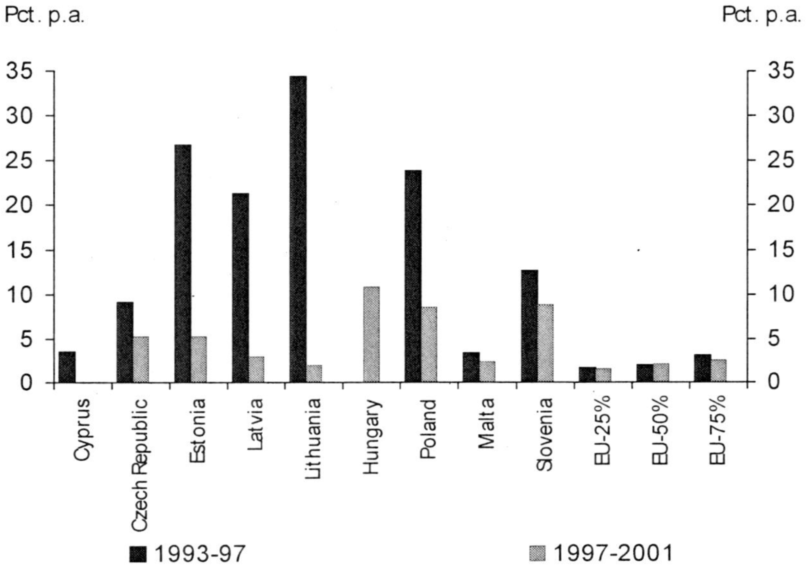

6. *INFRASTRUCTURE OF RESEARCH NETWORKS AND CO-OPERATION BETWEEN PRIVATE AND PUBLIC SECTOR*

A number of studies suggest that one of the most important public policy challenges in terms of boosting innovation is to review the whole architecture of public research institutions and their interaction with private counterparts. The EPC report touched upon this issue but not in depth. None the less, it was clear from last and present years EPC examinations that a number of countries are not happy with the present situation: the governance of public institutions is seen as being outmoded and is in the process of being reformed, not the least to make them more responsive to private firms looking for partners.

Going trough the available information sent out so far, it is not obvious where the new Member States are in this process. It seems clear that subsequent to the crisis following the break-down of the previous political system - see below - research appropriations to public institutions were cut substantially, but how much have the governance of institutions been reformed and do the concerns in the new Member States match those in the old?

7. *BROAD BRUSH INDICATORS OF INNOVATION*

Clearly the new Member countries are spending less on R&D as revealed by standard indicators, and consume less ICT.

Graph 6: R&D-spending relative to per capita incomea.

a. Research activity 1990

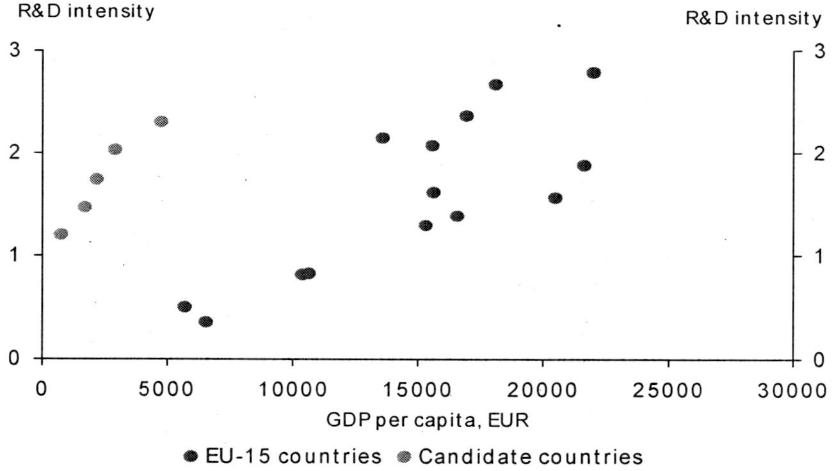

b. Research activity 1995

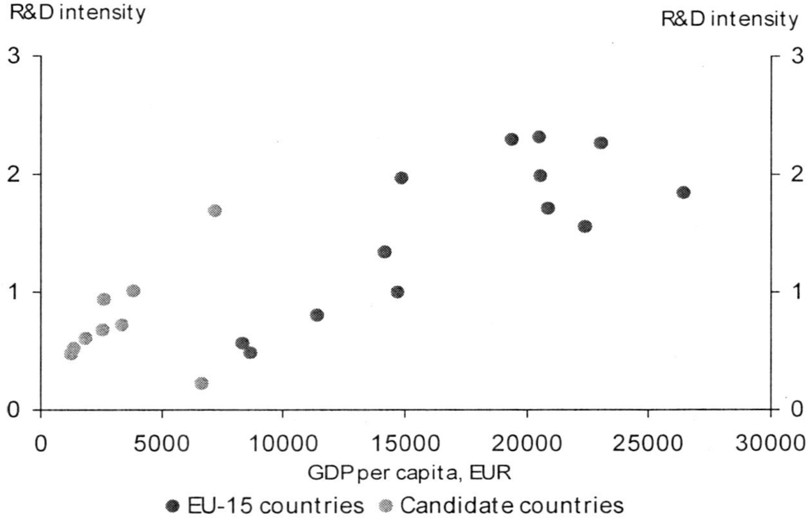

c. Research activity 2000

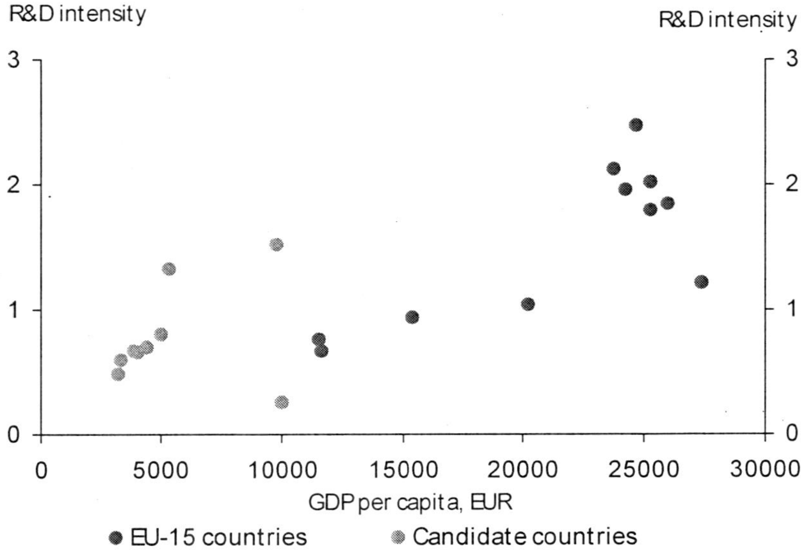

Source: Eurostat

The question is what conclusions can be derived from this. Prior to the regime changes, countries in Central and Eastern Europe spent more in terms of share per GDP than the relative income position would suggest. And the subsequent decline probably has been quite healthy in terms of moving manpower from perhaps poorly and overstaffed universities to firms looking for qualified personal.

Moreover, with relative incomes clearly well below EU-levels and market leaders elsewhere, in particular the US, it may indeed make much sense for some of the countries to focus more on technology transfer and gradual product and process improvement as opposed to large scale, long-term and risky industrial and public research investment

Graph 7: ICT spending (per cent of GDP), 2001

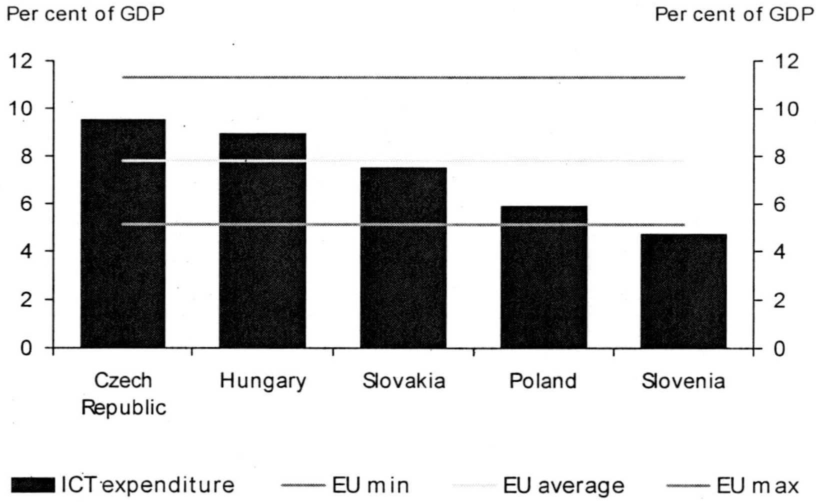

Source: World Bank Development Indicators

Spending on ICT appears on par with old Member States for the new Member States where data are available.

Some of the decline in formalised R&D spending in the new Member States may have been sensible in the wake of the regime change and one should avoid the temptation to suggest that countries at all levels of economic development should aim for the same innovation and R&D-strategy, at least in terms of public spending.

An alternative, and not necessarily conflicting hypothesis, may imply that the new Member States could become hot beds of privately financed investment in innovation given high degree of "academic" literacy and graduate production in hard core basic sciences as well as low wage costs.

EPC-Report

KEY STRUCTURAL CHALLENGES IN THE ACCEDING COUNTRIES: THE INTEGRATION OF THE ACCEDING COUNTRIES INTO THE COMMUNITY'S ECONOMIC POLICY CO-ORDINATION PROCESSES

ECONOMIC POLICY COMMITTEE[1]

PREFACE

In March 2000 in Lisbon, the European Union set itself the strategic ten-year goal

> "*to become the most competitive and dynamic knowledge-based economy in the world, capable of sustainable economic growth with more and better jobs and greater social cohesion*".

The Heads of State and Government, meeting in Lisbon and Stockholm, called for greater efforts to speed up structural change so as to raise the growth potential, aiming at five priority areas: (i) employment, (ii) innovation and research, (iii) economic reform on product and capital markets, (iv) social cohesion and (v) sustainable development. The Member States, recognising that a marked acceleration of structural reforms is required in order to bring the strategic Lisbon goal within reach, have taken steps to implement labour, product and capital market reforms embedded in a sound macroeconomic environment. The new Broad Economic Policy Guidelines (BEPGs) for 2003-05 recognise the imperative of attaining higher and sustainable growth rates. Sound macroeconomic conditions and policies are a prerequisite for a sustainable increase in economic prosperity. Better functioning and more competitive labour, product and capital markets are indispensable in achieving a

[1] EPC/ECFIN/114/03 final; Brussels, 29. April 2003

more dynamic economy and enhancing potential growth.

Enlargement in a medium- to long-term perspective is set to enhance considerably the prospects for growth of the EU economy. The acceding countries have achieved strong and solid progress with structural and institutional reforms. Progress (and the speed of structural change), however, has not been consistently strong across all countries and areas. Achieving real convergence with the EU and enhanced resilience to possible future shocks will depend on the scope and pace of progress in the implementation of the structural reform agenda.

The present Report should be a first step towards integrating the acceding countries, after enlargement, into the multilateral surveillance conducted by the Council under the Treaty, in line with the mandate given by the Ecofin ministers on 5 November 2002. The Report assesses the challenges faced by the acceding countries with regard to the Lisbon goal and the BEPGs, and identifies possible priorities for structural reforms in those countries by looking at the dynamics of a wide range of policy areas relative to the EU. The Report should also provide advice and oversight for the Council in concentrating the EU's monitoring on the priority areas where reform challenges are most evident.

The Report, which has been elaborated by a specific working group made up of experts from national administrations of the Member States, the European Commission and the European Central Bank (a list of members of the Working Group is annexed to this report), has to rely primarily on the Pre-Accession Economic Programmes and other secondary information, as the acceding countries do not yet participate in the Community's economic policy co-ordination processes. The outline of the Report follows the BEPGs and the EPC's annual reports on structural reforms. At this stage, its analytical part covers only the ten countries acceding in 2004 as the Report aims at preparing for their integration into the existing multilateral surveillance processes. Multilateral surveillance of the remaining three EU Candidate Countries (Bulgaria,

Romania and Turkey) will continue under the Pre-Accession Surveillance procedure. Moreover, the EPC considers that the latter should be assessed in a report similar to the present one before their actual EU accession. However, for the sake of completeness the comparative tables, if data is available, also cover those three countries (albeit for Turkey most data have been lacking).

KEY MESSAGES

Structural reform challenges

The Economic Policy Committee (EPC) has analysed structural challenges in the acceding countries, on the basis of the Lisbon strategy as implemented via the BEPGs. It found that the challenges of the acceding countries do not differ fundamentally in nature from those in the present Member States. However, some challenges are more demanding for the acceding countries. Consequently, the existing framework for multilateral surveillance of structural reforms, as outlined in the general recommendations of the BEPGs, seems broadly appropriate also for the acceding countries.

The gap with the EU average is still wide and in spite of experiencing higher growth rates than EU countries over the past few years the progress in catching-up with the EU in income levels has been limited in most acceding countries. Catching-up in income levels is a long-term process, but the challenge is to speed up the narrowing of the productivity gap and the gap in employment rates between the acceding countries and the EU Member States.

The Lisbon strategic goal of *"becoming the most competitive and dynamic economy"* remains unchanged in an enlarged Union. Yet the Lisbon targets are likely to be more difficult to achieve, simply because in most cases the average EU starting base is statistically lowered by the fact that most acceding countries are less well placed vis-à-vis the Lisbon targets than the existing Member States. It should also be recognised, though, that at least in some areas a number of acceding countries are already equally or even better placed than (some) present Member States.

Within the existing framework, the EPC considers that in the Cardiff process and the BEPGs, the focus for the acceding countries could rest more on the still incomplete structural shift. A number of product market issues, such as privatisation, administered prices and factors affecting the sectoral composition of the economy, and a number of challenges related to the knowledge-based economy, such as the performance of the education systems and R&D as well as innovation performance, need to be discussed more intensively than is currently the case for the existing Member States. A special focus for surveillance should be the institutional framework for market development and the business environment, and the effective implementation of competition policies. In the Luxembourg process, the focus for the acceding countries should, on account of the need for business restructuring, be more on the priority "promoting adaptability in the labour market". In regard of the specific elements of the Lisbon strategy and the BEPGs, the EPC would like to highlight the following priority areas:

- **Increasing employment and incentives to work.** Whilst the average employment rate in the EU has been rising, this is not the case for many acceding countries. In most of them, unemployment has remained unacceptably high. Major differences exist between the acceding countries in regard of employment rates and unemployment ratios. Even greater efforts than in the EU-15 will therefore be needed in order to achieve the Lisbon employment goals in an enlarged EU-25 as a whole. The measures that hold the key to "more and better jobs" include:
  - increasing the incentive effects of tax and benefit systems, in particular for low-wage earners by reducing unemployment traps ("increase incentives to work");

- ensuring that wage increases remain in line with productivity gains and price stability (wage bargaining systems are key);
- improving employment flexibility through an in-depth review of employment protection legislation;
- improving the skill level with a focus on lifelong learning;
- focusing on precisely targeted, effective and efficient active labour market policies.

Such reforms will speed up the acceding countries' convergence towards the EU's Lisbon employment targets.

- **Strengthening competition and efficiency in product and service markets.** While many challenges in product markets are key to both acceding countries and present Member States, the acceding countries are facing some specific challenges, especially with regard to sectoral changes in the economy, privatisation, administered prices and state aid. There are still several sectors in product and service markets, especially in the non-tradeable sector, where competition in the acceding countries seems to be lacking relative to EU-15. Across all sectors, for enterprise and entrepreneurship to thrive, measures to improve the business environment will be essential. The following should be priorities for further action:
  - In some countries, more progress is needed to strengthen competition rules and establish independent competition authorities. Despite good progress, significant deficiencies need to be addressed in most countries with regard to the regulatory burden on business, the effective implementation and, in some countries, the design of judicial reforms, and the quality and administrative capacity of the central and local authorities. Many segments of the public sector need to be made more efficient to facilitate the operation and growth of businesses.
  - In a number of countries, incomplete market-exit mechanisms should be addressed, in particular through the improvement of bankruptcy legislation and procedures. For network industries, it

will be key to reduce potential barriers to foreign and domestic competititon and ensuring effective and transparent supervision.

- After accession, particular attention will have to be devoted to the effective implementation of internal market obligations, which is a challenge notably with respect to achieving rapidly the targets for transposing EU directives, and eliminating barriers to cross-border trade.
- In many countries, further scope exists for privatisation/restructuring. Countries which have encountered problems in devising viable strategies should reinforce and press ahead their privatisation/restructuring programmes. State aid should be reduced and overhauled with the aim to both reduce the total and to redirect this aid towards horizontal objectives.

The implementation of competition policies should be a core focus for monitoring. Restructuring of the agricultural sector remains an urgent priority in many acceding countries.

- **Pressing ahead with financial market reforms.** Bank restructuring and privatisation have added to financial sector stability in the accession countries. Except for some notable exceptions, the privatisation process can be regarded as largely completed. As regards financial sector development, the acceding countries in transition clearly lag behind the EU average in terms of stock market capitalisation, the level of financial intermediation, and the degree of liquidity. The following reforms have been identified as being important for further action:
  - Continued reforms to deepen and widen the financial sector are required so as to avoid credit constraints. The legislative frameworks must support the development of financial markets and the institutional investor base. In this regard, the timely and effective implementation of EU financial services regulation, notably the Financial Services Action Plan is crucial.

  - The availability of low-cost loan finance and early-stage risk capital financing for SMEs is essential. The implementation of the Risk Capital Action Plan has an important role to play.
  - Whilst it appears that satisfactory progress has been made in putting into place adequate regulatory and supervisory capacities, substantial changes in the structure of financial markets create new demands for the organisation of financial supervision, which should proactively be addressed.

- **Improving the quality of public finance.** The Ecofin ministers in their meeting with their counterparts from the Candidate Countries on 5 November 2002 noted that reaching sound fiscal positions for some of the acceding countries will clearly require efforts over and above those described in the PEPs. The acceding countries, whilst after accession respecting the requirements of the Stability and Growth Pact, should enhance the efficiency of public spending and revenues by way of institutional and structural reforms. In order to foster a growth-enhancing environment providing sufficient scope and incentives for private-sector development, the structure of budget revenue and expenditure needs to be reassessed. Specifically:
  - On the revenue side, specific challenges should be addressed, such as the compared to present Member States narrow tax base with at the same time similar levels of public expenditure which characterises several acceding countries, and weaknesses in tax collection and administration.
  - On the expenditure side, the quality of services provided by the public sector and improvement of the efficiency of public administration set the framework for dynamic economic growth. Specific attention should be devoted to investment in key areas (such as R&D and innovation, public infrastructure and human capital) so as to underpin future competitiveness and growth, while the need for expenditure control rules at sub-national levels of government should be addressed.

- It is essential that the use of EU structural funds will be focused on those types of investments most conducive to long-term productivity gains, particularly human and knowledge capital, as well as on basic infrastructure.

- **Continuing pension and health care reforms.** Ageing populations could induce dramatic changes in potential growth rates, and a deterioration of public finances, which is the same challenge as in the present EU Member States. In the light of the Lisbon agenda:
  - In line with the three-pronged strategy developed by the Ecofin Council to prepare for the budgetary effects of ageing (i.e. debt reduction, raising employment rates and reform of pension systems) and in view of the current parameters of their pension systems, many acceding countries will have to implement comprehensive reform strategies. These will inter alia have to include initiatives aimed at offsetting the effects of ageing via reforms of the basic parameters of public pension systems (e.g. the retirement age, the replacement rate or the contribution rate), with a view to improving incentives to work and strengthening the actuarial link between contributions and benefits.
  - Due to growing GDP as well as technical progress and product innovation, health care expenditures are expected to grow fast. Containing such expenditures, while providing effective coverage, will entail steps to improve the efficiency of the health care systems.

- **Accelerating the transition to a knowledge-based economy.** The acceding countries have, in particular relative to their income levels, achieved high levels of educational attainment. However, they lag substantially behind present Member States in regard of the transition to a knowledge-based economy as reflected by lower investment in R&D. In regard of education, the lack of high skilled labour could indicate potential long-term difficulties in the light of the Lisbon agenda. To accelerate the catching-up process:

- The acceding countries should press ahead with educational reforms and improve their education and training systems in terms of educational attainment, skilled human resources, and R&D and innovation performance.
- They should improve the general framework conditions for R&D, including the entrepreneurial climate, access to risk capital, and the interrelationship between business and the research network.
- In view of the technology gap of several acceding countries vis-à-vis EU-15, increased focus should be laid on technology transfer and gradual product and process improvement as well as direct public educational and research efforts to underpin this process. The dynamics of foreign direct investment, which has a key role as mechanism of technology transfer, should be sustained.

The acceding countries, in their future Cardiff reports (and the remaining Pre-Accession Programmes in 2003), are invited to pay particular attention to the structural reform priorities identified above. The EPC considers that it is crucial for the acceding countries to maintain the current reform momentum, even in the event of lower growth performance, as some countries could face a risk of backtracking in certain areas undergoing reform. There should be a determined attempt in those countries to mobilise public opinion and build a solid political consensus amongst the various stakeholders backing the catching-up process.

Economic policy co-ordination processes and further work

In response to the mandate given by the Ecofin Council in November 2002 as to how the acceding countries could be integrated as early as possible into the Community's **structural reform co-ordination processes,** the EPC suggests including the acceding countries for the first time in:

- the BEPGs in 2004 (including in their country-specific part), taking into account their new three-year perspective (which for the current Member States is the period 2003-2005, and for the new Member

States should therefore be 2004-05), and accordingly the implementation report on the BEPGs in 2005;
- the EPC's annual report on structural reforms in 2005 (the Cardiff report), including specific country notes. However, the acceding countries should be invited to already provide Cardiff reports in October/November 2003 and participate at the annual examinations of the EPC for the 2004 annual report on structural reforms;
- the Luxembourg and Cologne processes in 2004; a (possible) upcoming report on the open method for pensions only after long-term projections for pension expenditures are made available in 2006 (the acceding countries have already been included in the Lisbon strategy in 2003).

In terms of further follow-up, in **its comprehensive monitoring report** in the structural reform area to be provided in November 2003, and in its Lisbon reports for the Spring European Council, the Commission is invited to devote particular attention to the most urgent challenges identified in this Report. Enlargement will be a special subject in the **EPC Annual Report on Structural Reforms in 2004**. With the Lisbon targets in mind, a special annex could be devoted to the areas of critical items identified by this report for the acceding countries, (such as privatisation, the share of public enterprises, administered prices, and tertiary and vocational education). The **EPC's working groups** are invited to extend their work to cover the acceding countries, for example the EPC's Ageing Working Group to include them into their next round of common projections for public spending on pensions, health and long-term care for the elderly in 2004/5, and the EPC's Working Group on Output Gaps with a special report being submitted to the Committee by the end of 2004. The EPC's Working Group on Structural Indicators is invited to explore whether there is any need for additions to, or changes to the scope of the existing list of structural indicators. The EPC as a whole should include the issue of regional disparities, and the role that Community and national policies could play over a broad range of fields to reduce standards of living within the Community.

The finance ministries and the statistical offices in the acceding countries should devote sufficient resources to the structural indicators to ensure best possible **coverage and quality of the data** used. The information content of the Pre-Accession Programmes should be improved for example as regards the data on the quality of public finances (revenue and expenditure) and the sustainability of public finances.

1. The Context for Meeting the Strategic Lisbon Goal

1. Since the outset of transition the economies of the acceding countries have made remarkable progress in regard of **macroeconomic stability**. For several years, output growth in most countries has exceeded the EU average. A number of macroeconomic imbalances remain for some countries, and this calls for renewed vigour, e.g. with regard to current account balances, the savings rate, the sustainability of the fiscal stance over the medium term, the commitment to fiscal consolidation and the stability of price developments. Additional macro- and microeconomic reforms, together with continued fiscal consolidation, will be necessary to increase further the efficiency of economic management and domestic co-ordination and raise the growth potential of the economy while tackling medium-term challenges. Stability-oriented macroeconomic policies as well as credible and viable exchange-rate strategies will be crucial for investment and economic growth. Stable macroeconomic conditions are a precondition for the acceding countries to cope successfully with enhanced competition, increased market flexibility and the possible economic vulnerabilities associated with the ongoing catching-up process.

Real convergence

2. The main challenge that acceding countries are facing is to catch up in terms of income levels. Whilst achieving income-per-capita levels close to the EU average will be a long-term process, there are also signs

that many acceding countries are slowly but steadily closing the economic gap with the EU even if, for a number of countries, some backtracking in convergence has been forecasted to take place in 2003. Despite overall progress, the gap in income-per-capita levels between the acceding countries and the EU average remains considerable. Taking account of differences in purchasing power, GDP per capita in the acceding countries is around 45% of the average EU level. This figure masks large differences between countries, as shown in Graph 1. In 2002 GDP per capita ranged from over 74% of the EU average in Cyprus to 35% in Latvia. While Cyprus and Slovenia are, in fact, as prosperous as some of the present, less affluent Member States, the Baltic countries and Poland have a GDP per capita which is less than 45% of the EU average.

Graph 1: GDP per capita in PPS in 1995 and 2002
(EU average = 100)

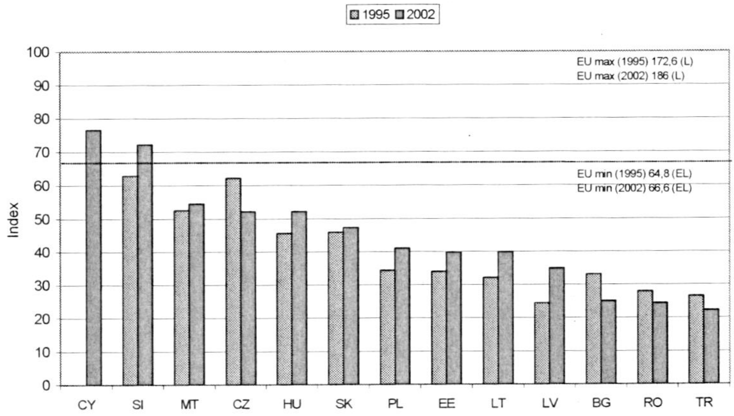

Source: Eurostat. Note: 2002: estimates. Data for Cyprus 2001 (data for 1995 not *comparable for Cyprus).*

3. Looking at the future prospects for real convergence and using a stylised set of assumptions, it is for illustrative purposes possible to derive a rather mechanistic long-term outlook for convergence trends in the acceding countries towards the EU-15 average. For that purpose, real in-

comes as a % of EU incomes have been calculated over a longer period, assuming for the years after 2004:

- the same growth rates as in the 2004 Commission's Spring 2003 forecasts for the Candidate Countries (see first column in Table 1);
- an EU growth rate of 2.4% based on the 2004 growth rates in the Commission's Spring 2003 economic forecasts;[2]
- constant prices and population size.

4. According to this calculation, Hungary, the Czech Republic, Estonia, Latvia, Malta and Slovakia would join Cyprus and Slovenia to reach 75% of the EU-15 income level over the next 25 years (see third column in Table 1). For other countries the catching-up process would take much longer. Indeed, it is likely to take one or two generations in the case of some of them.[3] This is perhaps unsurprising, given the lessons from the process of convergence for accession countries in the past. Yet the most noteworthy point is the sensitivity of the results to the assumptions made. Small changes in growth rates can significantly affect the speed of convergence. The fourth column in Table 1 shows the effect of increasing the growth rate assumptions in the Candidate Countries by 0.5 percentage point. In the case of Poland, for example, increasing the growth assumption by that amount would reduce the period needed to reach "75% convergence" with the EU by thirteen years (from 50 to 37 years).

---

2 Those figures are technical assumptions taken for purely illustrative purposes, and are not to be misunderstood as forecasts.

3 See also the conclusions of the Commission's report (DG ECFIN, November 2001) on "Real Convergence in the Candidate Countries": "*what is clear from that exercise is that for many countries catching-up even to levels of just 75% of the EU average will probably be a process spanning over more than one generation*". That paper provides also a good analysis of underlying growth-enhancing factors and an overview of the economic convergence of Portugal, Ireland, Spain and Greece before and after joining the EU.

Table 1: Period needed to reach 75% of the EU-15 average for GDP per capita (in PPS)

	Growth rate assumption as from 2004 (% p.a.) *	Average growth rate achieved 1995-2002 (% p.a.)	Period needed to reaching 75% of the EU average	Scenario: Period needed to reach 75% of EU average with 0.5 percentage point higher growth	
Cyprus	3.8	3.6	1	1	(-)
Czech Rep	3.9	1.7	19	15	(-4)
Estonia	5.1	4.9	23	19	(-4)
Hungary	4.1	3.9	24	19	(-5)
Latvia	6.0	5.6	24	21	(-3)
Lithuania	5.0	3.9	28	23	(-5)
Malta	3.7	3.3	25	18	(-7)
Poland	3.7	3.9	50	37	(-13)
Slovakia	4.5	3.7	22	18	(-4)
Slovenia	3.7	3.9	7	5	(-2)
Bulgaria	5.0	0.5	40	34	(-6)
Romania	5.0	0.4	44	37	(-7)
Turkey	4.5	2.9	61	49	(-12)

Source: Own calculations; AMECO, European Commission, April 2003. * Commission 2004 economic forecasts.

5. The general economic developments in acceding countries in recent years permit a more general, albeit simplistic, observation regarding the role of policy: those economies which have made the strongest progress in implementing wide-ranging reforms seem to have achieved higher growth rates.

Labour productivity, wage costs and the structure of the economy

6. In order to close the income gap with the EU, it will be important for the acceding countries to increase further labour productivity and total factor productivity, along with employment. As illustrated by Graph 2, six Candidate Countries are below half the EU average productivity level. Only three acceding countries have a labour productivity level above the lowest productivity level among the current Member States. However, labour productivity increased steadily for most acceding countries over the period from 1995 to 2002.

Graph 2: Labour productivity per person employed in 1995 and 2002 (EU average = 100)

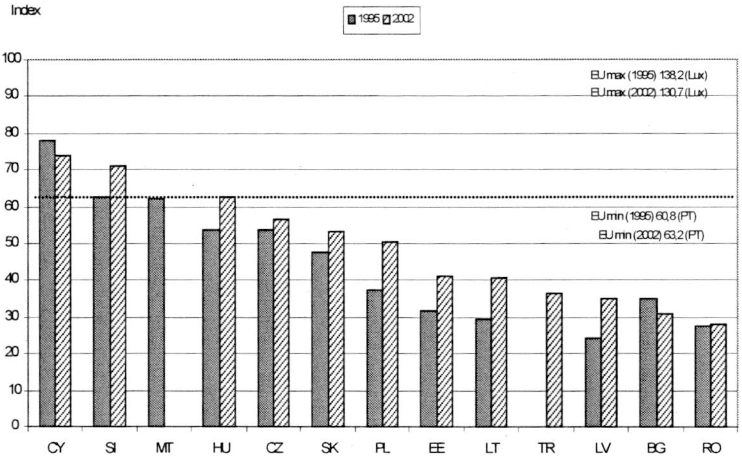

Source: Eurostat. Note: 2002: estimates.

7. Recent empirical work providing a breakdown of GDP growth into its various components for five acceding countries shows that in Hungary, Poland, and Slovenia a key driver behind cumulative output growth over the period 1991-99 was the relatively high total factor productivity growth (i.e. independent technical progress) (Table 2). In addition, fixed capital contributed strongly to the high cumulative output growth in Poland. The contribution of employment declined in all five countries, except Slovakia (however, in the late 1990s, production was catching up and the contribution of employment to growth was higher). This is also illustrated by a recent Commission analysis which highlights the essential characteristics of the economies of the central European acceding countries, featuring relatively low capital endowment and a low level of technology. It also asserts that their future speed of real convergence towards the EU average depends essentially on the rate of investment (including foreign direct investment), the growth in total factor produc-

tivity, and high labour force growth and participation[4]. In contrast, during the same period within the EU-15 the contribution of employment to GDP growth was stronger than in the acceding countries; and having a lower growth rate than the acceding countries the contribution of total factor productivity growth and capital deepening was weaker.

Table 2: Contributions to growth rates in central European countries 1991-99 (as %)

		Contribution of		
	Cumulative GDP growth	**TFP growth**	**Employment**	**Capital**
Czech Rep	9.1	4.6	-4.3	9.0
Hungary	16.6	20.2	-11.1	9.2
Poland	47.9	20.9	-1.6	24.3
Slovakia	21.8	2.0	6.2	12.4
Slovenia	25.6	21.0	-6.4	10.9

Source: IMF (2001), "Real Convergence to EU income levels: Central Europe from 1990 to the Long-Term", Doyle P., Kuijs L., and Jiang G., Discussion Paper, p. 31.

8. Labour costs differ markedly between the acceding countries and relative to the current Member States[5]. The level of total hourly labour costs in 2000 in industry and services ranged from 2.42 euros in Latvia to 10.74 euros in Cyprus (Graph 3). This compares with an EU average of 21.5 euros (1999 figure). In most of the acceding countries, labour costs were below one quarter of the EU average.

---

4 European Commission: The economic impact of enlargement, June 2001, pp. 27-31.

5 See Labour Costs Survey 2000, Eurostat Statistics in Focus 23/2002.

Graph 3: Hourly labour costs in industry and services in 2000 (in euros per hour)

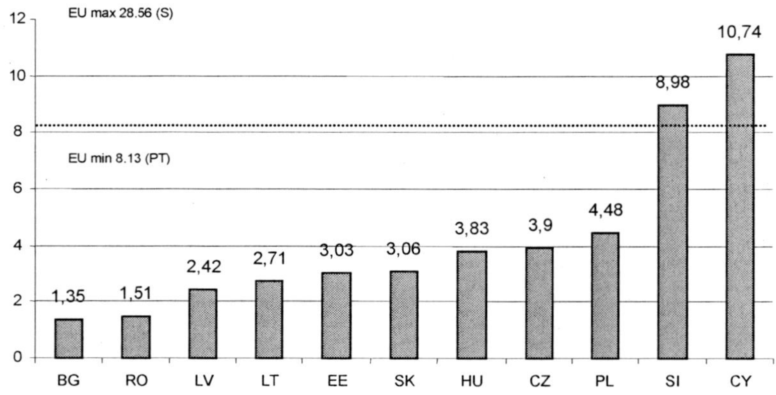

Source: Eurostat, Labour Cost Survey, Candidate Countries 2000.

9. The developments of unit labour costs between 1995 and 2002 diverged widely between countries and was very dynamic in some of them (Table 3). At the initial stage of transition, especially in labour-intensive industries, low and falling (nominal) wages, together with undervalued currencies, constituted the key comparative advantage of acceding countries. Since then, nominal wages went up substantially, outpacing in several countries labour productivity growth. It should also be taken into account that in the period 1995-2001 real exchange rate appreciation ranged from approximately 10% to a maximum of 100% (Slovenia, Malta and Cyprus being at the lower end and Lithuania and Latvia at the upper end; the other countries moved within a band of 35-60%). Accession countries are likely to face further real exchange rate appreciation, as inflation differentials with EU-15 will not, in general, diminish completely due to catching-up price movements[6], internal market integration in association with low initial price levels and further

[6] Through the so-called Balassa-Samuelson effect faster-growing countries tend to experience higher rates of inflation without necessarily suffering a deterioration in their cost competitiveness. Wage increases will, to a large extent, be determined by productivity growth in the tradable sector (c.f. manufacturing, agriculture), which is exposed to international competition.

adjustments in administered prices. Wage increases, if not matched by gains in productivity in the longer term, pose a challenge to external competitiveness in some acceding countries and could further aggravate the existing current account deficits. Unit labour costs being a key determinant of competitiveness, it is a major challenge for the candidates to ensure that real wage growth does not exceed productivity gains. Sustained wage moderation is therefore an important precondition for easing inflationary pressures, attracting foreign direct investment inflows, boosting growth and raising employment.

Table 3: Unit labour costs in 1995 and 2002; EUR-based, annual averages

	1995	2002	Relative change 1995-2002 (in %)
Czech Republic	110.3	202.7	+ 83.8
Hungary	110.9	187.4	+ 69.0
Poland	152.1	301.6	+ 98.3
Slovakia	93.1	120.5	+ 29.4
Slovenia	94.7	107.8	+ 13.8
Estonia	413.1	635.7	+ 53.9*
Latvia	508.2	794.7	+ 56.4*
Lithuania	472.7	997	+ 110.9*
Bulgaria	29	39.9	+ 37.6
Romania	60.8	90.1	+ 48.2

Source: Vienna Institute for International Economic Studies (WIIW), Research Report No. 293, February 2003. Note: Unit labour costs are exchange-rate adjusted, with 1989=100 for CZ, HU, PL, SK, SI BG, RO and 1992 = 100 for EE, LV and LI. 2002 data preliminary. * Note that the Baltic countries cannot be compared with the Central European countries as the base year for EE, LI and LT is 1992 instead of 1989.

10. As regards the structure of the economy, the private sector has expanded significantly over the last decade in most acceding countries. While in EU Member States the general government sector in 2001 accounted for between 8% and 20% of GDP, in Latvia and Slovenia the public sector still accounted for a third of GDP or more. Only in Estonia, the Slovak Republic and Hungary did the private sector generate more than 80% of GDP. The relatively small private sector in some

countries may indicate a lack of competition and ample room for efficiency gains. The sectoral composition of employment in acceding countries and in some countries the existence of large state-owned manufacturing companies with hidden unemployment help explain the low labour productivity (Graph 4 shows the sectoral shares of employment in 2001). Productivity growth in the acceding countries could be increased in the future by a further shift of emphasis within the sectoral composition of the economy towards sectors with a higher value added.

Graph 4: Sectoral share of employment in 2001 (%)

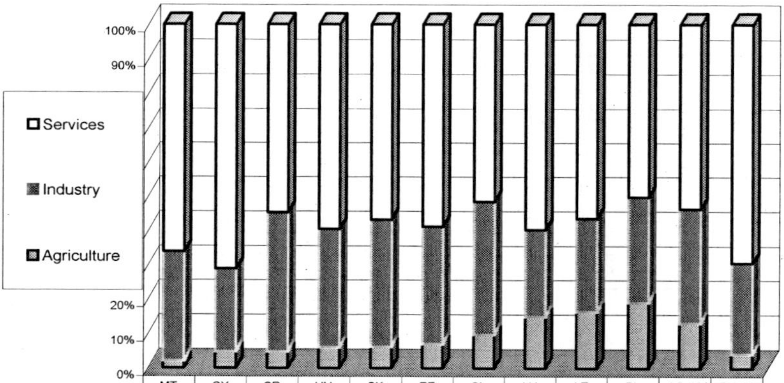

	MT	CY	CR	HU	SK	EE	SL	LV	LT	PL	AC-10	EU-15
Services	66,0	71,1	54,6	59,4	56,7	58,7	51,4	59,6	56,3	50,1	53,6	69,3
Industry	31,8	24,0	40,5	34,5	37,1	34,2	38,6	25,3	27,2	30,7	33,2	26,4
Agriculture	2,2	4,9	4,9	6,1	6,3	7,1	9,9	15,1	16,5	19,2	13,3	4,3

Source: Eurostat

11. The sectoral composition of output and employment is still biased towards agriculture, which accounts for a high percentage of employment in most of the acceding countries. The share of the agricultural sector in terms of employment is, on average, three times higher in the acceding countries than in the EU. The employment share of agriculture in the acceding countries are much higher than GDP shares, i.e. they suffer from very low productivity. In order to foster overall productivity, in most acceding countries agriculture (farms and agro-enterprises) needs urgent restructuring.

2. LABOUR MARKET REFORMS

12. A flexible labour market will be vital in achieving the strategic Lisbon goal. In Lisbon, viewing the EU as a whole, the EU Heads of State and Government set a 2010 target for the total employment rate of 70% and one of more than 60% for the employment rate of women. In Stockholm an overall target for the employment rate for those aged between 55 and 64 was set at 50% and intermediate targets of 67% and 57% were set for the overall employment rate and the employment rate of women respectively in 2005.

13. As for employment, there are major differences between countries; all the acceding countries except Cyprus report lower total employment rates than the EU average (see Graph 5). In 2001 total employment rates in acceding countries ranged from 50.7% to 67.9% of the working-age population as compared with 64% on average in the EU. The employment rates of older workers were in the 22.5%-50.5% range. This relatively low employment rate is explained by, among other things, widely used and relatively generous early retirement systems. Female employment rates are less dispersed and range between 47.9% and 57.4%. The comparatively high female participation is due partly to the rather easy access to childcare facilities, which did, however, deteriorate in the post-communist period.

Graph 5: Employment rates in the acceding countries in 2001 (as percentage)

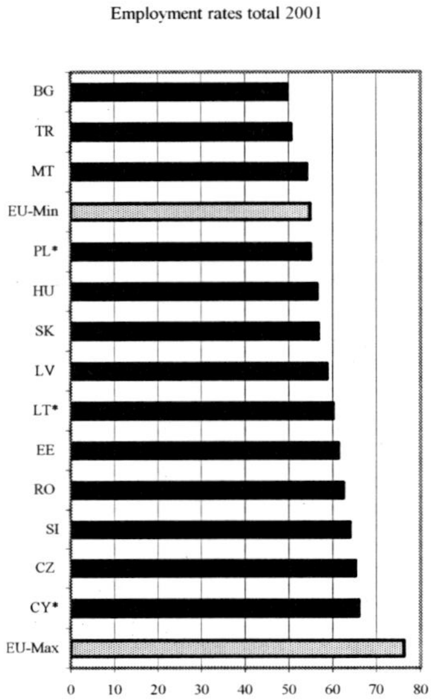

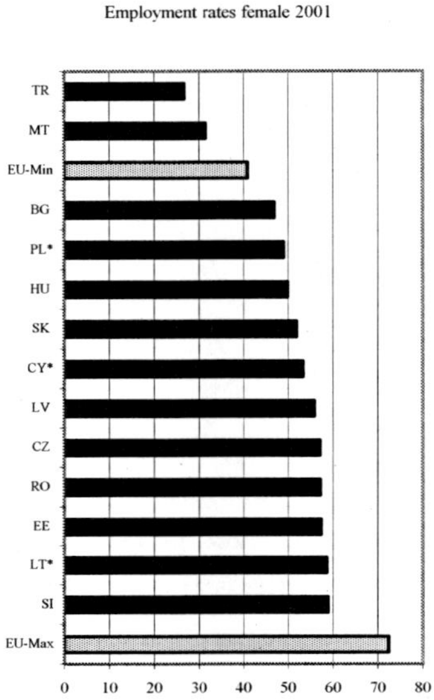

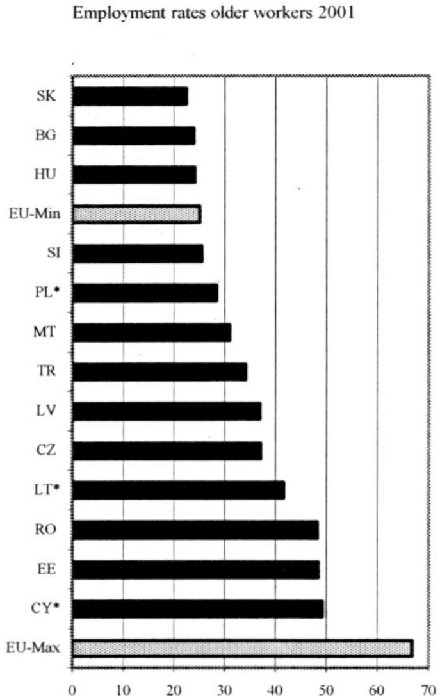

Source: Eurostat - Structural Indicators, April 2003. Note : * 2000 data.

14. **Unemployment** remains a serious problem in most countries, ranging between 4.5% and 19.7% in 2001 (Table 4). Unlike in the EU, the female unemployment rate is lower than the male unemployment rate in about half of the acceding countries. Special attention should be paid to high rates of long-term and youth unemployment and to high unemployment among low-skilled workers. Regional unemployment is rather high in most acceding countries, with Slovakia showing the widest gap between regions.

Table 4: Unemployment rates in 2001 (as %)

	Total	Long-term	Men	Women	Youth
Cyprus	4.5	0.9	3.0	6.5	3.5
Czech Rep	-	4.1	-	-	6.7
Estonia	12.2	5.8	12	12.5	8.8
Hungary	5.7	2.5	6.3	4.9	3.7
Lithuania	16.5	9.3	19.0	13.8	10.2
Latvia	12.9	7.7	14.2	11.5	8.6
Malta	-		-	-	
Poland	18.6	9.2	17.2	20.3	15.2
Slovenia	5.9	3.6	5.6	6.3	5.7
Slovakia	19.7	11.3	20.4	18.8	17.6
Bulgaria	19.6	12.5	20.5	18.6	13.6
Romania	6.5	3.2	7.0	5.9	7.0
EU:					
Average	7.3	3.2	6.4	8.5	7.1
Max	10.6	5.4	8.6	15.6	10.3
Min	2.0	0.5	1.7	2.4	2.7

Source: Employment in Europe 2001 and 2002 for long-term unemployment rates of acceding countries, structural indicators for EU and total unemployment rates in acceding countries.

15. Prospects for employment creation should, however, improve in the years to come as widespread labour shedding, which has been part of the business restructuring process, is likely to come to an end. Thus, employment could increase modestly in 2003-04. The pure statistical result for the ten acceding countries joining the EU in 2004 will increase the unemployment ratio in an enlarged EU. In the longer run, there are grounds for assuming that the positive effects of enlargement on eco-

nomic growth in Europe would bring about favourable employment developments as well. However, across the acceding countries, employment rates have decreased (see Annex 1) and unemployment rates increased since 1997 which is problematic in view of the Lisbon agenda.

16. Policies to raise employment levels in the acceding countries are not very different from the range of approaches observed in the present Member States, including macroeconomic stimulus. In some countries, **tax and benefit systems** seem to be important areas for further labour market reforms so as "*to make work pay and encourage the search for jobs*". In most acceding countries the newly introduced unemployment insurance systems appear to be less generous on average than in the EU. However, they appear to be especially generous for unemployed persons with a family, which creates possible unemployment traps. Several acceding countries devote, relatively speaking, more resources to non-employment benefits than the current Member States, undermining the incentives for low-productivity workers to seek and take up employment. The relatively high tax burden on labour, especially low-wage earners, is a particular problem in some acceding countries. Early retirement systems are in some cases used as a response to the decline in employment and, as in current Member States, excessive replacement rates and generous eligibility rules might be an issue, notably for unemployment and disability schemes that often lead to early retirement.

17. The **wage bargaining systems** in the acceding countries have evolved during the transition period. Minimum wages were introduced in almost all of them and currently amount to between 25% and 42% of the average wage. Lack of regional differentiation of the nominal minimum wage is a problem in Poland, but it is not clear whether it makes up for high regional differences in the labour market situation in other countries. Tripartite bargaining was common in the centrally planned economies; bilateral bargaining has developed as the degree of corporatism has declined rapidly. Nowadays, in most acceding countries, wage negotiations at firm level predominate, facilitating wage differentiation.

18. Labour market flexibility in a number of acceding countries is hampered by relatively strict labour market regulation, especially **employment protection legislation**. However, in many current Member States restrictions are similar to, or even more binding than, those in some acceding countries. In many acceding countries, factors such as complicated administrative procedures and unduly long minimum notice periods are at play. Working-time flexibility varies between acceding countries, with an increasing share of part-time and fixed-term contracts.

19. **Active labour market policies,** such as training, employment subsidies and job search assistance, have gained in importance in labour market policies of the present Member States, but also in acceding countries. While present EU countries spend around 1% of GDP on active labour market policies, the comparable figures in acceding countries are still much lower (on average 0.2% of GDP, though the share of expenditure for active labour market policies in total labour market expenditure is higher than in the present EU Member States). Spending patterns and the efficiency of spending differ widely. Finally, human capital formation is an important challenge for the acceding countries, as the education systems in the centrally planned economies did not prepare people for lifelong adaptability of their skills and focused too much on narrow job descriptions (see Chapter 6).

20. Overall, while in the EU the average employment rate has been rising, this is not the case in many acceding countries. In most of them, unemployment has remained unacceptably high and the challenges are to reduce the high (and especially long-term) unemployment rates among certain groups, especially the young and the low-skilled, to narrow regional disparities and to increase employment rates for older workers. Institutional arrangements on the labour market in many acceding countries need to be modernised. The authorities should, however, guard against adopting more rigid labour market policies. Measures such as increasing the incentive effects of tax and benefit systems so as to restore the financial benefits associated with a return to employment, reducing early retirement by offering incentives for people opting for later retirement, enforcing sustained wage moderation to strengthen or maintain the link between productivity growth and wages, improving employment flexibility through a thorough review of employment protection legislation, improving the skills level with the focus on lifelong learning, and focusing on precisely targeted, effective and efficient active labour market policies hold the key to "more and better jobs" in the Lisbon process.

3. *PRODUCT MARKETS*

21. An EU aspiring to become the most competitive and dynamic knowledge-based economy in the world needs strong competition and an effective competition policy. In the acceding countries, given their relatively low level of labour productivity, an appropriate regulatory and competition framework, including a right business environment conducive for entrepreneurship, and the liberalisation of network industries are central issues for increasing international competitiveness.

22. The economies of the acceding countries are very open economies, well-integrated into the EU. All the acceding countries except Lithuania, Latvia, Cyprus and Poland have a greater degree of trade openness than the average of the smaller EU Member States. **Transposing internal**

market directives into national legislation will be a major issue that will need to be monitored after accession to the EU. Integration is also being driven by foreign direct investment (FDI). In Estonia, the Czech Republic, Poland and Hungary annual FDI from the EU between 1996 and 2001 averaged more than 3% of GDP. This is considerably more than Slovenia and Latvia managed to attract; their average annual inflow of FDI from EU Member States was below 1.6% of GDP. As a comparison, FDI flows to EU Member States from other Member States during this period averaged 3%.

23. Accession countries made considerable progress in bringing high and volatile CPI inflation rates down from double to single-digit numbers and, thus, closer to EU-15 levels. In 2002, CPI inflation rates amounted to between 0.4% in Lithuania to 7.5% in Slovenia, compared to 2.1% in EU-15. Inflation differentials with EU-15 are related to the Balassa-Samuelson effect or to specific transition factors, such as deregulation, indirect tax harmonisation or relative price changes. **Consumer price levels** in most acceding countries are low compared with the EU. In 2001 the consumer price level, expressed in a common currency, was less than half the EU average in five acceding countries. This may be attributed in part to relatively low wage and income levels as well as to a residual need to liberalise administered prices (Graph 6 illustrates that in four acceding countries regulated prices account for more than one fifth of the CPI). Several acceding countries are undertaking reforms to reduce price controls (which, however, might also affect inflation) and to open up markets to competition.

Graph 6: Administered prices in 2001 as a share of CPI

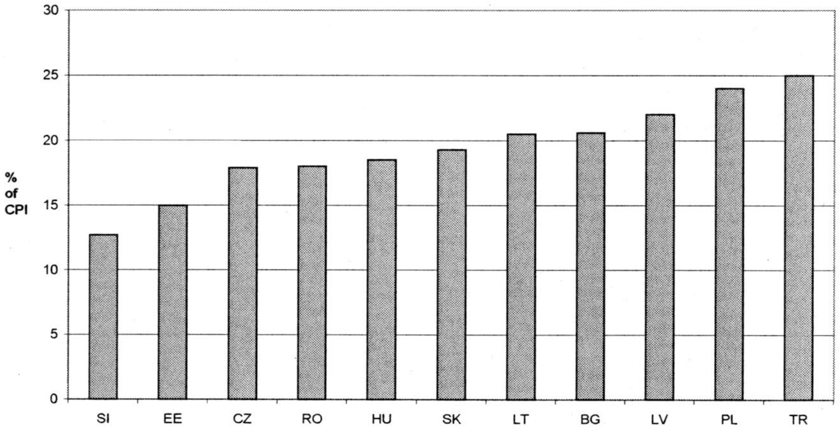

Source: Commission regular reports.
Note: Data for PL, SI and SK from 2000. No data for CY and MT.

24. A specific challenge on product markets for the acceding countries arises from the shift in the sectoral composition of output. Business **privatisation and restructuring** have made huge advances in most countries. Annual average privatisation receipts for the period 1994-99 in the acceding countries ranged from less than 1% of GDP to almost 4.5% of GDP. In a few countries, the privatisation process has been practically completed. In others, the public enterprise sector is still large (accounting for more than 25% of GDP in five acceding countries) and privatisation remains high on the structural reform agenda. Privatisation is an important element in raising economic efficiency further and in attracting sorely needed foreign capital and knowledge. A few countries have encountered problems devising viable privatisation and restructuring strategies for some sectors (e.g. steel in Poland). In this regard, it will be important to reinforce and press ahead forcefully with the privatisation programmes. Restructuring of the agricultural sector remains a major task. Agricultural modernisation is hindered notably by the lack of employment opportunities in other sectors. In many countries subsis-

tence farming, developed during transition as a form of social safety net, dampens the productivity. Generally, income on subsistence farms does not derive from the sale of agricultural products but from welfare payments, which provides no incentive for change. In some countries, the functioning of land markets needs to be improved.

25. In many acceding countries **competition in product and service markets**, which is a key driver of growth, productivity and job creation, is still relatively weak, especially in the non-tradable sector. This potentially holds back real income convergence. In most countries, the efecttive implementation of the legal framework for market entry and exit of companies should be further enhanced. Measures to liberalise, open up and increase competition in product and service markets should be key policy priorities. Many acceding countries have made encouraging headway in strengthening competition rules and establishing independent competition authorities, but in some countries more progress will be needed if EU competition policy is to be fully and effectively enforced. The **liberalisation of network industries**, which is important in view of its contribution to raising growth potential and lowering inflation, appears to vary considerably between acceding countries. Too little information is available, but it appears that in many countries effectments to market entry remain in certain industries and that regulation needs to be improved. Viable tariffs need to be in place to induce private sector investments. As in current Member States, it will be crucially important to improve market contestability by reducing (potential) barriers to foreign and domestic competition and by ensuring effecttive and transparent monitoring structures. In terms of the degree of energy market openness, progress has to date been fastest in Slovenia. For electricity, many acceding countries have already gone further than the current minimum requirements. For gas, very few measures have been taken in most countries to support competition and there is a problem of concentration of gas supply sources. Unbundling requirements are currently minimal.

26. A major issue in the acceding countries is the quantitative impact of **ad hoc state aid**[7], which has a distorting effect, deters new entrants and prevents the reallocation of resources to more competitive enterprises, thereby slowing down the restructuring of the economy. Total state aid in acceding countries, excluding aid to agriculture and fisheries, ranged from 0.4% of GDP in Slovakia to 1.7% of GDP in Hungary in 2000 (EU average: 0.8% of GDP) (Graph 7). Whilst Slovakia, Estonia, Lithuania and Latvia recorded lower total state aid than the EU average, in Hungary state aid was more than double the EU average. However, there might be some underestimation of state aid attributable to indirect state aid such as soft budget constraints for state-owned companies and tax exemptions. State aid in the acceding countries should therefore be analysed with caution. In several of them a large share of the aid was sectoral or ad hoc aid used for specific industries (notably for the steel and coal industries), which can have a particularly distorting effect on the economy. In a number of acceding countries it will be necessary to overhaul state aid with a view to both reducing total state aid and redirecting state aid towards horizontal measures.

Graph 7: State aid in 2000 (% of GDP)

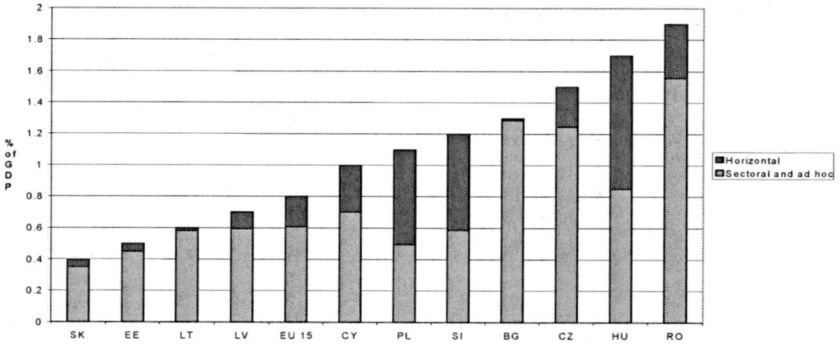

Source: State Aid Scoreboard special edition. Note: Figures exclude aid to fisheries and agriculture. Data not available for MT.

[7] which is subject to transition regulation until 2011.

27. A necessary component of strategies to accelerate real convergence is reforms improving the efficiency of the institutional framework, including **measures to improve the business environment**. The 2002 Regular Report[8] by the Commission states that the acceding countries have made good progress in institutional and legal convergence but also that significant deficiencies still have to be addressed in most countries. This particularly concerns the regulatory burden on business, the effective implementation and, in some countries, the design of judicial reforms, and the quality and administrative capacity of the central and local public sectors. There is a widespread perception that many segments of the public sector remain highly inefficient, creating obstacles to the operation and growth of businesses. According to the assessment made in the Commission's Regular Report, corruption remains a matter of serious concern in several of the acceding countries. In a number of countries incomplete market exit mechanisms should be rectified, in particular by improving bankruptcy legislation and procedures. Market entry and exit mechanisms are an area where additional analysis would be warranted.

28. Overall, EU accession will increase the pressure for further structural reforms in product markets for the acceding countries. While many challenges in product markets are common to both acceding countries and EU Member States, the acceding countries are facing specific challenges, especially with regard to sectoral changes in the economy, privatisation, administered prices and state aid. Reforms of product and service markets, including a strengthening of competition, measures to streamline the business environment, continuous reform in public administration and improvement of the entrepreneurial climate, are necessary. For countries which have encountered problems in devising viable privatisation and restructuring strategies, it will be important to reinforce and press ahead forcefully with the privatisation programmes. For

[8] Strategy Paper and Report by the European Commission on progress towards accession by each of the Candidate Countries (COM(2002)700) of 9 October 2002. On the business environment in the acceding countries, see also, in particular, Chapter 2 of the 2002 EBRD transition report.

network industries, as in current Member States, it will be key to improve market contestability by reducing potential barriers to foreign and domestic competititon and ensuring effective and transparent supervision structures. Together with the ongoing shift in the structural composition of the economy from agriculture and heavy industry to services and capital- and technology-intensive industries, these reforms will provide a basis for productivity growth in the acceding countries. Sufficient inflow of capital will be critical to unlock the possible potential in higher tech industries for those countries in which the specialisation structures are dependent on the labour-intensive, low-skill sectors. After accession, particular attention will have to be devoted to complying with internal market obligations, notably with respect to the targets for transposing EU directives and eliminating barriers to cross-border trade. A specific focus of monitoring should be the implementation of EU competition policies (actual compliance and appropriate administrative capacity). The efforts by many acceding countries to undertake additional important reforms in those areas, as evidenced out in the Pre-Accession Economic Programmes, are to be welcomed.

4. *FINANCIAL MARKET REFORMS*

29. Financial markets have an important role to play in achieving the Lisbon objectives. Financial sector development may stimulate real convergence via the mobilisation of savings, which is vital in view of high investment needs, and via the monitoring function as a key element of corporate performance. The full integration of the acceding countries' capital markets into the EU is a key issue.

30. As regards financial sector development, the acceding countries in transition clearly lag behind the EU average in terms of stock market capitalisation, the level of financial intermediation, and the degree of liquidity. The institutional investor base is weak. This points to the enormous potential for financial sector growth in these countries. Only Cyprus and Malta have a domestic financial sector that, in size, broadly

resembles that of the EU Member States. The financial sector of the eastern European acceding countries has undergone major changes since the beginning of the transition. At present, it is characterised by strong dominance of the generally well-capitalised banking sector on capital markets, a still relatively low level of financial intermediation and a relatively low degree of liquidity in many market segments. Capital ratios exceed the Basle recommendation of 8% in all countries. Domestic credit at the end of 2000 represented on average 60% of GDP (euro area: close to 140%). The average interest rate spread in 2002 in the accession countries was 5.8%, as compared to 3.5% in the euro area. Access to bank financing (i.e. by foreign parent banks) and capital markets abroad may somewhat alleviate domestic financial constraints, particularly after having become part of the EU Single Market.

31. Ownership of banks in the acceding countries has been largely converted from public to private and from domestic to foreign. Except for a few cases, the **privatisation** process can be regarded as largely completed, thanks to major efforts and funds from public authorities to consolidate and re-capitalise the banking system. Notable exceptions to private ownership of banks are Poland, where the government controls the largest bank, and Slovenia, where the government controls the second-largest bank and holds a significant share in the largest bank. Moreover, acceding countries have, in individual cases, retained interests in privatised banks by offering guarantees to cover future losses. The further consolidation and efficiency improvements in the banking sector remain a challenge.

32. Starting from a low level, lending to individuals in many acceding countries represents one of the fastest-growing areas of the banking system, as illustrated in Table 5 below. This largely reflects a catching-up phenomenon; in Hungary, for example, the level of gross debt of individuals (around 7% of disposable income in 2002) falls far short of the average figure of 50% in the EU. The availability of risk capital and low cost debt finance for small and medium-sized firms (SMEs), espe-

cially at the earliest stages of their life cycle, is important for funding innovation and development. Although some progress has been made here, it remains inadequate and risk capital is - by and large - too expensive.

Table 5: Commercial bank lending to households* (% of total at year-end)

	1998	2000	2001
Czech Rep	6	9	12
Estonia		20	22
Hungary		8	12
Latvia	10	15	15
Lithuania	11	10	11
Poland		24	27
Slovakia	8	14	21
Slovenia	22	30	27
Bulgaria	10	7	8
Romania		4	4
Euro area*	42	43	42

Source: National data, IFS, ECB staff calculations.
Note: * As % of total loans of euro-area residents excluding MFI.

33. Rapid integration of the acceding countries into the **Single Market for financial services** has an important role to play in achieving the Lisbon objectives. While many acceding countries have already addressed a few issues that are also dealt with under the Financial Services Action Plan, such as supervising capital-based pension funds, substantial challenges remain. For example, many countries still need to implement changes to the legislative frameworks for securities, pension and investment funds and life insurance. It would be useful if the newly created Financial Services Committee monitored effective implementation.

34. Progress on **financial sector regulation and supervision** remains uneven between countries and between different sectors but important progress has been achieved. The substantial changes in the structure of financial markets impose new demands on the organisation of financial

supervision (including cross-border co-operation) which should be addressed pro-actively by acceding candidates, as they seek fast integration into the Single Market for financial services. Maintaining the level playing field for institutions in an enlarged EU will be crucial for both current and future EU Member States with a view to preserving overall financial stability. Once they have joined the EU, acceding countries will face further challenges in regard to the regulatory framework.

35. Overall, EU accession represents an important structural challenge for both the banking and the non-banking sector. Financial markets in the acceding countries continue to be underdeveloped relative to the EU. Integration is viewed as speeding up the pace of concentration, boosting competition, adding to efficiency incentives, promoting the range of financial services available (e.g. mortgages, consumer credit, SME finance) and strengthening the competition for deposits. It can also be expected to provide an impetus for further liberalisation, fostering better regulation and imparting momentum especially for retail and insurance banking, which makes closer co-operation between national and foreign supervisors important. The legislative frameworks must support the development of financial markets and the institutional investor base. Timely and effective implementation of the Financial Services Action Plan will play a key role. The availability of risk capital and loan finance for small and medium-sized firms (SMEs), especially at the earliest stages of their life cycle, remains inadequate and mostly too expensive. The implementation of the Risk Capital Action Plan has an important role to play. The process of adjusting acceding countries' market infrastructure seems particularly challenging against the background of a continuously evolving market infrastructure within the euro area - this is relevant notably for payment systems.

5. *Improving the Quality and Sustainability of Public Finance*

36. Public expenditure and taxes account for significant proportions of national income. With a view to raising the growth potential of the EU economies in conformity with the Lisbon agenda, the quality and sustainability of public finances in recent years have become key policy objectives within the EU.

37. All Member States must achieve and sustain sound budgetary positions. In this respect, the Ecofin ministers, at their meeting with their counterparts from the Candidate Countries on 5 November 2002, already noted that a number of Pre-Accession Economic Programmes fall short on policy commitments that credibly underpin a medium-term path of fiscal consolidation and do not envisage sufficient efforts to correct the major imbalances and to meet the potential costs of structural reforms. Achieving sound fiscal positions for some of the acceding countries will clearly require efforts over and above those described in the Pre-Accession Economic Programmes (see Table 6 for fiscal developments). In line with the goals agreed in Lisbon and Stockholm, also referred to in the Broad Economic Policy Guidelines, public finances should maximise the contribution of public finances to growth and employment.

38. General government balances continue to be mostly negative in the acceding countries, but there are major differences among countries. For the acceding countries as a whole, aggregate general government deficits (in ESA 95 terms) reached 5.3% of GDP in 2002, mainly due to the sharp increase of the deficit in Hungary. In a context of declining privatisation receipts and some take over of private sector liabilities (in particular from the financial sector), debt developments should continue to be closely monitored. A detailed discussion relative to the Maastricht deficit and debt criterion is within the competence of the Economic and Financial Committee, and is therefore not elaborated here.

Table 6: Fiscal developments (percentage of GDP)

	Government deficit				Gross debt ratio	
	2001	**2002**	**2003**	**2004**	**2002**	**2004**
Cyprus	-3.0	-3.5	-4.0	-3.5	55.9	52.4
Czech Rep.	-5.5	-6.5	-6.3	-5.9	25.6	31.3
Estonia	0.5	1.3	-0.5	-0.6	4.4	3.9
Hungary	-4.2	-9.1	-4.9	-3.7	52.9	51.4
Lithua-nia	-2.3	-1.8	-1.9	-2.0	23.6	23.4
Latvia	-1.9	-2.5	-2.9	-2.6	16.8	18.6
Malta	-7.0	-6.1	-5.2	-4.1	64.9	62.8
Poland	-3.1	-4.2	-4.2	-4.0	43.3	46.0
Slovenia	-2.5	-1.8	-1.5	-1.2	27.9	25.2
Slovakia	-5.4	-7.7	-5.3	-3.8	39.3	38.8
Bulgaria	0.4	-0.7	-0.6	-0.5	59.2	50.2
Romania	-3.3	-2.6	-2.7	-2.7	24.6	26.4
Turkey	-28.9	-13.7	-9.8	-6.9	99.6	79.6
EU-15	-0.9	-1.9	-2.3	-2.2	62.7	63.2

Sources: Commission Spring 2003 Economic Forecast; Fiscal Notifications 2002.

Quality of public finances

39. The overall level of expenditure and, to a lesser degree, revenue in the acceding countries broadly resemble those of the present Member States, although significant differences for individual countries exist (Table 7). In most of the acceding countries, the ratio of public expenditure to GDP was above 40% of GDP in 2001. However, total government expenditure fell by several percentage points of GDP in the countries in transition from a centrally planned to a market economy in the late 1990s. The scale of government activities was reduced, state-owned enterprises were privatised to a varying degree, and complex systems of subsidies designed to equalise incomes between different enterprises and sectors were reformed or dismantled. As the large share of the public sector in the economy hampers the convergence process of these catching-up economies, most acceding countries envisage a continuing decline in GDP ratios for both public expenditure and public revenue in the medium term in the PEPs 2002, via overall spending restraint and

tax cuts.

Table 7: Size of general government spending (% of GDP)

	Revenue		Expenditure	
	2001	**2005**	**2001**	**2005**
Cyprus	40.5	42.2	43.5	42.5
Czech Rep.	42.1	41.3	47.1	46.8
Estonia	38.6	38.4	38.4	38.4
Hungary	46.1	42.5	50.2	45
Lithuania	34.2	36.1	36.1	37.6
Latvia	41.4	38.6	43	40.6
Malta	37.4	35.8	44.4	38.8
Poland	41.8	42.2	45.3	44.5
Slovenia	43.1	42.5	45.6	43.3
Slovakia	41.2	39.8	46.6	41.8
Bulgaria	40.6	35	40.3	35
Romania	36.7	34.6	40.1	37
Turkey	42.1	40.1	57.2	40.6
EU-15	46.4	-	47.2	-

Source: 2002 PEPs.

40. Table 8 presents the structure of general government revenue in the acceding countries. Total tax receipts in the acceding countries averaged about 35% of GDP in 2000, compared with 45% in the euro area. Financing the existing scale of public expenditure imposes a heavy burden on the tax base, which is much narrower in the acceding countries than in the present Member States. Nominal tax rates for earned and capital incomes are rather high (according to indications from the International Bureau of Fiscal Documentation), while many exemptions and tax evasion reduce effective rates. Social security contributions as a share of labour costs are also high. According to the IMF and the Commission, the distortions caused by high rates of taxation on labour

may be a serious impediment to a job-intensive growth strategy in several acceding countries[9].

Table 8: Structure of general government revenue in 2000 (% of GDP)

	Czech Rep	Estonia	Hungary	Latvia	Lithuania	Poland	Slovak Rep.	Slovenia	Euro area
Current revenue	39.2	38.7	41.8	36.8	30.4	41.6	36.6	41.5	45
Tax revenue	36.7	35.8	36.2	31.3	28.5	39.9	34.1	39.2	44.9
Personal income tax	5	7.8	7.2	6	7.8	4.6	4.6	7.6	9.9
Corporate income tax	3.9	1	2.2	1.7	0.7	2	3	-	3
Social security contributions	14.7	12.4	9.8	10.7	7.1	8.7	13	13.6	15.6
Property tax	0.5	0.4	0.9	1	0.6	-	-	2.3	1.5
Indirect tax	12.6	14.2	16	11.9	11.7	11.4	13.5	15.7	13.6
Total public revenue	40.6	-	44.5	-	-	41.6	46.1	-	-

Source: IMF/EU, OECD, Finmin of Poland.

41. There is a general intention, as spelt out in the 2002 PEPs, to gradually shift the tax burden from labour towards consumption. However, as nominal VAT rates are already close to or at EU levels, boosting effective consumption tax revenue should take place through a broadening of the tax base and through higher excise duties and eco-taxes. Furthermore, tax administration and the effectiveness of tax collection need to be improved significantly. According to the PEPs, a significant lowering of company taxation is planned in many countries.

42. As for the **expenditure side of budgets**, government consumption and social transfers as a percentage of GDP is comparable to that in the present Member States (Table 9). The World Bank estimates that up to

---

9 See European Commission: European Economy No 3, "Public finances in EMU 2002", 2002, pp. 114 ff.

80% of all government expenditure in these countries - as in most present Member States - is **mandatory and quasi-mandatory expenditure** in the sense that it is determined by rules outside the budgetary process. These are mainly expenditures in the areas of defence, old-age and disability pensions. The corresponding expenditure rigidity is often compounded by indexation clauses for pensions and public-sector wages. Moreover, the widespread lack of clear frameworks defining the fiscal relations between the state and sub-state levels is a challenge for delivering the medium-term adjustment efforts needed in many cases. As a result, spending at the lower levels of government is difficult to control. Some acceding countries apply budgetary rules and procedures to improve public expenditure efficiency and control, such as multi-annual budgets, expenditure rules with explicit limits on the annual growth rate and agreements between different levels of government. In some countries, these rules should be improved, both in design and/or enforcement as there continue to be large spending slippages.

43. In the 2002 PEPs public investment expenditure is set to be maintained at a level of 3% of GDP on average. The acceding countries are characterised by a relatively **low stock of public infrastructure**, which is often ill suited to the needs and standards of market economies. They face considerable challenges in replacing old technology and building new infrastructure networks, including through public-private partnership (PPP) arrangements (the implementation of which depend on viable tariffs). The sections below provide information on investment in human capital (health care, education).

Table 9: Structure of general government expenditure in 2000 (% of GDP)

	Czech Rep	Estonia	Hungary	Latvia	Lithuania	Poland *	Slovak Rep.	Slovenia	Euro area
Current expenditure	38.4	36.3	39.9	36.6	30.4	-	38.2	39.2	43.8
Government consumption	8.7	24.6	14.4	16.1	16.6	15	17.6	17.6	19.8
Interest payments	1.1	0.3	6.1	1.1	1.7	3	2.7	1.5	3.7
Subsidies and current transfers	28.6	11.4	19.4	18.9	12.1	-	17.9	20.1	19.8
Subsidies	8.1	0.8	2.8	5	0.2	-	4	1.5	1.4
Current transfers	20.5	10.6	16.6	13.9	11.9	-	13.9	17.9	18.4
Capital expenditure	5.9	3.2	7.1	4	1.9	2.8	3.9	4.1	1
Total public expenditure	46.1	40.1	47.5	40.6	32.3	45.5	52.2	43.3	44.8

Sources: IMF/EU, OECD, Finmin of Poland; *Year 2001.

44. It is critical to use the **EU's Structural and Cohesion Funds** efficiently in the interest of long-term sustainable economic growth. The acceding countries are currently preparing their national development strategies for EU part-financing of public investment and it is essential that these are focused on those types of measure most conducive to long-run productivity gains, particularly human and knowledge capital, as well as on basic infrastructure. Mechanisms must be put into place to ensure efficient implementation.

45. Overall, if fiscal policy is to play its role in supporting rapid and sustainable real convergence, further improvement in the quality of public finances will be crucial in a number of acceding countries. Given the still limited availability of data on the quality of public finances, urgent steps should be taken to improve data compilation and reporting to allow for a more detailed assessment. The following key issues can be identified. On the revenue side, the tax base in most acceding countries is narrow. The tax burden on labour is relatively high, and this is a challenge in light of the Lisbon agenda aimed at making tax and benefit systems more employment-friendly. Weaknesses in tax collection and administration should be addressed urgently so as to achieve an efficient and fair fiscal system, including a broader tax base. On the expenditure side, the quality of services provided by the public sector and improvement of the efficiency of public administration set the framework for dynamic economic growth. However, tackling the rapidly increasing nominal expenditure pressure on public services and fulfilling the higher EU standards for these services will be further challenges also on the financing side. It can be expected that social security expenditure (and public sector wages) will also rise in tandem with the gradual convergence of prices and wages towards EU levels. There is a need to control spending at all levels of government, which too is a challenge given the widespread lack of frameworks determining the fiscal relations between the state and sub-state levels. The need for public investment expenditure will remain high in the foreseeable future in the light of the development and convergence of the acceding countries. Some countries should devote particular attention to public spending on human capital in order to catch up with the present Member States. In sum, sound public finances should be achieved via spending restraint and growth friendly tax systems, with clear priorities on the composition of public expenditure.

The sustainability of public finances: pension and health care reforms

46. In view of the demographic challenges posed by ageing populations and the goal of the Lisbon strategy to ensure that public finances contribute to growth and employment, the sustainability of public finances within the EU has become a core policy objective in recent years. The Ecofin Council developed a three-pronged strategy to address the budgetary implications of ageing: raising employment and participation rates, reducing public debt and reforming pension and health care systems. This was endorsed by the Stockholm European Council and subsequently incorporated into the Broad Economic Policy Guidelines.

47. The already observed population decrease in the acceding countries will reinforce the diminution of the population of the present Member States foreseen in twenty years from now (after 2020). Most acceding countries have very low fertility rates, lower life expectancies at birth than the present Member States and in many cases strong negative migration balances. In most of them, the working-age population (aged between 20 and 64), the number of elderly persons aged over 65 and the old-age dependency ratio are expected to follow broadly similar trends as in the present Member States[10]. The dependency ratio is expected to surpass EU levels by around 2040 (see Table 10).

[10]See EPC report on budgetary challenges posed by ageing populations of 24 October 2001: http://europa.eu.int/comm/economy_finance/epc_en.htm

Table 10: Old-age dependency ratio (persons aged 65+ as a percentage of persons aged 15-64)

				Change 2000/50	
	2000	**2025**	**2050**	**Absolute**	**%**
Czech Rep	20	36	61	41	207
Cyprus	18	29	39	21	119
Estonia	21	30	47	26	122
Hungary	21	33	51	30	139
Latvia	22	31	50	28	128
Lithuania	20	29	51	31	156
Malta	18	37	47	28	154
Poland	18	31	50	32	180
Slovakia	17	27	50	33	200
Slovenia	20	38	66	46	233
Bulgaria	24	31	54	30	127
Romania	19	26	45	25	130
EU-15	24	36	49	24	100

Source: UN population projections 2002. AMECO for the EU-15.
Note: The old-age dependency ratio is defined as persons aged over 65 as a percentage of the working-age population (aged 15-64). Similar trends are expected for the economic dependency ratio, which expresses the population aged 15 and over not employed as a percentage of the number of persons employed.

48. The projected decline in the size of the active labour force involves a strong risk of lower economic growth, even under reasonable assumptions concerning the increase in total factor productivity. In the Lisbon agenda, the goal of higher factor productivity goes hand in hand with that of higher **participation and employment**. Higher participation rates, among men as well as among women and especially at older ages, and lower unemployment rates can help mitigate the challenges of ageing populations.

49. As regards the **size of current public spending on public pensions**, public pension expenditure in several countries is close to or above 10% of GDP (Cyprus, Latvia, Poland and Slovenia). Ageing populations could lead to a substantial increase in public expenditures in many acceding countries as long-term projections, where available, point to a

sharply rising expenditure trajectory (see Table 11)[11]. This development may make it more difficult to finance the impact of an ageing population on public spending on pensions. On the basis of the scenarios set out in the 2002 PEPs, six out of ten acceding countries have a debt level below 40% of GDP. Several acceding countries, with relatively low debt levels, and gradual build-up of assets in funded schemes, appear in a good position to cope with the budgetary impact of ageing populations. However, this could be very different for those acceding countries that have not yet proceeded with the introduction of a comprehensive reform of their first-pillar pension schemes. Given the fact that long-run budgetary projections are only available for a number of countries, and their limited comparability, a detailed case-by-case analysis by the EPC's Ageing Working Group seems warranted on the impact of population ageing on public expenditure on pensions.

Table 11: Public pension expenditures in 2000-50 (% of GDP)

	2000	2030	2050	Change 2000-50
Cyprus	8	11.9	14.8	+6.8
Czech Republic	7.8[5]	-	14.6[5]	+6.8
Estonia	6.9 [2,4]	-	-	
Hungary	6.0[5]	-	7.2[5]	+1.2
Latvia	9.8 [4]	-	-	
Lithuania	5.3	6	7	+1.7
Malta	5.4 [2,4]	-	-	
Poland	10.8	9.6	9.7	-0.9
Slovakia	7.9 [4]	-	-	
Slovenia	13.2	19.7	18.1	+4.9
Bulgaria	9.1 [2,4]	-	-	
Romania	6.4	7.8	8.2	+1.8
EU-15	10.4	13.0	13.3	+2.9

Sources: If not explicitly indicated, data are based on the 2002 Pre-Accession Economic Programmes.
Notes: -: not available; [1)]2002; [2)]2001; [3)] 2000; [4)] According to Gesellschaft für Versicherungswissen-schaft und -gestaltung e.V. (which in turn draws on national statistics). [5] OECD. Since definitions of public pension expenditures are not identical for each country, caution is warranted when making comparisons.

[11] It should be borne in mind, though, that public debt ratios in the acceding countries are at present generally lower than in the present Member States.

50. In several acceding countries **funded schemes** within the publicly financed pension systems have gradually become more prominent in recent years. Cyprus, Estonia, Hungary, Latvia and Poland have introduced a three-pillar pension system (compulsory and non-funded/compulsory and funded/voluntary and funded) and Lithuania and Slovakia are planning to do so in the near future. Funding does not by itself reduce future pressures on public expenditure; its benefits are in entrenching long-term budgetary consolidation efforts, by building reserves for the future pension liabilities of governments and introducing a flexible and long-term instrument of budgetary discipline to help to respond to the expected additional budgetary cost of ageing. Benefits of funding in the first pillar in the existing PAYG schemes include strengthening the financial basis of pension systems, increasing the security of future pension provision, and enhancing intergenerational equity in public finances. However, it should be recognised that, if funding is to make a meaningful contribution towards financing age-related expenditures, considerable resources will need to be devoted.

51. Recent pension reforms in the acceding countries have also focused on increasing the effective **retirement age,** which in most countries is relatively low. In addition, the legal retirement age in several countries appears too low and is, in many cases, several years lower than in most EU countries (it is close to 65 for men in most Member States[12], whilst it is two to five years lower in several acceding countries). It should be recalled here that the Barcelona European Council called for an increase in the effective average retirement age in the EU by some five years. Other challenges facing pension systems in the acceding countries, quite similar to those facing EU Member States, may include

[12]See EPC report on reform challenges facing public pension systems: the impact of certain parametric reforms on pension expenditure of 5 July 2002: http://europa.eu.int/comm/economy_finance/epc_en.htm.

the dynamics of early retirement arrangements (in some countries these have been introduced in response to the increase in unemployment), expenditure pressures due to indexation rules[13], and striking the right balance between contribution rates and the level of benefits paid out.

52. Comparable information on **health care spending** is available for only four acceding countries. Public expenditure on health care in 2000 amounted to 6.6% of GDP in the Czech Republic, 5.1% in Hungary, 4.2% in Poland and 5.3% in the Slovak Republic[14]. Public health care expenditure has increased sharply since the start of transition in some of the countries. It can be expected that, owing to general increases in welfare, technical progress and product innovation in the coming years, public health care expenditures will converge on EU levels (EU-15: 5.9% of GDP in 1998), which for certain countries implies a significant increase in such expenditure.

53. Overall, a decline in the size of the active labour force may dampen growth and thereby slow down the catching-up process, since it may not be possible to maintain the increase of total factor productivity continuously at a level which would offset the impact of a declining labour force. Higher employment and participation rates are necessary to mitigate the challenges of ageing populations. Many acceding countries have already introduced a wide range of pension reforms, including the introduction of a three-pillar system. However, in order to counter longer-term spending trends in line with the three-pronged strategy for tackling the budgetary implications of ageing populations, further reforms seem to be needed in some countries before the projected decline in the size of the active labour force fully materialises. Such reforms need to focus on raising the employment rate of older workers and the

[13]For example, with pensions indexed to wages, gains in total factor productivity will not have a large beneficial impact on pension expenditure.

[14]For the other Candidate Countries, the Gesellschaft für Versicherungswissenschaft und -gestaltung e.V. (2001) indicates health care expenditure as follows: Cyprus 5.7% of GDP in 2000, Estonia 5.5% in 2001, Latvia 3.5% in 2000, Lithuania 4.4% in 2000, Malta approximately 8% in 2000, Slovenia 7% in 2000, Bulgaria approximately 10% in 2001, Romania 4.1% in 2000, and Turkey 4.8% in 2000.

effective retirement age. In a number of countries, scope for further improvements is to be found in reforming pension systems in the direction of better financial sustainability (e.g. by moving towards actuarial neutrality). The EPC considers that a further case-by-case analysis is warranted on the impact of population ageing on public expenditure on pensions. Health-care expenditure is also likely to be severely affected by increasing life expectancy and associated improvements in the health of elderly persons, whilst other factors come into play such as technological developments. Containing future expenditure growth while providing effective coverage will necessitate steps to raise the efficiency of health care systems (several countries have to contend with overcapacities and face an urgent need for modernisation).

6. *FOSTERING THE KNOWLEDGE-BASED ECONOMY*

54. Within manufacturing, most acceding countries are experiencing a rather dynamic process of integration into the European division of labour. But all acceding countries except Malta, Estonia and Hungary have considerably lower levels of high-technology exports as a share of total manufactured goods than the EU average. The gap in export structures between most acceding countries and current Member States has narrowed considerably over the past decade, however, and the adjustment process out of commodities and labour-intensive products and into capital- and technology-intensive products is continuing at a fairly fast pace. In a few acceding countries dependence on labour-intensive branches in their export structures has increased since the late nineties[15]. While its share in the total economy has been increasing steadily, the service sector is generally less developed than manufacturing.

[15]See e.g. Michael Landesmann, "Structural features of economic integration in an enlarged Europe: patterns of catching-up and industrial specialisation", European Economy, January 2003.

Education and training systems

55. The education systems in not only the present Member States but also the acceding countries face similar challenges: to raise the quality of education and to ensure that the population is provided with skills adapted to the needs of working life and market requirements. The Lisbon strategy set several goals in education and training, including much higher per capita investment in human resources, access for all schools in the EU to the Internet and a halving in the number of 18 to 24 year-olds who have not completed at least secondary education.

56. Graph 8 shows that **public funding of education** in acceding countries is, on average, somewhat lower than the EU average of 5.3% of GDP. Two groups among the acceding countries can be identified: the Baltic states (Estonia, Latvia and Lithuania), with expenditure levels above 6% of GDP, which are higher than the EU average and rank them with the EU countries that have the highest levels of expenditure; and the Czech Republic and Slovakia, which have the lowest ratios of public expenditure not only relative to the EU-15 average but also on an EU-25 comparison. In Poland, the Czech Republic and Slovakia, public spending on education has registered a marked drop during the 1990s. In contrast, public spending has risen steadily in Estonia, Slovenia, Lithuania and Cyprus. No information is available on private funding, which for some countries might make a difference.

Graph 8: Public expenditure on education as % of GDP in 2000[16]

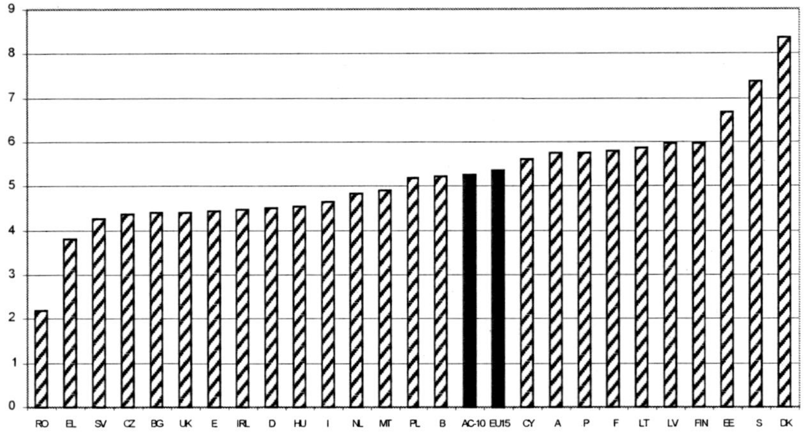

Source: Structural Indicators, New Cronos, Eurostat.

57. In terms of the **efficiency of education spending**, in some acceding countries there appear to be certain cost inefficiencies related to overstaffing, a duplication of facilities, inefficient class sizes, inefficiencies in available equipment and overemphasis on non-essential services, which push up the costs of education.

58. As regards the quality of the educational systems, curricula may be outdated in several respects, e.g. in terms of management skills or flexibility/adaptability more generally. With regard to output, available information suggests that many acceding countries share the common problem that the education system does not meet the needs of the private sector, in terms of the knowledge produced and adaptability of the labour force.[17] As a consequence, a sizeable proportion of workers in the

[16] It should be noted, though, that these figures are difficult to compare as they have not been adjusted for differences in demographic developments. Data comparability may be further impeded by differences in the efficiency of resource input.

[17] In terms of broader reforms to the education system, the literature has highlighted factors such as the decentralisation of schools or broader pedagogical aims of the educational system. See, for example, Andreas Ammermüller, Hans Heijke and Ludger Wössmann, "Schooling Quality in Eastern Europe: Educational Production During Transition", Kiel Working Paper No 1154, March 2003. http://www.uni-kiel.de/ifw/pub/kap/kap.htm.

acceding countries may not be sufficiently well prepared to meet the needs of the labour market.

59. Educational attainment of the population in acceding countries is high when measured as a proportion of the adult population that has completed at least **secondary education**. On average, a larger proportion of 25 to 64 year-olds in the acceding countries have completed at least upper secondary level than in the EU (the average in the acceding countries is 77%, compared to some 64% in the EU, with a number of acceding countries scoring higher than the EU countries). Similarly, the gross enrolment rate in secondary education exceeds that in most EU countries (the exception being Malta).

60. However, the situation is different as regards **tertiary education**, which in the acceding countries has been completed on average by only 19% of the 25 to 64 year-olds (compared with 22% in the EU). Only Lithuania, Estonia and Cyprus are above the EU average. Moreover, the situation is certainly less advanced than suggested by the quantitative indicators, as attainment levels do not usually differentiate between the narrow, often outdated, qualifications used in the former centrally planned economies, and the new, broad-based qualifications needed for the knowledge-based economy. In over half of the central European acceding countries the proportion of persons having completed tertiary education is lower in the younger age groups than in the older age groups. Graph 9 shows that the average gross enrolment ratio in the EU is 49% of the age group eligible for tertiary education[18] (ranging from 46% in Germany to 84% in Finland). Only four acceding countries (Poland, Latvia, Estonia and Slovenia) exceed the EU average gross enrolment ratio.

[18] A subgroup of university-age population.

Graph 9: Gross enrolment ratio at tertiary level in 1999

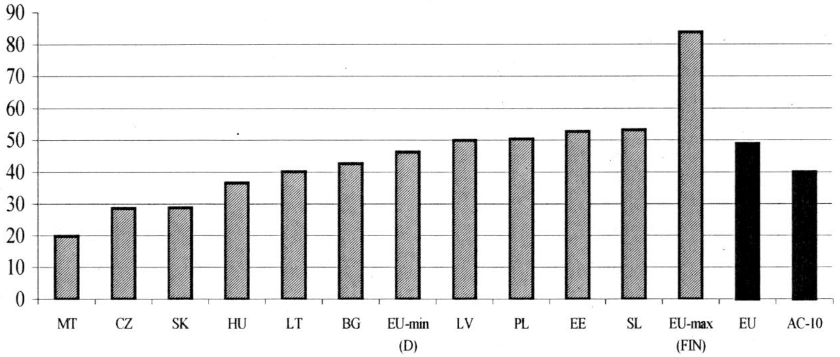

Source: UNESCO.

61. Recent reforms in education systems show increasing awareness of these issues, and in particular the need to boost participation at tertiary education level to satisfy the demand for high skill workers. As a result, almost all acceding countries are undertaking major efforts to catch up with the EU level of participation in tertiary education. Poland and Hungary had the highest percentage increase in enrolments in higher education between 1995 and 1999 in all OECD countries. Estonia also shows a significant increase (80%) in this same respect. Other countries also recorded large, albeit less marked increases.

62. The proportion of **tertiary graduates in science and technology** per 1000 persons in the age group 20-29 in the accession countries appears lower than in the EU Member States, even if it has increased considerably, especially in Estonia, Lithuania and Poland. The number of persons in 2000 ranged from 3.3 persons in Cyprus to 12.1 persons in Lithuania, compared with a range of between 23.2 persons (in Ireland) and 5.7 (in Italy) in the EU in 2000. On the basis of available information, however, it is not clear whether the ratio of tertiary graduates in science and technology to all tertiary graduates in the acceding countries is lower than the same ratio in the present Member States.

63. The number of **drop-outs and early leavers**, another indicator of the output of the education system, has substantially increased in accession countries, but it is still lower than in the EU countries (12.9% on average as against 19.3%). However, drop-outs remain a major problem (notably in vocational education and training).

64. Especially serious is the situation of **low-skilled workers**, who are in a much more disadvantaged situation than their high-skilled counterparts and even more so when compared with the EU. While unemployment rates of high-skilled workers in Candidate Countries are comparable to those in the EU (differences reflect mainly higher unemployment rates), the situation of the low-skilled is rather different. Unemployment rates are higher than in any EU country and the gap between high- and low-skilled workers is wider, reflecting a more pronounced dual labour market. This conclusion is reinforced when taking into account the extremely low employment rates for the low-skilled.

65. Education and training systems need to be better adapted to the needs of lifelong learning, and the capabilities of those systems to respond adequately to changes in skill requirements need to be enhanced. In this respect, in terms of participation in **continuing vocational education and training** in general for the 25 to 64 year-olds, data from the Labour Force Survey show large disparities between acceding countries and EU countries (3.6% on average in the accession countries compared with 8.4% on average in the EU).

66. Overall, the acceding countries have made major efforts to reform their education systems and to adapt them gradually to the challenges posed by a knowledge-based economy. On balance, people in the acceding countries have a high literacy rate and the educational infrastructure is well developed. Spending on human capital is higher than the EU average in several acceding countries. In some countries, however, spending on human capital has registered a marked drop during the 1990s. Some important challenges remain for the education systems in

the acceding countries, in terms of preparedness of the workers to meet the demands of the labour market, participation in tertiary education and cost-inefficiencies when compared with EU Member States, and in terms of the progress to be made if the Lisbon objectives are to be met. In certain areas and countries a gap might emerge in regard of the quality and output of education systems since educational attainment does not fully meet the needs of the private sector. This is of particular concern in terms of the knowledge and skills being produced and the adaptability of the workforce, notably for high skilled workers. Many members of the labour force might require time and investment to develop new skills needed for prospering in a knowledge-based economy. This could indicate potential long-term difficulties in the light of the Lisbon agenda.

R&D and innovation

67. The Barcelona European Council set the goal of raising overall spending on R&D so as to approach 3% of GDP by 2010. Two thirds of this investment should come from the private sector. This input indicator implies inter alia improved incentives for firms to invest in R&D.

68. Acceding countries spend relatively little on both **total and business R&D** as a share of GDP. In 2000 total R&D spending for those countries averaged well below 1% of GDP, compared with an average of almost 2% of GDP in the EU (Graph 10). This poor record was matched by weak business R&D investment in 2000, which was equivalent to less than 0.4% of GDP, i.e. not even a third of the EU average. Moreover, business expenditure on R&D in the acceding countries, expressed as a percentage of GDP, did not increase between 1995 and 2000. There is therefore no sign that this large gap in business R&D expenditures between those countries and the EU is about to disappear. The low level of R&D expenditure is also reflected in low patenting activities in the acceding countries.

Graph 10: R&D expenditure in 2000

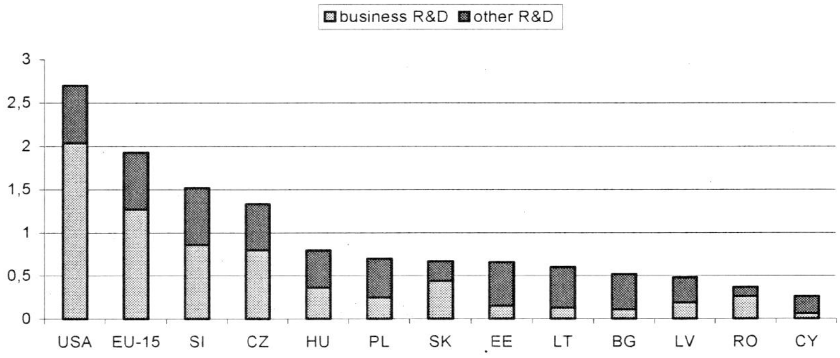

Source: Eurostat.
Note: *Estimated value for EU-15. No data available for Malta and Turkey.

69. The EPC's 2002 report on research and development[19] can provide a useful framework for comparing the situation in the acceding countries with that in the EU. It identified as key drivers of innovation activities a well-educated workforce, a strong climate for entrepreneurship, easy access to risk capital and other finance, infrastructure for research networks and co-operation between the private and public sector, an appropriate intellectual property regime and macroeconomic stability. It showed that the improvement of the **general framework conditions**, and above all a highly competitive environment, is vital. This means not only having the appropriate competition rules in place but also creating an environment in which smaller firms are able to grow extremely quickly and challenge less innovative incumbents to improve their performance. According to the Commission's 2002 Regular Report, the implementation of competition policies in several acceding countries was found to be insufficient, which also affects innovation. Many firms face disadvantageous conditions for financing innovation, either in terms of obtaining access to finance or in terms of its cost. One of the most important policy challenges for boosting innovation, not only in the present but also in the future Member States, is the overall govern-

---

19 http:www.europa.eu.int/comm/economy_finance/epc/documents/rdfinal_en.pdf.

ance of public research institutions and grant mechanisms and their responsiveness to the needs of their private counterparts. It may make sense for some of the acceding countries to focus more on technology transfer and gradual product and process improvement as opposed to large-scale, long-term and risky industrial and public research investment.

70. Three acceding countries, the Czech Republic, Hungary and the Slovak Republic, invested more in **information and communication technologies** (ICT) in 2000 than the EU average (7.4% of GDP). However, no acceding country except the Czech Republic could match the growth of ICT investments in the EU during the last six years (1995-2000). This trend points to a further widening of the gap in ICT maturity between the EU Member States and many acceding countries.

71. Overall, acceding countries lag substantially behind EU Member States in the transition to the knowledge-based economy. Low levels of investment in R&D and IT may hamper their catching-up with the EU mainstream and any improvement in their productivity levels. Present levels of spending on R&D in the acceding countries fall well short of the Lisbon objective, notably in the private sector. Those countries may well benefit most from continuing their reforms of educational and research institutions, raising the educational attainment in the areas most relevant for innovation performance and aim for gradual but steady progress towards the Barcelona target of 3% of GDP expenditure on R&D and innovation. It may make sense for some of the acceding countries to focus more on technology transfer and gradual product and process improvement. Measures should be taken to improve the general framework conditions, including the entrepreneurial climate, the efficiency of the education system, access to risk capital, the education of the workforce and the interrelationship between business and the research network so as to make them more responsive to private firms looking for partners. The effective implementation of competition policies should be a key priority with a view to fostering innovation.

7. ENVIRONMENTAL AND SOCIAL SUSTAINABILITY

72. Sustainable development is defined by the conclusions of the Gothenborg European Council as "to meet the needs of the present generation without compromising those of future generations" ... which "requires dealing with economic, social and environmental policies in a mutually reinforcing way". The Commission proposes to "focus on a small number of problems which pose severe or irreversible threats to the future well-being of European society", namely (1) global warming, (2) threats to public health, (3) poverty, (4) ageing of the population, (5) loss of bio-diversity and (6) transport congestion. The question of population ageing was addressed above.

Environmental sustainability

73. The 2002 Broad Economic Policy Guidelines state that the "*protection of environmental resources such as clean air, water and soil, maintaining biodiversity and reducing environmental threats to public health require an active environmental policy in order to ensure a responsible use of scarce natural resources and development which is economically, environmentally and socially sustainable in the long run. Commitments undertaken at international level, notably in the area of climate change, also call for policy action.*"

74. The **energy intensity** of the economy is more than three times higher in the acceding countries than the EU average (708.8 gross inland consumption of energy divided by GDP as opposed to 193.9 on average in the EU). Almost all accession countries exceed the figure of the EU Member State with the highest energy intensity. Urban air quality seems to be a major problem in the acceding countries. Freight transport volumes are about the same as the EU average. Freight transportation by road in all eastern and central European acceding countries plays a smaller role than in the EU as a whole. The same seems to be true for passenger transport.

75. **Greenhouse gas emissions** are much lower in the acceding countries than in the EU and are characterised by a decreasing trend in the accession countries as a whole. Several countries show, however, increasing emissions. It is likely that the declines observed in emissions are part of the sectoral shift away from heavy industry, and the increases in some countries are an indication that the transition process is substantially completed, so that increases in emissions due to rising levels of economic activity are now the dominant factor. The share of renewable resources, which must be seen in relation to the existing indicative target of 22% of gross electricity consumption by 2010, is on average lower in the acceding countries than in the EU. In 2000 it ranged from 0.2% in Estonia to 31.2% in Slovenia (average EU: 14.7%). As in the EU, no clear trend has been discernible in recent years.

Social cohesion

76. Data on social cohesion in the accession countries are particularly scarce. Nevertheless, one can draw some conclusions from the employment situation. According to the 2002 Broad Economic Policy Guidelines, "*... jobs are the best protection against poverty and social exclusion.*" The unemployment and employment rates discussed above demonstrate that there is scope for improving social inclusion. The high long-term unemployment rate in the accession countries, which ranges from 1.2% in Cyprus (in 2000) to 11.3% in the Slovak Republic (2001), further underpins this argument. However, the share of the population in a jobless household falls perfectly into the range recorded for EU countries.

77. Regional income dispersion does not seem to pose a greater problem than in the EU. The same is true for the share of early school-leavers. Generally speaking, those leaving the education system without sufficient skills are at a high risk of poverty and social exclusion.

8. *Implications for the Lisbon Strategy and Integration of the Acceding Countries into EU Structural Reform Processes*

The Lisbon strategy

- The Lisbon strategic goal of "becoming the most competitive and dynamic economy" remains unchanged in an enlarged Union. Yet the Lisbon targets are likely to be more difficult to achieve, simply because in most cases the average EU starting base is statistically lowered by the fact that most acceding countries are less well placed vis-à-vis the Lisbon targets than the existing Member States (for a summary of main Lisbon targets, see Annex 2)[20]. It should also be recognised, though, that at least in some areas a number of acceding countries are already equally or even better placed than (some) present Member States. Given the data collected recently and the specific characteristics of the accession countries, quantitative assessments should, however, be treated with care.
- As regards the Lisbon and Stockholm targets for employment rates, the total employment rate in an EU-25 would have been some 1.5 percentage points lower than in the EU-15 in 2001 (62.6% compared with 64%). The female employment rate in an EU-25 would have been 54.1% (compared with the actual female employment rate in the EU-15 of 54.9%). The employment rate of older workers would have been 37.2% in an EU-25 (compared with the actual employment rate of older workers in the EU-15 of 38.6%). Challenges facing labour markets in the acceding countries do not differ fundamentally in nature from those in the EU Member States, but the problems are often more severe.
- Integration implies the full transposition of internal market directives

[20]The complete Lisbon targets can be found in the Commission staff working paper in support of the Report from the Commission to the Spring European Council in Brussels ("The Spring Report"), SEC(2003) 25 of 14 January 2003.

in the area of product markets, and the removal of other barriers to trade and services, which is a challenge. The acceding countries face more severe problems than the present Member States as regards their efforts at reform intended to strengthen competition in several product markets, including the need to enhance the general business environment, to lower barriers imposed by market entry and exit mechanisms, and to reduce significantly sectoral or ad hoc state aid. In many acceding countries, the administrative capacity of the public sector also needs to be urgently enhanced. Many segments of the public sector are perceived as remaining highly inefficient which creates obstacles to the operation and growth of businesses. Necessary improvements particularly concern the regulatory burden on business, the effective implementation and in some countries the design of judicial reforms, and the quality and administrative capacity of the central and local public sectors. For network industries, it will be key to improve market contestability by reducing potential barriers to foreign and domestic competititon and ensuring effective and transparent supervision structures. A specific challenge is posed by the large share of employment represented by the agricultural sector in several countries, the modernisation of which is hampered by a lack of employment opportunities in other sectors.

- Financial markets in the acceding countries continue to be underdeveloped relative to the EU. The legislative frameworks must support the development of financial markets and the institutional investor base. Challenges may arise from the adjustment process of acceding countries' market infrastructure, and the access to and cost of loan and risk capital finance for SMEs. In line with the Financial Market Action Plan, continued reforms to deepen and widen the financial sector are required so as to avoid credit constraints. In addition, progress with financial sector supervision and regulation remains uneven between countries.

78. As regards the **quality of public finances**, there is a need in many acceding countries to reassess the structure of budget revenue and ex-

penditure in order to foster a growth-enhancing environment providing sufficient space and incentives for private sector development. Sound public finances should be achieved via spending restraint and growth friendly tax systems. On the revenue side, specific weaknesses may stem from the narrow tax base in several acceding countries, from the lack of a clear definition of fiscal relations between the national and sub-national level in terms of public expenditure control, and from tax collection and administration. On the expenditure side, challenges exist in the shape of the ever-rising needs of public-sector services and the need to improve the efficiency of public administration. Specific attention should be devoted to investment in key areas (such as R&D and innovation; public infrastructure and human capital) so as to underpin future competitiveness and growth.

79. In view of the current parameters of their **pension systems** (e.g. effective retirement ages, employment rates of older workers, contribution and replacement rates), many acceding countries in addition to reforms already introduced will have to implement comprehensive reform strategies. The goal of an increase in the effective retirement age is difficult to assess, as no reference point exists (there is probably no data on the retirement age in the EU-25 as a whole in 2002 - the reference year for which the goal was set at the European Council in Barcelona). However, the statutory retirement age in several acceding countries is two to five years lower than in present Member States which points to a problem.

80. Acceding countries lag substantially behind EU Member States in the **transition to a knowledge-based economy**. The industrial base of most of the acceding countries is still biased towards low to medium-technology sectors. The Lisbon target of R&D investment rising by 2010 to 3% of GDP, of which two thirds should come from the business sector, is likely to be somewhat more difficult to achieve in an enlarged Union (rough estimates suggest that the total R&D figure in EU-25 would be around 1.8% of GDP and the business R&D figure around

1.1% of GDP - as opposed to 1.9% in EU-15, of which 1.1% from business). In regard of education, the lack of high skilled labour could indicate potential long-term difficulties in the light of the Lisbon agenda. The acceding countries have to take steps to improve their education and training systems in terms of educational attainment, skilled human resources as well as R&D and innovation performance. More attention should be drawn onto technology transfer and gradual product and process improvement - this is often spurred by foreign direct investment.

EU structural policy co-ordination processes and further work

81. Within the EU, a number of economic policy co-ordination processes have been developed to foster economic reform and provide for appropriate peer pressure:

- the **Broad Economic Policy Guidelines**, which are at the centre of economic policy co-ordination and which reflect and guide all other co-ordination activities at EU level. They are specific about misalignments, structural imbalances and issues of competitiveness. The Council in December 2002 decided that in the future the BEPGs should focus on the medium-term economic policy strategy and should be reviewed only every three years (see Annex 3 for the set-up of the new economic policy co-ordination cycle). In the intermediate years, the focus is on implementation of the key recommendations.
- **other policy co-ordination processes** which deal with specific economic policy areas, such as employment (the Luxembourg process), structural reforms and competitiveness (the Cardiff process/report), the macroeconomic dialogue with the social partners (the Cologne process) and pension reforms (the open method of co-ordination on pensions).
- the **Lisbon strategy** with the Commission's annual synthesis report leading to the Spring European Council on economic reform.

82. The existing policy co-ordination processes, notably the Cardiff report, the Luxembourg process, the Lisbon strategy and the BEPGs, cover all economic aspects which are relevant for the present and the future Member States. It appears that the specific challenges facing the acceding countries can be dealt with within the existing multilateral surveillance framework. However, in their future Cardiff reports (and the remaining Pre-Accession Economic Programmes), the acceding countries should pay particular attention to the challenges spelt out above; there is sufficient leeway for them to do so under the current reporting priorities.

In response to the mandate given by the Ecofin Council as to how the acceding countries could be integrated as early as possible into the Community's **structural reform co-ordination processes,** the EPC suggests including the acceding states for the first time in:

- the BEPGs in 2004 (including in their country-specific part), taking into account the new three-year perspective of the BEPGs (which for the current Member States is the period 2003-2005), and accordingly the implementation report on the BEPGs in 2005;
- the EPC's annual report on structural reforms in 2005 (the Cardiff report), including specific country notes. As the acceding states will be observers in the EPC from 2004, they should be invited to already provide national Cardiff reports by October/November 2003 to allow them to already participate at the annual examinations of the EPC for the 2004 annual report on structural reforms[21];
- the Luxembourg and Cologne processes in 2004; and a (possible) upcoming report on the open method for pensions only after long-term projections for pension expenditures are made available in 2006. The acceding countries were already included in the Lisbon process in 2003.

---

[21] In this context, it might be interesting to note that the Commission also already receives Cardiff reports from Norway.

83. Within the existing framework, the EPC considers that:

- in the Cardiff report and the BEPGs, the focus for the acceding countries could rest more on the still incomplete structural shift. A number of product market issues, such as privatisation, administered prices and factors affecting the sectoral composition of the economy, and a number of challenges related to the knowledge-based economy, such as the performance of the education systems and R&D as well as innovation performance, need to be discussed more intensively than is currently the case for the existing Member States. A special focus for surveillance should be the institutional framework for market development and the business environment, and the effective implementation of competition policies;
- in the Luxembourg process, the focus for the acceding countries should, on account of the need for business restructuring, probably be more on the priority "promoting adaptability in the labour market"[22].

84. In view of the challenges outlined above, the **structural indicators** adopted under the Lisbon process appear generally adequate. The EPC Working Group on Indicators should explore whether there is any need for additions to, or changes to the scope of the existing list of structural indicators, e.g. in the areas of employment (tertiary education) or economic reform (privatisation/share of public enterprises, and administered prices).

85. The statistical offices of the acceding countries need to devote enough resources to the structural indicators to ensure the best possible **coverage and quality of the data** used in the structural indicators. For example, in order to allow for a thorough assessment of the quality of public finances, the acceding countries should aim at improving data quality on public revenue and expenditure; future updates of the Pre-Accession Economic Programmes, and indeed the first Convergence

---

[22] As proposed by the European Commission in COM(2003)6 final, 14.1.2003.

Programmes in 2004, would benefit from (i) a more extensive description of the pension reforms under way, (ii) the indication of available long-term projections for pension expenditures, and (iii) a description of the precise role of funding and the pace of asset accumulation in the funded pension systems.

86. The following recommendations are made for **further work in the EPC:**

- Enlargement will be a special subject in the **EPC Annual Report on Structural Reforms in 2004**. With the Lisbon targets in mind, a special annex could be devoted to the areas of critical items identified by this report for the acceding countries, (such as privatisation, the share of public enterprises, administered prices, and tertiary and vocational education).
- Taking account of the close linkages between employment policies and productivity growth, the EPC's **wage monitoring exercise and the Working Group on Labour Market Issues** should be called on to pay particular attention to the labour market challenges in acceding countries.
- So as to produce comparable long-term projections for pension expenditures for the Convergence Programmes, the acceding countries should be included in the next round of common projections for public spending on pensions, health and long-term care for the elderly by the EPC's **Ageing Working Group** in 2004/05.
- The methodological work on potential output and the computation of cyclically adjusted budget balances by the EPC's **Working Group on Output Gaps** should be extended to cover the acceding countries, with a report being submitted to the Committee by the end of 2004.
- The EPC's **Working Group on Structural Indicators** should explore whether there is any need for additions to, or changes to the scope of the existing list of structural indicators.
- The EPC as a whole should include the issue of regional disparities, and the role that Community and national policies could play over a

broad range of fields to reduce standards of living within the Community.

9. ANNEX

Annex 1: Employment rates in the acceding countries (as % of age-specific groups)

	Male											
	15-64						55-64					
	1996	1997	1998	1999	2000	2001	1996	1997	1998	1999	2000	2001
Bulgaria	--	--	--	--	56.1	53.6	--	--	--	--	34.9	34.2
Czech R.	--	77.1	76.1	74	73.1	73.2	--	38.5	37.5	37.6	36.1	36.9
Cyprus	--	--	--	78.7	78.9	79.7	--	--	--	66.3	67.1	67.9
Estonia	--	69.7	70.3	66.3	64.3	65.6	--	59.6	60.9	59.2	50.2	57.1
Hungary	59.4	59.6	60	62.4	62.7	63.3	27.1	27.1	26.3	29.3	33	35
Latvia	--	--	63.5	65.2	62.3	61.9	--	--	49.2	50.2	48.3	44.8
Lithuania	--	--	67.6	68.9	61.8	59.8			57	56.7	52.2	48.6
Malta	--	--	--	--	--	--	--	--	--	--	--	--
Poland	--	66.2	66.3	63.6	61.2	59.2	--	44.5	42.7	41.8	37.4	38.3
Romania	--	73.4	71.9	70.4	69.5	68:6	--	62.8	61.9	59.4	57.4	56
Slovakia	--	--	--	64	61.6	61.8	--	--	--	36.4	35.2	37.7
Slovenia	66	67.1	67.5	66.8	66.7	68.5	28.1	29.8	32.8	32.2	31	33
EU-15	70.1	70.3	71	71.7	72.5	73	47.2	47.1	47.3	47.5	48	48.6

	Female											
	15-64						55-64					
	1996	1997	1998	1999	2000	2001	1996	1997	1998	1999	2000	2001
Bulgaria	--	--	--	--	47.2	47.9	--	--	--	--	11.2	11.4
Czech R.	--	60.2	58.9	57.4	56.8	57	--	24	23.2	23.6	22.1	23
Cyprus	--	--	--	50.2	52.5	56.5	--	--	--	28.8	31.9	32.6
Estonia	--	60.6	60.7	58	57.1	56.9	--	40.5	42	39.3	37.5	41.9
Hungary	45.1	44.8	46.8	48.8	49.4	49.6	10.2	10.7	9.3	11.1	13	14.6
Latvia	--	--	54.2	54.1	53.5	56.1	--	--	28.1	26.4	25.9	30.1
Lithuania	--	--	58.5	61.4	58.5	57.4	--	--	27.4	31.8	34.5	31.8
Malta	--	--	--	--	--	--	--	--	--	--	--	--
Poland	--	51.6	52.2	51.6	49.3	48.4	--	27.7	25.2	24.5	21.8	23.8
Romania	--	61.1	60.1	59.7	59	58.2	--	48.2	48.4	47.3	47.3	45.8
Slovakia	--	--	--	52.1	51.1	51.8	--	--	--	10.6	10.2	10
Slovenia	57.5	58.4	59.5	58.1	58.5	58.6	12.9	16.4	19.4	14.9	14.3	14.4
EU-15	50.1	50.6	51.5	52.8	54	54.9	25.8	26.1	26.3	27.1	27.9	28.8

	Male and female											
	15-64						55-64					
	1996	1997	1998	1999	2000	2001	1996	1997	1998	1999	2000	2001
Bulgaria	--	--	--	--	51.5	50.7	--	--	--	--	22.1	23.9
Czech R.	--	68.6	67.5	65.6	64.9	65	--	54.8	53.4	53.2	51.6	52.4
Cyprus	--	--	--	64.2	65.5	67.9	--	--	--	47	49	49.8
Estonia	--	64.9	65.3	62	60.6	61.1	--	48.9	50.2	47.9	43	48.6
Hungary	52	52	53.2	55.4	55.9	56.3	17.6	17.9	16.7	19.1	21.9	23.7
Latvia	--	--	58.6	59.4	57.7	58.9	--	--	37	36.6	35.4	36.4
Lithuania	--	--	62.9	65	60.1	58.6	--	--	40.2	42.6	42.2	39.1
Malta	--	--	--	--	--	--	--	--	--	--	--	--
Poland	--	58.8	59.2	57.5	55.1	53.8	--	35.5	33.3	32.5	29	30.5
Romania		67.2	65.9	65	64.2	63.3	--	55	54.7	52.9	52	50.5
Slovakia	--	--	--	58	56.3	56.7	--	--	--	22.2	21.4	22.5
Slovenia	61.7	62.8	63.5	62.5	62.7	63.6	19.9	22.7	25.9	23.4	22.3	23.4
EU-15	60.1	60.5	61.2	62.3	63.2	63.9	36.2	36.3	36.6	37.1	37.8	38.5

Source: Employment in Europe 2002 - European Commission and EPC Ageing Working Group 2001.

Annex 2: Summary of main Lisbon targets and objectives

The Lisbon strategy entails a variety of targets and objectives, agreed not only at the Lisbon Council itself (March 2000) but also at Stockholm (March 2001), Göteborg (June 2001) and Barcelona (March 2002). Not all are quantified or time-specific, but those which are include:

Employment

- an overall employment rate of 67% in 2005 (Stockholm) and 70% in 2010 (Lisbon);
- a female employment rate of 57% in 2005 (Stockholm) and 60% in 2010 (Lisbon);
- an employment rate for workers aged 55-64 of 50 per cent in 2010 (Stockholm);
- an increase of five years by 2010 in the average effective retirement age (Barcelona); and
- available childcare by 2010 for 90% of pre-school children over three and for 33% of children under three (Barcelona).

Research and innovation

- R&D spending equivalent to 3% of GDP by 2010, with two thirds of the total coming from business (Barcelona);
- 100% of schools to be connected to the Internet by 2002; and
- All teachers to have training in digital skills by 2003.

Economic reform

- full implementation of the Risk Capital Action Plan by 2003 and of the Financial Services Action Plan by 2005 (Lisbon);
- a transposition rate into national law for internal market directives of 98.5% (Stockholm);
- no internal market directives to be more than two years overdue in their transposition (Barcelona);
- open energy markets for business customers in 2004 and subse-

quently for domestic users (Barcelona);
- cross-border energy transmission capacity equal to at least 10% of installed production capacity by 2005 (Barcelona); and
- a single European sky by 2004 (Barcelona).

Social cohesion
- to halve by 2010 the number of early school-leavers not continuing with further education (Lisbon); and
- to reduce by 2010 the numbers living at risk of poverty (Barcelona).

Environment/sustainable development
- visible progress on reducing greenhouse gas emissions by 2005 (Göteborg);
- an indicative target for electricity generated from renewable sources of 22% of gross electricity consumption in 2010 (Göteborg); and
- Combating Climate Change: meet the indicative target of 22% for the contribution of electricity produced from renewable energy sources to gross electricity consumption by 2010 (Gothenborg).

Annex 3: Flowchart of the improved economic policy co-ordination cycle

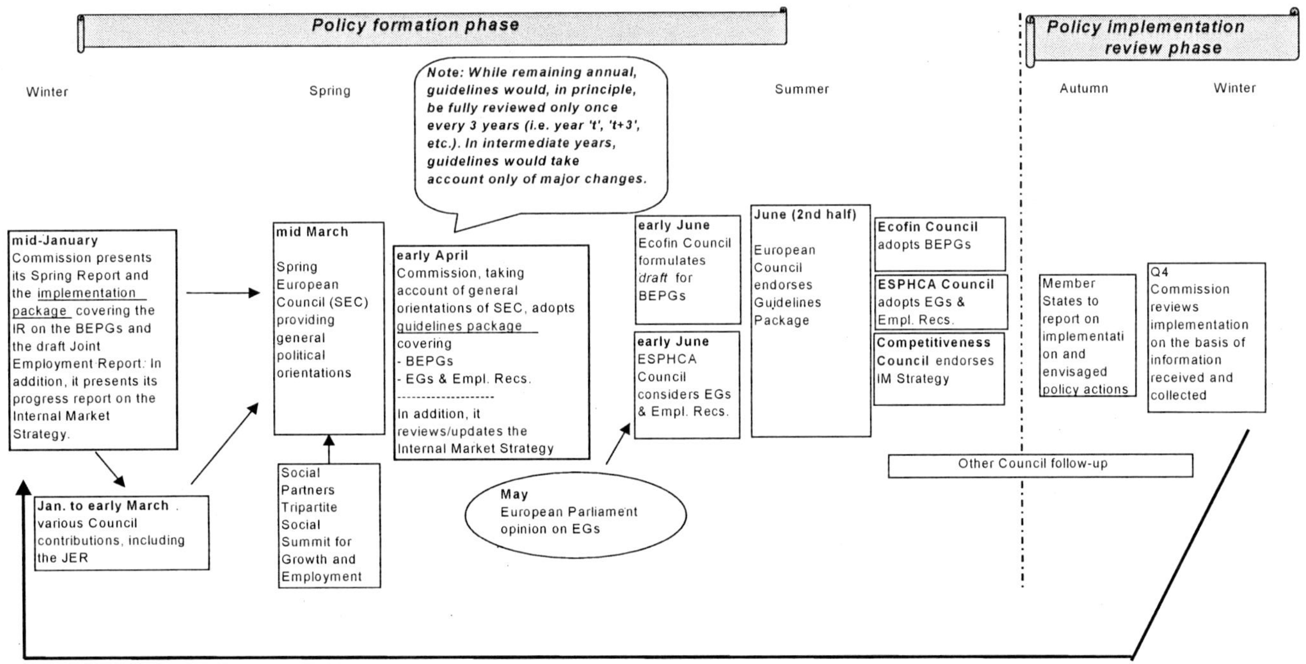

10. References

AMMERMÜLLER A., HEIJKE H., WÖSSMANN L., "Schooling Quality in Eastern Europe: Educational Production During Transition", Kiel Working Paper No 1154, March 2003. http://www.uni-kiel.de/ifw/pub/kap/kap.htm.

BARRO, R.J., JONG-WHA L. (2000), "International Data on Educational Attainment: Updates and Implications" CID Working Paper No 42, Centre for International Development, Harvard University.

Economic Policy Committee, "Budgetary challenges posed by ageing populations", Brussels, 24 October 2001. http://europa.eu.int/comm/economy_finance/epc_en.htm.

CARREIRO, P., HECKMAN, J. (2003), "Human Capital Policy", NBER Working Paper 9495.

DANG T.-T et al. (2001), "The fiscal implications of ageing", OECD Economics Department Working Papers No 305.

EBRD (2002), "Transition Report", 2002.

Economic Policy Committee, "Reform challenges facing public pension systems: the impact of certain parametric reforms on pension expenditure", Brussels, 5 July 2002. http://europa.eu.int/comm/economy_finance/epc_en.htm.

Economic Policy Committee, "Report on Research and Development", Brussels, 22 January 2002. http://europa.eu.int/comm/economy_finance/epc_en.htm.

EUROPEAN COMMISSION (2001), "Real Convergence in the Candidate Countries", DG ECFIN, November 2001.

EUROPEAN COMMISSION, "Employment in Europe", 2001 and 2002.

EUROPEAN COMMISSION (2002), "Human Capital in a Global and Knowledge-based Economy", DE LA FUENTE, A., CICCONE, A., Final Report for the DG Employment and Social Affairs.

EUROPEAN COMMISSION (2002), "Employment in Europe 2002. Recent Trends and Prospects", DG Employment and Social Affairs.

EUROPEAN COMMISSION (2002), "European Report on Quality

Indicators of Lifelong Learning", DG Education and Culture.
EUROPEAN COMMISSION (2002), "Regular Reports on Candidate Countries' Progress towards Accession".
EUROPEAN COMMISSION (2002), "Summary Sheets on Education Systems in Europe: Slovakia, Slovenia, Estonia, Lithuania, Latvia, Malta, Poland, Czech Republic, Romania, Cyprus, Bulgaria", EURYDICE.
EUROPEAN COMMISSION (2002), "Strategy Paper" and "Report by the European Commission on the Progress Towards Accession" (for each of the Candidate Countries), COM (2002) 700.
EUROPEAN COMMISSION (2003), "Spring Economic Forecasts".
EUROPEAN COMMISSION (2003), "Key Data on Education in Europe 2002", EURYDICE, Education and Culture, EUROSTAT.
EUROPEAN COMMISSION (2003), Decision COM (2003) 6 final (http://www.cc.cec/home/dgserv/sg/i/college/dec.htm)
EUROPEAN COMMISSION (2002), Public Finances in EMU 2002, European Economy No 3/2002.
EUROPEAN COMMISSION (2003), Commission staff working paper in support of the Report from the Commission to the Spring European Council in Brussels ("The Spring Report"), SEC(2003) 25 of 14 January 2003.
EUROPEAN COMMISSION, State Aid Scoreboard, special edition.
EUROPEAN TRAINING FOUNDATION (2002), "Key indicators on vocational education and training".
EUROPEAN TRAINING FOUNDATION (2002), "Preparation by Candidate Countries for involvement in the EU lifelong learning policy: achievements, gaps and challenges. Synthesis of the Monographs exercise Interim Report".
EUROPEAN TRAINING FOUNDATION, Statistics database.
EUROSTAT (2002), "Statistics in Focus", "Labour Costs Survey 2000 - Candidate Countries", Theme 3 - 23.
EUROSTAT, NEWCRONOS STATISTICS DATABASE.
Gesellschaft für Versicherungswissenschaft und -gestaltung e.V., Proceedings of the 2002 workshop on the social protection systems of

the Candidate Countries, Brussels 25 March 2003: http://www.gvg-koeln.de/deutsch/projekte.html

HIRSCH, D. (2002), "How good is our global education? The PISA Survey", OECD Observer. Centre for Educational Research and Innovation.

IMF (2001), "Real Convergence to EU Income Levels: Central Europe from 1990 to the Long-Term", Doyle, P.;Kuijs, L.;Jiang, G., Discussion Paper, 2001.

IMF (2002), "Into the EU, Policy Frameworks in Central Europe".

Landesmann Michael, "Structural features of economic integration in an enlarged Europe: patterns of catching-up and industrial specialisation", European Economy, January 2003.

OECD (2002), "Education at a Glance 2002", OECD.

OECD (2002), "Investment in Human Capital Through Post- Compulsory Education and Training: Selected Efficiency and Equity Aspects", OECD Economic Department Working Paper No 333.

Pre-Accession Economic Programmes (2002), for each Candidate Country.

SIANESI, B., REENE, J. V. (2002), "The Returns to Education: a review of the Empirical Macro-Economic Literature", The Institute for Fiscal Studies WP02/05.

UNESCO (2002), "Education Sector", UNESCO Institute For Statistics.

UNESCO INSTITUTE FOR STATISTICS, "Education Indicators. Technical Guidelines", UNESCO.

UNITED NATIONS, Population Forecasts 2002.

WORLD BANK (2000), "Hidden Challenges to Education Systems in Transition Economies", The World Bank, Europe and Central Asia Region, Human Development Sector.

11. Members of the EPC Working Group on Enlargement

CHAIRMAN

Mr Heinz HANDLER	*Bundesministerium für Wirtschaft and Arbeit, Vienna, Austria*

BELGIQUE

Mr Henri BOGAERT	*Commissaire au Plan*
Ms Micheline LAMBRECHT	*Bureau du Plan*

DANMARK

Mr Sigurd NÆSS-SCHMIDT	*Finansministeriet*

BUNDESREPUBLIK DEUTSCHLAND

Mr Willi KOLL	*Bundesministerium für Wirtschaft und Arbeit*

ESPANA

Ms Ana MARTINEZ SÁEZ	*Ministerio de Economia e Hacienda*

FRANCE

Mr Christophe BLANC	*Ministère de l'Economie, des Finances et de l'Industrie*

LUXEMBOURG

Ms Alexandra GUARDA-RAUCHS	*Ministry of the Economy*

ÖSTERREICH

Mr Peter PART	*Bundesministerium für Finanzen*
Ms Christina BURGER	*Bundesministerium für Wirtschaft und Arbeit*

SUOMI FINLAND

Mr Kari VARIS	*Ministry of Finance*

UNITED KINGDOM

Mr Matthew SALTER	*HM Treasury*

EUROPEAN CENTRAL BANK

Mr Reiner MARTIN

EUROPEAN COMMISSION

Mr Jan Host SCHMIDT
Mr Peter GRASSMANN
Mr Lars ÖSTLING
Ms Fabienne ILZKOVITZ

Secretariat of the ECONOMIC POLICY COMMITTEE

Mr Heinz SCHERRER

APPENDIX

AUTHORS

Christophe BLANC, Head of the Agrigulture and Environment Department, Forecasting Directorate, Ministry of Economics, Finance and Industry, France

Patrick van BRUSSELEN, Economist, Federal Planning Bureau, Belgium

Willem BUITER, Chief Economist of the European Bank for Reconstruction and Development

Christina BURGER, Director, Economic Policy Center, Ministry for Economic Affairs and Labour, Austria; previously Economist, European Commission, Directorate General for Economic and Financial Affairs

Giacomo CAVIGLIA, Economist in the EU Neighbouring Regions Division, Directorate General International and European Relations, European Central Bank

Christian FEHLKER, Expert in the Financial Stability Division in the Financial Stability and Supervision Directorate, European Central Bank

Esther GORDO, Economist, Bank of Spain

Heinz HANDLER, Director General, Economic Policy Center, Ministry for Economic Affairs and Labour, Austria

András INOTAI, Director General of the Institute for World Economics, Hungarian Academy of Sciences, Hungary

Micheline LAMBRECHT, Economist, Federal Planning Bureau, Belgium

Michael LANDESMANN, Director of the Vienna Institute for International Economic Studies, Austria

Felix LOWINSKI, Economist, Witten/Herdecke University, previously Trainée, Secretariat of the Economic Policy Committee

Reiner MARTIN, Principal Economist in the EU Countries Division, Directorate General Economics, European Central Bank

Ana MARTINEZ SÁEZ, Advisor to the General Director for Economic Policy, Ministry of Economics and Finance, Spain

Sigurd NÆSS-SCHMIDT, Head of Division, Ministry of Finance, Denmark

Lars ÖSTLING, Economist, European Commission, Directorate General for Economic and Financial Affairs

Peter PART, Deputy Director, Ministry of Finance, Austria

Matthew SALTER, Head of EU Enlargement Branch, Macroeconomic Policy and International Finance Directorate, HM Treasury, United Kingdom

Heinz SCHERRER, Economist, Secretariat of the Economic Policy Committee

Dominique SIMONIS, European Commission, Enterprise Directorate General; previously Economist, Federal Planning Bureau, Belgium

Lauri TARO, Economist, Economics Department, Ministry of Finance, Finland

Kari VARIS, Financial Counsellor, Economics Department, Ministry of Finance, Finland

List of Abbreviations

ACs:	Accession countries
AT:	Austria (A)
BE:	Belgium (B)
BEPGs:	Broad Economic Policy Guidelines
BG:	Bulgaria
CEECs:	Central and Eastern European Countries
CEFTA:	Central European Free Trade Association
CPI:	Consumer price index
CY:	Cyprus
CZ:	Czech Republic (CR)
DE:	Germany (D)
DK:	Denmark
EBRD:	European Bank for Reconstruction and Development
ECB:	European Central Bank
ECOFIN:	Council of Economic and Financial Ministers
EE:	Estonia
EEK:	Estonian kroon
EFC:	Economics and Financial Committee
EL:	Greece
EMU:	European Monetary Union
EPC:	Economic Policy Committee
ERM II:	Exchange Rate Mechanism II
ES:	Spain (E)
EU:	European Union
EU-MS:	European Union Member States
FDI:	Foreign direct investment
FI:	Finland (FIN)
FIEs:	Enterprises with some degree of foreign ownership
FR:	France (F)
FSAP:	Financial Services Action Plan
GDP:	Gross domestic product
GER:	Gross enrolment rate

HICP: Harmonised Index of Consumer Prices
HU: Hungary
IALS: International Adult Survey
ICT: Information and communication technologies
IE: Ireland (IRE)
IMF: International Monetary Funds
ISCED: International Standard Classification of Education
IT: Information technology
IT: Italy (I)
JAP: Joint Assessment of Employment Priorities
LE: Life expectancy
LFS: Labour force survey
LT: Lithuania
LU: Luxembourg (L, LUX)
LV: Latvia
LVL: Latvian Lat
MT: Malta
na: not available
NL: Netherlands
OECD: Organisation for Economic Co-operation and Development
OeNB: Oesterreichische National Bank (Austrian National Bank)
OFE: Open Pension Funds
PAYG: Pay-as-you-go-scheme
PEPS Pre-Accession Economic Programmes
PISA: Programmes for International Student Assessment
PL: Poland
PPS: Purchasing Power Standards
PSE: Producer Support Estimate
PT: Portugal (P)
R&D: Research and Development
RO: Romania
SDR: Special drawing rights
SE: Sweden (S)
SI: Slovenia (SL)

SK:	Slovak Republic
SMEs:	Small and medium-sized enterprises
TFP:	Total factor productivity
UK:	United Kingdom
UN:	United Nations
USD:	US-Dollar
VAT:	Valued added tax
WIFO	Wirtschaftsforschungsinstitut (Austrian Institute of Economic Research)
WIIW:	Wiener Institut für Internationale Wirtschaftsvergleiche (Vienna Institute for Comparative Economic Studies)

INDEX

A

Accession Partnership 192, 193
accounting standards 178, 181
acquis communautaire 21, 120, 132, 186, 191, 192
acquisition 29, 155, 217
actuarial system 289
administrative burden 99, 128, 157
administrative capacity 6, 157, 360, 386, 387, 415
agricultur 7, 19, 34, 36, 144, 146, 147, 170, 174, 175, 189, 198, 361, 375, 383, 384, 415
aid, structural 88
allocation of resources 187
Amsterdam 191
appreciation 97, 121, 123, 125, 126, 128, 129, 130, 132, 133, 373
Austria 41, 42, 45, 49, 54, 55, 101, 130, 166, 185, 233, 317, 327, 430, 434, 435, 436

B

Balassa-Samuelson effect 126, 127, 129, 373, 382
Baltic states 32, 63, 69, 113, 170, 185, 267, 269, 277, 279, 315, 332, 404
banking sector 19, 24, 25, 177, 180, 182, 187, 347, 388, 390
bankruptcy legislation 6, 361, 386
banks 71, 126, 177, 181, 184, 185, 188, 304, 388
Barcelona European Council 292, 401, 409
Belgium 34, 151, 185, 194, 195, 206, 207, 209, 219, 233, 322, 326, 327, 328, 434, 435, 436
benchmark 41, 54, 199, 343
benefit 5, 120, 128, 193, 199, 200, 201, 202, 203, 206, 207, 210, 240, 251, 285, 293, 304, 360, 379, 381, 397, 411, 420
big bang 88
Broad Economic Policy Guidelines 9, 210, 237, 251, 356, 391, 398, 412, 413, 417, 436
budget 7, 26, 27, 89, 103, 158, 189, 217, 245, 255, 259, 284, 288, 302, 312, 314, 316, 362, 385, 416, 421
business environment 6, 20, 117, 136, 144, 164, 359, 360, 381, 386, 415, 419

C

capital deepening 274, 372
capital market 100, 311, 356
capital-intensive 61, 62
Cardiff process 10, 359, 418
catching-up 4, 5, 9, 14, 16, 28, 29, 30, 31, 32, 38, 47, 55, 56, 57, 58, 64, 69, 72, 77, 79, 83, 94, 97, 99, 100, 111, 124, 127, 129, 132, 134, 136, 140, 178, 182, 276, 289, 290, 292, 358, 364, 367, 369, 373, 388, 393, 402, 403, 411, 429
central bank 187, 357
child care 199
co-financing 103
Cologne process 10, 418
Commission regular reports 383
common agricultural policy 26, 89
comparative advantage 57, 58, 61, 64, 79, 83, 106, 107, 129, 373
competition 6, 7, 80, 96, 124, 128,

136, 141, 142, 148, 150, 156, 158, 163, 164, 165, 169, 175, 188, 249, 260, 341, 347, 359, 360, 361, 366, 373, 375, 381, 382, 384, 386, 390, 410, 412, 415, 419
competition authorities 6, 158, 163, 360, 384
competition rules 384
competitiveness 4, 8, 10, 14, 31, 48, 55, 69, 81, 82, 91, 92, 93, 96, 97, 98, 99, 100, 101, 103, 117, 120, 121, 123, 125, 129, 131, 132, 134, 140, 165, 167, 170, 171, 232, 362, 373, 374, 381, 416, 417, 418
consumer credit 183, 188, 390
Consumer Price Index 89, 142, 304
consumption 12, 90, 106, 131, 170, 230, 254, 256, 277, 394, 396, 412, 413, 425
convergence 4, 5, 7, 16, 17, 27, 29, 33, 47, 83, 99, 106, 108, 110, 111, 112, 113, 114, 120, 121, 124, 129, 133, 139, 167, 177, 178, 179, 257, 258, 260, 289, 290, 357, 360, 367, 368, 369, 371, 384, 386, 387, 392, 397
Convergence Programm 285, 293, 294, 420
co-ordination process 1, 4, 9, 10, 13, 356, 357, 364, 417, 418, 426
Copenhagen 2, 106, 115, 120, 135, 186, 192
corporate governance 20, 115, 178
costs 24, 31, 47, 48, 56, 98, 103, 108, 117, 118, 119, 130, 170, 171, 175, 188, 214, 219, 220, 222, 224, 225, 254, 258, 260, 318, 341, 346, 353, 370, 372, 373, 391, 393, 405
coverage 9, 38, 216, 302, 363, 366, 403, 420
credit constraints 7, 361, 416
currency 48, 56, 97, 123, 124, 125, 131, 259, 382
currency board 123, 124, 125

D

demographic projection 263
Denmark 40, 71, 151, 194, 201, 202, 204, 207, 232, 315, 316, 317, 322, 326, 327, 328, 435, 436
dependency ratio 8, 263, 281, 282, 283, 302, 398, 399
deregulation 129, 164, 382
derogation 257
disability 207, 255, 289, 292, 379, 395
downturn 90, 91, 113, 276, 277
drop-outs 233, 336, 408

E

early school leavers 233, 336, 408
ECOFIN 1, 436
education, compulsory 327, 330, 331, 333
education, higher 190, 312, 314, 324, 334, 336, 338, 407
education, secondary 74, 76, 309, 312, 317, 319, 320, 321, 325, 327, 328, 329, 330, 331, 332, 337, 338, 404, 406
education, tertiary 74, 76, 77, 309, 312, 313, 314, 317, 319, 322, 323, 324, 332, 333, 334, 338, 406, 407, 409, 420
educational attainment 9, 31, 73, 74, 79, 218, 313, 319, 322, 323, 332, 343, 363, 364, 409, 411, 417
efficiency 6, 7, 9, 19, 23, 24, 102, 107, 148, 177, 180, 188, 199, 202, 251, 261, 306, 313, 314, 315, 318, 360, 362, 363, 366, 375, 380, 383, 386, 388, 390, 395, 397, 403, 405,

411, 416
efficiency gain 148, 375
employment protection 6, 172, 220, 221, 240, 360, 380, 381
employment rates 4, 5, 8, 73, 108, 116, 194, 195, 230, 240, 251, 278, 279, 282, 292, 325, 358, 359, 363, 376, 379, 381, 408, 413, 414, 416
EMU 14, 18, 27, 124, 132, 133, 257, 258, 261, 394, 428, 436
energy market 384
energy sector 142
enlargement 1, 4, 14, 27, 28, 31, 79, 88, 89, 93, 96, 104, 106, 107, 116, 133, 135, 163, 166, 167, 169, 175, 189, 357, 372, 378
enlargement, Mediterranean 88
enrolment ratio 233, 314, 329, 330, 333, 344, 406, 407, 437
entrepreneurship 6, 157, 165, 167, 341, 346, 360, 381, 410
EPC 1, 2, 4, 10, 115, 199, 262, 281, 282, 301, 341, 349, 355, 356, 357, 358, 359, 364, 365, 398, 400, 401, 403, 410, 418, 419, 420, 421, 423, 430, 436
ERM-II 124, 132, 133
Essen European Council 192
EU Directive 6, 361, 387
EU structural funds 8, 260, 363
Europe Agreements 139
European Council 10, 106, 192, 193, 194, 199, 291, 365, 398, 412, 414, 416, 418, 428
exchange rate 2, 5, 49, 56, 120, 121, 122, 123, 124, 125, 126, 127, 128, 129, 130, 131, 132, 133, 141, 257, 373
exchange rate, nominal 125
exchange rate, pegged 123
exchange rate, real 120, 128, 141
excise duty 254, 394
expenditures 9, 98, 161, 200, 232, 252, 253, 255, 284, 285, 293, 294, 306, 363, 365, 395, 399, 400, 401, 402, 409, 419, 420
export 57, 60, 61, 62, 63, 66, 70, 73, 90, 91, 92, 101, 151, 152, 153, 154, 156, 171, 403
export quotas 171

F

FDI 30, 31, 58, 69, 71, 72, 80, 94, 95, 96, 98, 117, 131, 150, 151, 154, 155, 156, 260, 276, 382, 436
financial discipline 115
financial intermediation 145, 146, 155, 178, 180, 181, 182, 186, 361, 387
financial market 7, 177, 178, 180, 184, 185, 291, 293, 361, 362, 390, 415
financial services 7, 24, 58, 181, 182, 218, 362, 389, 390
Financial Services Action Plan 11, 187, 362, 389, 390, 424, 436
Finland 185, 206, 322, 328, 333, 406, 435, 436
fiscal balance 89
flexibility 6, 19, 21, 100, 113, 124, 125, 133, 199, 220, 225, 226, 236, 293, 360, 366, 380, 381, 405
forecast 110, 112, 258, 264, 278
foreign direct investment (FDI) 30, 69, 79, 150, 154, 184, 364, 371, 374, 382, 417
France 23, 34, 151, 185, 204, 209, 221, 222, 265, 317, 327, 328, 434, 436
free movement 186, 188, 193

G

Germany 34, 89, 92, 101, 185, 200, 204, 209, 220, 221, 222, 277, 320, 322, 326, 327, 406, 436
Gerschenkron hypothesis 29, 55, 56, 68, 79
goods 6, 57, 86, 87, 92, 93, 142, 150, 151, 152, 153, 310, 403
Göteborg European Council 11, 12, 424, 425
Greece 16, 34, 62, 113, 114, 139, 140, 151, 161, 163, 185, 194, 197, 198, 201, 202, 203, 227, 228, 232, 238, 244, 315, 316, 322, 327, 328, 369, 436
greenfield investment 94, 155
growth potential 5, 8, 29, 127, 150, 356, 357, 363, 366, 384, 391

H

headquarters 96
health care system 2, 8, 9, 363, 398, 403
health insurance 255
Heckscher-Ohlin model 92
human capital 8, 69, 98, 199, 251, 310, 311, 362, 380, 395, 397, 408, 416

I

ICT 9, 160, 161, 162, 318, 350, 352, 411, 437
implementation 2, 6, 7, 10, 11, 120, 158, 178, 183, 186, 187, 192, 242, 306, 308, 347, 357, 359, 360, 361, 362, 365, 384, 386, 387, 389, 390, 395, 396, 410, 412, 415, 418, 419, 424
incentive 5, 249, 360, 381, 384
incumbent 347, 410
indexation 211, 245, 255, 286, 289, 307, 308, 395, 402
infrastructure 8, 14, 19, 21, 23, 98, 165, 178, 188, 191, 250, 255, 313, 362, 363, 390, 395, 396, 408, 410, 416
innovation 6, 9, 11, 127, 183, 341, 342, 345, 346, 347, 349, 350, 353, 356, 359, 362, 363, 364, 389, 402, 409, 410, 411, 416, 417, 419, 424
integration 1, 2, 4, 28, 31, 79, 83, 89, 90, 108, 120, 124, 126, 132, 133, 134, 136, 139, 150, 152, 177, 185, 187, 188, 225, 239, 276, 356, 357, 373, 387, 389, 390, 403, 414, 429
interest rate 122, 126, 132, 388
internal market directives 158, 382, 415, 424
internal market obligation 6, 361, 387
Internet 11, 314, 318, 404, 424
internet penetration 162, 163
Ireland 113, 138, 139, 151, 157, 200, 201, 204, 209, 228, 265, 326, 327, 328, 331, 369, 407, 437
Italy 101, 151, 157, 185, 194, 195, 196, 198, 201, 202, 204, 207, 220, 221, 222, 265, 322, 327, 407, 437

J

Joint Assessment Paper 192, 242

K

know-how 69, 155
knowledge-based economy 2, 4, 9, 115, 135, 136, 144, 154, 160, 161, 163, 165, 166, 193, 309, 311, 313, 320, 335, 356, 359, 363, 381, 403, 406, 408, 409, 411, 417, 419

L

labour costs 48, 118, 119, 219, 372
labour demand 77, 79, 189, 190, 199, 202, 226
labour shedding 378
labour supply 199, 266
labour-intensive 40, 61, 62, 63, 64, 65, 79, 92, 108, 129, 373, 387, 403
Lamfalussy Procedure 187
Lisbon European Council 11, 107, 279, 356, 424
Lisbon objectives 2, 4, 5, 6, 11, 116, 240, 250, 266, 290, 309, 337, 357, 358, 359, 360, 365, 376, 387, 389, 409, 414, 420, 424
Lisbon strategy 1, 2, 4, 8, 9, 10, 11, 100, 107, 115, 135, 167, 193, 262, 278, 309, 337, 358, 359, 363, 364, 365, 379, 391, 397, 398, 399, 404, 409, 414, 417, 418, 424
loans 71, 182, 183, 185, 238, 389
long-term care 10, 294, 365, 421
Luxembourg 151, 196, 197, 198, 201, 237, 327, 328, 333, 437
Luxembourg process 10, 191, 192, 210, 359, 365, 418, 419

M

Maastricht criteria 103
macroeconomic environment 10, 31, 32, 120, 133, 170, 257, 258, 348, 366
manufacturing 31, 32, 33, 37, 38, 39, 40, 43, 45, 54, 55, 58, 60, 71, 79, 82, 87, 130, 144, 145, 152, 153, 155, 157, 218, 246, 334, 335, 373, 375, 403
market capitalisation 25, 180, 182, 361, 387
market share 91
merger 155
migration 214, 264, 265, 398
mobility 193, 199, 213, 214, 220, 312
monetary policy 14, 126, 133
multilateral surveillance 4, 357, 358, 418
multinational companies 93, 101

N

Netherlands 151, 185, 197, 201, 202, 203, 204, 206, 227, 228, 244, 322, 326, 328, 437
network industries 96, 163, 255, 256, 349, 361, 381, 384, 387, 395, 410, 415
non-tariff barriers 102

O

old age pension 207
older workers 5, 8, 194, 195, 207, 240, 279, 282, 286, 291, 292, 376, 381, 403, 415, 416
open method of co-ordination 10, 418
output 19, 32, 39, 40, 41, 42, 44, 46, 47, 48, 113, 120, 121, 122, 128, 133, 170, 171, 173, 269, 272, 273, 274, 275, 290, 319, 336, 342, 366, 371, 375, 383, 405, 408, 409, 421

P

peer review 107
pension system 8, 251, 284, 285, 286, 289, 291, 292, 293, 302, 363, 401, 403, 416, 420, 427
PISA 236, 237, 319, 325, 326, 339, 343, 429, 437
Portugal 16, 34, 62, 113, 114, 138, 139, 140, 151, 157, 206, 212, 219, 220, 221, 222, 317, 320, 322, 326,

327, 328, 331, 369, 437
poverty 12, 199, 206, 219, 233, 255, 261, 412, 413, 414, 425
Pre-Accession Economic Programmes (PEPs) 4, 7, 124, 126, 129, 135, 157, 163, 164, 165, 166, 193, 253, 254, 255, 256, 259, 260, 285, 286, 289, 294, 302, 346, 362, 364, 393, 394, 395, 400
pre-transition 68, 128, 169, 170, 171
price control 141, 142, 149, 165, 382
price liberalisation 115, 128
price regulation 142
private sector 7, 20, 131, 148, 149, 156, 190, 218, 229, 240, 247, 260, 284, 313, 314, 374, 384, 391, 405, 409, 411, 416
privatisation 7, 19, 24, 69, 94, 115, 131, 132, 148, 149, 155, 164, 165, 166, 174, 177, 184, 190, 219, 253, 257, 260, 359, 360, 361, 365, 383, 386, 388, 391, 419, 420
productivity gains 8, 107, 117, 132, 360, 363, 374, 396
productivity gap 5, 47, 54, 108, 358
prosperity 108, 111, 114, 137, 356
public expenditure 7, 10, 207, 251, 252, 254, 256, 257, 260, 261, 262, 266, 284, 294, 312, 315, 316, 317, 353, 362, 365, 392, 393, 395, 396, 397, 399, 400, 401, 403, 404, 416, 421
public procurement 158
public revenue 7, 8, 185, 200, 253, 254, 362, 366, 392, 393, 394, 397, 416, 420
public sector 18, 126, 147, 148, 163, 189, 190, 217, 218, 238, 240, 255, 259, 261, 342, 349, 360, 362, 374, 386, 392, 397, 410, 415

R

R&D 8, 9, 11, 61, 94, 100, 160, 161, 164, 314, 341, 350, 353, 359, 362, 364, 409, 410, 411, 416, 417, 419, 424, 437
rail networks 256
raw-material-intensive 92
red tape 157, 346
regional disparities 5, 116, 366, 381, 421
resource-intensive 40, 41, 42, 47, 48, 54, 72
retention 328
retirement age 8, 225, 286, 287, 289, 292, 293, 302, 363, 401, 416
retirement age, effective 11, 286, 292, 401, 403, 416, 424
retirement age, statutory 208, 303, 416
retirement, early 199, 200, 207, 210, 286, 289, 292, 302, 376, 379, 381, 402
risk capital 7, 183, 341, 362, 364, 389, 390, 410, 411, 416
Risk Capital Action Plan 11, 183, 362, 390, 424
road networks 256

S

school attainment 310, 311
science 234, 235, 311, 314, 334, 335, 338, 346, 407
sectoral composition 6, 114, 144, 147, 166, 359, 375, 383, 419
self-employment 189, 191, 198
service sector 34, 93, 128, 145, 152, 403
services 6, 19, 33, 34, 36, 38, 57, 60, 81, 92, 93, 99, 101, 118, 119, 127, 150, 178, 186, 188, 198, 214, 218,

229, 255, 256, 261, 310, 312, 313, 318, 346, 362, 372, 373, 387, 397, 405, 415, 416
shadow economy 209, 210
Single Market 106, 107, 388, 389, 390
skilled, high skilled 325, 338, 364, 409, 417
skilled, low skilled 5, 196, 239, 325
skills 9, 76, 77, 85, 94, 98, 190, 203, 231, 233, 236, 247, 269, 309, 310, 311, 312, 313, 323, 325, 335, 336, 338, 364, 378, 380, 381, 404, 405, 408, 409, 414, 417, 424
small- and medium-sized companies (SMEs) 7, 95, 101, 102, 136, 157, 164, 165, 183, 189, 198, 214, 362, 389, 390, 416, 438
social assistance 200, 203, 206, 210
social cohesion 4, 99, 100, 193, 309, 310, 311, 356, 413
social security 191, 206, 209, 255, 287, 291, 302, 304, 307, 397
Spain 16, 34, 62, 113, 114, 138, 139, 140, 151, 196, 197, 198, 206, 220, 227, 228, 233, 322, 327, 328, 369, 434, 435, 436
Stability and Growth Pact 257, 362
stakeholder 9, 364
standard of living 16, 211
start-up 157
state aid 6, 159, 347, 361, 385
state assets 253
state-owned companies 115, 144, 147, 157, 177, 217, 240, 249, 252, 375, 385, 392
stock exchange 184
stock market 25, 180, 184, 361, 387
Stockholm European Council 11, 194, 195, 240, 251, 279, 291, 356, 376, 391, 398, 414, 424
structural reform 2, 4, 7, 10, 14, 19, 97, 109, 114, 115, 116, 120, 127, 129, 132, 133, 135, 136, 139, 144, 149, 150, 163, 164, 166, 251, 356, 357, 358, 362, 364, 365, 383, 386, 391, 414, 418, 419
subsidies 128, 158, 214, 217, 238, 246, 252, 311, 341, 380, 392
subsistence farms 22, 169, 174, 384
supervision 165, 186, 187, 293, 361, 362, 387, 390, 415, 416
supervisory 7, 186, 187, 188, 307, 362
Sweden 161, 163, 185, 206, 265, 317, 322, 326, 327, 438

T

tariffs 102, 384, 395
tax administration 254, 394
tax base 8, 254, 260, 362, 393, 394, 397, 416
tax burden 208, 210, 240, 254, 260, 379, 394, 397
tax collection 8, 255, 362, 394, 397, 416
tax evasion 254, 393
tax exemption 287
tax harmonisation 129, 382
taxation 128, 254, 287, 393, 394
technology leader 29
telecommunication 341
tertiarization 33, 38
total factor productivity 120, 272, 273, 274, 290, 291, 292, 370, 371, 372, 438
trade deficit 93
trade policy 94
trade surplus 93
trade theory 68, 91, 93
training 9, 91, 191, 199, 214, 217, 232, 234, 235, 237, 238, 239, 309, 310, 311, 312, 314, 318, 319, 332,

336, 337, 339, 364, 380, 404, 408, 417, 424, 428
transition period 102, 189, 190, 193, 200, 208, 218, 230, 240, 269, 379
transposition 6, 11, 187, 415, 424
Turkey 111, 112, 136, 145, 151, 152, 155, 162, 165, 264, 358, 370, 392, 393, 402, 410

U

unemployment benefit 203, 204, 205, 206, 210, 223, 292
unemployment, hidden 144, 189, 375
unemployment, long-term 5, 195, 196, 378, 413
unit labour costs 5, 48, 49, 50, 55, 56, 117, 118, 121, 129, 130, 373, 374
unit price 92
United Kingdom 23, 34, 82, 83, 87, 151, 204, 206, 207, 209, 220, 221, 222, 238, 320, 322, 326, 327, 328, 435, 438
university 82, 312, 332, 338, 340, 352, 427, 434
USA 23, 91, 184, 220, 352, 438

V

value added 6, 34, 35, 36, 37, 95, 144, 145, 146, 147, 375
vocational training 190, 245, 337

W

wage differentiation 128, 131, 380

Y

youth 5, 198, 378

PUBLICATIONS BY THE ECONOMIC POLICY CENTER

Wirtschaftsstandort Österreich - Wettbewerbsstrategien für das 21. Jahrhundert (Handler [Hrsg.]); Februar 1996; 2. Aufl. Februar 1998

Wettbewerbsbericht; März 1996

Deregulierung im Wirtschaftsrecht (Winner); Oktober 1996

Reform des Betriebsanlagenrechts (Schwarzer); März 1997

Vom Schilling zum Euro - Wirtschaftspolitische Aspekte des Überganges (Handler [Hrsg.]); März 1997

Ansätze zur Sicherung der Nahversorgung; Juli 1997

Der Euro - Aspekte der Umsetzung in den Unternehmen (Handler, Takacs [Hrsg.]); August 1997

Der österreichische Außenhandel 1997; Dezember 1997

Holz als Standortfaktor - Bauen mit Holz; Jänner 1998

Wirtschaftsstandort Österreich - Rahmenbedingungen im Umbruch (Handler [Hrsg.]); Februar 1998

Wirtschaftsstandort Österreich - Globalisierung - Tourismus - Beschäftigung (Handler [Hrsg.]); Juli 1998

Anreize zur Beschleunigung von Genehmigungsverfahren und zur Aufdeckung freier Kapazitäten im öffentlichen Sektor (Wieser); September 1998

Auswirkungen der Liberalisierung der Ladenöffnungszeiten (Burger); Oktober 1998

Better Regulation Serves Employment (Handler [Ed.]); October 1998

Das österreichische Gründungsgeschehen (Wanzenböck); Oktober 1998

Future Competitiveness of Europe (Darlap, Handler [Ed.]); December 1998

Freie Berufe - Regulierungssysteme (Buchinger); Mai 1999

Wirtschaftsstandort Österreich - Ernährungswirtschaft (Buchinger, Handler [Hrsg.]); August 1999

Der Euro - Aspekte der Umsetzung für den Verbraucher (Frauwallner, Handler [Hrsg.]); Oktober 1999

Der Unternehmer und die Banken - Neue Herausforderungen auf Finanzmärkten (Frauwallner, Handler [Hrsg.]); November 1999

Zahlungsbilanz - Einst und Jetzt (Burger, Handler [Hrsg.]), Februar 2000

Wohnbauforum - Mehr Markt oder mehr Staat für Gemeinnützige? (Handler, Sommer [Hrsg.]); April 2000

Eastern Enlargement: The Sooner, The Better? (Arndt, Salvatore, Handler [Hrsg.]); Juli 2000

Bürgernahes Wirtschaftsrecht - Eine Utopie? (Fuchs, Handler [Hrsg.]); November 2000

Festschrift Heinz Handler - Wirtschaftsstandort Österreich, Von der Theorie zur Praxis (Fuchs, Horvath [Hrsg.]), Jänner 2001

Mittel- und Osteuropa - Technologietransfer im Wohnbau (Abteilung Wohnungspolitik [Hrsg.]); April 2001

Euro-Währungsangabengesetz (EWAG) (Fuchs [Hrsg.]); Mai 2001

Wohnungspolitiken in der Europäischen Union (Handler, Sommer [Hrsg.]); September 2001

Gründerland Österreich (Buchinger [Hrsg.]); April 2002

Working Paper: Sustainability in the European Context - Spotlights on Recent Incidents (Reichert [Hrsg.]); May 2002

Working Paper: European Employment Strategy - A description and critical assessment (Burger [Hrsg.]); May 2002

Competition and Competitiveness in a New Economy (Handler, Burger [Ed.]); July 2002

Neue Herausforderungen für ein europäisches Lauterkeitsrecht, Studie von Hon.Prof.Dr. Gamerith im Auftrag des BMWA, Dezember 2002; 2. Auflage, Jänner 2003

The above mentioned publications may be ordered, as far as still available, from the Federal Ministry for Economic Affairs and Labour (Fax: ++43-1-714 27 22; Tel.: ++43-1-71100-5653).